HIGH SEAS

STORIES OF BATTLE AND ADVENTURE
FROM THE AGE OF SAIL

HIGH SEAS

STORIES OF BATTLE AND ADVENTURE
FROM THE AGE OF SAIL

EDITED BY CLINT WILLIS

adrenaline®

Thunder's Mouth Press
New York

HIGH SEAS: STORIES OF BATTLE AND ADVENTURE FROM THE AGE OF SAIL

Adrenaline® and the Adrenaline® logo are trademarks of
Avalon Publishing Group Incorporated, New York, NY.

An Adrenaline Book®

Published by
Thunder's Mouth Press
An Imprint of Avalon Publishing Group Incorporated
161 William Street, 16th floor
New York, NY 10038

Book design: Sue Canavan

frontispiece photo: Up Aloft by Montague Dawson, © Christie's
Images/Corbis

Library of Congress Cataloging-in-Publication Data

High seas: stories of battle and adventure from the age of sail / edited by
Clint Willis.
    p.cm.
  "An Adrenaline book"--T.p. verso.
    ISBN 1-56025-434-3
    1. Sea stories, English. 2. Historical fiction, English. 3. Great Britain--
History, Naval--Fiction. 4. Great Britain--History, Naval--Anecdotes. I. Willis,
Clint.

PR1309.S4 H44 2002
823.009'32162--dc21   2002141671

Printed in Canada

Distributed by Publishers Group West

For
Charles Perry Willis, Sr.

And his shipmates:
Bruce Baird
Allen Lill
John Caraway
Charley Blum

contents

p h o t o g r a p h s

introduction

M y childhood—bookish, landlocked—exists partly as memories of memories and partly as knowledge or theories about
how to live in the world. Many of the theories I picked up
in books. Many of the books I picked up were about sailors
and many were written by men who had lived and worked at sea
during the age of sail.

Those writers were among my teachers. They taught me the way
writers teach, by way of fable and invention. They served as my companions. The characters they imagined gave voice to what the writers
knew and wondered, and served as the writers' responses to difficulty
and mystery and beauty.

The writers often were concerned with matters of character. Was
Fletcher Christian, leader of the *Bounty* mutineers, a good man or a
foolish one? What were we to make of his behavior? His story as told
and imagined by Charles Nordhoff and James Norman Hall in their
1932 novel *Mutiny on the Bounty* suggested that such questions mattered. This somehow meant that my own behavior and decisions
mattered—perhaps even apart from their consequences.

Writers want you to know what they know. What Joseph Conrad

knew and wanted his readers to know was what he'd learned at sea; he had learned to value for their own sakes certain old-fashioned virtues—community, competence, integrity, courage, awareness—necessary to survive nature's power and its seeming indifference.

Such values surface again and again in the best literature about the age of sail. They animate Patrick O'Brian's Aubrey-Maturin series and C.S. Forester's Hornblower books, as well as the seagoing memoirs of men such as Eric Newby and Richard Henry Dana, Jr. The writers' values—often learned at sea—animate not merely the stories and the characters who inhabit them but also the writing itself, which is careful and resourceful, courteous and bold.

These stories are populated by men, many of them very young. I knew some of them when I was a boy. A few, along with the writers who invented some of them, remain the kind of friends whose examples inform my decisions. I revisit the stories and come away refreshed, aware that life is at hand and that my task is to find my strength and my desire.

Always, too, the stories remind me of what we have lost: vast oceans virtually empty of men and their contraptions, a world that even then was as alluring as innocence or as something already lost. What boys will run away to sea in the 21st century?

Smitten by such change, some of us seek escape or consolation in these stories of an earlier age; happily, we find more than that. The best of the stories in this collection remind us of what we knew at the beginning of our lives: that our work includes meeting and embracing adventure where it finds us—and that it will find us no matter where or when or even how we live.

—CLINT WILLIS
SERIES EDITOR, ADRENALINE BOOKS

from The Ionian Mission
by Patrick O'Brian

This selection is from the eighth novel in Patrick O'Brian's (1914–2000) 20-book series about Captain Jack Aubrey and ship's surgeon Stephen Maturin. The Ionian Mission finds the two friends in the Greek islands aboard H.M.S. Surprise. Aubrey and his crew are preparing to engage a Turkish man-of-war whose captain has rebelled against the Sultan.

For the ten thousandth time Jack woke to the sound of holystones on deck: the *Surprise* might be going into action later in the day, but she was certainly going into it titivated to the nines, and the first lieutenant could be heard calling with unusual insistence for the removal of three spots of tar. Jack's whole massive form was utterly relaxed, yielding to the slow easy lift and roll: he had been on deck twice during the graveyard watch, but since then he had had some hours of deep, deep velvet sleep, and he felt perfectly rested, actively and positively well. The tension of that interminable waiting for the transports was gone, and with it his uncertainty and his immediate distress about Kutali and all the falsity and double-dealing on shore: his present course of action was clear-cut and perfectly direct at last, an operation that he was fully qualified to undertake by training, inclination, and the splendid instrument at his disposal, and one in which he needed no man's advice.

Yet although he had been a great way down, the thought of their probable encounter with the *Torgud* had never left him: he had fallen asleep working out the weight of her broadside and now that he was awake his mind carried on the sum. But could the shocking great thirty-six-pounders be counted? Was the renegade to be believed when he said there were only nine rounds for them altogether? And then what was the Turks' gunnery like? A great deal would depend on that. If it was no better than their seamanship it would not be very formidable; but the two did not necessarily go together. As for numbers, the *Torgud* probably had about a hundred and fifty more men than *Surprise* when he saw her, but she would have lost a good many in her prize-crews, more than enough to compensate for the Surprises now in Malta or on their way back in the *Dryad*. He was on the point of exclaiming 'Thank God *Dryad* ain't here,'—for even an unhandy butter-box of her size would upset the fairly even match and take all the glory away—when he realized that nothing could be more presumptuous or unlucky, and choking back even the enunciation of the thought he sprang out of his cot, singing 'The lily, the lily, a rose I lay, The bailey beareth the bell away,' in his powerful melodious bass.

Like a horizontal jack-in-a-box Killick shot in, carrying shaving-water; and lathering away Jack said to him, 'Breeches today, Killick. There are chances we may see action.'

With Killick's goodwill Jack would never have worn anything but scrubbed old nankeen pantaloons and a threadbare coat with the lace taken off, while his good uniforms all lay in tissue-paper where no damp or sun could get at them. He now objected to any change on the grounds that a Turk and above all a rebellious Turk did not rate breeches. 'Lay out the breeches and top your boom,' said Jack firmly, when the nagging had been going on for some time. But when he pulled off his nightshirt and turned, he found that although the letter of the order had been obeyed the spirit, as usual, had not—before him lay a barely reputable pair of darned breeches, thread stockings, yesterday's shirt, and the coat whose sleeve he had ruined in Ismail's dinner. Of his own authority he opened a locker and took out the splendid affair he wore to visit admirals, pashas and governors; in this he walked on to the already crowded quarterdeck, and after a general 'Good morning' he surveyed the scene. A brilliant day with a high dappled sky and the sun a handsbreadth up astern; the breeze steady; the sea flecked with white where the wind caught the remains of the dying northern swell. From the traverse-board and the log-board it was clear that the *Surprise* was almost exactly where he had meant her to be: Cape Doro would lie a little abaft the beam over the starboard horizon, and right ahead Phanari should loom up within an hour or two. He took a couple of turns the whole length of the ship, breathing the sea-smell deep in after the closeness of his sleeping-cabin, and with it the damp fresh scent of newly-scrubbed planks: most of the ship's company were on deck, and he moved among faces he knew perfectly well. The men had had their breakfast, and they looked at him cheerfully, knowingly, expectantly, with a certain connivance or complicity; some were engaged in beautifying the long seams of the larboard gangway with a shining black preparation invented by Mr. Pullings, but most were busy with such things as the breechings of the great guns or the chipping of round-shot to make it more perfectly spherical, truer in its flight, more deadly. The armourer was at his grindstone under the forecastle with a group of seamen round him relaying one another, at the crank and giving advice; he had rows of shining cutlasses and boarding axes and officers' swords at his feet, and his mates were checking pistols by the score, while in a separate body a little farther aft the Marines, looking quite human in their shirt-sleeves, polished their already spotless muskets and bayonets.

A couple of turns, and then saying to the officer of the watch, 'Mr. Gill, pray lend me your glass,' he swung up over the hammocks, tightly packed in their netting, and so up and up for the pleasure of climbing, the strong easy motion of going aloft. The lookout, warned by the creaking of the shrouds, moved out apelike on the topgallant yard to make room and Jack installed himself at the crosstrees, gazing all round the vast blue disc spread taut below him and reaching to the sky on every hand: there to starboard lay Cape Doro, where it ought to be within half a point; and he believed he could just make out Phanari ahead. 'Simms,' he called to the man on the yard, 'keep a good lookout, d'ye hear me there? Our gentleman is likely to come up from the south, but since he is a Turk, he might come from anywhere.'

With this he returned to the deck, where he found Stephen and Graham. He invited them to breakfast, together with Pullings and two youngsters, Calamy and Williamson; and while it was preparing he talked to the gunner about the amount of cartridge filled and to the carpenter about the provision of plugs to deal with forty-pound-ball shot-holes. 'For,' he said, 'our possible adversary—and I say only *possible*, Mr. Watson . . .'

'Or hypothetical, as you might put it, sir.'

'Exactly so—is the *Torgud*, and she carries two Portuguese thirty-sixes, which is our forty-pounder, give or take a trifle.'

'Hypothetical,' muttered Killick with great contempt, and then very loud, drowning the carpenter's reply, 'Wittles is up, sir, if you please.'

It was a cheerful meal. Jack was a good host, and when he had time to concern himself with them he was fond of the little brutes from the midshipmen's berth; furthermore he was in remarkably high spirits and he amused himself and the young gentlemen extremely by dwelling at length on the fact that the country they had just quitted was practically the same as Dalmatia—a mere continuation of Dalmatia—so famous for its spotted dogs. He himself had seen quantities of spotted dogs—had even hunted behind a couple of braces—spotted dogs in a pack of hounds, oh Lord!—while the town of Kutali was positively infested with spotted youths and maidens, and now the Doctor swore he had seen spotted eagles . . . Jack laughed until the tears came into his eyes. In a Dalmatian inn, he said, by way of pudding you could call for spotted dick, give pieces of it to a spotted dog, and throw the remains to the spotted eagles.

While the others were enlarging upon the possibilities, Graham said to Stephen in a low voice, 'What is this spotted eagle? Is it a joke?'

'The *aquila maculosa* or *discolor* of some authors, Linnaeus' *aquila clanga*. The Captain is pleased to be arch. He is frequently arch of a morning.'

'I beg your pardon, sir,' cried the midshipman of the watch, fairly racing in. 'Mr. Mowett's duty and two sail on the larboard beam, top-sails up from the masthead.'

'Two?' said Jack. 'Are they ships?'

'He cannot make out yet, sir.'

'May I go, sir?' asked Pullings, half out of his chair, his face alive with eagerness.

'Aye, do,' said Jack. 'We will eat up your bacon for you.'

Ships they were. Turkish ships they were, although it was so early, and men-of-war: the *Torgud* and the *Kitabi*. Mustapha had sailed far sooner than had been expected; and being now perhaps less confident of Ali's good faith he had brought his consort with him.

'Oh what a damnable thing,' cried Graham, when this was established beyond the tremor of a doubt. 'Oh what a bitter, bitter disappointment. Yet I am sure Osman gave me the best intelligence he had.' He fairly wrung his hands, and Jack said, 'Never be so concerned, sir: it will be somewhat harder, to be sure, but we must not despair of the republic.'

'You cannot possibly attack both of them,' said Graham angrily. 'The *Torgud* carries thirty-two guns in all and nearly four hundred men, and the *Kitabi* twenty guns and a hundred and eighty. You are outnumbered by more than a hundred and eighty. There is no shame in retiring before such odds.'

As he said this some of the people on the quarterdeck nodded; others adopted reserved, remote expressions; only Pullings and Mowett frowned with evident disapproval. Stephen thought he detected a predominant sense of agreement with Graham's remark: for his own part he did not feel qualified to form a naval opinion, but he did know how passionately Jack wished to wipe out the wretched affair at Medina and he suspected that desire might warp his judgement.

'Why, Professor,' said Jack pleasantly, 'I believe you are almost in danger of poaching upon my province,' and Graham, recollecting himself, begged pardon and withdrew.

Leaning over the hammocks in the starboard netting Jack watched them over the sparkling sea: the frigate and the twenty-gun ship were now not much above two miles away, keeping steadily to their original course under all plain sail while the *Surprise* stood towards them on the larboard tack, the south-east wind one point free.

'Lord, how glad I am we weighed directly,' he said to himself. He smiled at the thought of his mad frustration had they arrived too late, all for the sake of the cables and hawsers ashore: he smiled and even chuckled aloud.

By now the quarterdeck had all its officers and young gentlemen, all its proper foremast hands, signalmen, messengers and timoneers, together with everyone else in the ship who had a right to walk upon it, and Stephen and Professor Graham were wedged against the hances, behind the Captain's clerk and the purser.

'It seems an uncouth long wait before anything happens,' said Graham in a low voice. 'I dare say you have seen many actions at sea?'

'I have seen the beginnings of several,' said Stephen, 'but as soon as it grows dangerous I retire to a place of safety below.'

'You are all very arch and jocose this morning,' said Graham discontentedly. Then, nodding towards the other side, where Jack and Pullings were discussing some point of their approach and laughing heartily as they did so, he said, 'Do you know the word *fey*, that we use in the north?'

'I do not,' said Stephen. He was perfectly well acquainted with the word, but he did not wish to discuss his friend's dangerous high spirits with Graham.

'I am not a superstitious man; but if those gentlemen are married and if their wives . . .'

'All hands aft,' said Jack, and the howling of the calls and the sound of hundreds of feet drowned Graham's words.

'I am not going to make a speech,' said Captain Aubrey to his men. 'We know one another too well to go on about duty. Very well. Now when we were in Medina I had to tell you not to fire into the enemy first, and since he would not begin we were obliged to come away without doing anything. Some of you were not quite pleased. This time it will be different. Those two Turkish men-of-war over there have rebelled against their Sultan.' The wrongs of the Sultan of Turkey left the Surprises quite unmoved: their expressions did not change in the slightest degree: they looked attentively at their Captain, who continued, 'And what is more they have taken our transports. So it stands to reason we must knock some sense into their heads, and get our prisoners and ships and cannon back. As I dare say you know, they have a good many men in them, so we are not likely to board very soon, but rather hammer them from a distance. You must fire into their hulls, right into their hulls, mind: fire low and true, deliberate fire with post paid on every ball. Mr. Pullings, we may clear for action, and beat to quarters.'

Very little required doing. All the warrant and petty officers had had plenty of warning and they had taken their measures: Mr. Hollar, for example, had had his puddings and dolphins in the tops these hours past. Killick had already taken Jack's better clothes and possessions below, and Diana's dressing-case, horribly ringed and stained by Graham's cocoa, lay in its elaborate double case in the bread-room. All that remained was for the galley fires to be put out, for the carpenters to knock down the bulkheads of Jack's and the master's cabins, and for the gun-crews to take possession of the massive brutes that had been Jack's stable-companions, and it was done.

The various officers reported to Pullings, and Pullings stepped up to Jack, saluted and said, 'A clean sweep fore and aft, sir, if you please.'

'Thank you, Mr. Pullings,' said Jack, and they stood there side by side, smiling and looking forward, over the starboard bow, at the immediate future coming towards them.

The *Surprise* was silent, most of her men grave, as they usually were before action: grave, but not very much concerned, since there were few who had not run down on the enemy like this many times over. On the other hand, not many had run down to quite such odds, and some thought the skipper had bitten off more than he could chew. Most hands knew very well that Medina rankled at his heart, and the few stupid fellows were soon told. 'That is all wery fine and large,' said

William Pole, on hearing the news. 'All wery fine and large, so long as I don't have to pay for it with my skin.'

'For shame, Bill Pole,' said the rest of the gun-team.

The *Surprise* bore down, therefore, under her fighting-sails, with her master at the con, her guns run out, powder-boys sitting well behind them on their leather cartridge-cases, shot-garlands full, splinter-netting rigged, scuttle-butts all along, decks damped and sanded, and wet fearnought screens over the hatches leading to the magazine far below, where the gunner sat among his little deadly kegs. Mowett had the forward division of guns on the maindeck, Honey, the senior master's mate, the after division, with midshipmen attending three aside each—the oldsters, that is to say, for Jack kept the boys who had breakfasted with him on the quarterdeck as aides-de-camp. Those Marines who were not quartered at the guns lined the gangway, looking particularly trim, their red coats strikingly brilliant against the white hammock-cloths and the now intense blue of the sea, in this powerful sunlight. Their lieutenant now stood amidships, with the purser and the captain's clerk, none of them speaking but all looking steadily forward at the Turks.

In this silence Graham turned to Stephen, who had not yet gone below to his battle-station, and close to his ear said, 'What did Mr. Aubrey mean by desiring the men to put *post paid* on every ball?'

'In English law it is a capital offence to stop His Majesty's mails: by extension the stopping of any object marked post paid is also mortal. And indeed the man who stops a cannon-ball is unlikely to survive.'

'So it was a joke?'

'Just so.'

'A joke at a time like this, good God forgive us? Such a man would be facetious at his father's burial.'

In the last few minutes the ships had approached to within random shot, the Turks on *Surprise*'s starboard bow holding their course without the slightest deviation with the *Kitabi* abreast of the *Torgud*, a quarter of a mile to leeward. Bonden, the captain of the gun, kept the starboard chaser steadily trained on the *Torgud*'s bows, perpetually shifting it with his handspike. They were drawing together at a combined speed of ten miles an hour, and just before they came to point-blank range the silence was ripped apart by a great screaming blast of Turkish trumpets, harsh and shrill.

'God, how it lifts your heart,' said Jack, and he gave the orders 'Colours at the fore and main.' With his glass he watched the crowded Turkish deck: saw the man at the halyards, followed the flags as they ran up in reply, and on seeing the regular Turkish ensign break out he reflected, 'He thinks we do not know yet: perhaps he hopes to slip by. But his guns are manned,' and aloud he called 'Professor Graham, pray come and stand by me. Mr. Gill, wear round to the starboard tack and lay me within pistol-shot of his starboard side.'

Now high seamanship showed its splendid powers: the sail-trimmer sprang from their guns; forecourse, staysails and jibs flashed out; the frigate leapt forward like a spurred horse and made her quick tight turn, as Jack knew she would do, bringing her larboard guns to bear when the Turks were still expecting her on the other side.

'Shiver the foretopsail,' called Jack, with his eye on the *Torgud*'s quarterdeck and her burly captain right under his lee. 'Mr. Graham, call out to him that he must surrender directly. Larboard guns stand by.'

Graham shouted loud and clear. Jack saw Mustapha's red beard part in a white gleam as he roared back his answer, a long answer.

'In effect he refuses,' said Graham.

'Fire.'

The *Surprise*'s entire broadside went off in a single explosion that shook both ships from truck to keelson and for a moment deadened the air; and now in the thick smoke rolling to leeward over the *Torgud* began the great hammering, red flashes in the gloom, iron crashing into the hulls on either side or howling overhead, an enormous all-pervading din, with ropes parting, blocks falling, jagged pieces of wood struck from the rails, the bulwark, the decks, and whistling across. After their hesitant start, they being caught on the wrong foot, the Turks fired hard and fast, though with no attempt at regularity, and the first shot of their starboard thirty-six-pounder tore a great gap in the hammocks, scored an eighteen-inch groove in the mainmast yet extraordinarily killed no men. But if the *Torgud* was firing pretty well or at least pretty fast, the *Surprise* was excelling herself: now that the broadsides were no longer simultaneous, the guns being out of step after the third or fourth discharge, it was hard to be sure, but judging by number seven, just under him, they were achieving something like a round in seventy seconds, while the quarterdeck carronades were doing even better; and Jack was very sure that their aim was a great deal truer than the Turks'. Glancing to windward he saw a wide area of sea torn up by Turkish grape and round-shot that must have missed by as much as twenty or thirty yards, and then as he paced up and down he stared to leeward, trying to pierce the smoke: 'I wonder the Turk bears it so long,' he said, and as he spoke he saw the *Torgud*'s topsails bracing round as she edged away to join the *Kitabi* to leeward. He caught the master's eye: Gill nodded—he was already following the movement.

After a few minutes of this gradual turn the smoke would blow away ahead and the sharpshooters would have a chance. He bent to his youngsters, and shouting loud through the uproar and the general deafness that affected all hands he said, 'Mr. Calamy, jump up to the tops and tell them to annoy the Turk's thirty-six-pounder. Mr. Williamson, tell Mr. Mowett and Mr. Honey we are reducing the charges up here by a third. Mr. Pullings, make it so.'

At this furious rate of fire the guns heated excessively and they kicked with even greater force when they went off: indeed, as he moved towards the taffrail, trying to see through the smoke, one of the quarterdeck carronades did in fact break its breeching and overset.

As he bent to snub a trailing side-tackle the waft of the thirty-six-pound ball sweeping over the deck a foot from his head made him stagger; and now, as the iron hail beat furiously on and about the *Surprise*, ball, grape and bar flying through the continuous thunder, with the crackle of musketry above it, there was a new note. The *Torgud*, with the *Surprise* following her, had edged down much closer to the *Kitabi*, and now the *Kitabi* opened with her shrill twelve-pounders. Up until this point the *Surprise* had not suffered badly, except perhaps in her hull; but this present hail knocked one of the forward guns half across the deck, striking it on its own recoil and maiming three of its crew, and again the thirty-six-pounder roared out: its great crash was followed by a screaming below that for two minutes pierced even the united gunfire. And now a bloody trail on the deck showed where the wounded were carried down to the orlop.

Yet the frigate's fire scarcely slackened from its first tremendous pace: powder and shot ran smoothly up from the magazines, the gun-teams rattled their massive pieces in and out with a magnificent zeal, sponging, loading, ramming, heaving up and firing with a racing coordination that it was a pleasure to watch. Although it was still impossible to see at all clearly Jack was sure that they must already have mauled the *Torgud* very severely; she was certainly not firing so fast nor from so many guns, and he was expecting her to wear in the smoke, either to run or to present her undamaged larboard broadside, when he heard the fierce harsh trumpets bray out again. The *Torgud* was going to board.

'Grape,' he said to Pullings and his messengers, and very loud, 'Sail-trimmers stand by.' The *Torgud*'s fire died away except for her bow guns; the smoke cleared, and there she was, turning into the wind, steering straight for the *Surprise*, her bowsprit and even her jibboom crowded with people, willing to take the risk of a raking fire for the sake of boarding. 'Wait for it,' cried Jack. To tack his ship before the Turk could run her aboard, to tack her in so short a space of time and sea as though she were a cutter, was appallingly dangerous; but he knew her through and through, and as he calculated the wind's strength, the ship's impetus, and the living force of the water he called again, 'Wait for it. Wait. Fire.' And then the second his voice could be heard, 'Hands about ship.'

The *Surprise* came about, but only just: the *Torgud* did not. She lay there, taken aback; and as they passed, the Surprises cheering like maniacs, Jack saw that the storm of grape had cleared her head of men, a most shocking butchery.

'Warm work, Professor,' he said to Graham in the momentary pause.

'Is it, indeed? This is my first naval battle of any consequence.'

'Quite warm, I assure you: but the Turks cannot keep it up. That is the disadvantage of your brass guns. If you keep on firing at this rate, they melt. They are pretty, to be sure; but they cannot keep it up. Mr. Gill, we will lie on her larboard quarter, if you please, and rake her from there.'

The *Torgud*, falling off, had put before the wind, and now the *Surprise* bore up and made sail in pursuit; no guns but the bow-chaser could be trained round far enough to bear, and all up and down the ship men straightened and stood easy. Some went to the scuttle-butts to drink or dash the water in their faces; most were stripped to the waist, shining with sweat; all were in tearing spirits. At one of the quarterdeck carronades a young fellow was showing his mates a lost finger. 'I never noticed it,' he kept saying. 'Never noticed it go at all.'

But now here, against all expectation, was the *Kitabi*, coming up fast with the obvious intention of passing between the *Surprise* and the *Torgud* and then presumably of hauling her wind to take the *Surprise* between two fires.

'That will not do, my friend,' said Jack, watching her approach. 'It is very gallant, but it really will not do. Round-shot,' he called, 'and fire steady from forward aft: fire at the word.' Some minutes later, when the relative positions of the three ships were such that the *Torgud* was directly to leeward of her consort and unable to give her any support, Jack shivered the main and mizzen topsails, slanting down towards the *Kitabi*, making no reply to her high, rapid, nervous, largely ineffectual fire until they were a cable's length apart, no more.

They gave her six deliberate rolling broadsides, beating five of her midships gun-ports into one and silencing her entirely. At the sixth there was a violent explosion aboard her, and the beginning of a fire: the *Surprise* passed on, leaving her drifting before the wind, her people running with buckets and hose.

The breeze had faded, perhaps stunned by the cannonade, and the *Surprise* set her topgallantsails to pursue the *Torgud*: not that the Turk was evidently flying—he had no great speed of canvas—but he was steering steadily on his original course, perhaps in the hope of reaching Ali Pasha; and right ahead the mainland could now be seen, mountain-peaks nicking the horizon, while the low Morali islands must be nearer still. In this wonderfully silent pause, while the bosun and his mates sprang about the rigging, knotting and splicing, Jack stared at the *Torgud* for a moment, watching them throw their dead over the side—a trail of dead in her wake—and then made a quick tour of the ship. He found less damage than he had feared: one gun dismounted, the side pierced by three thirty-six-pounder balls and some others, but none of the holes dangerously low, while in Stephen's hands there were no more than six badly wounded men and three sewn into their hammocks, remarkably few for such a furious bout.

On deck again he saw that the breeze had recovered, and that the *Surprise* was overhauling the *Torgud* fast. They were already within gun-shot, but with land in sight it seemed to Jack that so long as he could avoid being boarded close action was called for, and it was not until they were drawing abreast, close enough to see men's faces clearly, that he reduced sail and the hammering began again. This was the *Torgud*'s larboard broadside, hitherto unengaged and undamaged, and the Turks blazed away with as much spirit as before: again a thirty-six-pound ball passed so close to Jack's head that it made him stagger—he actually saw the dark blur of its passing—and he said to Driver of the Marines, 'Let your men amidships concentrate on the loader of that damned heavy gun.' Graham, who was just at hand, said 'May I take a musket, sir? I might do some good, and I feel uneasy, useless and exposed standing here.'

He was indeed exposed. Now that both ships had the wind aft the smoke blew clear away forward; the *Torgud* was shooting more accu-rately than before and as her shot hit the *Surprise*'s bulwark or upper hull so showers of splinters flew across her deck, some trifling, some deadly. Graham had already been knocked over twice, and most of those on deck had been more or less banged about.

The *Torgud* was still full of fight, and she still had a surprising number of men. After a particularly violent salvo she clapped her helm hard over, meaning to board again, and again her people crowded thick into her bows and along her bowsprit. This time the *Surprise* had no room to tack, but she had her forecourse in the brails for just such an emergency, and dropping it now she shot ahead: though none too fast, since the *Torgud*'s jibboom caught in her mizzen topgallant backstays. She shot ahead nevertheless, her stern-chasers blasting grape into the close-packed Turks, a red slaughter that checked even the gun-crew's cheers; and the moment she had way enough she crossed the *Torgud*'s stern, raking her as she did so. The *Surprise* let fly her sheets, and the *Torgud*, ranging up, engaged again with her starboard broad-side, shockingly ravaged from that first bout, with at least seven guns dismounted, ports blackened and battered in, the scuppers and even the bare sides thick with blood.

Ravaged, but still dangerous: now, when some opponents might have struck, she let fly with a dozen or thirteen guns and two of these did more damage than all she had fired hitherto. One struck the uppermost pintle and wedged the rudder, and another, the last of her huge round-shot, caught the *Surprise* just as she was on the lift, showing her copper, and made a shocking great hole under her waterline. And a third, fired as Jack was giving Williamson orders to carry forward, took the boy's arm off at the elbow. Jack saw his amazed face go paper-white—not pain but amazement and concern and disbelief—whipped a handkerchief round the stump, twisted it tight, staunched the jetting blood and passed him to a quartermaster to carry below.

By the time the *Surprise* had dealt with the steering and the leak the *Torgud* was much nearer the land. Apart from a few shots from her stern-chasers as she drew ahead she had not tried to profit by her advantage, still less to board. It was possible that she was unaware of the damage she had inflicted: it was certain that the last encounter, the last raking, had killed a great number of her men. She sailed away, therefore, and in her wake there now sailed the *Kitabi*, she having pursued a course with no turnings since the *Surprise* left her; and both Turks were clearly steering for the same port.

'All sail she will bear, Mr. Pullings,' said Jack, going forward to study the *Torgud* through a borrowed telescope—a musket-shot had broken his own as he held it: the tube shattered, his hand untouched. The *Torgud* had suffered terribly, there was no doubt of that; she was sailing low and heavy and although the *Surprise* was now gathering way fast as Pullings spread topgallantsails and even weather studdingsails in his passionate eagerness, the *Torgud* seemed unwilling and unable to make any increase. And even now the bodies were still splashing over the side.

'No,' said Jack to Bonden at the starboard bow-chaser as they came within easy range of the Turk's stern, moving faster every moment. 'Do not fire. We must not check her way. Boarding is the only thing for it, and the sooner the better.'

'Anyhow, sir,' said Bonden, 'that damned fool is in the way.' This was the *Kitabi*. Convinced that the *Surprise* was in pursuit of her, she had cracked on the most extraordinary amount of canvas to rejoin the *Torgud* and now she lay directly between the two.

Jack walked aft, and as he passed the boarders in each gun-crew smiled at him, or nodded, or said 'Coming up now, sir,' or cheerful words of that kind; and again he felt the rising of that enormous excitement of immediate battle, greater than any other he had ever known in the world.

He spoke to the Marines, who were now to come into their own, and after a few more turns he ran down the ladders to the lantern-lit orlop. 'Stephen,' he said privately, 'how is the boy?'

'He will do, I believe.'

'I hope so, indeed. As soon as we come up, we mean to board.'

They shook hands and he ran on deck again. Pullings was already taking in the studdingsails, not to overrun the *Torgud:* and there, still absurdly ahead, fled the *Kitabi*, between the two frigates. She fired not a gun: she seemed to have lost her head entirely. 'Forward, there,' called Jack to the bow-chaser guns. 'Send a ball over her deck.'

'By God,' cried the master, as the *Kitabi* jigged at the shot, 'she'll run the *Torgud* aboard if she don't take care—by God, she can't avoid her— by God, she's doing it.'

With a rending, crashing sound that came clear to their ears at four hundred yards the *Kitabi* ground slanting into the *Torgud*'s starboard side, her foremast falling over the frigate's waist.

'Lay me athwart her stern,' cried Jack, and then very loud, 'One broadside at the word, and board her in the smoke.'

As the *Surprise* began her turn he stepped forward to the great gap in the starboard hammock-netting torn by the Turks, loosening his sword, easing his pistols. Pullings was at his right hand, his eyes sparkling, and from nowhere had appeared the grim man Davis, jostling against Bonden on the left, looking perfectly mad with a line of white spittle between his lips and a butcher's cleaver in his hand.

The last sweeping movement, the easy, yielding crunch of the ship's sides, and the roar of the great guns as Jack gave the word. Then calling 'Boarders away' he leapt through the smoke down to the *Kitabi*'s deck. Perhaps forty Turks stood against them, an irresolute line almost instantly overwhelmed and beaten back, and there in the clearing eddies was an officer holding out his sword, hilt first, and crying, 'Rendre, rendre.'

'Mr. Gill, take charge,' said Jack, and as the *Torgud* fired her remaining after-guns straight into the *Kitabi* he raced through the billowing smoke into the bows, roaring 'Come on, come on, come on with me.'

It was no great leap across, for the *Torgud* was low, low in the water, the sea washing into her shattered midship ports and flowing out red, and one flying stride took him on to her quarterdeck rail.

Here it was different. Here though her decks were bloody and ploughed with shot they were still full of men: most were facing aft into the smoke, but one whipped around and cut at him directly. Jack caught the blade on his sword and from his height on the rail gave the Turk a great thrust with his foot that sent him flying into the waist of the ship—into the water that swilled over the waist of the settling, almost sinking ship.

He leapt down on to the deck: he had never felt stronger or more lithe or more wholly in form and when a pike came piercing through the confusion, thrusting straight at his belly, he slashed it with such force and precision that he struck the point clean from its shaft. Almost at once the fight took on a pattern. Jack, Pullings and most of the boarders were crowding into the forward starboard corner of the *Torgud*'s quarterdeck, trying to force their way aft from there and the gangway. Some others and all the Marines were doing their best to storm the stern-windows and the taffrail.

It was the usual furious melée, with a huge amount of shouting and striving, very little room to move because of both friends and enemies, little in the way of skill in swordsmanship—an enormous pushing, thrusting, lashing out at a venture, quick stabs in the tumult, short-armed blows, kicking: the physical weight of both sides and the moral weight of both sides.

The mass heaved to and fro: turbans, skull-caps, yellow bloodshot eyes, swarthy bearded faces on the one hand, pale on the other, but both with the same extremity of naked murderous violence; a prodigiously strenuous, vehement mass, sometimes clearing between the two fronts for a short burst of individual, direct and often deadly fighting: then it closed again, the men face to face, even chest to chest, immediately touching. And hitherto neither had a clear advantage: Jack's hundred or so had won a few yards to fight in, but there they were blocked; and the people astern seemed to have lost their foothold. Jack had felt two or three wounds—the searing lash of a pistol-ball across his ribs, a sword-thrust, half-parried, on the other side, while once Davis had very nearly brought him down with the back-stroke of his cleaver that opened a blunt gash on his forehead—and he knew that he had given some very shrewd blows. And all the time he looked for Mustapha: never a glimpse of him, though his enormous voice could be heard.

Abruptly there was room in front of him, breathing-space as some of the Turks eased back, still fighting. On Jack's right Pullings lunged into this space, thrusting at his opponent, caught his foot on a ring-bolt and fell. For a fragment of time his ingenuous face was turned to Jack, then the Turk's sword flashed down and the fight closed in again.

'No, no, no,' roared Jack, driving forward with enormous strength. He had his heavy sabre in both hands and taking no guard he hacked and slashed, standing astride over Pullings' body. Now men scattered before his extreme fury; they fell back; the moral advantage was established. Shouting to Davis to stand by, to stand guard, to carry the body under the ladder, he charged aft, followed by all the rest. At the same time the Marines repulsed from the stern and reformed farther forward, came thundering down both gangways with bayonets fixed.

The crowd of Turks thinned, some running, most retreating steadily towards the taffrail, and there abaft the tottering mizzen sat Mustapha at a table covered with pistols, most of them discharged. His leg had been broken early in the day and it rested on a blood-stained drum. Two of his officers were holding his hands down and a third called to Jack 'We surrender.' This was Ulusan, who had come aboard the *Surprise* with Mustapha: he stepped forward, hauled down the colours and slipped the ensign free. The others at last made Mustapha give up his sword: Ulusan, wrapping the flag about it, offered both to Jack in the unearthly silence. Mustapha rose up, grasping the table, and flung himself on the deck in a paroxysm of rage or grief, his head striking against the wood like a mallet. Jack glanced at him with frigid indifference. 'Give you joy, sir,' said Mowett at his side. 'You have come it the Nelson's bridge at last.'

Jack turned a pale, hard face on him. 'Have you seen Pullings?' he asked.

'Why, yes, sir,' said Mowett, looking surprised. 'They have fairly ruined his waistcoat and knocked his wits astray; but that don't depress his spirits, I find.'

'You had better get back to the barky, sir,' said Bonden in a low voice, tucking the ensign and the other officers' swords under his arm. 'This here is going to Kingdom Come.'

Frigate Engagement
by Samuel Leech

Samuel Leech manned the fifth gun on the British 38-gun man-of-war H.M.S. Mace-donian when it encountered the 44-gun U.S.S. United States in 1812. Advances in American shipbuilding had brought the U.S. Navy a long way from the ragtag assemblage that fought during the Revolutionary War. The crew of the Macedonian learned firsthand the strength of the new Yankee frigates.

A t Plymouth we heard some vague rumors of a declaration of war against America. More than this, we could not learn, since the utmost care was taken to prevent our being fully informed. The reason of this secrecy was, probably, because we had several Americans in our crew, most of whom were pressed men, as before stated. These men, had they been certain that war had broken out, would have given themselves up as prisoners of war, and claimed exemption from that unjust service, which compelled them to act with the enemies of their country. This was a privilege which the magnanimity of our officers ought to have offered them. They had already perpetrated a grievous wrong upon them in impressing them; it was adding cruelty to injustice to compel their service in a war against their own nation. But the difficulty with naval officers is, that they do not treat with a sailor as with a *man*. They know what is fitting between each other as officers; but they treat their crews on another principle; they are apt to look at them as pieces of living mechanism, born to serve, to obey their orders, and administer to their wishes without complaint. This is alike a bad morality and a bad philosophy. There is often more real manhood in the forecastle than in the ward-room; and until the common sailor is treated *as a man*, until every feeling of human nature is conceded to him in naval discipline—perfect, rational subordination will never be attained in ships of war, or in merchant vessels. It is needless to tell of the intellectual degradation of the mass of seamen. "A man's a man for a' that", and it is this very system of discipline, this treating them as automatons, which keeps them degraded. When will human nature put more confidence in itself?

Leaving Plymouth, we next anchored, for a brief space, at Torbay, a small port in the British Channel. We were ordered thence to convoy a huge East India merchant vessel, much larger than our frigate and having five hundred troops on board, bound to the East Indies with money to pay the troops stationed there. We set sail in a tremendous gale of wind. Both ships stopped two days at Madeira to take in wine and a few other articles. After leaving this island, we kept her company two days more; and then, according to orders, having wished her success, we left her to pursue her voyage, while we returned to finish our cruise.

Though without any positive information, we now felt pretty certain that our government was at war with America. Among other things, our captain appeared more anxious than usual; he was on deck almost all the time; the "look-out" aloft was more rigidly observed; and every little while the cry of "Mast-head there!" arrested our attention.

It is customary in men-of-war to keep men at the fore and main mast-heads, whose duty it is to give notice of every new object that may appear. They are stationed in the royal yards, if they are up, but if not, on the topgallant yards: at night a look-out is kept on the fore yard only.

Thus we passed several days; the captain running up and down and constantly hailing the man at the mast-head: early in the morning he began his charge "to keep a good look-out", and continued to repeat it until night. Indeed, he seemed almost crazy with some pressing anxiety. The men felt there was something anticipated, of which they were ignorant; and had the captain heard all their remarks upon his conduct, he would not have felt very highly flattered. Still, everything went on as usual; the day was spent in the ordinary duties of man-of-war life, and the evening in telling stories of things most rare and wonderful; for your genuine old tar is an adept in spinning yarns, and some of them, in respect to variety and length, might safely aspire to a place beside the great magician of the north, Sir Walter Scott, or any of those prolific heads that now bring forth such abundance of fiction to feed a greedy public, who read as eagerly as our men used to listen. To this yarn-spinning was added the most humorous singing, sometimes dashed with a streak of the pathetic, which I assure my readers was most touching; especially one very plaintive melody, with a chorus beginning with,

> "Now if our ship should be cast away,
> It would be our lot to see old England no more,"

which made rather a melancholy impression on my boyish mind, and gave rise to a sort of presentiment that the *Macedonian* would never return home again; a presentiment which had its fulfilment in a manner totally unexpected to us all. The presence of a shark for several days, with its attendant pilot fish, tended to strengthen this prevalent idea.

The Sabbath came, and it brought with it a stiff breeze. We usually made a sort of holiday of this sacred day. After breakfast it was common to muster the entire crew on the spar deck, dressed as the fancy of the captain might dictate; sometimes in blue jackets and white trowsers, or blue jackets and blue trowsers; at other times in blue jackets, scarlet vests, and blue or white trowsers with our bright anchor buttons glancing in the sun, and our black, glossy hats, ornamented with black ribbons, and with the name of our ship painted on them. After muster, we frequently had church service read by the captain; the rest of the day was devoted to idleness. But we were destined to spend the Sabbath, just introduced to the reader, in a very different manner.

We had scarcely finished breakfast, before the man at the mast-head shouted, "Sail ho!"

The captain rushed upon deck, exclaiming, "Mast-head there!"

"Sir!"

"Where away is the sail?"

The precise answer to this question I do not recollect, but the captain proceeded to ask, "What does she look like?"

"A square-rigged vessel, sir", was the reply of the look-out.

After a few minutes, the captain shouted again, "Mast-head there!"

"Sir!"

"What does she look like?"

"A large ship, sir, standing toward us!"

By this time, most of the crew were on deck, eagerly straining their eyes to obtain a glimpse of the approaching ship and murmuring their opinions to each other on her probable character. Then came the voice of the captain, shouting, "Keep silence, fore and aft!" Silence being secured, he hailed the look-out, who, to his question of "What does she look like?" replied, "A large frigate, bearing down upon us, sir!"

A whisper ran along the crew that the stranger ship was a Yankee frigate. The thought was confirmed by the command of "All hands clear the ship for action, ahoy!" The drum and fife beat to quarters; bulk-heads were knocked away; the guns were released from their confinement; the whole dread paraphernalia of battle was produced; and after the lapse of a few minutes of hurry and confusion, every man and boy was at his post, ready to do his best service for his country, except the band, who, claiming exemption from the affray, safely stowed themselves away in the cable tier. We had only one sick man on the list, and he, at the cry of battle, hurried from his cot, feeble as he was, to take his post of danger. A few of the junior midshipmen were stationed below, on the berth deck, with orders, given in our hearing, to shoot any man who attempted to run from his quarters.

Our men were all in good spirits; though they did not scruple to express the wish that the coming foe was a Frenchman rather than a Yankee. We had been told, by the Americans on board, that frigates in the American service carried more and heavier metal than ours. This, together with our consciousness of superiority over the French at sea, led us to a preference for a French antagonist.

The Americans among our number felt quite disconcerted at the necessity which compelled them to fight against their own countrymen. One of them, named John Card, as brave a seaman as ever trod a plank, ventured to present himself to the captain, as a prisoner, frankly declaring his objections to fight. That officer, very ungenerously, ordered him to his quarters, threatening to shoot him if he made the request again. Poor fellow! He obeyed the unjust command and was killed by a shot from his own countrymen. This fact is more disgraceful to the captain of the *Macedonian* than even the loss of his ship. It was a gross and a palpable violation of the rights of man.

As the approaching ship showed American colors, all doubt of her character was at an end. "We must fight her", was the conviction of every breast. Every possible arrangement that could insure success was accordingly made. The guns were shotted; the matches lighted; for, although our guns were all furnished with first-rate locks they were also provided with matches, attached by lanyards, in case the lock should miss fire. A lieutenant then passed through the ship, directing the marines and boarders, who were furnished with pikes, cutlasses, and pistols, how to proceed if it should be necessary to board the enemy. He was followed by the captain, who exhorted the men to fidelity and courage, urging upon their consideration the well-known motto of the brave Nelson, "England expects every man to do his duty." In addition to all these preparations on deck, some men were stationed in the tops with small-arms, whose duty it was to attend to trimming the sails and to use their muskets, provided we came to close action. There were others also below, called sail trimmers, to assist in working the ship should it be necessary to shift her position during the battle.

My station was at the fifth gun on the main deck. It was my duty to supply my gun with powder, a boy being appointed to each gun in the ship on the side we engaged, for this purpose. A woollen screen was placed before the entrance to the magazine, with a hole in it, through which the cartridges were passed to the boys; we received them there, and covering them with our jackets, hurried to our respective guns. These precautions are observed to prevent the powder taking fire before it reaches the gun.

Thus we all stood, awaiting orders, in motionless suspense. At last we fired three guns from the larboard side of the main deck; this was followed by the command, "Cease firing; you are throwing away your shot!"

Then came the order to "wear ship", and prepare to attack the enemy with our starboard guns. Soon after this I heard a firing from some other quarter, which I at first supposed to be a discharge from our quarter deck guns; though it proved to be the roar of the enemy's cannon.

A strange noise, such as I had never heard before, next arrested my attention; it sounded like the tearing of sails, just over our heads. This I soon ascertained to be the wind of the enemy's shot. The firing, after a few minutes' cessation, recommenced. The roaring of cannon could now be heard from all parts of our trembling ship, and, mingling as it did with that of our foes, it made a most hideous noise. By-and-by I heard the shot strike the sides of our ship; the whole scene grew indescribably confused and horrible; it was like some awfully tremendous thunder-storm, whose deafening roar is attended by incessant streaks of lightning, carrying death in every flash and strewing the ground with the victims of its wrath: only, in our case, the scene was rendered more horrible than that, by the presence of torrents of blood which dyed our decks.

Though the recital may be painful, yet, as it will reveal the horrors of war and show at what a fearful price a victory is won or lost, I will present the reader with things as they met my eye during the progress of this dreadful fight. I was busily supplying my gun with powder, when I saw blood suddenly fly from the arm of a man stationed at our gun. I saw nothing strike him; the effect alone was visible; in an instant, the third lieutenant tied his handkerchief round the wounded arm, and sent the groaning wretch below to the surgeon.

The cries of the wounded now rang through all parts of the ship. These were carried to the cockpit as fast as they fell, while those more fortunate men, who were killed outright, were immediately thrown overboard. As I was stationed but a short distance from the main hatchway, I could catch a glance at all who were carried below. A glance was all I could indulge in, for the boys belonging to the guns next to mine were wounded in the early part of the action, and I had to spring with all my might to keep three or four guns supplied with cartridges. I saw two of these lads fall nearly together. One of them was struck in the leg by a large shot; he had to suffer amputation above the wound. The other had a grape or canister shot sent through his ankle. A stout Yorkshireman lifted him in his arms and hurried him to the cockpit. He had his foot cut off, and was thus made lame for life. Two of the boys stationed on the quarter deck were killed. They were both Portuguese. A man, who saw one of them killed, afterwards told me that his powder caught fire and burnt the flesh almost off his face. In this pitiable situation, the agonized boy lifted up both hands, as if imploring relief, when a passing shot instantly cut him in two.

I was an eye-witness to a sight equally revolting. A man named Aldrich had one of his hands cut off by a shot, and almost at the same moment he received another shot, which tore open his bowels in a terrible manner. As he fell, two or three men caught him in their arms, and, as he could not live, threw him overboard.

One of the officers in my division also fell in my sight. He was a noble-hearted fellow, named Nan Kivell. A grape or canister shot struck him near the heart: exclaiming, "Oh! my God!" he fell, and was carried below, where he shortly after died.

Mr Hope, our first lieutenant, was also slightly wounded by a grummet, or small iron ring, probably torn from a hammock clew by a shot. He went below, shouting to the men to fight on. Having had his wound dressed, he came up again, shouting to us at the top of his voice, and bidding us fight with all our might. There was not a man in the ship but would have rejoiced had he been in the place of our master's mate, the unfortunate Nan Kivell.

The battle went on. Our men kept cheering with all their might. I cheered with them, though I confess I scarcely knew for what. Certainly there was nothing very inspiriting in the aspect of things where I was stationed. So terrible had been the work of destruction round us, it was termed the slaughter-house. Not only had we had several boys and men killed or wounded, but several of the guns were disabled. The one I belonged to had a piece of the muzzle knocked out; and when the ship rolled, it struck a beam of the upper deck with such force as to become jammed and fixed in that position. A twenty-four-pound shot had also passed through the screen of the magazine, immediately over the orifice through which we passed our powder. The schoolmaster received a death wound. The brave boatswain, who came from the sick bay to the din of battle, was fastening a stopper on a back-stay which had been shot away, when his head was smashed to pieces by a cannon-ball; another man, going to complete the unfinished task, was also struck down. Another of our midshipmen also received a severe wound. The unfortunate ward-room steward, who, the reader will recollect, attempted to cut his throat on a former occasion, was killed. A fellow named John, who, for some petty offence, had been sent on board as a punishment, was carried past me, wounded. I distinctly heard the large blood-drops fall pat, pat, pat, on the deck; his wounds were mortal. Even a poor goat, kept by the officers for her milk, did not escape the general carnage; her hind legs were shot off, and poor Nan was thrown overboard.

Such was the terrible scene, amid which we kept on our shouting and firing. Our men fought like tigers. Some of them pulled off their jackets, others their jackets and vests; while some, still more determined, had taken off their shirts, and, with nothing but a handkerchief tied round the waistbands of their trowsers, fought like heroes. Jack Sadler, whom the reader will recollect, was one of these. I also observed a boy, named Cooper, stationed at a gun some distance from the magazine. He came to and fro on the full run and appeared to be as "merry as a cricket". The third lieutenant cheered him along, occasionally, by saying, "Well done, my boy, you are worth your weight in gold."

I have often been asked what were my feelings during this fight. I felt pretty much as I suppose every one does at such a time. That men are without thought when they stand amid the dying and the dead is too absurd an idea to be entertained a moment. We all appeared cheerful, but I know that many a serious thought ran through my mind: still, what could we do but keep up a semblance, at least, of animation? To run from our quarters would have been certain death from the hands of our own officers; to give way to gloom, or to show fear, would do no good, and might brand us with the name of cowards, and ensure certain defeat. Our only true philosophy, therefore, was to make the best of our situation by fighting bravely and cheerfully. I thought a great deal, however, of the other world; every groan, every falling man, told me that the next instant I might be before the Judge of all the earth. For this, I felt unprepared; but being without any particular knowledge of religious truth, I satisfied myself by repeating again and again the Lord's prayer and promising that if spared I would be more attentive to religious duties than ever before. This promise I had no doubt, at the time, of keeping; but I have learned since that it is easier to make promises amidst the roar of the battle's thunder, or in the horrors of shipwreck, than to keep them when danger is absent and safety smiles upon our path.

While these thoughts secretly agitated my bosom, the din of battle continued. Grape and canister shot were pouring through our portholes like leaden rain, carrying death in their trail. The large shot came against the ship's side like iron hail, shaking her to the very keel, or passing through her timbers and scattering terrific splinters, which did a more appalling work than even their own death-giving blows. The reader may form an idea of the effect of grape and canister, when he is told that grape shot is formed by seven or eight balls confined to an iron and tied in a cloth. These balls are scattered by the explosion of the powder. Canister shot is made by filling a powder canister with balls, each as large as two or three musket balls; these also scatter with direful effect when discharged. What then with splinters, cannon balls, grape and canister poured incessantly upon us, the reader may be assured that the work of death went on in a manner which must have been satisfactory even to the King of Terrors himself.

Suddenly, the rattling of the iron hail ceased. We were ordered to cease firing. A profound silence ensued, broken only by the stifled groans of the brave sufferers below. It was soon ascertained that the enemy had shot ahead to repair damages, for she was not so disabled but she could sail without difficulty; while we were so cut up that we lay utterly helpless. Our head braces were shot away; the fore and main topmasts were gone; the mizzen mast hung over the stern, having carried several men over in its fall: we were in the state of a complete wreck.

A council was now held among the officers on the quarter deck. Our condition was perilous in the extreme: victory or escape was alike hopeless. Our ship was disabled; many of our men were killed, and many more wounded. The enemy would without doubt bear down upon us in a few moments, and, as she could now choose her own position, would without doubt rake us fore and aft. Any further resistance was therefore folly. So, in spite of the hot-brained lieutenant, Mr Hope, who advised them not to strike, but to sink alongside, it was determined to strike our bunting. This was done by the hands of a brave fellow named Watson, whose saddened brow told how severely it pained his lion heart to do it. To me it was a pleasing sight, for I had seen fighting enough for one Sabbath; more than I wished to see again on a week day. His Britannic Majesty's frigate *Macedonian* was now the prize of the American frigate *United States*.

Before detailing the subsequent occurrences in my history, I will present the curious reader with a copy of Captain Carden's letter to the government, describing this action. It will serve to show how he excused himself for his defeat, as well as throw some light on those parts of the contest which were invisible to me at my station. My mother presented me with this document on my return to England. She had received it from Lord Churchill and had carefully preserved it for twenty years.

• • •

"ADMIRALTY OFFICE,
Dec. 29, 1812.
"Copy of a letter from Captain John Surman Carden, late com-
mander of His Majesty's ship the Macedonian, *to John Wilson*
Croker, Esq., dated on board the American ship United States,
at sea, the 28th October, 1812:—

"SIR: It is with the deepest regret, I have to acquaint you, for the
information of my Lords Commissioners of the Admiralty, that
His Majesty's late ship Macedonian *was captured on the 25th*
instant, by the United States ship United States, *Commodore*
Decatur commander. The detail is as follows:
"A short time after daylight, steering NW by W, with the
wind from the southward, in latitude 29° N, and longitude 29°
30' W, in the execution of their Lordships' orders, a sail was seen
on the lee beam, which I immediately stood for, and made her
out to be a large frigate, under American colors. At nine o'clock
I closed with her, and she commenced the action, which we
returned; but from the enemy keeping two points off the wind, I
was not enabled to get as close to her as I could have wished.
After an hour's action, the enemy backed and came to the wind,
and I was then enabled to bring her to close battle. In this situa-
tion I soon found the enemy's force too superior to expect success,
unless some very fortunate chance occurred in our favor; and
with this hope I continued the battle to two hours and ten min-
utes; when, having the mizzen mast shot away by the board, top-
masts shot away by the caps, main yard shot in pieces, lower
masts badly wounded, lower rigging all cut to pieces, a small pro-
portion only of the fore-sail left to the foreyard, all the guns on
the quarter deck and forecastle disabled but two, and filled with
wreck, two also on the main deck disabled, and several shot
between wind and water, a very great proportion of the crew
killed and wounded, and the enemy comparatively in good order,
who had now shot ahead and was about to place himself in a

raking position, without our being enabled to return the fire, being a perfect wreck and unmanageable log; I deemed it prudent, though a painful extremity, to surrender His Majesty's ship; nor was this dreadful alternative resorted to till every hope of success was removed, even beyond the reach of chance; nor till, I trust their Lordships will be aware, every effort had been made against the enemy by myself, and my brave officers and men, nor should she have been surrendered whilst a man lived on board, had she been manageable. I am sorry to say our loss is very severe; I find by this day's muster, thirty-six killed, three of whom lingered a short time after the battle; thirty-six severely wounded, many of whom cannot recover, and thirty-two slightly wounded, who may all do well; total, one hundred and four.

"The truly noble and animating conduct of my officers, and the steady bravery of my crew, to the last moment of the battle, must ever render them dear to their country.

"My first lieutenant, David Hope, was severely wounded in the head, towards the close of the battle, and taken below; but was soon again on deck, displaying that greatness of mind and exertion, which, though it may be equalled, can never be excelled. The third lieutenant, John Bulford, was also wounded, but not obliged to quit his quarters; second lieutenant, Samuel Mottley, and he deserves my highest acknowledgments. The cool and steady conduct of Mr. Walker, the master, was very great during the battle, as also that of Lieutenants Wilson and Magill, of the Marines.

"On being taken on board the enemy's ship, I ceased to wonder at the result of the battle. The United States *is built with the scantling** * *of a 74-gun ship, mounting thirty long 24-pounders (English ship-guns) on her main deck, and twenty-two 42-pounders, carronades, with two long 24-pounders, on her quarter deck and forecastle, howitzer guns in her tops, and a*

---

* Structure

travelling carronade on her upper deck, with a complement of
four hundred and seventy-eight picked men.

"The enemy has suffered much in masts, rigging, and hull,
above and below water. Her loss in killed and wounded I am not
aware of; but I know a lieutenant and six men have been thrown
overboard.

JNO. S. CARDEN
"To J. W. CROKER, Esq., Admiralty."

Lord Churchill sent the above letter, with a list of the killed and
wounded annexed, to inform my mother that the name of her son was
not among the number. The act shows how much he could sympathize
with a mother's feelings.

I now went below, to see how matters appeared there. The first
object I met was a man bearing a limb, which had just been detached
from some suffering wretch. Pursuing my way to the ward-room, I
necessarily passed through the steerage, which was strewed with the
wounded: it was a sad spectacle, made more appalling by the groans and
cries which rent the air. Some were groaning, others were swearing most
bitterly, a few were praying, while those last arrived were begging most
piteously to have their wounds dressed next. The surgeon and his mate
were smeared with blood from head to foot: they looked more like
butchers than doctors. Having so many patients, they had once shifted
their quarters from the cockpit to the steerage; they now removed to
the ward-room, and the long table, round which the officers had sat
over many a merry feast, was soon covered with the bleeding forms of
maimed and mutilated seamen.

While looking round the ward-room, I heard a noise above, occa-
sioned by the arrival of the boats from the conquering frigate. Very
soon a lieutenant, I think his name was Nicholson, came into the
ward-room and said to the busy surgeon, "How do you do, doctor?"

"I have enough to do," replied he, shaking his head thoughtfully;
"you have made wretched work for us!" These officers were not

strangers to each other, for the reader will recollect that the commanders and officers of these two frigates had exchanged visits when we were lying at Norfolk some months before.

I now set to work to render all the aid in my power to the sufferers. Our carpenter, named Reed, had his leg cut off. I helped to carry him to the after ward-room; but he soon breathed out his life there, and then I assisted in throwing his mangled remains overboard. We got out the cots as fast as possible; for most of them were stretched out on the gory deck. One poor fellow, who lay with a broken thigh, begged me to give him water. I gave him some. He looked unutterable gratitude, drank, and died. It was with exceeding difficulty I moved through the steerage, it was so covered with mangled men and so slippery with streams of blood. There was a poor boy there crying as if his heart would break. He had been servant to the bold boatswain, whose head was dashed to pieces. Poor boy! he felt that he had lost a friend. I tried to comfort him by reminding him that he ought to be thankful for having escaped death himself.

Here, also, I met one of my messmates, who showed the utmost joy at seeing me alive, for, he said, he had heard that I was killed. He was looking up his messmates, which he said was always done by sailors. We found two of our mess wounded. One was the Swede, Logholm, who fell overboard, as mentioned in a former chapter, and was nearly lost. We held him while the surgeon cut off his leg above the knee. The task was most painful to behold, the surgeon using his knife and saw on human flesh and bones as freely as the butcher at the shambles does on the carcass of the beast! Our other messmate suffered still more than the Swede; he was sadly mutilated about the legs and thighs with splinters. Such scenes of suffering as I saw in that ward-room, I hope never to witness again. Could the civilized world behold them as they were, and as they often are, infinitely worse than on that occasion, it seems to me they would forever put down the barbarous practices of war, by universal consent.

Most of our officers and men were taken on board the victor ship. I was left, with a few others, to take care of the wounded. My master, the sailing-master, was also among the officers, who continued in their ship. Most of the men who remained were unfit for any service, having broken into the spirit-room and made themselves drunk; some of them broke into the purser's room and helped themselves to clothing; while others, by previous agreement, took possession of their dead messmates' property. For my own part, I was content to help myself to a little of the officer's provisions, which did me more good than could be obtained from rum. What was worse than all, however, was the folly of the sailors in giving spirit to their wounded messmates, since it only served to aggravate their distress.

Among the wounded was a brave fellow named Wells. After the surgeon had amputated and dressed his arm, he walked about in fine spirits, as if he had received only a slight injury. Indeed, while under the operation, he manifested a similar heroism—observing to the surgeon, "I have lost my arm in the service of my country; but I don't mind it, doctor, it's the fortune of war." Cheerful and gay as he was, he soon died. His companions gave him rum; he was attacked by fever and died. Thus his messmates actually killed him with kindness.

We had all sorts of dispositions and temperaments among our crew. To me it was a matter of great interest to watch their various manifestations. Some who had lost their messmates appeared to care nothing about it, while others were grieving with all the tenderness of women. Of these was the survivor of two seamen who had formerly been soldiers in the same regiment; he bemoaned the loss of his comrades with expressions of profoundest grief. There were, also, two boatswain's mates, named Adams and Brown, who had been messmates for several years in the same ship. Brown was killed, or so wounded that he died soon after the battle. It was really a touching spectacle to see the rough, hardy features of the brave old sailor streaming with tears, as he picked out the dead body of his friend from among the wounded and gently carried it to the ship's side, saying to the inanimate form he bore, "O Bill, we have sailed together in a number of ships, we have been in many gales and some battles, but this is the worst day I have seen! We must now part!" Here he dropped the body into the deep, and then, a fresh torrent of tears streaming over his weather-beaten face, he added, "I can do no more for you. Farewell! God be with you!" Here was an instance of genuine friendship, worth more than the heartless professions of thousands, who, in the fancied superiority of their elevated position in the social circle, will deign nothing but a silly sneer at this record of a sailor's grief.

The circumstance was rather a singular one, that in both the contending frigates the second boatswain's mate bore the name of William Brown, and that they both were killed; yet such was the fact.

The great number of the wounded kept our surgeon and his mate busily employed at their horrid work until late at night; and it was a long time before they had much leisure. I remember passing round the ship the day after the battle. Coming to a hammock, I found some one in it apparently asleep. I spoke; he made no answer. I looked into the hammock; he was dead. My messmates coming up, we threw the corpse overboard; that was no time for useless ceremony. The man had probably crawled to his hammock the day before, and, not being perceived in the general distress, bled to death! O War! who can reveal thy miseries!

When the crew of the *United States* first boarded our frigate to take possession of her as their prize, our men, heated with the fury of the battle, exasperated with the sight of their dead and wounded shipmates, and rendered furious by the rum they had obtained from the spirit-room, felt and exhibited some disposition to fight their captors. But after the confusion had subsided and part of our men were snugly stowed away in the American ship, and the remainder found themselves kindly used in their own, the utmost good feeling began to prevail. We took hold and cleansed the ship, using hot vinegar to take out the scent of the blood that had dyed the white of our planks with crimson. We also took hold and aided in fitting our disabled frigate for her voyage. This being accomplished, both ships sailed in company toward the American coast.

I soon felt myself perfectly at home with the American seamen; so much so that I chose to mess with them. My shipmates also participated in similar feelings in both ships. All idea that we had been trying to shoot out each other's brains so shortly before seemed forgotten. We eat together, drank together, joked, sung, laughed, told yarns; in short, a perfect union of ideas, feelings, and purposes seemed to exist among all hands.

A corresponding state of unanimity existed, I was told, among the officers. Commodore Decatur showed himself to be a gentleman as well as a hero in his treatment of the officers of the *Macedonian*. When Captain Carden offered his sword to the commodore, remarking, as he did so, "I am an undone man. I am the first British naval officer that has struck his flag to an American": the noble commodore either refused to receive the sword or immediately returned it, smiling as he said, "You are mistaken, sir; your *Guerriere* has been taken by us, and the flag of a frigate was struck before yours." This somewhat revived the spirits of the old captain; but, no doubt, he still felt his soul stung with shame and mortification at the loss of his ship. Participating as he did in the haughty spirit of the British aristocracy, it was natural for him to feel galled and wounded to the quick, in the position of a conquered man.

We were now making the best of our way to America. Notwithstanding the patched-up condition of the *Macedonian*, she was far superior, in a sailing capacity, to her conqueror. The *United States* had always been a dull sailer, and had been christened by the name of the Old Wagon. Whenever a boat came alongside of our frigate and the boatswain's mate was ordered to "pipe away" the boat's crew, he used to sound his shrill call on the whistle and bawl out, "Away, *Wagoners*, away", instead of "away, *United States* men, away". This piece of pleasantry used to be rebuked by the officers, but in a manner that showed they enjoyed the joke. They usually replied, "Boatswain's mate, you rascal, pipe away *United States* men, not Wagoners. We have no wagoners on board of a ship." Still, in spite of rebuke, the joke went on, until it grew stale by repetition. One thing was made certain however by the sailing qualities of the *Macedonian*; which was, that if we had been disposed to escape from our foe before the action, we could have done so with all imaginable ease. This however, would have justly exposed us to disgrace, while our capture did not. There was every reason why the *United States* should beat us. She was larger in size, heavier in metal, more numerous in men, and stronger built than the *Macedonian*. Another fact in her favor was that our captain at first mistook her for the *Essex*, which carried short carronades, hence he engaged her at long shot at first; for, as we had the weather gage, we could take what position we pleased. But this maneuver only wasted our shot and gave her the advantage, as she actually carried larger metal than we did. When we came to close action, the shot from the *United States* went "through and through" our ship, while ours struck her sides and fell harmlessly into the water. This is to be accounted for both by the superiority of the metal and of the ship. Her guns were heavier and her sides thicker than ours. Some have said that her sides were stuffed with cork. Of this, however, I am not certain. Her superiority, both in number of men and guns, may easily be seen by the following statistics. We carried forty-nine guns; long eighteen-pounders on the main deck, and thirty-two-pound carronades on the quarter deck and forecastle. Our whole number of hands, including officers, men and boys, was three hundred. The *United States* carried four hundred and fifty men and fifty-four guns: long twenty-four-pounders on the main deck, and forty-two-pound carronades on the quarter deck and forecastle. So that in actual force she was immensely our superior.

To these should be added the consideration that the men in the two ships fought under the influence of different motives. Many of our hands were in the service against their will; some of them were Americans, wrongfully impressed and inwardly hoping for defeat: while nearly every man in our ship sympathized with the great principle for which the American nation so nobly contended in the war of 1812. What that was, I suppose all my readers understand. The British, at war with France, had denied the Americans the right to trade thither. She had impressed American seamen and forcibly compelled their service in her navy; she had violated the American flag by insolently searching their vessels for her runaway seamen. Free trade and sailors' rights, therefore, were the objects contended for by the Americans. With these objects our *men* could but sympathize, whatever our officers might do.

On the other hand, the crew of our opponent had all shipped *voluntarily* for the term of two years only (most of our men were shipped for life). They understood what they fought for; they were better used in the service. What wonder, then, that victory adorned the brows of the American commander? To have been defeated under such circumstances would have been a source of lasting infamy to any naval officer in the world. In the matter of fighting, I think there is but little difference in either nation. Place them in action under equal circumstances and motives, and who could predict which would be victor? Unite them together, they would subject the whole world. So close are the alliances of blood, however, between England and America, that it is to be earnestly desired, they may never meet in mortal strife again. If either will fight, which is to be deprecated as a crime and a folly, let it choose an enemy less connected by the sacred ties of consanguinity.

Our voyage was one of considerable excitement. The seas swarmed with British cruisers, and it was extremely doubtful whether the *United States* would elude their grasp and reach the protection of an American port with her prize. I hoped most sincerely to avoid them, as did most of my old shipmates; in this we agreed with our captors, who wisely desired to dispose of one conquest before they attempted another. Our former officers, of course, were anxious for the sight of a British flag. But we saw none, and, after a prosperous voyage from the scene of conflict, we heard the welcome cry of "Land ho!" The *United States* entered the port of New London; but, owing to a sudden shift of the wind, the *Macedonian* had to lay off and on for several hours. Had an English cruiser found us in this situation, we should have been easily recovered; and, as it was extremely probable we should fall in with one, I felt quite uneasy, until, after several hours, we made out to run into the pretty harbor of Newport. We fired a salute as we came to an anchor, which was promptly returned by the people on shore.

With a few exceptions, our wounded men were in a fair way to recover by the time we reached Newport. The last of them, who died of their wounds on board, was buried just before we got in. His name was Thomas Whittaker; he had been badly wounded by splinters. While he lived, he endured excessive torture. At last his sufferings rendered him crazy, in which sad state he died. He was sewed up in his hammock by his messmates and carried on a grating to the larboard bow port. There Mr. Archer, a midshipman of the *Macedonian*, read the beautiful burial service of the church of England. When he came to that most touching passage, "we commit the body of our brother to the deep", the grating was elevated, and, amid the most profound silence, the body fell heavily into the waters. As it dropped into the deep, a sigh escaped from many a friendly bosom, and an air of passing melancholy shrouded many a face with sadness. Old recollections were busy there, calling up the losses of the battle; but it was only momentary. The men brushed away their tears, muttered "It's no use to fret", and things once more wore their wonted aspect.

from Mutiny on the Bounty
by Charles Nordhoff and
James Norman Hall

The H.M.S. Bounty in 1787 set out for Tahiti to collect breadfruit trees for agricultural research. First mate Fletcher Christian on the return trip led the crew in a mutiny against Captain William Bligh. Charles Nordhoff (1887–1947) and James Norman Hall (1887–1951) in 1932 published their classic novel about the mutiny.

Shortly after daybreak I was awakened by someone shaking me roughly by the shoulder, and at the same time I was aware of loud voices, Mr. Bligh's among them, and the heavy trampling of feet on deck. Churchill, the master-at-arms, stood by my hammock with a pistol in his hand, and I saw Thompson, holding a musket with the bayonet fixed, stationed by the arms chest which stood on the gratings of the main hatch. At the same time two men, whose names I do not remember, rushed into the berth, and one of them shouted, "We're with you, Churchill! Give us arms!" They were furnished with muskets by Thompson and hurried on deck again. Stewart, whose hammock was next to mine in the larboard berth, was already up and dressing in great haste. Despite the confused tumult of voices overhead, Young was still asleep.

"Have we been attacked, Churchill?" I asked; for my first thought was that the *Bounty* must have drifted close to one of the islands thereabout, and that we had been boarded by the savages.

"Put on your clothes and lose no time about it, Mr. Byam," he replied. "We have taken the ship and Captain Bligh is a prisoner."

Aroused suddenly from the deepest slumber, I did not even then grasp the meaning of what he said, and for a moment sat gazing stupidly at him.

"They've mutinied, Byam!" said Stewart. "Good God. Churchill! Are you mad? Have you any conception of what you're doing?"

"We know very well what we're doing," he replied. "Bligh has brought all this on himself. Now, by God, we'll make him suffer!"

Thompson shook his musket in menacing fashion. "We're going to shoot the dog!" he said; "and don't you try any of your young gentlemen's tricks on us, or we'll murder some more of you! Seize 'em up, Churchill! They're not to be trusted."

"Hold your tongue and mind the arms chest," Churchill replied. "Come, Mr. Byam, hurry into your clothes. Quintal, stand fast by the door there! No one's to come forward without my orders—understand?"

"Aye, aye, sir!"

Turning my head, I saw Matthew Quintal at the rear entrance to the berth. Even as I looked, Samuel appeared behind him, dressed only in his trousers, his thin hair standing awry and his pale face considerably paler than its wont. "Mr. Churchill!" he called.

"Go back, you fat swine, or I'll run you through the guts!" Quintal shouted.

"Mr. Churchill, sir! Allow me to speak to you," Samuel called again.

"Drive him back," Churchill said, and Quintal made so fierce a gesture with his musket that Samuel vanished without waiting to hear more. "Give him a prod in the backside, Quintal," someone shouted, and, looking up, I saw two more armed men leaning over the hatchway.

Without weapons of any sort, there was nothing that Stewart and I could do but obey Churchill's orders. Both he and Thompson were powerful men and we should have been no match for them even had they been unarmed. I immediately thought of Christian, a man as quick in action as in decision, but I knew there could be no hope of his still being at liberty. He was the officer of the morning watch and had doubtless been rushed and overwhelmed at the very outset of the mutiny, even before Bligh had been secured. Catching my eye, Stewart shook his head slightly, as much as to say, "It's useless. There's nothing to be done."

We dressed in short order, and Churchill then ordered us to precede him along the passage to the fore ladderway. "Keep the others in the berth, Thompson," he called back. "Leave 'em to me; I'll mind 'em!" Thompson replied. There were several armed guards at the fore-hatch, among them Alexander Smith, my hammock man, whose loyalty in whatever situation I should have thought unquestionable. It was a shock to see him in Churchill's party, but the scene that presented itself as we came on deck made me forget the very existence of Smith.

Captain Bligh, naked except for his shirt, and with his hands tied behind his back, was standing by the mizzenmast. Christian stood before him, holding in one hand the end of the line by which Bligh was bound and in the other a bayonet, and around them were several of the able seamen, fully armed, among whom I recognized John Mills, Isaac Martin, Richard Skinner, and Thomas Burkitt. Churchill then said to us, "Stand by here. We mean no harm to either of you unless you take part against us." He then left us.

Stewart and I had taken it for granted that Churchill was the ringleader of the mutineers. As already related, after his attempted desertion at Tahiti he had been severely punished by Bligh. I knew how deeply he hated him, and it was conceivable that such a man could goad himself even to the point of mutiny. But that Christian could have done so, no matter what the provocation, was beyond anything I could have dreamed of as possible. Stewart's only comment was, "Christian! Good God! Then there's no hope."

The situation looked hopeless indeed. At this time the only unarmed men I saw on deck were Captain Bligh and ourselves. The ship was entirely in the hands of the mutineers. Evidently we had been brought up to divide the party of midshipmen below, thus preventing any opportunity for our taking concerted action. In the confusion we made our way aft a little way, and as we approached the spot where Bligh was standing, I heard Christian say, "Will you hold your tongue, sir, or shall I force you to hold it? I'm master of this ship now, and, by God, I'll stand no more of your abuse!" Sweat was pouring down Bligh's face. He had been making a great outcry, shouting, "Murder! Treason!" at the top of his voice.

"Master of my ship, you mutinous dog!" he yelled. "I'll see you hung! I'll have you flogged to ribbons! I'll . . ."

"*Mamu*, sir! Hold your tongue or you are dead this instant!"

Christian placed the point of his bayonet at Bligh's throat with a look in his eye there was no mistaking. "Slit the dog's gullet!" someone shouted; and there were cries of "Let him have it, Mr. Christian!" "Throw him overboard!" "Feed the bastard to the sharks!" and the like. It was only then, I think, that Captain Bligh realized his true situation. He stood for a moment breathing hard, looking about him with an expression of incredulity on his face.

"Mr. Christian, allow me to speak!" he begged hoarsely. "Think what you do! Release me—lay aside your arms! Let us be friends again, and I give you my word that nothing more shall be said of this matter."

"Your word is of no value, sir," Christian replied. "Had you been a man of honour things would never have come to this pass."

"What do you mean to do with me?"

"Shoot you, you bloody rogue!" cried Burkitt, shaking his musket at him.

"Shooting's too good for him! Seize him up at the gratings, Mr. Christian! Give us a chance at him with the cat!"

"That's it! Seize him up! Give him a taste of his own poison!"

"Flay the hide off him!"

"Silence!" Christian called, sternly; and then, to Bligh: "We'll give you justice, sir, which is more than you have ever given us. We'll take you in irons to England . . ."

A dozen protesting voices interrupted him.

"To England? Never! We won't have it, Mr. Christian!"

Immediately the deck was again in an uproar, all the mutineers clamouring against Christian's proposal. Never was the situation with respect to Bligh so critical as at that moment, and it was to his credit that he showed no sign of flinching. The men were in a savage mood, and it was touch and go as to whether he would be shot where he stood; but he glared at each of them in turn as though challenging them to do so. Luckily a diversion was created when Ellison came dashing up flourishing a bayonet. There was no real harm in this lad, but he loved mischief better than his dinner, and, being thoughtless and high-spirited, he could be counted upon to get himself into trouble whenever the opportunity presented itself. Evidently he considered joining in a mutiny nothing more than a fine lark, and he now came dancing up to Bligh with such a comical expression upon his face that the tension was relieved at once. The men broke into cheers. "Hooray, Tommy! Are you with us, lad?"

"Let me guard him, Mr. Christian!" he cried. "I'll watch him like a cat!" He skipped up and down in front of Bligh, brandishing his weapon. "Oh, you rogue! You old villain! You'd flog us, would you? You'd stop our grog, would you? You'd make us eat grass, would you?"

The men cheered him wildly. "Lay on, lad!" they shouted. "We'll back you! Give him a jab in the guts!"

"You and your Mr. Samuel! A pair of swindlers, that's what you are! Cheating us out of our food! You've made a pretty penny between you! You old thief! You should be a bumboat man. I'll lay you'd make your fortune in no time!"

It was a bitter experience for Bligh to be baited thus by the least of his seamen, but as a matter of fact nothing more fortunate for him could have happened. His life at that moment hung in the balance, and Ellison, in giving vent to his feelings, relieved the pent-up emotions of men who were not glib of speech and could express their hatred of Bligh only in action. Christian realized this, I think, and permitted Ellison to speak his mind, but he soon cut him short and put him in his place.

"Clear the cutter!" he called. "Mr. Churchill!"

"Aye, aye, sir!"

"Fetch up Mr. Fryer and Mr. Purcell! Burkitt!"

"Here, sir!"

"You and Sumner and Mills and Martin—stand guard here over Mr. Bligh!"

Burkitt took the end of the line in one of his huge hairy fists.

"We'll mind him, sir! I'll lay to that!"

"What's your plan, Mr. Christian? We've a right to know," said Sumner. Christian turned quickly and looked at him. "Mind what you're about, Sumner!" he said quietly. "I'm master of this ship! Lively, men, with the cutter."

Several men climbed into the boat to clear out the yams, sweet potatoes, and other ship's stores which were kept there, while others unlashed it and got ready the tackle for hoisting it over the side. Burkitt stood directly in front of Captain Bligh, holding the point of a bayonet within an inch of his breast. Sumner stood behind him with his musket at ready, and the other men on either side. Thompson excepted, they were the hardest characters among the sailors, and Bligh wisely said nothing to arouse them further. Others of the mutineers were stationed about the decks, and there were three at each of the ladderways. I wondered how the affair had been so well and secretly planned. I searched my memory, but could recall no incident of a character in the least suspicious.

I had been so intent in watching the scene of which Bligh was the centre that I had forgotten Stewart. We had become separated, and while I was searching for him Christian saw me for the first time. He came at once to where I was standing. His voice was calm, but I could see that he was labouring under great excitement.

"Byam, this is my affair," he said. "Not a man shall be hurt, but if any take part against us it will be at the peril of the entire ship's company. Act as you think best."

"What do you mean to do?" I asked.

"I would have carried Bligh to England as a prisoner. That is impossible; the men won't have it. He shall have the cutter to go where he chooses. Mr. Fryer, Hayward, Hallet, and Samuel shall go with him."

There was no time for further talk. Churchill came up with the master and Purcell. The carpenter, as usual, was surly and taciturn. Both he and Fryer were horror-stricken at what had happened, but they were entirely self-possessed. Christian well knew that these two men would seize the first opportunity, if one presented itself, for retaking the ship, and he had them well guarded.

"Mr. Byam, surely you are not concerned in this?" Fryer asked.

"No more than yourself, sir," I replied.

"Mr. Byam has nothing to do with it," said Christian. "Mr. Purcell . . ."

Fryer interrupted him.

"In God's name, Mr. Christian! What is it you do? Do you realize that this means the ruin of everything? Give up this madness, and I promise that we shall all make your interest our own. Only let us reach England . . ."

"It is too late, Mr. Fryer," he replied, coldly. "I have been in hell for weeks past, and I mean to stand it no longer."

"Your difficulties with Captain Bligh give you no right to bring ruin upon the rest of us."

"Hold your tongue, sir," said Christian. "Mr. Purcell, have your men fetch up the thwarts, knees, and gear bolts for the large cutter. Churchill, let the carpenter go below to see to this. Send a guard with him."

Purcell and Churchill went down the forward ladderway.

"Do you mean to set us adrift?" Fryer asked.

"We are no more than nine leagues from the land here," Christian replied. "In so calm a sea Mr. Bligh will have no difficulty in making it."

"I will stay with the ship."

"No, Mr. Fryer; you will go with Captain Bligh. Williams! Take the master to his cabin while he collects his clothes. He is to be kept there until I send word."

Fryer requested earnestly to be allowed to remain with the vessel, but Christian well knew his reason for desiring this and would not hear to the proposal. He put an end to the matter by sending the master below.

Purcell now returned, followed by Norman and McIntosh, his mates, carrying the gear for the cutter. Purcell came up to me at once.

"Mr. Byam, I know that you have no hand in this business. But you are, or have been, a friend to Mr. Christian. Beg him to give Captain Bligh the launch. The cutter is rotten and will never swim to the land."

This, I knew, was the case. The cutter was riddled with worms and leaked so badly as to be almost useless. The carpenters were to have started repairing her that same morning. Purcell would not come with me to speak of the matter, giving as a reason Christian's dislike of him. "He would not care to grant any request of mine," he said. "If the cutter is hoisted out, it will be almost certain death for Captain Bligh and all who are permitted to go with him."

I wasted no time, but went to Christian at once. Several of the mutineers gathered round to hear what I had to say. Christian agreed at once. "He shall have the launch," he said. "Tell the carpenter to have his men fit her." He then called, "Leave off with the cutter, my lads! Clear the launch."

There were immediate protests, led by Churchill, against this new arrangement.

"The launch, Mr. Christian?"

"Don't let him have it, sir! The old fox'll get home in her!"

"She's too bloody good for him!"

There was an argument over the matter, but Christian forced his will upon the others. In fact, they made no determined stand. All were eager to be rid of the captain, and they had little reason to fear that he would ever see England again.

The mutineers were in such complete control of the situation that Christian now gave orders for the rest of those who were not of his party to be brought on deck. Samuel, Bligh's clerk, was among the first to appear. He was anything but a favourite with the ship's company, and was greeted with jeers and threats by his particular enemies. I had supposed that he would make a poor showing in such a situation. On the contrary, he acted with spirit and determination. Disregarding the insults of the sailors, he went directly to Captain Bligh to receive his orders. He was permitted to go to Bligh's cabin with John Smith, the captain's servant, to fetch up his clothes. They helped him on with his boots and trousers and laid his coat over his shoulders.

I saw Hayward and Hallet standing aft by the rail. Hallet was crying, and both of them were in a state of great alarm. Someone touched my shoulder and I found Mr. Nelson standing beside me.

"Well, Byam, I'm afraid that we're even farther from home than we thought. Do you know what they plan to do with us?"

I told him the little I knew. He smiled ruefully, glancing toward the island of Tofoa, now a faint blur on the horizon.

"I suppose that Captain Bligh will take us there," he said. "I don't much relish the prospect of meeting any more Friendly Islanders. Their friendliness is of a kind that we can well dispense with."

The carpenter appeared at the ladderway, followed by Robert Lamb, the butcher, who was helping to bring up his tool chest.

"Mr. Nelson," he said, "we know whom we have to thank for this."

"Yes, Mr. Purcell, our unlucky stars," Nelson replied.

"No, sir! We have Captain Bligh to thank for it, and him alone! He has brought it upon us all by his damnable behaviour!"

Purcell had the deepest hatred for Bligh, which was returned with interest. The two men had not spoken for months save when absolutely necessary. Nevertheless, when Mr. Nelson suggested that be might be permitted to stay with the ship if he chose, the carpenter was horrified.

"Stop aboard? With rogues and pirates? Never, sir! I shall follow my commander."

At this moment Churchill, who was everywhere about the decks, caught sight of us.

"What are you about there, Purcell? Damn your blood! You'd steal our tools, would you?"

"Your tools, you scoundrel? They're mine, and they go where I go!"

"You shan't take a nail from the ship if I have my way," Churchill replied. He then called out to Christian, and there was another argument, not only with respect to the tool chest, but as to the carpenter himself. Christian was partly in the mind to keep him on the vessel, knowing his value as a craftsman, but all the others urged against it. Purcell had a violent temper and was regarded by the men as a tyrant second only to Bligh.

"He's a damned old villain, sir!"

"Keep the carpenter's mates, Mr. Christian. They're the men for us."

"Make him go in the boat!"

"Make me go, you pirates?" he cried. "I'd like to see the man who'll *stop* me!"

Unfortunately, Purcell was as thick-headed as he was fearless, and he now so far forgot the interests of Bligh's party as to boast of what we would do as soon as we should be clear of the mutineers.

"Mark my word, you rogues! We'll bring every man of you to justice! We'll build a vessel to carry us home . . ."

"So he will, Mr. Christian, if we give him his tools," several men shouted.

"The old fox could build a slip with a clasp knife!"

Purcell realized too late what he had done. I believe that Christian would have given him many of his tools, of which there were duplicates on board, but having been reminded of what he might do with them, he now ordered the tool chest to be examined, and Purcell was permitted to have nothing but a hand saw, a small axe, a hammer, and a bag of nails. Bligh, who had overheard all that was said, could contain himself no longer. "You infernal idiot!" he roared at Purcell, and was prevented from saying more by Burkitt, who placed a bayonet at his throat.

The decks were now filled with people, but Christian took good care that those not of his party should be prevented from coming together in any numbers. As soon as the launch had been cleared, he ordered the boatswain to swing her out. "And mind yourself, Mr. Cole! If you

spring a yard or carry anything away it will go hard with you!" Fifteen
or more of us were ordered to assist him, for the mutineers were too
canny to lay aside their arms and bear a hand.

"Foresail and mainsail there! All ready?"

"Aye, aye, sir!"

"Let go sheets and tacks!"

"All clear, sir!"

"Clew garnets—up with the clews!"

The breeze was still so light as barely to fill the sails, and the clews
of the mainsail and foresail went smoothly up to the quarters of the
yards. The yards were now squared and the braces made fast, and with
half a dozen men holding the launch inboard she was hoisted, swung
out over the bulwarks, and lowered away.

One of the first men ordered into her was Samuel. Hayward and
Hallet followed next. Both were shedding tears and crying for mercy,
and they were half carried to the gangway. Hayward turned to Christian, clasping his hands imploringly.

"Mr. Christian, what have I ever done that you should treat me so?"
he exclaimed. "In God's name, permit me to stay with the ship!"

"We can dispense with your services here," Christian replied, grimly.
"Into the boat, the pair of you!"

Purcell went next. He required no urging. I think he would have
died rather than remain in the ship now that she had been seized by
mutineers. His few tools were handed down to him by the boatswain,
who followed. Christian ordered Bligh to be brought to the gangway,
and his hands were freed.

"Now, Mr. Bligh, there is your boat, and you are fortunate to have
the launch and not the cutter. Go into her at once, sir!"

"Mr. Christian," said Bligh, "for the last time I beg you to reflect! I'll
pawn my honour—I pledge you my word never to think of this again
if you will desist. Consider my wife and family!"

"No, Mr. Bligh. You should have thought of your family long
before this, and we well know what your honour is worth. Go into
the boat, sir!"

Seeing that all pleading was useless, Bligh obeyed, and was followed by Mr. Peckover and Norton, the quartermaster. Christian then handed down a sextant and a book of nautical tables.

"You have your compass, sir. This book is sufficient for every purpose, and the sextant is my own. You know it to be a good one."

With his hands freed and once more in command, though only of his ship's launch, Bligh became his old self again.

"I know you to be a bloody scoundrel!" he shouted, shaking his fist in Christian's direction. "But I'll have vengeance! Mind that, you ungrateful villain! I'll see you swinging at a yardarm before two years have passed! And every traitor with you!"

Fortunately for Bligh, Christian's attention was engaged elsewhere, but several of the mutineers at the bulwarks replied to him in language as forceful as the captain's, and it was a near thing that he was not fired upon.

In the confusion I had lost sight of Stewart. We had been hauling together at one of the braces when the launch was hoisted out, but now I could find him nowhere. It soon became clear that many were to be allowed to go with Bligh, and Mr. Nelson and I, who had been standing together by the bulwarks, were hastening toward the after ladderway when we were stopped by Christian.

"Mr. Nelson, you and Mr. Byam may stay with the ship if you choose," he said.

"I have sympathy with you for the wrongs you have suffered, Mr. Christian," Nelson replied, "but none whatever with this action to redress them."

"And when have I asked you for sympathy, sir? Mr. Byam, what is your decision?"

"I shall go with Captain Bligh."

"Then make haste, both of you."

"Have we permission to fetch our clothes?" Nelson asked.

"Yes, but look sharp!"

Nelson's cabin was on the orlop deck directly below that of Fryer. Two guards stood by the ladderway on the lower deck. We parted there and I went to the midshipmen's berth, where Thompson was still on guard over the arms chest. I had seen nothing of Tinkler and Elphinstone, and was about to look into the starboard berth to see if they were still there. Thompson prevented me.

"Never you mind the starboard berth," he said. "Get your clothes and clear out!"

The berth was screened off from the main hatchway by a canvas-covered framework. To my surprise, I found Young still asleep in his hammock. He had been on watch from twelve to four, and this was his customary time for rest, but it was strange that he could have slept through such a turmoil. I tried to rouse him, but he was a notoriously heavy sleeper. Finding the matter hopeless, I left off and began to ransack my chest for things I should most need. Stacked in the corner of the berth were several Friendly Island war clubs that we had obtained from the savages of Namuka. They had been carved from the *toa*, or ironwood tree, which well deserved its name, for in weight and texture the wood was indeed like iron. At the sight of them the thought flashed into my mind, "Could I strike Thompson down with one of these?" I glanced quickly out the doorway. Thompson was now seated on the arms chest with his musket between his knees, facing the passageway leading aft. But he saw me thrust out my head and, with an oath, ordered me to "look sharp and clear out of there."

At this moment Morrison came along the passageway, and as luck would have it Thompson's attention was attracted by someone calling him from above. I beckoned Morrison into the berth, and he dodged in without having been seen. There was no need for words. I handed him one of the war clubs and took another for myself; then, together, we made a last effort to waken Young. Not daring to speak, we nearly shook him out of his hammock, but we might have spared ourselves the trouble. I heard Thompson call out, "He's getting his clothes, sir. I'll have him up at once." Morrison drew back by the door and raised his club, and I stood at ready on the other side, for we both expected Thompson to come in for me. Instead of that he shouted, "Out of there, Byam, and be quick about it!"

"I'm coming," I called, and again looked out of the doorway. My heart sank as I saw Burkitt and McCoy coming along from the fore hatchway. They stopped by the arms chest to speak to Thompson. Both had muskets, of course. Our chance to get at Thompson and the arms chest was lost unless they should pass on. Fortune was against us. We waited for at least two minutes longer and the men remained where they were. I heard Nelson's voice calling down the hatchway: "Byam! Lively there, lad, or you'll be left behind!" And Tinkler's: "For God's sake, hasten, Byam!"

It was a bitter moment for Morrison and me. The opportunity had been a poor one at best, but had there been time something might have come of it. We quickly put the war clubs aside and rushed out, colliding with Thompson, who was coming to see what I was about.

"Damn your blood, Morrison! What are you doing here?"

We didn't wait to explain, but ran along the passage to the ladderway. Morrison preceded me, and in my haste to reach the deck, cumbered as I was with my bag of clothes, I slipped and fell halfway down the ladder, giving my shoulder a wrench as I struck the gratings. I clambered up again and was rushing toward the gangway when Churchill seized me. "You're too late, Byam," he said. "You can't go." "Can't go? By God, I *will*!" I exclaimed, giving him a shove which loosened his hold and all but toppled him over. I was frantic, for I saw the launch being veered astern, one of the mutineers carrying the painter aft. Burkitt and Quintal were holding Coleman, the armourer, who was begging to go into the boat, and Morrison was struggling with several men who were keeping him back from the gangway. We were, in fact, too late; the launch was loaded almost to the point of foundering, and I heard Bligh shouting: "I can take no more of you, lads! I'll do you justice if ever we reach England!"

When the launch had drifted astern, the man holding the painter took a turn with it around the rail and threw the free end to someone in the boat. Those left in the ship now crowded along the rail, and I had difficulty in finding a place where I could look over the side. I was sick at heart, and appalled at the realization that I was, indeed, to be left behind among the mutineers. Norton was in the bow of the launch holding the end of the painter. Bligh was standing on a thwart, astern. Of the others, some were seated and some were standing, and the boat was so heavily loaded as to have no more than seven or eight inches of freeboard. There was a great deal of shouting back and forth, and Bligh was contributing his full share to the tumult by bellowing out orders to those in the boat, and curses and imprecations against Christian and his men.

Some of the mutineers looked on silently and thoughtfully, but others were jeering at Bligh, and I heard one of them shout: "Go and see if you can live on half a pound of yams a day, you bloody villain!" Fryer called out, "In God's name, Mr. Christian, give us arms and ammunition! Think where we go! Let us have a chance to defend our lives!" Others, the boatswain among them, joined earnestly in this plea.

"Arms be damned!" someone shouted back.

"You don't need 'em."

"Old Bligh loves the savages. He'll take care of you!"

"Use your rattan on 'em, boatswain!"

Coleman and I sought out Christian, who was standing by one of the cabin gratings, out of sight of the launch. We begged him to let Bligh have some muskets and ammunition.

"Never!" he said. "They shall have no firearms."

"Then give them some cutlasses at least, Mr. Christian," Coleman urged, "unless you wish them to be murdered the moment they set foot on shore. Think of our experience at Namuka!"

Christian consented to this. He ordered Churchill to fetch some cutlasses from the arms chest, and a moment later he returned with four, which were handed into the boat. Meanwhile, Morrison had taken advantage of this opportunity to run below for some additional provisions for the launch. He and John Millward brought up a mess kit filled with pieces of salt pork, several calabashes of water, and some additional bottles of wine and spirits, which they lowered into the boat.

"You cowards!" Purcell shouted, as the cutlasses were handed in. "Will you give us nothing but these?"

"Shall we lower the arms chest, carpenter?" Isaac Martin asked, jeeringly. McCoy threatened him with his musket. "You'll get a bellyful of lead in a minute," he shouted.

"Bear off and turn one of the swivels on 'em!" someone else called. "Give 'em a whiff of grape!"

Burkitt now raised his musket and pointed it at Bligh. Alexander Smith, who was standing beside him, seized the barrel of the musket and thrust it up. I am convinced that Burkitt meant to shoot Bligh, but Christian, observing this, ordered him to be dragged back, deprived of his arms, and placed under guard. He made a terrific struggle, and it required four men to disarm him.

Meanwhile, Fryer and others were urging Bligh to cast off lest they should all be murdered. This Bligh now ordered to be done, and the launch dropped slowly astern. The oars were gotten out, and the boat, so low in the water that she seemed on the point of foundering, was headed toward the island of Tofoa, which bore northeast, about ten leagues distant. Twelve men made a good load for the launch. She now carried nineteen, to say nothing of the food and water and the gear of the men.

"Thank God we were too late to go with her, Byam!"

Morrison was standing beside me.

"Do you mean that?" I asked.

He was silent for a moment, as though considering the matter carefully. Then he said, "No, I don't. I would willingly have taken my chance in her—but it's a slim chance indeed. They'll never see England again."

Tinkler was sitting on a thwart. Mr. Nelson, and Peckover, Norton, Elphinstone, the master's mate, Ledward, the acting surgeon—all were as good as dead, more than a thousand miles from any port where they might expect help. About them were islands filled with the cruellest of savages, who could be held at bay only by men well armed. Granted that some might escape death at the hands of the Indians, what chance had so tiny a boat, so appallingly loaded, to reach any civilized port? The possibility was so remote as to be not worth considering.

Sick at heart, I turned away from the sight of the frail craft, looking so small, so helpless, on that great waste of waters. There had been a cheer from some of the mutineers: "Huzza for Tahiti!" as Christian had ordered, "Get sail on her!" Ellison, McCoy, and Williams had run aloft to loose the fore-topgallant sail. Afterward a silence had fallen over the ship, and the men stood by the bulwarks, gazing at the launch growing smaller and smaller as we drew away from her. Christian, too, was watching, standing where I had last seen him, by the cabin grating. What his thoughts were at this time it would be impossible to say. His sense of the wrongs he had suffered at Bligh's hands was so deep and overpowering as to dominate, I believe, every other feeling. In the course of a long life I have met no others of his kind. I knew him, I suppose, as well as anyone could be said to know him, and yet I never felt that I truly understood the workings of his mind and heart. Men of such passionate nature, when goaded by injustice into action, lose all sense of anything save their own misery. They neither know nor care, until it is too late, what ruin they make of the lives of others.

It was getting on toward eight o'clock when the launch had been cast off. Shortly afterward the breeze, from the northeast, freshened, and the *Bounty* gathered way quietly, slipping through the water with a slight hiss of foam. The launch became a mere speck, seen momentarily as she rose to the swell or as the sunlight flashed from her oars. Within half an hour she had vanished as though swallowed up by the sea. Our course was west-northwest.

from Lieutenant Hornblower
by C.S. Forester

C.S. Forester (1899–1966) wrote 11 novels chronicling Horatio Hornblower's rise through the British Navy's ranks during the Napoleonic Wars. Here Hornblower patrols the Caribbean aboard H.M.S. Renown, whose captain had lost his mind and been relieved of command.

Lieutenant Buckland, in acting command of the H.M.S. *Renown*, of seventy-four guns, was on the quarterdeck of his ship peering through his telescope at the low mountains of Santo Domingo. The ship was rolling in a fashion unnatural and disturbing, for the long Atlantic swell, driven by the northeast trades, was passing under her keel while she lay hove-to to the final puffs of the land breeze which had blown since midnight and was now dying away as the fierce sun heated the island again. The *Renown* was actually wallowing, rolling her lower deck gunports under, first on one side and then on the other, for what little breeze there was was along the swell and did nothing to stiffen her as she lay with her mizzen topsail backed. She would lie right over on one side, until the gun tackles creaked with the strain of holding the guns in position, until it was hard to keep a foothold on the steep-sloping deck; she would lie there for a few harrowing seconds, and then slowly right herself, making no pause at all at the moment when she was upright and her deck horizontal, and continue, with a clattering of blocks and a rattle of gear, in a sickening swoop until she was as far over in the opposite direction, gun tackles creaking and unwary men slipping and sliding, and lie there unresponsive until the swell had rolled under her and she repeated her behaviour.

"For God's sake," said Hornblower, hanging on to a belaying pin in the mizzen fife rail to save himself from sliding down the deck into the scuppers, "can't he make up his mind?"

There was something in Hornblower's stare that made Bush look at him more closely.

"Seasick?" he asked, with curiosity.

"Who wouldn't be?" replied Hornblower. "How she rolls!"

Bush's cast-iron stomach had never given him the least qualm, but he was aware that less fortunate men suffered from seasickness even after weeks at sea, especially when subjected to a different kind of motion. This funereal rolling was nothing like the free action of the *Renown* under sail.

"Buckland has to see how the land lies," he said in an effort to cheer Hornblower up.

"How much more does he want to see?" grumbled Hornblower. "There's the Spanish colours flying on the fort up there. Everyone on shore knows now that a ship of the line is prowling about, and the Dons won't have to be very clever to guess that we're not here on a yachting trip. Now they've all the time they need to be ready to receive us."

"But what else could he do?"

"He could have come in in the dark with the sea breeze. Landing parties ready. Put them ashore at dawn. Storm the place before they knew there was any danger. Oh, God!"

The final exclamation had nothing to do with what went before. It was wrenched out of Hornblower by the commotion of his stomach. Despite his deep tan there was a sickly green colour in his cheeks.

"Hard luck," said Bush.

Buckland still stood trying to keep his telescope trained on the coast despite the rolling of the ship. This was Scotchman's Bay—the Bahia de Escocesa, as the Spanish charts had it. To the westward lay a shelving beach; the big rollers here broke far out and ran in creamy white up to the water's edge with diminishing force, but to the eastward the shore-line rose in a line of tree-covered hills standing bluffly with their feet in blue water; the rollers burst against them in sheets of spray that climbed far up the cliffs before falling back in a smother of white. For thirty miles those hills ran beside the sea, almost due east and west; they constituted the Samana peninsula, terminating in Samana Point. According to the charts the peninsula was no more than ten miles wide; behind them, round Samana Point, lay Samana Bay, opening into the Mona Passage and a most convenient anchorage for privateers and small ships of war which could lie there, under the protection of the fort on the Samana peninsula, ready to slip out and harass the West Indian convoys making use of the Mona Passage. The *Renown* had been given orders to clear out this raiders' lair before going down to leeward to Jamaica—everyone in the ship could guess that—but now that Buckland confronted the problem he was not at all sure how to solve it. His indecision was apparent to all the curious lookers-on who clustered on the *Renown*'s deck.

The main topsail suddenly flapped like thunder, and the ship began to turn slowly head to sea; the land breeze was expiring, and the trade winds, blowing eternally across the Atlantic, were resuming their dominion. Buckland shut his telescope with relief. At least that was an excuse for postponing action.

"Mr. Roberts!"

"Sir!"

"Lay her on the port tack. Full and by!"

"Aye aye, sir."

The after guard came running to the mizzen braces, and the ship slowly paid off. Gradually the topsails caught the wind, and she began to lie over, gathering way as she did so. She met the next roller with her port bow, thrusting boldly into it in a burst of spray. The tautened weather-rigging began to sing a more cheerful note, blending with the music of her passage through the water. She was a live thing again, instead of rolling like a corpse in the trough. The roaring trade wind pressed her over, and she went surging along rising and swooping as if with pleasure, leaving a creamy wake behind her on the blue water while the sea roared under the bows.

"Better?" asked Bush of Hornblower.

"Better in one way," was the reply. Hornblower looked over at the distant hills of Santo Domingo. "I could wish we were going into action and not running away to think about it."

"What a fire-eater!" said Bush.

"A fire-eater? Me? Nothing like that—quite the opposite. I wish— oh, I wish for too much, I suppose."

There was no explaining some people, thought Bush, philosophically. He was content to bask in the sunshine now that its heat was tempered by the ship's passage through the wind. If action and danger lay in the future he could await it in stolid tranquility; and he certainly could congratulate himself that he did not have to carry Buckland's responsibility of carrying a ship of the line and seven hundred and twenty men into action. The prospect of action at least took one's mind off the horrid fact that confined below lay an insane captain.

At dinner in the wardroom he looked over at Hornblower, fidgety and nervous. Buckland had announced his intention of taking the bull by the horns the next morning, of rounding Samana Point and forcing his way straight up the bay. It would not take many broadsides from the *Renown* to destroy any shipping that lay there at anchor. Bush thoroughly approved of the scheme. Wipe out the privateers, burn them, sink them, and then it would be time to decide what, if anything, should be done next. At the meeting in the wardroom when Buckland asked if any officer had any questions Smith had asked sensibly about the tides, and Carberry had given him the information; Roberts had asked a question or two about the situation on the south shore of the bay; but Hornblower at the foot of the table had kept his mouth shut, although looking with eager attention at each speaker in turn.

During the dogwatches Hornblower had paced the deck by himself, head bent in meditation; Bush noticed the fingers of the hands behind his back twisting and twining nervously, and he experienced a momentary doubt. Was it possible that this energetic young officer was lacking in physical courage? That phrase was not Bush's own—he had heard it used maliciously somewhere or other years ago. It was better to use it now than to tell himself outright that he suspected Hornblower might be a coward. Bush was not a man of large tolerance; if a man were a coward he wanted no more to do with him.

Half-way through next morning the pipes shrilled along the decks; the drums of the marines beat a rousing roll.

"Clear the decks for action! Hands to quarters! Clear for action!"

Bush came down to the lower gundeck which was his station for action; under his command was the whole deck and the seventeen twenty-four-pounders of the starboard battery, while Hornblower commanded under him those of the port side. The hands were already knocking down the screens and removing obstructions. A little group of the surgeon's crew came along the deck; they were carrying a strait-jacketed figure bound to a plank. Despite the jacket and the lashings it writhed feebly and wept pitifully—the captain being carried down to the safety of the cable tier while his cabin was cleared for action. A hand or two in the bustle found time to shake their heads over the unhappy figure, but Bush checked them soon enough. He wanted to be able to report the lower gundeck cleared for action with creditable speed.

Hornblower made his appearance, touched his hat to Bush, and stood by to supervise his guns. Most of this lower deck was in twilight, for the stout shafts of sunlight that came down the hatchways did little to illuminate the farther parts of the deck with its sombre red paint. Half a dozen ship's boys came along, each one carrying a bucket of sand, which they scattered in handfuls over the deck. Bush kept a sharp eye on them, because the guns' crews depended on that sand for firm foothold. The water buckets beside each gun were filled; they served a dual purpose, to dampen the swabs that cleaned out the guns and for immediate use against fire. Round the mainmast stood a ring of extra fire buckets; in tubs at either side of the ship smouldered the slow matches from which the gun captains could rekindle their linstocks when necessary. Fire and water. The marine sentries came clumping along the deck in their scarlet coats and white crossbelts, the tops of their shakos brushing the deck beams over their heads. Corporal Greenwood posted one at each hatchway, bayonet fixed and musket loaded. Their duty was to see that no unauthorised person ran down to take shelter in the safety of that part of the ship comfortably below waterline. Mr. Hobbs, the acting-gunner, with his mates and helpers made a momentary appearance on their way down to the magazine. They were all wearing list slippers to obviate any chance of setting off the loose powder which would be bound to be strewn about down there in the heat of action.

Soon the powder boys came running up, each with a charge for the guns. The breechings of the guns were cast off, and the crews stood by the tackles, waiting for the word to open the ports and run out the guns. Bush darted his glance along both sides. The gun captains were all at their posts. Ten men stood by every gun on the starboard side, five by every gun on the port side—maximum and minimum crews for twenty-four-pounders. It was Bush's responsibility to see to it that whichever battery came into action the guns were properly manned. If both sides had to be worked at once he had to make a fair division, and when the casualties began and guns were put out of service he had to redistribute the crews. The petty officers and warrant officers were reporting their subdivisions ready for action, and Bush turned to the midshipman beside him whose duty was to carry messages.

"Mr. Abbott, report the lower deck cleared for action. Ask if the guns should be run out."

"Aye aye, sir."

A moment before the ship had been full of noise and bustle, and now everything down here was still and quiet save for the creaking of the timbers; the ship was rising and swooping rhythmically over the sea—Bush as he stood by the mainmast was automatically swaying with the ship's motion. Young Abbott came running down the ladder again.

"Mr. Buckland's compliments, sir, and don't run the guns out yet."

"Very good."

Hornblower was standing farther aft, in line with the ringbolts of the train tackles; he had looked round to hear what message Abbott bore, and now he turned back again. He stood with his feet apart, and Bush saw him put one hand into the other, behind his back, and clasp it firmly. There was a rigidity about the set of his shoulders and in the way he held his head that might be significant of anything, eagerness for action or the reverse. A gun captain addressed a remark to Hornblower, and Bush watched him turn to answer it. Even in the half-light of the lower deck Bush could see there were signs of strain in his expression, and that smile might be forced. Oh well, decided Bush, as charitably as he could, men often looked like that before going into action.

Silently the ship sailed on; even Bush had his ears cocked trying to hear what was going on above him so as to draw deductions about the situation. Faintly down the hatchway came the call of a seaman.

"No bottom, sir. No bottom with this line."

So there was a man in the chains taking casts with the lead, and they must be drawing near the land; everyone down on the lower deck drew the same conclusion and started to remark about it to his neighbour.

"Silence, there!" snapped Bush.

Another cry from the leadsman, and then a bellowed order. Instantly the lower deck seemed to be filled solid with noise. The maindeck guns were being run out; in the confined space below every sound was multiplied and reverberated by the ship's timbers so that the gun-trucks rolling across the planking made a noise like thunder. Everyone looked to Bush for orders, but he stood steady; he had received none. Now a midshipman appeared descending the ladder.

"Mr. Buckland's compliments, sir, and please to run your guns out."

He had squealed his message without ever setting foot on deck, and everyone had heard it. There was an instant buzz round the deck, and excitable people began to reach for the gunports to open them.

"Still!" bellowed Bush. Guiltily all movement ceased.

"Up ports!"

The twilight of the lower deck changed to daylight as the ports opened; little rectangles of sunshine swayed about on the deck on the port side, broadening and narrowing with the motion of the ship.

"Run out!"

With the ports open the noise was not so great; the crews flung their weight on the tackles and the trucks roared as the guns thrust their muzzles out. Bush stepped to the nearest gun and stooped to peer out through the open port. There were the green hills of the island at extreme gunshot distance; here the cliffs were not nearly so abrupt, and there was a jungle-covered shelf at their feet.

"Hands wear ship!"

Bush could recognise Roberts' voice hailing from the quarterdeck. The deck under his feet steadied to the horizontal, and the distant hills seemed to swing with the vessel. The masts creaked as the yards came round. That must be Point Samana which they were rounding. The motion of the ship had changed far more than would be the result of mere alteration of course. She was not only on an even keel but she was in quiet water, gliding along into the bay. Bush squatted down on his heels by the muzzle of a gun and peered at the shore. This was the south side of the peninsula at which he was looking, presenting a coastline toward the bay nearly as steep as the one on the seaward side. There was the fort on the crest and the Spanish flag waving over it. The excited midshipman came scuttling down the ladder like a squirrel.

"Sir! Sir! Will you try a ranging shot at the batteries when your guns bear?"

Bush ran a cold eye over him.

"Whose orders?" he asked.

"M—Mr. Buckland's, sir."

"Then say so. Very well. My respects to Mr. Buckland, and it will be a long time before my guns are within range."

"Aye aye, sir."

There was smoke rising from the fort, and not powder smoke either. Bush realised with something like a quiver of apprehension that probably it was smoke from a furnace for heating shot; soon the fort would be hurling red-hot shot at them, and Bush could see no chance of retaliation; he would never be able to elevate his guns sufficiently to reach the fort, while the fort, from its commanding position on the crest, could reach the ship easily enough. He straightened himself up and walked over to the port side to where Hornblower, in a similar attitude, was peering out beside a gun.

"There's a point running out here," said Hornblower "See the shallows there? The channel must bend round them. And there's a battery on the point—look at the smoke. They're heating shot."

"I daresay," said Bush.

Soon they would be under a sharp crossfire. He hoped they would not be subjected to it for too long. He could hear orders being shouted on deck, and the masts creaked as the yards came round; they were working the *Renown* round the bend.

"The fort's opened fire, sir," reported the master's mate in charge of the forward guns on the starboard side.

"Very well, Mr. Purvis." He crossed over and looked out. "Did you see where the shot fell?"

"No, sir."

"They're firing on this side, too, sir," reported Hornblower.

"Very well."

Bush saw the fort spurting white cannon smoke. Then straight in the line between his eye and the fort, fifty yards from the side of the ship, a pillar of water rose up from the golden surface, and within the same instant of time something crashed into the side of the ship just above Bush's head. A ricochet had bounded from the surface and had lodged somewhere in the eighteen inches of oak that constituted the ship's side. Then followed a devil's tattoo of crashes; a well-aimed salvo was striking home.

"I might just reach the battery on this side now, sir," said Hornblower.

"Then try what you can do."

Now here was Buckland himself, hailing fretfully down the hatchway.

"Can't you open fire yet, Mr. Bush?"

"This minute, sir."

Hornblower was standing by the centre twenty-four-pounder. The gun captain slid the rolling handspike under the gun carriage, and heaved with all his weight. Two men at each side tackle tugged under his direction to point the gun true. With the elevating quoin quite free from the breech the gun was at its highest angle of elevation. The gun captain flipped up the iron apron over the touchhole, saw that the hole was filled with powder, and with a shout of "Stand clear" he thrust his smouldering linstock into it. The gun bellowed loud in the confined space; some of the smoke came drifting back through the port.

"Just below, sir," reported Hornblower standing at the next port. "When the guns are hot they'll reach it."

"Carry on, then."

"Open fire, first division!" yelled Hornblower.

The four foremost guns crashed out almost together.

"Second division!"

Bush could feel the deck heaving under him with the shock of the discharge and the recoil. Smoke came billowing back into the confined space; acrid, bitter, and the din was paralysing.

"Try again, men!" yelled Hornblower. "Division captains, see that you point true!"

There was a frightful crash close beside Bush and something screamed past him to crash into the deck beam near his head. Something flying through an open gunport had struck a gun on its reinforced breech. Two men had fallen close beside it, one lying still and the other twisting and turning in agony. Bush was about to give an order regarding them when his attention was drawn to something more important. There was a deep gash in the deck beam by his head and from the depths of the gash smoke was curling. It was a red-hot shot that had struck the breech of the gun and had apparently flown into fragments. A large part—the largest part—had sunk deep into the beam and already the wood was smouldering.

"Fire buckets here!" roared Bush.

Ten pounds of red-hot glowing metal lodged in the dry timbers of the ship could start a blaze in a few seconds. At the same time there was a rush of feet overhead, the sound of gear being moved about, and then the clank-clank of pumps. So on the maindeck they were fighting fires too. Hornblower's guns were thundering on the port side, the gun-trucks roaring over the planking. Hell was unchained, and the smoke of hell was eddying about him.

The masts creaked again with the swing of the yards; in spite of everything the ship had to be sailed up the tortuous channel. He peered out through a port, but his eye told him, as he forced himself to gauge the distance calmly, that the fort on the crest was still beyond range. No sense in wasting ammunition. He straightened himself and looked round the murky deck. There was something strange in the feel of the ship under his feet. He teetered on his toes to put his wild suspicions to the test. There was the slightest perceptible slope to the deck—a strange rigidity and permanence about it. Oh my God! Hornblower was looking round at him and made an urgent gesture downwards to confirm the awful thought. The *Renown* was aground. She must have run so smoothly and slowly up a mudbank as to lose her speed without any jerk perceptible. But she must have put her bows far up on the bank for the slope of the deck to be noticeable. There were more rending crashes as other shots from the shore struck home, a fresh hurrying and bustle as the fire parties ran to deal with the danger. Hard aground, and doomed to be slowly shot to pieces by those cursed forts, if the shots did not set them on fire to roast alive on the mudbank. Hornblower was beside him, his watch in his hand.

"Tide's still rising," he said. "It's an hour before high water. But I'm afraid we're pretty hard aground."

Bush could only look at him and swear, pouring out filth from his mouth as the only means of relieving his overwrought feelings.

"Steady there, Duff!" yelled Hornblower, looking away from him at a gun's crew gathered round their gun. "Swab that out properly! D'ye want your hands blown off when you load?"

By the time Hornblower looked round at Bush again the latter had regained his self-control.

"An hour to high water, you say?" he asked.

"Yes, sir. According to Carberry's calculations."

"God help us!"

"My shot's just reaching the battery on the point, sir. If I can keep the embrasures swept I'll slow their rate of fire even if I don't silence them."

Another crash as a shot struck home, and another.

"But the one across the channel's out of range."

"Yes," said Hornblower.

The powder boys were running through all the bustle with fresh charges for the guns. And here was the messenger-midshipman threading his way through them.

"Mr. Bush, sir! Will you please report to Mr. Buckland, sir? And we're aground, under fire, sir."

"Shut your mouth. I leave you in charge here, Mr. Hornblower."

"Aye aye, sir."

The sunlight on the quarterdeck was blinding. Buckland was standing hatless at the rail, trying to control the working of his features. There was a roar and a spluttering of steam as someone turned the jet of a hose on a fiery fragment lodged in the bulkhead. Dead men in the scuppers; wounded being carried off. A shot, or the splinters it had set flying, must have killed the man at the wheel so that the ship temporarily out of control had run aground.

"We have to kedge off," said Buckland.

"Aye aye, sir."

That meant putting out an anchor and heaving in on the cable with the capstan to haul the ship off the mud by main force. Bush looked round him to confirm what he had gathered regarding the ship's position from his restricted view below. Her bows were on the mud; she would have to be hauled off stern first. A shot howled close overhead, and Bush had to exert his self-control not to jump.

"You'll have to get a cable out aft through a stern port."

"Aye aye, sir."

"Roberts'll take the stream anchor off the launch."

"Aye aye, sir."

The fact that Buckland omitted the formal "Mister" was significant of the strain he was undergoing and of the emergency of the occasion.

"I'll take the men from my guns, sir," said Bush.

"Very good."

Now was the time for discipline and training to assert themselves; the *Renown* was fortunate in having a crew more than half composed of seasoned men drilled in the blockade of Brest. At Plymouth she had only been filled up with pressed men. What had merely been a drill, an evolution, when the *Renown* was one of the Channel Fleet, was now an operation on which the life of the ship depended, not something to be done perfunctorily in competition with the rest of the squadron. Bush gathered his guns' crews around him and set about the task of rousing out a cable and getting it aft to a port, while overhead Roberts' men were manning stay tackles and yard tackles to sway out the launch.

Down below the heat between the decks was greater even than above with the sun glaring down. The smoke from Hornblower's guns was eddying thick under the beams; Hornblower was holding his hat in his hand and wiping his streaming face with his handkerchief. He nodded as Bush appeared; there was no need for Bush to explain the duty on which he was engaged. With the guns still thundering and the smoke still eddying, powder boys still running with fresh charges and fire parties bustling with their buckets, Bush's men roused out the cable. The hundred fathoms of it weighed a trifle over a couple of tons; clear heads and skilled supervision were necessary to get the unwieldy cable laid out aft, but Bush was at his best doing work which called for single-minded attention to a single duty. He had it clear and faked down along the deck by the time the cutter was under the stern to receive the end, and then he watched the vast thing gradually snake out through the after port without a hitch. The launch came into his line of vision as he stood looking out, with the vast weight of the stream anchor dangling astern; it was a relief to know that the tricky business of getting the anchor into her had been successfully carried out. The second cutter carried the spring cable from the hawsehole. Roberts was in command; Bush heard him hail the cutter as the three boats drew off astern. There was a sudden jet of water among the boats; one or other, if not both, of the batteries ashore had shifted targets; a shot now into the launch would be a disaster, and one into a cutter would be a serious setback.

"Pardon, sir," said Hornblower's voice beside him, and Bush turned back from looking out over the glittering water.

"Well?"

"I could take some of the foremost guns and run 'em aft," said Hornblower. "Shifting the weight would help."

"So it would," agreed Bush; Hornblower's face was streaked and grimy with his exertions, as Bush noted while he considered if he had sufficient authority to give the order on his own responsibility. "Better get Buckland's permission. Ask him in my name if you like."

"Aye aye, sir."

These lower deck twenty-four-pounders weighed more than two tons each; the transfer of some from forward aft would be an important factor in getting the bows off the mudbank. Bush took another glance through the port. James, the midshipman in the first cutter, was turning to look back to check that the cable was out in exact line with the length of the ship. There would be a serious loss of tractive effort if there was an angle in the cable from anchor to capstan. Launch and cutter were coming together in preparation for dropping the anchor. All round them the water suddenly boiled to a salvo from the shore; the skipping jets of the ricochets showed that it was the fort on the hill that was firing at them—and making good practice for that extreme range. The sun caught an axe blade as it turned in the air in the sternsheets of the launch; Bush saw the momentary flash. They were letting the anchor drop from where it hung from the gallows in the stern. Thank God.

Hornblower's guns were still bellowing out, making the ship tremble with their recoil, and at the same time a splintering crash over his head told him that the other battery was still firing on the ship and still scoring hits. Everything was still going on at once; Hornblower had a gang of men at work dragging aft the foremost twenty-four-pounder on the starboard side—a ticklish job with the rolling handspike under the

transom of the carriage. The trucks squealed horribly as the men struggled to turn the cumbersome thing and thread their way along the
crowded deck. But Bush could spare Hornblower no more than a glance
as he hurried up to the maindeck to see for himself what was happening at the capstan.

The men were already taking their places at the capstan bars under
the supervision of Smith and Booth; the main-deck guns were being
stripped of the last of their crews to supply enough hands. Naked to
the waist, the men were spitting on their hands and testing their
foothold—there was no need to tell them how serious the situation
was; no need for Booth's knotted rattan.

"Heave away!" hailed Buckland from the quarterdeck.

"Heave away!" yelled Booth. "Heave, and wake the dead!"

The men flung their weight on the bars and the capstan came round,
the pawls clanking rapidly as the capstan took up the slack. The boys
with the nippers at the messenger had to hurry to keep pace. Then the
intervals between the clanking of the pawls became longer as the capstan turned more slowly. More slowly; clank—clank—clank. Now the
strain was coming; the bits creaked as the cable tightened. Clank—
clank. That was a new cable, and it could be expected to stretch a trifle.

The sudden howl of a shot—what wanton fate had directed it here
of all places in the ship? Flying splinters and prostrate men; the shot
had ploughed through the whole crowded mass. Red blood was
pouring out, vivid in the sunshine; in understandable confusion the
men drew away from the bloody wrecks.

"Stand to your posts!" yelled Smith. "You, boys! Get those men out
of the way. Another capstan bar here! Smartly now!"

The ball which had wrought such fearful havoc had not spent all its
force on human flesh; it had gone on to shatter the cheekpiece of a gun
carriage and then to lodge in the ship's side. Nor had human blood
quenched it; smoke was rising on the instant from where it rested.
Bush himself seized a fire bucket and dashed its contents on the
glowing ball; steam blended with the smoke and the water spat and
sputtered. No single fire bucket could quench twenty-four pounds of

red-hot iron, but a fire party came running up to flood the smouldering menace.

The dead and the wounded had been dragged away and the men were at the capstan bars again.

"Heave!" shouted Booth. Clank—clank—clank. Slowly and more slowly still turned the capstan. Then it came to a dead stop while the bitts groaned under the strain.

"Heave! Heave!"

Clank! Then reluctantly, and after a long interval, clank! Then no more. The merciless sun beat down upon the men's straining backs; their horny feet sought for a grip against the cleats on the deck as they shoved and thrust against the bars. Bush went below again, leaving them straining away; he could, and did, send plenty of men up from the lower gundeck to treble-bank the capstan bars. There were men still hard at work in the smoky twilight hauling the last possible gun aft, but Hornblower was back among his guns supervising the pointing. Bush set his foot on the cable. It was not like a rope, but like a wooden spar, as rigid and unyielding. Then through the sole of his shoe Bush felt the slightest tremor, the very slightest; the men at the capstan were putting their reinforced strength against the bars. The clank of one more pawl gained reverberated along the ship's timbers; the cable shuddered a trifle more violently and then stiffened into total rigidity again. It did not creep over an eighth of an inch under Bush's foot, although he knew that at the capstan a hundred and fifty men were straining their hearts out at the bars. One of Hornblower's guns went off; Bush felt the jar of the recoil through the cable. Faintly down the hatchways came the shouts of encouragement from Smith and Booth at the capstan, but not an inch of gain could be noted at the cable. Hornblower came and touched his hat to Bush.

"D'you notice any movement when I fire a gun, sir?" As he asked the question he turned and waved to the captain of a midship gun which was loaded and run out. The gun captain brought the linstock down on the touchhole, and the gun roared out and came recoiling back through the smoke. Bush's foot on the cable recorded the effect.

"Only the jar—no—yes." Inspiration came to Bush. To the question he asked Bush already knew the answer Hornblower would give. "What are you thinking of?"

"I could fire all my guns at once. That might break the suction, sir."

So it might, indeed. The *Renown* was lying on mud, which was clutching her in a firm grip. If she could be severely shaken while the hawser was maintained at full tension the grip might be broken.

"I think it's worth trying, by God," said Bush.

"Very good, sir. I'll have my guns loaded and ready in three minutes, sir." Hornblower turned to his battery and funnelled his hands round his mouth. "Cease fire! Cease fire, all!"

"I'll tell 'em at the capstan," said Bush.

"Very good, sir." Hornblower went on giving his orders. "Load and double-shot your guns. Prime and run out."

That was the last that Bush heard for the moment as he went up on the maindeck and made his suggestion to Smith, who nodded in instant agreement.

" 'Vast heaving!" shouted Smith, and the sweating men at the bars eased their weary backs.

An explanation was necessary to Buckland on the quarterdeck; he saw the force of the argument. The unfortunate man, who was watching the failure of his first venture in independent command, and whose ship was in such deadly peril, was gripping at the rail and wringing it with his two hands as if he would twist it like a corkscrew. In the midst of all this there was a piece of desperately important news that Smith had to give.

"Roberts is dead," he said, out of the side of his mouth.

"No!"

"He's dead. A shot cut him in two in the launch."

"Good God!"

It was to Bush's credit that he felt sorrow at the death of Roberts before his mind recorded the fact that he was now first lieutenant of a ship of the line. But there was no time now to think of either sorrow or rejoicing, not with the *Renown* aground and under fire. Bush hailed down the hatchway.

"Below, there! Mr. Hornblower!"

"Sir!"

"Are your guns ready?"

"Another minute, sir."

"Better take the strain," said Bush to Smith, and then louder, down the hatchway, "Await my order, Mr. Hornblower."

"Aye aye, sir."

The men settled themselves at the capstan bars again, braced their feet, and heaved.

"Heave!" shouted Booth. "Heave!"

The men might be pushing at the side of a church, so little movement did they get from the bars after the first inch.

"Heave!"

Bush left them and ran below. He set his foot on the rigid cable and nodded to Hornblower. The fifteen guns—two had been dragged aft from the port side—were run out and ready, the crews awaiting orders.

"Captains, take your linstocks!" shouted Hornblower. "All you others, stand clear! Now, I shall give you the words 'one, two, three.' At 'three' you touch your linstocks down. Understand?"

There was a buzz of agreement.

"All ready? All linstocks glowing?" The gun captains swung them about to get them as bright as possible. "Then one—two—three!"

Down came the linstocks on the touchholes, and almost simultaneously the guns roared out; even with the inevitable variation in the amounts of powder in the touchholes there was not a second between the first and the last of the fifteen explosions. Bush, his foot on the cable, felt the ship heave with the recoil—double-shotting the guns had increased the effect. The smoke came eddying into the sweltering heat, but Bush had no attention to give to it. The cable moved under his foot with the heave of the ship. Surely it was moving along. It was! He had to shift the position of his foot. The clank of a newly gained pawl on the windlass could be heard by everyone. Clank—clank. Someone in the smoke started a cheer and others took it up.

"Silence!" bellowed Hornblower.

Clank—clank—clank. Reluctant sounds; but the ship was moving. The cable was coming in slowly, like a mortally wounded monster. If only they could keep her on the move! Clank—clank—clank. The interval between the sounds was growing shorter—even Bush had to admit that to himself. The cable was coming in faster—faster.

"Take charge here, Mr. Hornblower," said Bush, and sprang for the maindeck. If the ship were free there would be urgent matters for the first lieutenant to attend to. The capstan pawls seemed almost to be playing a merry tune, so rapidly did they sound as the capstan turned.

Undoubtedly there was much to be attended to on deck. There were decisions which must be made at once. Bush touched his hat to Buckland.

"Any orders, sir?"

Buckland turned unhappy eyes on him.

"We've lost the flood," he said.

This must be the highest moment of the tide; if they were to touch ground again, kedging off would not be so simple an operation.

"Yes, sir," said Bush.

The decision could only lie with Buckland; no one else could share the responsibility. But it was terribly hard for a man to have to admit defeat in his very first command. Buckland looked as if for inspiration round the bay, where the red-and-gold flags of Spain flew above the banked-up powder smoke of the batteries—no inspiration could be found there.

"We can only get out with the land breeze," said Buckland.

"Yes, sir."

There was almost no longer for the land breeze to blow, either, thought Bush; Buckland knew it as well as he did. A shot from the fort on the hill struck into the main chains at that moment, with a jarring crash and a shower of splinters. They heard the call for the fire party, and with that Buckland reached the bitter decision.

"Heave in on the spring cable," he ordered. "Get her round, head to sea."

"Aye aye, sir."

Retreat—defeat; that was what that order meant. But defeat had to be faced; even with that order given there was much that had to be done to work the ship out of the imminent danger in which she lay. Bush turned to give the orders.

" 'Vast heaving at the capstan, there!"

The clanking ceased and the *Renown* rode free in the muddy, churned-up waters of the bay. To retreat she would have to turn tail, reverse herself in that confined space, and work her way out to sea. Fortunately the means were immediately available; by heaving in on the bow cable which had so far lain idle between hawsehole and anchor the ship could be brought short round.

"Cast off the stern cable messenger!"

The orders came quickly and easily; it was a routine piece of seamanship, even though it had to be carried out under the fire of red-hot shot. There were the boats still manned and afloat to drag the battered vessel out of harm's way if the precarious breeze should die away. Round came the *Renown*'s bows under the pull of the bow cable as the capstan set to work upon it. Even though the wind was dying away to a sweltering calm it was possible, by hard work, to move the ship out of range of that accursed artillery. While the capstan was dragging the ship up to her anchor the necessity for keeping the ship on the move occurred to Bush. He touched his hat to Buckland again.

"Shall I warp her down the bay, sir?"

Buckland had been standing by the binnacle staring vacantly at the fort. It was not a question of physical cowardice—that was obvious—but the shock of defeat and the contemplation of the future had made the man temporarily incapable of logical thought. But Bush's question prodded him back into dealing with the current situation.

"Yes," said Buckland, and Bush turned away, happy to have something useful to do which he well knew how to do.

Another anchor had to be cockbilled at the port bow, another cable roused out. A hail to James, in command of the boats since Roberts' death, told him of the new evolution and called him under the bows for the anchor to be lowered down to the launch—the trickiest part of the whole business. Then the launch's crew bent to their oars and towed ahead, their boat crank with the ponderous weight that it bore dangling aft and with the cable paying out astern of it. Yard by yard, to the monotonous turning of the capstan, the *Renown* crept up to her first anchor, and when that cable was straight up and down the flutter of a signal warned James, now far ahead in the launch, to drop the anchor his boat carried and return for the stream anchor which was about to be hauled up. The stern cable, now of no more use, had to be unhitched and got in, the effort of the capstan transferred from one cable to the other, while the two cutters were given lines by which they could contribute their tiny effort to the general result, towing the ponderous ship and giving her the smallest conceivable amount of motion which yet was valuable when it was a matter of such urgency to withdraw the ship out of range.

Down below Hornblower was at work dragging forward the guns he had previously dragged aft; the rumble and squeal of the trucks over the planking was audible through the ship over the monotonous clanking of the capstan. Overhead blazed the pitiless sun, softening the pitch in the seams, while yard after painful yard, cable's length after cable's length, the ship crept on down the bay out of range of the red-hot shot, over the glittering still water; down the bay of Samana until at last they were out of range, and could pause while the men drank a niggardly half-pint of warm odorous water before turning back to their labours. To bury the dead, to repair the damages, and to digest the realisation of defeat.

The Cheerful Tortoise
from Doctor Dogbody's Leg
by James Norman Hall

James Norman Hall (1887–1951) is famous for collaborating with Charles Nordhoff to write adventure books such as Mutiny on the Bounty *(see page 43). His 1940 collection of fictional sketches about a loquacious ship's surgeon is a different kettle of fish.*

On a dreary autumn evening when the clouds hung low in the heavens and the masts and yards of the tall men-of-war in the harbour were obscured by a chill drizzle of rain, there was no more inviting spot in Portsmouth than the taproom of Will Tunn's Cheerful Tortoise. But times were dull, now that Napoleon had been safely exiled to Saint Helena; half the fleet was paid off, ships laid up, and the Royal Dockyards, which had hummed with activity two years before, were reduced to the peacetime establishment.

The Cheerful Tortoise had suffered with the rest of the community from the return of peace, although the creature which gave the inn its name smiled down upon passers-by with its old-time air of wistful geniality. The inn sign, as Mr. Tunn himself was willing to admit, was a veritable work of art. Carved from a huge slab of oak by an old seaman, many years before, it was impervious to wind and weather; only the strongest gale would cause it to swing slightly on its heavy gilded chain. Many a thirsty seaman, just ashore, would stop short to gaze in admiration at Will Tunn's tortoise, touch his hat to it with a grin, and seek no farther for refreshment. The carapace was a bright sea-green, the calipee pale blue, and the flippers yellow, while the head, with its eager smiling face, was richly ornamented and picked out in gold leaf. But the tortoise was greater than the sum of its parts, thanks to a happy stroke of seaman's genius. Its attitude of absorbed interest as it craned its neck to one side, as though to gaze past the lintel of the doorway into the taproom, combined with its smile, in which sadness at thought of its own deprivations seemed to be mingled with unselfish delight at thought of the good cheer and good company within, had made it a famous tavern animal amongst innumerable swans, blue boars, cocks, dogs and ducks, red lions, green dragons, white harts, and horses that adorned the highroad between Portsmouth and London.

Mr. Tunn's house stood on a corner a short distance from the waterfront. Although not one of the great posting-inns of the time, it was a place of call for some of the principal London coaches, and was especially frequented by men who followed the sea. It was a brick building of three stories which had been raised in the substantial manner of the period, to last for centuries. A door studded with brass nails gave directly upon the taproom with its dark paneled wainscoting, its floor of red bricks, well worn and scrubbed, its casks on trestles with a line of bright spigots behind the high old-fashioned bar, and its comfortable recesses with oaken tables, the chairs and settees upholstered in breeches-polished leather. One such recess alongside a mighty fireplace at the far end of the room was reserved for the "props" of the house, as the landlord called them, old friends and steady patrons who well deserved the name.

Beyond the taproom and connected with it by a wide passageway was the kitchen, an apartment equally spacious, whose dusky rafters were festooned with sides of bacon, hams, sausages, strings of onions, and parcels of dried herbs. Pots and pans polished to a degree of brightness something past perfection hung on pegs about the fireplace, where an entire bullock might almost have turned on the spit. At one side of the kitchen stood a long deal table, scrubbed white, where guests of the humbler sort were furnished with food and drink. On the floor above, reached by a staircase from the taproom, was the handsome apartment in which Tunn's famous dinners were served, and where four tall windows looked to the westward toward the Royal Dockyards and the shipping in the harbour. Along a carpeted passageway were the sitting rooms and bed-chambers for travelers. On the third floor, where mullioned windows projected from the steep slope of the roof, were the quarters for postboys, coachmen, and hostlers, and for the landlord and his staff.

Mr. Tunn was a stoutly built, muscular man of sixty, with a clear ruddy complexion, a solid paunch, and a fringe of iron-gray hair framing a bald head. His had been a blameless, useful life, and he deserved well of the world if any man did; but on a certain evening in November his thoughts were as cheerless as the autumn day. He stood in the kitchen, superintending with little of his wonted relish the preparations for supper. Bilges, the kitchen boy, was seated on a stool opening a cask of oysters fresh from Newport. Another boy stood at the spit where a stubble goose and a splendid saddle of mutton were turning under the landlord's direction. So pleasant a prospect would have caused Tunn's mouth to water at another time.

His worries were unselfish ones, for he was not a man to permit his own troubles to weigh heavily upon him. Mr. Tunn was a widower who revered the memory of his wife. A cousin of hers, a Mrs. Quigg, had done well with a lodginghouse during the long years of war, and although times grew hard after the defeat of the French, she had clung to her lease, waiting and hoping for lodgers who seldom came. Mrs. Quigg was a sturdy independent woman who would accept no help from her kin, and it worried Mr. Tunn to see a connection of his beloved Sarah reduced to such straitened circumstances. Thinking of this, he sighed, wiped his hands on his apron, and walked along the passage to the taproom, just in time to see one of his drawers toss off a pint-pot of ale. Tunn stopped short.

"Tom!"

The drawer, a spindle-shanked cadaverous fellow with a colourless face and a surprisingly round belly, turned his head with a grin, half guilty, half impudent.

"Tuppence in the till, ye rogue!" said the landlord, indignantly. "Tom Tapleke! Curse me if ever a man was better named! It's so ye help your master, is it? And custom fallen away to naught in these days! Tuppence in the till, I say!"

Tapleke, who knew to a shade his master's moods, sighed with the doleful air of a deeply wronged man, produced the coins with reluctant ostentation, and dropped them in the till. Tunn was about to say more when the drawer nodded toward the window. Dimly discernible through the frosted panes, a hackney coach was drawing up outside. The landlord turned in that direction as a smallish active man flung open the door and stumped in on a wooden leg. He wore a cocked hat of a style somewhat past the fashion, a handsomely embroidered waistcoat, and a coat which, though plain, was well cut and of the best materials. The buckle of the single shoe below the white silk stocking was of silver.

"Mr. Tunn?" he asked, briskly.

"Will Tunn, sir, at your service."

"Doctor Dogbody, at yours, sir. I was directed to you . . . but damme, I'm parched! You've good rum here?"

"The best old Port Royal, sir."

"Then I'll thank you to take a glass with me while I tell my errand."

The visitor seated himself at a table and removed his hat, displaying a head of thick white hair, brushed neatly back and gathered in a queue. Doctor Dogbody's eyes, of the clearest blue, twinkled with shrewdness and good humour, in a face as ruddy as a winter sunset. It would have been difficult to guess his age with any exactness, although he appeared to be on the latter side of seventy. But the vigour of his movements, his erect carriage, and his small, well-shaped, muscular hands were those of a much younger man. Taking up the small glass of spirits the drawer had set before him, he nodded to the landlord and drained the contents at a gulp.

"Hah! That's better!" he exclaimed. "Ahoy, you at the tap! What's your name?"

"Tom, sir."

"Another of the same presently, Tom. And draw a pint of ale for yourself."

"Thankee, sir," said the delighted Tapleke, with a malicious grin for the landlord's benefit. The doctor turned to his host.

"Of all the drawers, Mr. Tunn," he said, "in all the inns between London and Portsmouth, five in six are named Tom. On the Dover road the ratio is seven Dicks to four Toms, whilst on the Exeter road there's naught but Joes as far as the King's Arms, Salisbury, whence, curiously enough, the Toms begin again and continue without break to the Elephant, in Exeter itself."

"You're a great traveler, sir?" Mr. Tunn asked, politely.

"By sea, yes. By land, no. But when I do travel, ashore, there's little I miss by the way, sir."

The doctor lifted his refilled glass, holding it toward the light as he examined the contents, critically.

"A prime old spirit, landlord. It has made a new man of me, I declare! Now, sir, to my errand. But before I proceed, just send out a tankard of your best to the coachman. The fellow's waiting for me and looks as dry as ashes.

"For some fifty years, Mr. Tunn, I've been a surgeon in His Majesty's Navy. For the moment I'm ashore, but London doesn't suit me. Damme, no! Portsmouth's the place for an old seaman, where he can cross tacks with shipmates now and again. At the Angel, in Town, the landlord told me that Will Tunn, of the Cheerful Tortoise, was the man for me. It's lodgings I'm after, with a well-found inn, like yours, sir, close at hand. Now then, do you know of a snug berth near by? My compliments once more!"

Tunn raised his glass with a pleased smile and pretended to reflect for a moment before he spoke. "I know the very place, sir. A quiet house, and kept by a decent woman, a Mrs. Quigg."

"I'm no ordinary lodger, Tunn. It's not every woman would put up with me. I might make a bit of a noise abovestairs, getting about on my larboard leg. Then, it's not easy to cook for me, and there'll be times I want to dine in. Not that I demand any fiddle-faddle fare. I'm an old seaman; I've been nourished, and well nourished, on pease, oatmeal, good salt beef, cheese, and such simple food, but I'll have it dressed as I want it, in the best old Navy fashion. Would this Mrs. . . . what's her name again? Quigg?—would she be the woman for my money?"

"The very one, Doctor Dogbody! Her husband was a warrant officer, and as choice a man about his victuals as ever I see. You could ransack Portsmouth from the waterside up without finding a woman with her knack for making a man comfortable."

"There's another thing. I'll have no bed. I must have my hammock battens made fast to the wall."

"No trouble about that, sir. Mrs. Quigg's lodged none but seamen since her house was opened."

"Then, Tunn, if you'll show me there, we'll board the coach." The surgeon fumbled in his waistcoat pocket and tossed a sovereign on the table. "Credit me with the balance of that," he said. "You've not seen the last of me, here."

"I trust not, sir, indeed," said the landlord in a pleased voice; then, taking his hat from a peg on the wall, he glanced from Tom Tapleke to the line of spigots with a look conveying a warning and a menace, and followed the surgeon out through the door.

The hour had gone six before Mr. Tunn again appeared in the tap-room, entering from the kitchen with the air of a man who has dined well and is deeply content with the world. Two old patrons of the house came in at this moment, and with a nod to the landlord went to their customary corner at the left of the fireplace. The first, Ned Balthus, was a burly man of middle stature, dressed in a worn and weather-stained coat, with anchor-buttons of silver, and wearing a wig of the kind called "Grizzle Major." There was not a better old fellow in Portsmouth, nor one with a kinder heart, but his face was marked with the scar of a deep cutlass slash that gave him a most forbidding frown.

He had been a Navy gunner for nearly half a century, and now, at the age of retirement, some small employment had been found for him at the Portsmouth Arsenal. His companion, Mr. Ostiff, engraver of charts to the Admiralty, was a tall spare man in middle life, whose small mouth, sharp nose, and long upper lip gave him an air of solemnity belied by a pair of nearsighted grey eyes with a twinkle of mischief in them. As the drawer was attending to their wants, the landlord joined his two old friends.

"Gad, Tunn," Mr. Ostiff remarked, drily. "You look as though you'd come into a fortune."

"And so I have, Mr. Ostiff," said Tunn, taking a seat at the end of the table, with a comfortable sigh. "I do believe it! A landlord's fortune is the guests who choose his house. I've had the luck to add one to-day, a rare gentleman, if I'm a judge. If ye'll allow me to say so, he'd make a companion to those of ye who favour this corner."

"We'd best decide that for ourselves," said Ostiff, still more drily.

"I'd be far from wishing to foist him amongst ye, Mr. Ostiff," Tunn replied; "and he'd be the last to permit it. But he's to lodge close by, at Mrs. Quigg's, and he's done me the honour to say the Tortoise will suit him well for his evenings."

"What name?"

"Doctor Dogbody."

Mr. Balthus set down his pot with a bang.

"Dogbody!" he exclaimed. "Not F. Dogbody?"

"There could be only the one, surely," said Ostiff. "You mean to say it's the man's true name?"

"Tunn, is it F. Dogbody?" Balthus repeated, eagerly.

"I'll not be certain as to that," said the landlord.

"One leg?"

"Aye. His left one's off above the knee."

The gunner brought his hand down on his thigh with a resounding smack. "Damn my eyes! He's here? In Portsmouth?"

"He was in this room not two hours gone. Ye know him, then, do ye, Mr. Balthus?"

"Know him!" said Balthus. "God's rabbit! Where's the old Navy man that don't know Doctor Dogbody? I'm astonished at the pair of ye who've not heard of him till this day. But there's this to be said: he's none of your half-pay surgeons. I'll warrant he's not spent six weeks ashore in a quarter of a century. A better-loved man never trod a ship's deck."

"How did he lose his leg?" asked Tunn.

Balthus sat back in his seat with a look of pleased recollection on his face. "Well may ye ask, Tunn! I've heard him tell the tale a dozen times if I've heard it once, and never twice the same."

"The man must be the very king of liars," said Ostiff, testily.

The gunner smiled. "Say ye so! I'll say naught. My belief is that *all* his tales are true! And mark ye this, Mr. Ostiff! If ever a man lost his leg in some strange way and survived the loss miracle-fashion, as ye might say, that man is Surgeon F. Dogbody. There's nothing humdrum about him. If he no more than spits to leeward he does it with an air of his own."

The door opened at this moment and another old patron of the Tortoise entered. Captain Thankful Runyon was a merchant from Boston, in America, who owned two Nantucket whaling vessels commanded by his sons. He was also half-owner of a vessel which plied chiefly between Boston and Portsmouth with sperm oil, for which the British Admiralty was an excellent customer. Captain Runyon, whose business it was to dispose of the oil, spent most of each year in Portsmouth, and, despite his being a Yankee, was well liked at the Tortoise. He was in his early sixties, rawboned, wiry, with a sunburned leathery face and neck. Although he had spent much of his life at sea, he was a man of excellent education, most of which he had acquired himself.

"Here's one will bear me out, I'll warrant," said Balthus, as Captain Runyon took his place amongst them. "Mr. Runyon, ye must have heard of one of our old Navy surgeons, F. Dogbody?"

"Never, Balthus, never," Runyon replied, in his curt manner. "Hot pot for me, Tom," he added to the drawer, who stood at his side. He turned again to the gunner. "Peabodys, yes; ye can raise three or four in a ten-minute walk anywhere in New England. I know a Fairbody or two, and one Angelbody in the West India trade. But a Dogbody or a Catbody it's not been my fortune to meet. Friend of yours, Balthus?"

"I'd wish him to think me one," the gunner replied gravely, and the reproach implied by his manner was obvious.

"No offense, Balthus," Captain Runyon replied. "We've names on our side as odd as any of yours. My partner, in Boston, is Ralph Soilbibb, and well he lives up to the allegation. And the best friend I had in the world, in my younger days, was George Pigwart. Lost at sea, off Cape Horn, poor fellow! But what did ye wish to say of Surgeon Dogbody?"

"He's here, gentlemen!" Tunn put in, in a low voice. The street door swung open, admitting the surgeon himself, and a gust of damp air that made the lamps flicker for a moment. Balthus half rose from his seat, thought better of it, and dropped back once more. "Wait!" he cautioned the landlord. "Say naught!"

After a sweeping glance around the room, Doctor Dogbody was about to take a seat at a vacant table on the other side of the fireplace when Balthus roared out: "Clean sponges, damn your eyes, and be quick about it!" The surgeon stopped short, spun round on his peg, and brought down his bushy eyebrows as he peered through the dimly lighted room. Then he stumped across to the table, his blue eyes twinkling.

"Not Ned Balthus?" he exclaimed. "Not that corny-faced gunner of the old *Minerva*? Gentlemen, does the man call himself Balthus?"

"Aye, that he does!" said the gunner, heartily. The surgeon took him by the shoulders and held him at arm's length. "By God, Ned! I've mourned ye as dead these five years! D'ye mind Captain Farshingle, of the *Trent*? 'Twas him that told me. You were back on the West India station, he said, and went off with the yellow fever."

"He might well have heard it, Doctor," Balthus replied. " 'Twas a near thing. I was in the *Acteon* that year, and a good half of the ship's company left their bones in the cursed place. But let me make ye known to these gentlemen."

There was a gleam of honest triumph in the gunner's eyes as he noted the reception accorded the surgeon. That the others approved of him was plain, and it was Ostiff himself, hard to please in company, who invited him to take his place amongst them. The surgeon, sensing the sincerity of these overtures, needed no further urging.

"So ye've come ashore at last, Doctor?" Balthus asked, when the drawer had attended to the wants of the company.

"Ashore? Damn my eyes! Who says it?" the surgeon replied, with a snort.

"I understood as much from the landlord here."

"Begging your pardon, sir, if I took your meaning wrong," Mr. Tunn put in, hastily. "I was telling these gentlemen ye'd honoured the Tortoise with a call this afternoon, and I'd the notion ye'd retired from the service."

"Temporarily, sir, but not for good. No, no! There's a score of years' use in me yet. But I won't say I'm not pleased with a bit of a holiday, now that old Boney is safely caged."

"And well ye might be, Doctor," said Balthus. "Ye've not been ashore long, then?"

"Six weeks, come next Thursday. I was paid off out of the *Bedford*. She's to be broken up."

Mr. Ostiff shook his head. "Many's the good ship will go that way now," he said. "I wish we may not live to regret them."

"As to that, sir, I'm of the same mind as yourself," said the surgeon. "It tears my heart to see them go. But since go they must, the Admiralty might better have scuttled 'em all, off soundings. The oldest and the least of them deserve a better fate than the breaking yard."

"Your Admiralty Board had fewer for that end at the close of the American War," said Runyon, with a sly grin.

"Pay no heed to this Pompkinshire Yankee, Doctor," said Ostiff. "By God's grace, the Americans managed to raise up one seaman amongst them—Paul Jones, and even he was born on this side. But Runyon will boast of him, in season and out. To hear him you'd think Paul Jones had destroyed the entire British Navy."

"I'll do them the honour to say they'd more than one of his mettle," the surgeon remarked.

"Handsomely admitted, sir!" said Runyon, warmly. "I've never had such an acknowledgment from Ostiff. You've met them at sea, I take it?"

"Aye, to both my pleasure and my sorrow."

Captain Runyon turned to Ostiff, with a triumphant smile.

"There, sir! The best of testimony for the defense!"

"For the defense?" said Ostiff. "Gad, sir, I like the way you put it! I'll leave it to Balthus, here, if you've ever taken a defensive position."

"He'll not acknowledge, Doctor Dogbody," said Runyon, "that an American ship of war ever came off best, in a battle against odds. There was the old *Protector*, for example. You may have heard of her?"

"The *Protector*? Captain John Foster Williams?"

"The same, sir! You knew her, then?"

"From truck to keelson," the surgeon replied, quietly. "Oddly enough, it was the *Protector* that cost me my leg."

"You don't tell me!" said Runyon, an expression of keen interest upon his face. "Would you be willing, sir, to favour us with the circumstances?"

"Quite, if these other gentlemen are of the same mind as yourself."

"We'd esteem it a privilege, Doctor Dogbody," said Ostiff, with a slight bow. Balthus stole a cautious glance at the surgeon, who was gazing before him with a grave, musing, abstracted expression.

"You'll mind, Ned," the surgeon began, with a glance at the gunner, "the first time we were on the West India station together, and I came so near to a taking-off with the cursed yellow jack?"

"Aye, well, sir," said Balthus, with an emphatic nod. "And how grieved we was at thought of leaving ye behind."

"I need say nothing of the two months that followed. I took what comfort the place afforded in the way of convalescence, and when recovered was appointed surgeon for the homeward voyage to a Company ship, the *Admiral Duff*, returning to England with a cargo of sugar and tobacco which we'd taken on at Saint Kitts. The *Duff* was a well-found ship. We had a crew of two hundred and fifty, and, for the weight of armament, thirty-six twelve-pounders on the gun deck. Her captain was Richard Strange—Mad Dick he was called behind his back, and well he deserved the name! But mind you, he was mad in the way of genius. His men worshiped him; it was a happy ship, and we'd not been a week at sea when I was perfectly recovered, and as content as an old Navy surgeon could be in a merchantman.

"Well, sir, Dick Strange thought no more of the valuable cargo he was taking to London than did his men. It was so much ballast, and his owners could whistle for it. He was a born fighter and I saw how matters stood before we'd lost the land. We were for prizes, so I spent my time with my loblolly boys preparing sponges, dressings, tourniquets, and the like, certain that we'd have use for a plenty before Dick Strange would consent to sail home.

"We took two Yankee brigs the first week and a third the week after, and sent all to Saint Kitts; then b'gad, you'd have said the seas had been swept clean. Not a sail did we spy, though we were in the direct track of shipping up and down the Atlantic coast. We had dirty easterly weather and could scarce see a mile; even so we'd expected better luck than that.

"We got well north, and crept to within ten leagues of the American coast. On a morning in June, after a thick fog had cleared away—this was in 1780—a sail was sighted to the eastward not two leagues off. We made sure he was a Yankee by the cut of his royals and were ready to eat him up. Damme, I had my share of the prize money already spent! But we had to reach him first, and there was not wind enough to lift a feather.

"In ten minutes we'd four boats out, towing. The men put their backs into it, but you'll know what headway they made with a thousand-ton ship. Nevertheless, we moved. Captain Strange was halfway up the mizzen ratlins, egging them on, one minute with his eye to his spyglass, the next, roaring out encouragement to the seamen. Then he made out that the Yankee was towing as well, and in our direction, so we felt easier. It was clear they wanted to engage.

"So it went for near an hour, but the breeze came at last. The Yankee had it first, and as soon as we spied their boats at the falls, in came ours. Being to windward, they edged down toward us, and it was a near thing but they'd have caught us without so much as steerageway, the breeze was that light. But the *Duff* felt it at last. Long before this we had the hammocks up and stuffed into the nettings, decks wet and sanded, matches lighted, and the bulkheads hooked up. They flew the English ensign, but Strange was not deceived by that. As we passed him, Strange called out, 'What ship is that?' The only reply was from their sailing master bawling out orders to his men. They steered to cross our stern and hauled up under our quarter. At that moment up went their true colours and their captain replied: 'Continental ship, *Protector*! Come on! We're ready for you!'

"B'gad, gentlemen, they were! But no more ready than ourselves. We'd caught a tartar, as we learned, directly we were abreast of him once more. He let go every gun on his starboard side, and every shot hulled us, I'll take my oath! The *Duff* was a higher ship, and our gunners were hard put to bring their guns to bear where they would do the most damage. But the noble fellows performed prodigies, and, for all the advantage of the Yankees, our fire was near as murderous as their own.

"The action began within easy pistol shot, and it was yardarm to yardarm from then on. We were fairly matched as to armament, but they had seventy marines amongst them whilst we had none, and seamen are no match for marines in the use of small arms. They killed our topmen as fast as we could replace them, and they'd not forgotten, the rascals, that there were fair targets, aft. But Dick Strange's quizzing-glass never dropped from his eye, save for an instant when the ribbon to it was cut by a musket ball. He caught the eyepiece before it could fall, twirled it carelessly by the bit of frayed ribbon, and replaced it just as our lads let go a broadside that might have taught them better manners.

"Aye, it was warm work, but the end of it was that they made a sieve of us from wind to water. Down came our foremast, then the main, and, b'gad, the mizzen followed! There was nothing left a yard high to hoist our colours on. The Yankee thought we'd struck and ceased firing. Little he knew Dick Strange. D'ye know what he did, sir?"

Doctor Dogbody paused and took up his glass. Finding it empty, he turned to the drawer, who was standing near by, forgetful of his duties while he listened. "Here, Tom, you rascal! I might positively die of thirst with you looking on!" Tapleke, galvanized into action by the abrupt summons, was away to the bar and back in an instant. The surgeon then resumed.

"Well, sir, Strange was fairly beside himself, though you'd not have guessed it by his manner. To have been thought to have struck was an insult so rank he could scarce bear it. He glanced coolly around the quarter-deck—the place was a shambles of the dead and dying—and his eye fell upon a lad standing near by. 'Fetch me a boat flag,' said Strange, 'and be quick about it!' The lad was back with one in twenty seconds. Strange fastened it to his cane, for he fancied his little stick even on shipboard. With this he sprung onto the bulwark and roared out to Williams: 'I've not struck, sir! Tell your bloody bang-straws to try and hit my stick!'

"Gentlemen, I give you my word: he stood there, holding that small flag aloft for a full ten minutes. But in the end, hit it they did. The shot from a carronade clipped off the stick within three inches of Strange's hand. Meanwhile, our three remaining guns continued to fire when they could be brought to bear, but without a rag of sail left you can imagine our situation.

"I and my assistants were at work on the orlop, but with the best will in the world we could not keep pace with the stream of shattered bleeding fellows that were carried or came crawling down to us. Aye, it was raw-meat day, one of the worst in my experience; the tubs were heaped high with arms and legs. Busy as we were at the bloody work, we'd no time to know what was taking place above us, and you can imagine my astonishment when one of the lieutenants came with orders to move all my wounded to the gun deck. We were sinking. It was the first intimation I'd had of the seriousness of our situation.

"Serious, do I say? Damme, it was hopeless, as I saw a moment after, but Dick Strange would not call it so. And there was that in his spirit to have made a ravening lion out of the veriest sheep in his ship's company, had there been any such, which there were not. By God, they fought like devils, even the lads of fourteen. The Yankee was right alongside, and we'd not carried above a dozen of our wounded up from the orlop when, even above the uproar overhead, we heard Strange bellow out: 'Boarders! Boarders! Every man on deck!'

"There was no more thought of the wounded then, nor would they have wished us to think of them. My cutlass and pistols were in my cabin, and I seized the nearest weapon that came to hand, a toma-hawk, and rallied with the others at the starboard bulwarks. There were not above a score of us left, but with Strange to lead us we felt equal to a gross of Yankees. He'd a pistol in one hand and a cutlass in the other, and his quizzing-glass with the frayed ribbon was still at his eye. I was pleased that he should have a word for me at such a moment, with the Yankee closing in, not twenty yards off. 'Dogbody,' said he, coolly, with a nod toward the *Protector*, 'we'll have a noggin of rum directly, in my cabin yonder.' And I've not the least doubt that he was perfectly con-vinced we should.

"There had been no time to get out our nettings, and the Yankees swarmed into us the moment they grappled. They were five to one, and the *Duff* had settled to such an extent that our bulwarks were now lower than their own. Two stout fellows were upon me at once, to their cost, if I may be permitted to say so. The third I did not see until too late, else I might have lost both legs in the place of one. I had my right foot raised and resting on a casing by the bulwark, when I felt a most peculiar numbing sensation in my left leg, and immediately fell back on my buttocks. As I did so I beheld my severed leg lying beside me, and a gigantic Indian—he looked all of eight feet high, although I later found he was but six feet six—who by this time had rushed by me, drawing back his cutlass for a swing at the man beyond. Him he fairly cut in two, at one ferocious blow.

"I spare you the details. It is enough to say that we were taken, but the Americans had little good of their prize. There was no surrender. We sunk under their very feet, not five minutes after they had boarded. Strange went down with his ship, by a miracle unwounded, but he was not one to suffer the humiliation of capture. Lacking his delicacy of feeling in this respect, I seized the first floating object I could get my hands upon in the swirl of waters that closed over the *Duff*. Fortunately, I had had the presence of mind, after my leg was off, to tie up the femoral artery with a bit of marline, and had then plunged the stump into a bucket of tar, else I should have died before I could be taken up. As it was, I'd lost a deal of blood by the time I was laid amongst the wounded, both ours and theirs, aboard the *Protector*.

"Their surgeons were working at top speed, but with so many to be served, they were obliged to choose those most likely to live. Two of their dressers were about to take up a fellow, one of their own men, lying beside me, but the surgeon said, 'Let Little lie. Attend to the others first. He will die.' Indeed, he might well have thought so, for the poor fellow had been horribly wounded in the face by a charge of grape. I rose on my elbow and turned to look at him. The man was perfectly sensible, and I saw that within his eye which gave me a most vivid impression of indomitable courage. It was curious: as our glances met, something passed between us—complete sympathy, mutual respect—and I was convinced not only that the man would not die, but that I could learn to love him like a brother.

"My professional interest in his case was immediately aroused. I have a brusque way with me in my capacity as surgeon, and in an instant I had one of their dressers fetching for me. He brought me a basin of water, sponges and lint, and, managing to raise myself to a sitting position, I proceeded to dress Little's wounds. Strangely enough, I then felt no sensation of pain in my severed leg, and suffered but little inconvenience from it.

"Little had been wounded by three balls: one between the neck bone and windpipe, one through the jaw, lodging in the roof of his mouth and taking off a piece of his tongue, and the third through the lip, which had destroyed nearly all of his upper teeth. I worked over him for an hour, removed the lodged ball, cleansed the wounds, sewed up his lip, and staunched the flow of blood. The event of it was that he perfectly recovered."

Doctor Dogbody rose abruptly. "I ask you leave for one moment, gentlemen," he said; then, turning to Tapleke: "Tom, your necessary-house."

"This way, sir," said the drawer, leading him toward a passageway to the left, and the surgeon followed him out with great dignity.

Mr. Ostiff looked after him with a faint smile, in which puzzlement and admiration were mingled.

"Balthus," said he, "I can scarcely believe our friend to be the liar you've pictured him."

"A liar!" said Runyon. "The tale has the very stamp of truth upon it! Some of the details are inexact, but I've often heard, at home, of the fight between the *Protector* and the *Duff*, and I'll take my oath that the latter was conquered as the surgeon has related the circumstances. What's this, Balthus?"

"I said naught of his being a liar," Balthus replied, warmly. "What I did say was that I've heard him tell the tale of his lost leg a dozen times, and never twice . . ." He broke off, for the surgeon was again approaching. Captain Runyon waited with impatience for him to be seated.

"Sir," he said, "the man whose wounds you dressed could have been no other than Captain Luther Little."

"So it was, sir," said Dogbody, "though he was not a captain at this time. He was a young man on the *Protector* and served in her as midshipman and prize-master. An older brother, George Little, was a lieutenant in the same vessel. They belong to a family, Little in name only, from the town of Marshfield, in the Massachusetts colony."

"I've no doubt that you became excellent friends, after such a meeting?" said Runyon.

"The very best, sir. Mr. Luther Little was considerably my junior, but the small service I was able to render him whilst wounded, combined, as I have said, with something compatible in our natures, served to draw us together upon terms of sincere liking and deep understanding. His elder brother, George, became no less my friend. For the next eight months I was a guest in the Little home. I was, to be sure, a prisoner-of-war, but not the least restraint was put upon my liberty, nor upon my sentiments as a loyal Englishman. And I came to understand the sentiments of our late colonists better, perhaps, than many an Englishman who has never had occasion to live amongst them. They are an admirable nation, and I have little doubt will be a great one in the course of time. It could scarcely be otherwise when one considers the stock from which they sprung."

The surgeon paused to give Captain Runyon a keen glance. "You are acquainted with the Littles, sir?" he asked.

"I have not that honour," Runyon replied, "although I have more than once passed through the town of Marshfield. The place was as famous at one time for a gigantic Indian follower of the Little boys as for the family itself."

"Of the name of Powana?" the surgeon asked.

"Bless my soul! The very same! . . . Jehoshaphat! Could it have been . . ."

"Yes, sir. It could have been, and was, Powana who deprived me of my leg, and a cleaner blow was never given with a cutlass. I could not have made a better amputation at leisure, with my saws and razors, than was done by the Indian before I could have said 'Oh!' His name, Powana, signifies 'whale' in the Natick tongue, and a whale he was in stature. He carried me about like an infant at Marshfield, whilst my stump was healing, and when it had healed he made me a very serviceable wooden leg to replace that he had taken."

"Is it the one you are wearing, Doctor?" Will Tunn asked.

"No, Mr. Tunn, it is not. Curiously enough, Powana's leg was to serve me but a short time, as I shall explain in a moment. . . . Nine months, almost to a day, from the time of our first meeting, Little and I were again at sea, though not, to be sure, as companions-in-arms. He was now in virtual command of the letter-of-marque brig *Jupiter*, carrying twenty-one guns and one hundred and fifty men. I say in virtual command, for the owner and nominal captain was a merchant of the town of Salem, in Massachusetts, a man of the name of Gorme. My status was still that of a prisoner-of-war. Little had gone bail for me to the American authorities, and whilst he would have liked nothing better than to release me, that he was in honour bound not to do until

I could be exchanged for some American prisoner of my own rank. He meant to arrange for this at sea, at the first opportunity.

"We cruised for a full three weeks, in a southerly direction, without any particulars worthy of mention, but I am bound to say that this result was due to the excessive timidity of Captain Gorme. We often sighted English vessels, whereupon Gorme would examine them through his spyglass with the fluttery apprehension of an old woman, and would not allow Little to approach nearer than two leagues. His mouth watered for prizes, but he could not bring himself to take the least risk in obtaining them.

"One morning whilst crossing the Gulf Stream not far off the American coast, we sighted an object a mile or so distant to leeward which Gorme, for once, was willing to approach for a nearer view. There was a light breeze from the northeast, and a curious popple, due perhaps to the action of the Gulf Stream itself. We soon made out the object to be a floating log of considerable size, and clinging to it were three men whom we first took to be Indians. They were dressed in skins resembling that of the raccoon, though there were but three rings on the tail instead of five. Their hair was long, straight and black, like that of the Iroquois, but strangely enough their eyes were of the deepest blue, and their skins almost as light as those of Englishmen. They were nearly dead when picked up, and in spite of my ministrations and those of my Yankee colleague on the *Jupiter*, they lived but a few days. Powana, who was, of course, on board, was unable to exchange a word with them, either in the Natick tongue or in any of the other Indian dialects with which he was familiar. But, astounding as it may seem, a Welsh quartermaster discovered that they spoke a language closely akin to his own. To the great loss of science, they died before he was able to learn whence they came.

"But what I wished to say was that we took on board the log as well as the Indians, if such they were, who had clung to it, for Captain Gorme hoped that it might be useful for spars. We found it to be of a nature as strange as the mysterious castaways. No one on board could identify the wood. The heartwood was almost as hard as iron, and yet it could be worked. When sawn, its peculiar fragrance attracted clouds of butterflies from the main; they appeared in countless thousands, so that, for some days, the ship could scarcely be navigated. I discovered, later, that this heartwood sank like lead in the water, and, strangest of all perhaps, it was impervious to the teredo worm, the ruination of our ships in warm seas.

"The log, though useless for spars, was a valuable find, and Captain Gorme was beside himself with vexation that he had not been able to learn, from the Indians, whence it came. From a morsel of the heartwood, Mr. Colbarch, the ship's carpenter, fashioned me a leg to replace the temporary one made by Powana, and a more comfortable, serviceable peg, once I was accustomed to it, I have never had the pleasure of wearing. It is the one I have on at the moment.

"We proceeded on our voyage, and, as the days passed, my friend Little and the entire ship's company became more and more impatient with their fainthearted captain. At last the captain himself, finding himself incapable of making a resolute decision, placed Little in command. Thereafter, Gorme kept to his cabin. As the event proved, he had not long to keep it.

"The following morning, at dawn, we sighted a schooner which showed no colours, though Little was convinced, as well as myself, that she was English. 'Dogbody,' said he, 'if she proves to be such, and has American prisoners on board, you shall be exchanged immediately.' He then ran up a signal of a parley and we bore down on the vessel. As we approached, we made her out to be a smart little privateer of eighteen guns. I went to my cabin to prepare for quitting the *Jupiter*, and whilst there, I heard the parley which followed.

" 'What ship is that?' Little roared through his speaking trumpet.

" '*Lion*, of London,' came the reply, so clearly that though I could not see the schooner, I knew that she was right alongside. 'Who are you?'

" '*Jupiter*, of Salem,' Little replied. 'Have you prisoners to exchange?'

" 'That's as may be,' replied the British captain. 'What d'ye offer?'

" 'A one-legged surgeon,' said Little, 'and better with one than any you've got with two.'

" 'A sawbones? What name?'

" 'Dogbody.'

" 'Dogbody!' came the reply. 'Ye don't mean F. Dogbody, late of the *Duff*?

" 'Aye, the same,' said Little.

" 'You mean ye've got him there, on board?'

" 'Aye,' said Little, 'all but his larboard leg.'

" 'By God, sir,' said the British captain, 'for Dogbody I'll give ye two Yankee lieutenants, a boatswain, a gunner and a gunner's mate, three quartermasters, and a half-dozen reefers for a makeweight. Will ye trade?'

" 'Send 'em across. He's yours,' said Little, and within the quarter-hour the boatload of Yankee prisoners came on board, the *Lion*'s captain with them. I knew him well. We'd served together three years earlier in the *Lowestoffe*, frigate, under Captain William Locker. His name was Irons, and he had been a lieutenant in the *Lowestoffe*.

" 'Dogbody,' said he, clasping my hand warmly, 'I hate to buy ye home at so cheap a rate, but these'—with a nod toward his prisoners—'are all I have on hand at the moment. I sent threescore off, a fortnight since, in one of my prizes. Well, sir' he added, turning to Little, 'for once I've got the best of a Yankee in a trade, but a bargain's a bargain, as your countrymen say.'

"He had a provoking way with him, did Irons. He was tough as an old lanyard knot, and, fine seaman that he was, I regret to say that he had no delicacy of feeling. Indeed, he had a deep respect for the seagoing American, but he took pleasure in showing the contrary.

"Little nodded, with a grim smile. 'I'm content,' said he. He then clasped my hand. 'Good-bye, Dogbody, and God bless you!'

" 'Little,' said I, 'I would not have believed that a prisoner-of-war could ever leave the hands of his captors with any degree of reluctance, but so it is in my case. I respect you as a man, sir, and, if you will permit me to say so, esteem you as a friend.'

" 'Then why leave him, Dogbody?' said Irons. 'Shall we take his little ship with us?'

"Little's eyes blazed. 'By God, sir! Will ye fight?' he asked.

"Irons, who was a short thickset man, bristled up like a bulldog. 'Have ye ever met an Englishman that wouldn't?' said he.

" 'Then get ye gone to your vessel,' said Little, 'for ye've not long to command her.'

"Captain Gorme, who had come out of his cabin meanwhile, stood by, pressing his hands together with an expression of perfect anguish on his face, but Little paid no heed to him. The *Jupiter* buzzed like a nest of hornets before we were down the side. 'Irons,' said I, as we were being rowed across to the *Lion*, 'you've a wildcat by the tail this time.' 'Never ye mind, Dogbody,' said he. 'I'll have him by the throat, directly.' He was silent for a moment, then he added: 'I must make him strike within the half-hour, for I'm damned short of ball.'

"And, b'gad, gentlemen, we did! 'Twas a miracle, no less, for we deserved to have been taken. Irons had told the plain truth: he'd powder a plenty, but only sufficient ball for six charges for each of his guns. But the man was a veritable firebrand and would have used his own head for ammunition had it been necessary. We were over-matched, both as to men and guns, but the *Lion* had a picked crew and was a worthy foe for a ship twice her size. I've never seen a vessel better handled; every shot from our guns went home. The *Jupiter*'s mainmast went over the side in the first five minutes of the action, and the mizzen followed shortly; and whilst the *Lion* received her share of pun-ishment, she'd lost nothing in her sails. Little performed prodigies with his disabled ship. He was tearing to board, but we kept clear. Damme, I was more than glad, for I could see Powana towering above the *Jupiter*'s bulwark, and I knew he'd as soon cut off my other leg as look at me. What cost them the victory was, past question, the cow-ardice of Gorme. He was for running away, and gave orders counter to those of Little, which confused the Yankee seamen. But having shot and to spare, they poured them into us at an appalling rate. More than half our company was either dead or wounded.

"I'd removed my wooden peg directly upon boarding the *Lion*, for the stump of the limb was still tender. I could not bear the heavy peg for long at a time, and so would make shift, for an hour or two, with a crutch. Fortunate it was that I did so on this occasion, for it was the indirect means of victory.

"The *Lion*'s gunners had fired their last broadside, and a murderous one it was, but we'd not a ball left. One shot had all but shattered their foremast, and Irons was dancing round our quarter-deck shouting, 'Fall, blast ye! Fall!' At this moment the gunner came aft; he was dripping with sweat and breathing heavily. 'Sir,' said he to Irons, 'we've fired our last shot.' 'What's that to me?' Irons bellowed at him. 'Get back to your guns! Use marlinspikes! Get back to your guns, damn your blood! Use deadeyes, chain plates! Get back to your guns, I say!'

"And, b'gad, gentlemen, he did! All the rusty raffle in the ship went into the guns and on to the *Jupiter*, and with it my new peg which might well be classed as hardware. One of the gunners, seeing it resting by the bulwark, seized upon it and rammed it down the muzzle of his piece amongst iron spoons, bolts, nuts, and fragments of brick prized up from the galley floor. I was told afterward, upon unimpeachable authority, for I was, of course, then at my own bloody work below, that it was my leg that cost the Yankees the day. It caromed off the *Jupiter*'s tottering foremast and then struck my friend Little a glancing blow on the head, which, thank God, only knocked him unconscious. The other oddments of the charge worked great havoc as well, amongst the ship's company, and Gorme, who was then forced to take command, immediately struck his colours."

Doctor Dogbody broke off, refreshed himself at his glass, and touched his lips with a richly coloured silk bandana.

"And what then, sir?" Will Tunn inquired, when it seemed apparent that the surgeon had no intention of proceeding.

"What then, Will Tunn? Why, nothing then. What more could there be save that, when we had made temporary repairs on the two ships, we carried our prize to the West Indies? It was a sad blow for Little, but he took it like the man he was, and whilst he must have despised Gorme with all the strength of his being, no word of censure crossed his lips. I was not surprised, later, when Gorme jumped his parole.

Little refused to give his. Despite my protestations, he insisted on being put aboard the *Regulus*, a dismantled seventy-four, moored in the harbour of Saint Kitts, and used to confine prisoners-of-war. 'Never fear, Dogbody,' said he. 'I shall not remain long aboard of her, and I refuse that you should be compromised by my escape.' Two days later, when I went aboard the *Regulus* to visit him and to bring him some delicacies from shore, he was gone, and Powana with him. I have never heard of either of them from that day to this."

"It is my pleasure, sir," said Runyon, "to tell you that he is still living, and an honoured citizen of the town of Marshfield. Powana, as well, survives."

"I am profoundly glad to hear it, sir," the surgeon replied.

"You have said, Doctor Dogbody," Ostiff put in, "that the strange wood of which your peg was made was impervious to the teredo worm. How could you be certain of that?"

"It was a piece of good fortune for me, sir, that the peg was not lost when fired into the *Jupiter*. After wounding Little, it struck the bulwark, and the smaller end penetrated four inches into the oak. Captain Irons recovered it for me when he went on board to receive the ship. Some months later, whilst we were lying at Port Royal, in Jamaica, I lost the leg overboard, having unstrapped it, as my custom then was of an evening, to rest my stump. I offered a hogshead of the finest rum the island produced to the man who could fetch it up. During the next fortnight, scores of negroes attempted to secure it, and one poor fellow was taken by the sharks. I immediately withdrew the reward and ordered that no further search should be made. Imagine my surprise, six months later, upon returning from Barbadoes, to find that one persevering fellow had dived it up! He was a veritable sea otter, else he could never have reached bottom at such a depth. Needless to say, I rewarded him handsomely. The peg was as good as upon the day I'd lost it; not the mark of a worm appeared upon it. It was like meeting an old friend to strap it on once more, and my stump being perfectly hardened by that time, I never again exposed myself to the risk of losing it. . . . Bless me, Tunn! What's this?"

A great commotion was heard in the kitchen, and a few seconds later a huge black rat came running into the taproom, followed by Hodge the dwarflike waiter, Bilges, the kitchen boy, and several others, all in a mad chase after the rodent. Doctor Dogbody, who had already donned his hat and coat in preparation for going home, skipped across the taproom with the agility of a boy, and, with a dexterous side blow with his wooden leg, caught the rat fairly in the middle and sent it hurtling through the air against the tavern wall, where it fell lifeless. Then, with a slight bow, "Gentlemen," he said, "I bid you good evening," and a moment later the door closed behind him.

Rule Britannia
from Doctor Dogbody's Leg
by James Norman Hall

Doctor F. Dogbody, fictional protagonist of James Norman Hall's (1887–1951) 1940 book, lost his left leg during a 50-year career as a ship's surgeon in England's Royal Navy. The gregarious Dogbody here offers one version of the events that led to losing his limb. (See page 83 for another—very different—version.)

The evening was a busy one at the Cheerful Tortoise, and Will Tunn's staff of servants were at the stretch, caring for the wants of the numerous company, above and below. In the taproom all the tables were occupied; the Argand lamps were blurs of mellow light in the haze of tobacco smoke, and a lively hum of conversation filled the air. Tom Tapleke shuffled from table to table on his flat feet, resentful of the unaccustomed activity, while Hodge, who had been pressed into the taproom service for the evening, made rapid zigzag sorties, answering the calls of thirsty patrons. With his bandy legs twinkling under him and his fusty wig askew, he resembled an elderly and disreputable gnome who had strayed into the place by accident and was frantically seeking some means of escape. Will Tunn, delighted at seeing custom pick up, strolled among the tables exchanging greetings with his guests, all the while keeping a watchful eye upon the two pretty barmaids busy at spigots and decanters behind the high zinc-covered bar. He halted at the table where Doctor Dogbody, Mr. Ostiff, Ned

Balthus, and Captains Runyon and Murgatroyd were seated. Mr. Ostiff glanced up indignantly.

"How now, Tunn?" he remarked. "Is it first come, last served at the Tortoise, and we the props of the house?"

The landlord was profuse in his apologies and immediately hurried away to attend to their wants.

Doctor Dogbody had been gazing from time to time at a gentleman in the uniform of a merchant captain who was seated alone at a table on the far side of the room.

"Ned," he remarked, "I'll take my oath I know the officer yonder."

"It's like enough," the gunner replied. "He's the cut of an old Navy man."

"An admiral, surely, in such a rig," said Runyon, with an air of disapproval. "Or a nabob, no less."

The stranger was, indeed, handsomely dressed in broadcloth of robin's-egg blue, richly embellished with gold braid, with lace ruffles of the finest material at his cuffs. His white hair was tied with a ribbon of the same colour as his coat.

"Aye, Runyon," Captain Murgatroyd replied, "he'll look so to an American, no doubt. There's none of your Yankee plainness and poverty in the India service. They'll have their captains dressed as befits their station. Shouldn't wonder if he commands the *Hindostan*; she came in this morning. Four months from Calcutta."

"He's the same advantage as yourself, Dogbody," said Ostiff. "A leg off just above the knee, and on the same side."

"You don't tell me," said the surgeon, craning his neck for a better view.

"I was here when he came. A handsome peg he's wearing if ever I saw one. Ivory it looks to be, inlaid with silver and gold."

At this moment the officer in question turned in his seat for a casual view of the company. Dogbody stared hard at him. "Damn my bones and blood!" he exclaimed. " 'Tis Dick Rodd!" Immediately he sprang from his seat and crossed the room to where the captain was sitting. His companions looked on with interest at the meeting which then took place; indeed, the attention of all the company was suddenly fixed upon the two old fellows who stood with hands clasped, beaming at each other as though scarcely able to credit their good fortune at the chance encounter. Nothing more nautical in appearance could have been seen in the whole of Portsmouth. Then Dogbody linked his arm in that of his companion and marched him across the room to his own table.

"Gentlemen," he announced, "you've heard me speak times without number of my old friend Dick Rodd."

"Captain Rodd, you rogue," his friend replied. "You'd deny me my rank, would you?"

"What you will, Dick, what you will," the surgeon replied, airily. "B'gad, had you left it to me to kick you upstairs I'd have made a handsomer job of it. You'd have stopped in the Navy and been Lord High Admiral by this time."

He then proceeded with the introductions, whereupon the company took seats again. "Now, Dick, bring me up to date," said Dogbody. "And first, ye renegade, what are ye doing in the merchant service?"

"He asks me that!" Captain Rodd replied, addressing the company in general. "Gentlemen, it was this same rascally surgeon who maimed me as you see me now. I'd a scratch on the leg, a mere nothing, and before I could draw breath to protest, he'd deprived me of the scratch and the leg with it."

"Tut, man," said Dogbody. "You'd not grudge a surgeon the practice of his trade? If ye recollect, 'twas a slack time with us when I took the limb. I'd the need to keep my hand in."

"I harbour no ill feelings, Dogbody. You might have the right leg as well, if I was as sure to get as handsome a peg to replace it as I have for the left."

"Whalebone, Captain?" the gunner asked.

"No, Mr. Balthus. Elephant's tusk. Dogbody, have ye ever seen such a work of art? The carving and inlay were all of a year in the execution. The leg is worth a prince's ransom. As a matter of fact, 'twas an Indian prince that gave it to me."

" 'Tis a pretty kickshaw. I wouldn't cheapen it, Dick, since ye seem to prize it so highly."

"Sour grapes!" said Captain Rodd, with a grin. "And small wonder, with such a common-looking thing on your own stump. You couldn't have bought it, surely?"

" 'Twas a gift, like your own," said the surgeon, stretching out his peg and regarding it with a complacent air. "I'd not exchange it for a dozen elephants' tusks."

"And who from? Some of your Scotch friends, I doubt not?"

"Ye really wish to know?"

"Aye; but first I'd learn how a sawbones managed to get sawn, for once, in his turn. Would ye bear with me, gentlemen?" he added, with a glance at the others. "I've not seen this fellow in better than twenty years. His history since we last met is a blank to me."

"With pleasure, Captain," Ostiff replied. "We are as curious as yourself. The doctor has been with us these four months past, but not a word will he say of his lost leg. Wild horses will not drag the tale from him."

"Nonsense, friend Ostiff," the surgeon replied, with a deprecatory wave of the hand. "What could be duller, in a seafaring, war-faring race like ours, than the tale of a missing leg? As far as interest goes, ye might as well ask Ned Balthus here what food he was wont to eat on banyan day."

"Damme if ye get off with that excuse," Captain Rodd replied. "You chopped off my leg, you villain! I'll have yours, now, in retrospect."

"You'd force me to it, would you?"

"We'd be pleased to learn, first, of your own loss, Captain," said Runyon. "The doctor will then be bound to oblige, in his turn."

"I can tell you that, sir, in scarcely more than a breath," Captain Rodd replied. "Dogbody and I were serving on the *Bedford* at the time. The *Bedford*, the *Prince Frederick*, and the *Magnanime*, under the command of Lord Howe, in the latter ship, were sent to reduce a fort on the little island of Dumet, on the French coast. The place was of no consequence, but there was excellent water upon it, wanted for servicing our fleet, then on blockade duty. The fort was silenced without the loss of a man, but one of their salvos shattered the *Bedford*'s mizzenmast, and a splinter from the mast grazed the calf of my left leg. I would have bound up the little wound with my handkerchief and gone about my business. As it chanced, this butcher, Dogbody, was on deck at the moment. For all my protests, he, with his dressers and loblolly boys, seized and bore me to the after cockpit, and before I could have said 'Oh,' my leg was in his meat tub. Mine was the only casualty on our side."

The surgeon smiled. "You'll mind, Dick, how we carried you ashore, on the evening of that day, and buried the leg below the fort, with you looking on? You might give me credit for that, at least. 'Tis not every man who has the honour of witnessing his own partial interment. Did you know that the place is called Rodd's Island to this day, by Navy men?"

"So I've heard," the captain replied. "I've often thought to go back there and fetch the bones. They'd make a pretty keepsake for my grandchildren. I remember the very spot where you laid them."

"Bones? Bone meal is what we buried, and well ye know it! I've never seen a worse-shattered leg. You've me to thank, Dick Rodd, for a stump to set a peg on. Most surgeons would have had that, as well, in the state it was."

"I'll give you your due, Dogbody. It may have been more than a scratch I had. Now then, where's your own leg? Did ye buy an island with it?"

"I made a better bargain than that, sir. As in your own case, France has it, and a pretty penny it cost them!"

The surgeon paused to draw out his snuffbox, laid a train of the powder along the back of his left hand, snuffed it in with one deft movement, and replaced the box in his pocket.

"Dick, did ye ever know Bob Fingott?" he then asked.

"Fingott . . . Fingott . . . The name's familiar. A lieutenant, wasn't he? And a perfect ass?"

" 'Twas the reputation he bore, and I'll not say without some cause," the surgeon proceeded. "But for all his lack of judgment and his madcap ways, a better friend and comrade never trod the deck of a King's ship."

"Mind you, I never knew him personally, Dogbody. I don't remember that I ever set eyes on him. But I've heard mention more than once of a Lieutenant Fingott. Always in hot water, I believe. Court-martialed four times, or was it five?"

"Six," the surgeon corrected, "and came through with flying colours every time. I was his fellow culprit before the fifth court, and more than proud of the company. B'gad, I'd sooner be hung with Bob Fingott than sit at the Admiralty Board, bedecked with all the stars and garters in His Majesty's gift of disposal. Near enough I came to that end at the time I speak of."

"When was this?" Captain Rodd asked.

"In 1809, and Basque Roads was the place. You'll recollect, Dick, what happened there in the month of April, in that year. Lord Gambier's Channel fleet had eleven French ships of the line bottled up before Rochefort, to say nothing of frigates, sloops, and bombs without number. And there were ourselves, outside, in the Roads, under the command of Rear Admiral Robert Stopford, doing what brave men could to taunt the enemy out to battle. For all their numbers, the French squadron, under Admiral Allemande, lay where they were, week after week, moored in two compact lines, as close as they could get under their batteries on the island of Aix, in Rochefort Harbour. 'Twas an all but impossible thing to get at them with ships of any draught. But to be certain of immunity, they'd erected booms and impediments of every description. And there they lay, snug and safe, as they thought."

"There is thus to be said for Admiral Allemande, Doctor," Captain Murgatroyd put in. "The French had some new ships of the line building in Rochefort Harbour at that time. The admiral was waiting till he could add them to his strength."

"So he was, Inky," the surgeon replied. "I cast no reflections upon his courage. All I say is that we were tired of waiting till he would consent to come out."

"As I remember it, Admiral Wiliaumez was in command of the French fleet, then at Rochefort," said Ostiff.

"Under Admiral Allemande, Ostiff, as Admiral Stopford was under Lord Gambier, on our side. 'Twas Wiliaumez who got the blame for what we did to them, as it was Lord Gambier who reaped most of the glory with us, over Admiral Stopford's head, but 'twas the latter who deserved the credit.

"Well, having cooled heels and keels in Basque Roads for an unconscionable time, it was decided that we must, somehow, drive the enemy from their lair or destroy them where they lay. Admiral Stopford called a conference of his ships' captains on board the *Caesar*, in which ship I had the honour to be surgeon. Bob Fingott was one of the *Caesar*'s lieutenants. A most gallant project was there formed for destroying the enemy by means of fire-ships, transports of light draught, loaded with explosives and combustibles, which should be sailed in amongst them. There is no need to tell old Navy men of the hazardous nature of such a project: hazardous in itself, and for this additional reason, that, by the laws of war, men taken by the enemy on such an expedition suffer death. For this reason it was to be a volunteer affair.

"Bob Fingott was one of the first lieutenants to volunteer, and the first to be accepted by Admiral Stopford. You may think this strange, in view of Fingott's reputation throughout the service, but Admiral Stopford knew what he was about. Bob was sure to go wrong in carrying out whatever orders, but, by a kind of genius, he invariably mounted on his mistakes to the most brilliant successes.

"There were to be twelve fire-ships and three explosion-ships, sailed in by a crew of five men each, in charge of a lieutenant. The lieutenants were to have the choosing of their own crews. Immediately after the conference on the *Caesar*, Fingott called me aside.

" 'Dogbody,' said he, 'was there ever such glorious luck? Now then, I want your advice as to the four men to go with me.'

" 'Four?' said I. 'I thought the number was five.'

" 'So it is,' said he, 'but I've already chosen the first,' and he put his forefinger, like the muzzle of a pistol, against my breastbone.

" 'Thank you kindly, Bob,' said I; 'but I'll not be burned up or blown up for any lieutenant in His Majesty's service. Furthermore, ye know damned well they'll never permit a ship's surgeon to volunteer for any such expedition as this.'

" 'They?' said he. 'What have *they* got to do with it? I'm to choose my own men, and, by God, you're to be one of them!"

"Well, the long and the short of it was that I let him win me over. He'd the most engaging, peremptory way with him, and I loved the man, of course. B'gad, had he wished to set his mind to it, he could have persuaded a Scotch parson to leap with him into the fiery pit. I knew this was about what it would come to, in my own case, with such a leader. 'Bob,' said I, ' 'twill be as much as my commission is worth if the matter is discovered. I'll be broke and dismissed the service as sure as sunrise.' But he had a ready answer to every objection I could make. It was to be a night expedition, of course, and we'd be either killed, captured, or safe back well before daylight. In the latter case, he'd pawn his honour to get me aboard the *Caesar* once more, and no one the wiser."

The surgeon paused to taste his grog, and Murgatroyd took advantage of the opportunity to remark: "I believe I once met Fingott, at Christmas time, in the North Sea. A short fellow, wasn't he, and none too tidy about his person?"

"*Believe* you met him?" said the surgeon. "Damme, you could never be in any doubt, if you had! As for his person, he was short and dirty as a winter's day. Ye'd have had a merry Christmas, if he was of the party."

"We did that! And at the end of it, Fingott swum back to his own ship for a two-pound wager. A calm still day it was, but cold as Greenland. Such a bath would have killed another man."

" 'Twas Fingott, certain. There's nothing he wouldn't do for a wager. When we were serving together in the *Marlborough*, at the time of the Duke of York's visit to Spithead, Fingott got to the very top of the vane of the mainmast and stood there upon his head, waving a little Union

Jack which he held in his bare toes. At so great a height he looked no larger than your little finger. He was a mid at the time, and such a prank would have gotten anyone else into a peck of trouble. But His Royal Highness was so taken with the lad's daring, damme if he didn't get Bob his lieutenant's commission for it!"

"How was your fire-ships fitted out?" Balthus asked, fearful lest the surgeon should branch off on one of his long digressions.

"Where's the need to tell an old Navy gunner of that?" said Dog-body. "Ye must have prepared fire-ships yourself, more than once."

"So I have," said Balthus, "and never twice the same."

"In truth, Ned, 'twas a matter of great interest to me, for I'd never seen it done till then. Two of the vessels, the *Thomas* and the *Whiting*, old transports of three hundred and fifty tons, were fitted out by the *Caesar's* men. For the *Thomas*, narrow troughs were made, with others to cross them, and in these were laid trains of quick-match. In the square openings of these troughs were put the combustibles: open casks of resin, turpentine, and coal tar. Tarred canvas hung above, fixed to the beams, and great loose bundles of tarred shavings. Four port-holes were cut on each side for the fire to burst through, and thick ropes of twisted oakum, well tarred, led from each of the ports to carry the fire up the standing rigging to the sails and mastheads. B'gad, nothing was wanting to make a very furnace of each vessel, the moment they were set aflame.

"The *Whiting* was to be an explosion-ship. In her hold there were stowed, upright, thirty-six barrels of gunpowder, of ninety pounds each. The heads of the casks were out and on each was placed a ten-pound shell, with a short fuse, in order to burst quickly. A canvas hose filled with prime powder was laid for a train from the barrels through a small hole in the ship's quarter to the outside. It was there she was to be touched off, with a fuse to burn from twelve to fifteen minutes to give the men in her time to get well away in their boat before the explosion.

"The preparations were of the most thorough description. Lord Cochrane, who was to command the expedition, was a very genius at this work and left nothing to chance.

"On the eleventh of April, all was in readiness: three explosion-ships and twelve fire-ships completely equipped, and their little crews eager to be off. The night could not have been more perfect. The tide was making, the sky overcast, and the wind fresh from the north. At eight o'clock the signal was made to weigh . . ."

"Pawl there, Dogbody," Captain Rodd interrupted. "I'll not have the details scanted at this rate. You were not to go without convoy, surely? And what was the order of your going?"

"I should have spoken of that. We were not, of course, sent in without support. With us went the sloops *Aigle*, *Pallas*, and *Unicorn*: they were to lie near the Boyard shoal, to receive the boats returning from the fire-and-explosion ships when the work was done. The *Indefatigable* and the *Foxhound* were to lie near the island of Aix, to protect the *Aetna*, bomb, whilst she threw shells into the batteries there. The *Emerald*, *Dotterel*, *Beagle*, *Insolent*, *Conflict*, and *Growler* were to make a diversion on the east side of Aix. All these latter vessels were fitted with Congreve rockets, to spread terror and confusion amongst the enemy. The *Lyra* and *Redpole* were sent ahead of all to anchor, with lights showing, the first on the Boyard side, the other on the Aix side. They were to serve as a guide to the channel to the rest that followed. Lord Cochrane, in the *Impérieuse*, was to act as circumstances would permit, but going in as far as possible to take up the men escaping in the boats, in case they should miss the vessels told off for rescue. There was the order of it, Dick. Is all clear now?"

"Aye, proceed," said the captain.

"There is one particular I have not yet mentioned. The French had placed, amongst their other obstructions for safety, a heavy boom across the channel to the inner roads where their ships of the line were moored. That had to be broken. To effect this, the old *Mediator*, frigate, also equipped as a fire-ship, was to lead the way, crashing through the boom and opening up the channel for the ships of light draught that followed.

"Fingott got me aboard the *Thomas* at dusk without a soul aware of the fact save our little crew. The four others, all of the *Caesar*, were a quartermaster's mate and three seamen. One of these latter, Runyon, chanced to be a countryman of yours in our service, a brisk lad, Jack Ellis, known as Yankee Jack to his shipmates.

"Fingott was tearing to be off, but we had to wait our signal. The *Mediator* went first, then the three explosion-ships, then the fire-ships in a particular order, each one about half a cable's length from the next ahead. We were fifth in the line, following the third of the explosion-ships. Fingott had put the lot of us, in the *Thomas*, in French uniforms stole from amongst the effects of some prisoners we had in the *Caesar*, off the *Jalouse*, frigate, which had struck to us the week before. As I've said, men taken by the enemy on a fire-ship expedition suffered death. Very well, said Fingott. Since we would run no greater risk by doing so, we'd go disguised as Frenchmen, and we might well meet with opportunities denied to the others. He spoke French near as well as myself and was dressed in a captain's outfit. Mine was that of a lieutenant of marines, and the fellow must have had an admiral's belly. However, I stuffed out waistcoat and breeches with a feather pillow and the rig did well enough."

"Was ye cool, Doctor?" Runyon asked.

"At this time? B'gad, no! I was shaking in my shoes, but I'd the vanity not to let Fingott see it. But mind you, Runyon: scared as I was, there was an exhilaration in the venture to have made a very sheep happy to be a part of it. Fingott was in his glory. He'd no imagination, not an atom. I doubt if ever the man knew the least tremor of fear. He had the wheel at the start, and was humming 'Rule Britannia' to himself in his deep bass voice.

"The place where our fleet lay was a good fifteen miles out, which gave Bob plenty of room for starting his mischief.

" 'Dogbody,' said he, presently, 'we'll be first in, what d'ye say? Show the lot of 'em a clean pair of heels.'

" 'Not with my consent,' said I. 'Damn your eyes, Bob! Stick to orders for once. We're to keep fifth place.'

"He clapped me on the back. 'Never fear, old cock! I'll earn ye more glory in the next three hours than ye'd hoard up in fifty years as a sawbones.'

" 'I've no wish to have it in a lump,' said I. 'Be prudent, Bob, for God's sake!'

"I might have saved my breath. There was no reasoning with such a madcap, once he'd made up his mind. The *Thomas* was a fast-sailing little vessel, and Fingott had been ordered to use none but his head-sails so as to be sure to keep his place. But nothing would do now, but we must hoist more, and we began to surge forward. There never was a blacker night, at the start, but each vessel had a light showing astern to guide the one behind her. We were scarce two miles on our way when we passed the explosion-ships. What they thought I don't know. They may have believed us some French merchantman slipping in unawares of what the British were up to. In any case, not a hail did they give as we passed. But Captain Woodridge, in command of the *Mediator*, had sharper eyes. We passed almost within spitting distance, though we were a mere shadow, and he guessed what was up.

" 'What ship is that?' he roared through his speaking-trumpet. 'Is it you, Bob Fingott?'

"No reply from Bob save a low chuckle. Then, gentlemen, we were treated to the most accomplished explosion of blasphemous rage it has been my privilege to hear in more than sixty years at sea. But it trailed away behind us and became inaudible. The *Mediator* had all sails set, but she was deeply and heavily ballasted for the sake of the great boom she was to break, and she'd not yet full way on her."

"Damn his soul!" Captain Rodd broke in. "Was Fingott so great a fool as to endanger the success of the entire expedition?"

"He was, Dick. And he feared neither man, beast, devil, nor Admiral Gambier himself. I reminded him of the boom ahead and asked if he thought we'd break it with our little three-hundred-and-fifty-ton transport. 'Never ye fret about that, Dogbody,' said he. 'The boom will be well sunk for ships of deeper draught than this. I'll take my oath we'll pass over it with a foot or two to spare.'

"By this time we could see, far ahead, the lights of the *Lyra* and *Red-pole*, marking the way for us. As soon as they came within view, commanders had only to hold a course midway between them, and they'd be right for the channel where the boom was fixed."

"Ye fetched over it?" Balthus asked.

"I'm coming to that," said the surgeon. "We're not there yet. You'll recollect, Dick, how the harbour of Rochefort lies, with the Ile d'Oléron enclosing it to the west and south? When you've passed the Antioch Rock, off the northern tip of Oléron, there's another ten miles, or thereabout, before you fetch the island of Aix. Fingott said he knew the place better than the palm of his hand and held his course with the utmost confidence, all the while quizzing me for being a sour old bachelor, as he called it. Unless I made haste to wed, there'd be no children for me to tell my tales to as an old man, above all, the story of the glorious night of April eleventh, when Lieutenant Robert Fingott was first in with his fire-ship and destroyed the entire French fleet. Presently he left off his banter, and I could see he was worried.

" 'Where's the blasted boom?' said he. 'Ought to be hereabout. Blast me if I don't believe we've sailed over it!'

"We hadn't long to wait to know where the thing lay. The words were scarce out of his mouth when we struck it.

" 'Twas no honest, downright, shattering blow that tells ye the worst at once. The thing played with us as though it had a kind of intelligence. Fingott had not been far off in reckoning how deep it would lie, but he was just wrong enough to do us all the damage necessary. The little *Thomas* slipped up on it, heeled over to starboard, and there we stuck. Then the boom swung back slow and we slid along a bit more till we were slightly down by the head. This gave us hope that she'd inch along over it, for the wind was fresh and coming from right aft, and our mainsail had the full good of it. We began to slip down, ever so slowly.

" 'We'll make it lads! By God, we will!' said Fingott. 'Half a minute more and we'll be clear. Dogbody, what d'ye say now? Was I right to take the chance?' "

The surgeon paused to draw out his silk bandana, and blew his nose loudly. "I'd no need to answer that question, gentlemen," he then resumed. " 'Twas answered for me by a frigate of fourteen hundred tons."

"God's rabbit!" Balthus exclaimed. "I was about to ask ye, Doctor, what space ye had with the *Mediator* right astern."

"About thrice the length of this taproom, Ned, at the moment when we cleared the boom, for clear it we did. Will ye believe it? In the excitement of getting off we'd clean forgot the frigate. 'Twas Jack Ellis that spied her first. 'Hold hard!' he yelled; then we all saw her. The sky was clearing to seaward, and there she came, seething down upon us, her sails seeming to reach the very stars. She had way enough on her now, b'gad! Fingott put his helm hard over, and much good it did him! The *Mediator* struck the boom, lifting the great beams clear of the water and tearing them apart with a rending and crashing of chains and timbers. On she came as though the impediment had been so many ropes of straw. There was no room to stand clear of us. Out went my feet from under me; I saw all the stars in the mind's firmament, and when I came round I was lying in the bottom of our jolly boat, with Jack Ellis spilling some of Fingott's flask of brandy over my chin.

" 'What's this, Jack?' said I. 'Where are we, and where's the *Thomas*?'

"His reply was lost in a shuddering roar that Vesuvius could scarce have made, in full eruption. The first of the explosion-ships had been touched off, not half a mile from where we lay. By the light, I saw the *Thomas* near by, settling by the stern. Down she went as I looked at her, with all her combustibles intact. Then the second of the explosion-ships blew up. We bobbed about in our little boat with burning wreckage falling on every side. The men had their oars out, awaiting Fingott's orders. He sat with the tiller under his arm, staring at the spot where the *Thomas* had sunk, blood streaming down the side of his face from a cut he'd got.

" 'Dogbody,' said he, 'we've disgraced ourselves forever!'

"I could have spared his generosity in sharing the blame with me, but I said nothing and waited to see what he'd do next."

"What! Not a word?" said Captain Rodd. "You were a blessed saint, Dogbody, if you'd so firm a command of your feelings. Damn his blood! I'd have had the last drop of it if he'd gotten me into such a mess!"

"No, Dick. Not if you'd known Fingott. 'Twas at just such a moment, when bogged to the chin in a mess of his own making, that his guardian angel took him by the hand and raised him out of it. The man was a genius at falling on his feet.

"He got to those feet now, in the stern sheets of the jolly boat, and looked about him. We were about a mile to the west of Aix. I wish it were within my power to give you a picture of Rochefort Harbour as we saw it then. 'Twas a spectacle truly awe-inspiring. The third of the explosion-ships now blew up, whilst the fire-ships, with flames roaring hundreds of feet into the air, were drifting in every direction. Land and sea for miles around stood out in clear relief in the awful light. The French batteries on Aix were in full action, endeavouring to sink the fire-ships and the convoy that had followed us in, and these latter were replying as hotly with shells and Congreve rockets. A more infernal sight could scarce be conceived. 'Twas fit to mimic the Day of Judgment.

"Fingott wiped the blood from his face with his coatsleeve and took the tiller. 'To the oars, lads,' he said. 'Break your backs! Our luck's been out thus far, but, by God, we'll better it before the night's done!' The men pulled with a will, and Fingott steered us straight for the French fleet. The instant we were under way he was his old self again. 'Dogbody,' said he, 'how's the feather belly? Full of courage?' He was alluding to the pillow I had under my borrowed French waistcoat and breeches.

" 'Lead on,' said I. 'I'd as soon be killed or taken by the French as be flung out of His Majesty's Navy in disgrace. Ye promised me glory, Bob Fingott. If ye miscarry a second time, I'll smother you with that same belly!"

"We proceeded into the midst of a scene of the wildest confusion. One of the fire-ships had run afoul of the *Océan*, a one-hundred-gun ship, which was all aflame, her men pouring out of her like rats. The ships on either side were being unmoored in frantic haste; we saw the *Aquilon* and the *Tonnerre* already free and drifting toward the Palais

Shoal, where they soon grounded and heeled over. The sea all round their fleet was alive with boats rushing about like water spiders on various errands. No notice was taken of us, and Fingott steered right on. He was awaiting the inspiration of the moment, and presently spied it through flame and smoke: a ship of the line anchored a good half mile from where the fleet lay. We found a six-oared boat alongside, empty, and a boarding ladder let down as though for our convenience. 'Twas the *Varsovie*, a brand-new ship, though not yet in commission. She was lying there to take in her guns.

"We made the painter of our boat fast and followed Fingott up the ladder, not knowing what we'd find the next moment. We found no one. 'Twas such luck as would come only to a Fingott, but aft, in the ward room, still smelling of gilding and new paint, was a detachment of ten marines, under a lieutenant, all stretched out on the bare deck, asleep. On guard duty, and snoring through all that uproar!

"There was Fingott's chance. As I've said, he was near as perfect in his French as myself, and even better skilled to speak the argot of their Navy. We roused them out, and Fingott gave the lieutenant a dressing-down would have done credit to a post captain. They were scared as rabbits at having been caught asleep, and must have thought the end of the world had come when they saw what was taking place outside. They never doubted us French. Fingott drove them before him to the gangway and told the lieutenant he was to report at once with his men aboard the *Aquilon*. They sprang into their boat and off they went.

"Not a moment did we lose. We rushed down to the main gun deck where a dozen new thirty-two-pounders were already in place. Fingott seized a swab, plunged it into a bucket of tar, and this was set aflame. Down he led us into the bowels of the ship, and, with that flaring torch to light us, we gathered up shavings, oakum, bits of new boards and beams left by the shipwrights, and within twenty minutes we had the ship burning fiercely in half-a-dozen places. 'Twas a crime, no less, for she was a splendid ship, but we did it for Old England's sake, to say nothing of our own. By the time we cleared out, nothing could have saved her.

" 'Bob,' said I, as we scrambled into our boat once more, 'there's glory enough for the six of us. We'd best push home now whilst we've whole skins.'

" 'Home!' said he. 'We've only just started.' He was rapt clean out of himself with so huge a success and thought no more of our safety than he did of his own. For all that, I'd never have believed he was daft enough to do what he did next.

"We passed three frigates, still at moorings, but he gave them scarce a glance. He was so flushed with success that nothing less than a ship of the line was game for us. The *Foudroyant* lay next.

" 'Lads,' said he to the seamen as we made toward her, 'the surgeon and I are going aboard yonder. Do you lie close by within hail. If we fail to appear within twenty minutes, make the best of your way out to one of the rescue ships.' Then, with a nod to me, up the side he went, as cool as though he were the captain himself, coming aboard after a night in town.

"Everything was in confusion on deck, for rockets and bombs from our sloops were bursting on every side. Wounded men were being carried below and some still lay as they'd fallen. Fingott strode aft with me at his heels. We found a lieutenant in charge of the quarter-deck. 'Where's your commander?' demanded Fingott. The lieutenant stared hard at him. 'He's been hit, sir,' he then said. 'You are in charge of the deck?' asked Bob. 'I am, sir,' replied the other. 'Then slip your cables without an instant's delay!' said Fingott. What he hoped to do was to get the *Foudroyant* adrift and grounded where she could be destroyed at leisure, and damme if he didn't come within an ace of succeeding! But a Congreve rocket, fired at that moment from one of our sloops, did for the pair of us. The thing came flaming over and burst almost upon us, and a fragment of the iron casing ripped open my belly. Or, to be more exact, it ripped open what would have been my belly had I been as fat in the middle part as the French lieutenant whose uniform I wore. The result was that I was damaged only in the feathers, but these flew out in a blinding cloud."

The surgeon paused to glance at Captain Rodd.

"I'm coming to the leg, Dick," he resumed, "but 'twas the belly that went first. Large as the pillow was I was stuffed with, ye'd never have believed there could be such a mort of feathers in it. They came and they came, and when I thought I was all but emptied, another cloud greater than the last would be teased out by the wind, which was still blowing fresh, and whirled aloft and about the decks.

"We were lost from that moment. I knew it and Fingott knew it. Nevertheless, we stood our ground, trying to make it appear that nothing was amiss and that all wounded men, upon occasion, were as like as not to bleed feathers.

" '*Tonnerre de Dieu!*' Fingott roared, when he could see once more. 'Do ye stand there gaping, Lieutenant? Unmoor, I say! Slip your cables at once, sir!'

"The fellow spat out two or three feathers that he had inadvertently drawn in with his breath. 'By whose authority?' he then replied.

" 'That of Admiral Wiliaumez,' said Fingott. 'I've come from him this instant.'

"But it wouldn't do. He had no more than spoken when a voice at our backs replied: 'From *me*, sir? I am Admiral Wiliaumez.'

"We turned quickly, and there in truth was the admiral himself, who had just emerged from the companionway with the *Foudroyant*'s captain, the latter's head bound round with a bloody cloth.

"Fingott saw that the game was up, but he lost none of his self-possession. With a faint smile, he drew his borrowed French sword, and, with great dignity, tendered it by the blade to the admiral. 'Then I am your prisoner, sir,' he replied. 'Lieutenant Robert Fingott, of His Majesty's ship *Caesar*. . . . Surgeon F. Dogbody, likewise of the *Caesar*,' he added as I proffered my blade, and with it another storm of feathers, largess for the entire ship's company."

"Damn your eyes and feathers, Dogbody," Captain Rodd broke in, with a chuckle. "A wonder it is that the pair of you were not guillotined as you stood, with your own swords. Well you deserved to be!"

"We expected no less," the surgeon replied; "but the French honour reckless courage as well as ourselves. We were secured at once, of course, but treated with the utmost courtesy. As my hands were being tied behind my back, Admiral Wiliaumez stepped forward to inspect my wounded middle part, thrust his hand into the aperture, and drew forth the tattered pillow. Then, gentlemen, followed a white storm that even surpassed the earlier ones. 'Twas like the fairy tale of the mill that makes the sea salt: there was magic in the pillow; its contents seemed to come from an inexhaustible supply. With the utmost gravity, the admiral handed the not-yet-emptied casing to a midshipman, who made haste to carry it to leeward and toss it over the bulwark. The admiral turned to me, and I could see that he maintained his composure with some difficulty. 'Surgeon Dogbody,' said he, 'I wish the wounds of my own men were of as light a nature as this.' He then gave orders that we were to be carried aboard the *Calcutta* and placed under a strict guard."

"The *Calcutta*? Was she not destroyed in the Basque Roads affair?" Captain Murgatroyd asked.

"She was, Inky, but not until the day following the running-in of the fire-ships. All of these latter had miscarried save the one that burned the *Océan*; nevertheless, Admiral Stopford's purpose had been well served. The French had been forced to unmoor, and on the morning of April twelfth, all save two of their ships were aground on the Palais Shoal, some of them helpless and exposed to our further damage. Admiral Stopford ordered the *Caesar* and the *Theseus* into Rochefort Harbour, and the *Caesar* was able to get close enough to the *Calcutta* to effect her destruction. 'Twas then that Fingott and I, with the *Calcutta's* men, were treated to a dose of British ball from our own ship that I shudder to think of to this day. My leg went in one of the first salvos, and this time I bled something worse than feathers! Fingott was wounded as well, though not gravely. The end of it was that the *Calcutta* was abandoned, a complete wreck, and the pair of us were taken to the naval hospital in Rochefort.

"With your leave, Dick, I will now pass over the next four months. They were not, in truth, eventful for prisoners-of-war. Fingott never lost his spirits, but I was sad enough, at times, knowing what we had in prospect as soon as we had recovered from our wounds: the final wound of all, either strung up at a yardarm, or stood up against a wall, facing a firing squad. We hoped for the latter, but never doubted it would be one or the other. Fingott was up and about long before myself. There never was such a man to make friends with no matter whom. He knew everyone in the hospital, from the chief surgeon down to the girls who brought the bread, and was on first-name terms with most of them. At last, when I was able to hobble with a crutch, we were ordered before a naval court.

"We were tried on the *Foudroyant*, Admiral Wiliaumez himself presiding. The examination was as brief as it was fair and unprejudiced. We made no attempt to defend ourselves, but freely admitted our part in the fire-ship expedition. The evidence having been heard, we were dismissed to await sentence.

"A quarter of an hour later we were again escorted to the admiral's great cabin. Court and spectators rose as we entered, and stood in deep silence, awaiting the words of Admiral Wiliaumez. He was a man of noble bearing, with a countenance grave, serene, and commanding. He stood with his hands resting lightly on the table before him. The interval seemed endless to me. Then he spoke.

" 'Lieutenant Robert Fingott, Surgeon F. Dogbody: Having heard the evidence in support of the charges made against you, and having heard your own freely offered testimony which confirms that evidence, and having maturely and deliberately weighed the whole, this Court is of the opinion that the charges have been proved. It doth, therefore, judge that you shall die.'

"He paused, and we waited in numb despair to learn whether we were to suffer the ignominy of being hung, or whether we were to be accorded the melancholy honour of a firing squad.

" 'But,' continued the admiral—and never has that small word produced in me so profound an emotion—'but . . . it is neither the desire nor the intention of this Court to hasten that judgment. On the contrary, it is the wish of my officers and myself that it may be carried out only through natural causes, in the fullness of time, when you are as distinguished in years as, by your courage and hardihood, on the night of April the eleventh last, you are ennobled by the honours which your grateful country will, doubtless, confer upon you. Lieutenant Robert Fingott, Surgeon F. Dogbody: I sentence you to be returned to that country with all the honours of war.' "

"What! Ye was let off?" Balthus exclaimed.

"You may well be astonished, Ned. Imagine our own amazement at the moment. I was so shaken with relief and joy that the crutch I balanced with slid from under my shoulder and down I went before the assembled Court! As I was helped to my feet, or, better, my foot, Admiral Wiliaumez smiled and remarked that I'd best be furnished now with another feather pillow for the reverse side of my anatomy, which set them all to laughing."

"Nonsense, Dogbody!" Ostiff remarked. "You tell us that a court-martial in an admiral's ship was as informal as this comes to?"

"It was, Ostiff, but I'd be the last to say it was a common thing. It could never have happened with us, for British officers stand too much on their dignity. The French are vastly our superiors in the gracious art of unbending, upon suitable occasions. They excel us in magnanimity to an even greater extent. Can you imagine a British court that would forgive two officers of an enemy nation that had stolen into one of our very harbours and destroyed a ship of the line? 'Tis not conceivable. They might have called them brave fellows, but they'd have hung them like dogs."

"There was pride in it, to my thinking," said Ostiff. "The French wished to belittle Admiral Stopford and the fire-ship expedition by making it appear that they considered you harmless and not worth the hanging."

"Never, Ostiff, never," the surgeon replied. "Say what you may, you'll not lower my opinion of that most noble action. 'Twas pure magnanimity."

"How were you sent home?" asked Runyon.

"Admiral Wiliaumez fulfilled his promise to the letter. The following day we were brought once more on board the *Foudroyant*, where, to my infinite surprise, I was presented with the leg that I wear at this moment, the gift of the admiral and his officers.

" 'Surgeon Dogbody,' said the admiral, in making the presentation, 'you have been deprived of a leg by your own countrymen. Accept this substitute, the gift of your country's enemies, and may it bring you to France, under more happy auspices, when we are again at peace.' He then paused, and a smile in which grimness and humour mingled crossed his face. 'But you are not to try our good nature too far,' he added. 'Should you venture amongst us again whilst our nations are at war, we will require the return of our gift. And not only the leg, sir! Though you should come adorned, or stuffed, with the feathers of all the plucked geese of Arcady, they will not suffice, a second time, to save your head.' "

"I should think not, indeed," said Murgatroyd, with a laugh. "It was undoubtedly the pillow that saved you, Dogbody."

"So I believe," said the surgeon, "though Fingott would never acknowledge this. Had I not bled feathers in so astonishing and seemingly inexhaustible a fashion, which touched Admiral Wiliaumez's sense of humour, the pair of us would have been dead these nine years. I have since had an affection amounting to idolatry for both ducks and geese. I would not taste the flesh of the noblest bird of either species that Will Tunn might roast upon his spits."

"Did ye wear the peg home?" asked Balthus.

"I did; it was attached to my stump there and then. When Fingott and I had made our grateful *adieux* to the admiral and his officers, four longboats, under a flag and manned by seamen in their dress uniforms, conducted us out to Basque Roads where our fleet still lay. We were, of course, thought to be dead by our comrades, and you can imagine the amazement in the *Caesar* as we approached that ship, with a band of music playing in the leading boat. Our comrades swarmed on the yards and lined the bulwarks, and, as we came on deck, wild cheering burst forth from all ranks. But it was soon silenced. Captain Woodridge, who had taken in the *Mediator* on the night of April eleventh, was now in command of the *Caesar*, and what did he do but clap us under arrest the moment our French escort was gone! We were, later, court-martialed, as I've said, and it was no thanks to Woodridge that we were not dismissed the service. As it was, Navy discipline demanded that we be found guilty of disobeying orders and sentenced to be reprimanded.

" 'Twas Admiral Stopford himself who delivered the reprimand, in the privacy of his own cabin. He ushered us in, and locked the door behind him; then he brought out a bottle of his best French brandy. Having filled our glasses, he raised his own.

" 'Lads,' said he, 'God bless you! Here's to Old England, and to Surgeon Dogbody's feather belly!' "

" 'Twas a handsome way of letting ye down," said Balthus.

"Was it not? He kept us with him a full hour, for he wanted all the details of the burning of the *Varsovie*, and I took pride in showing him my new peg."

"I'd have spared calling his attention to such a clumsy-looking thing," said Captain Rodd. "The poorest carpenter's mate in our service could have made you a better one."

The surgeon stretched out his peg, regarding it fondly for a moment. "Hodge!" he called.

The little waiter was still bustling about the taproom on his tasks, though the place was half empty by now. Setting down a tray of glasses on the bar, he hastened to the call.

"Unstrap my peg," said Dogbody.

Hodge had performed this service more than once for the doctor when he wished to rest his stump. He knelt down and quickly loosed the straps, whereupon Dogbody set the peg upright on the table before the company.

"I'll show you, Dick, why I prize it so highly, beyond its associations," he remarked, with a glint of triumph in his eye. " 'Twas not the gift of an Indian prince, to be sure, but I fancy it nonetheless."

The cylindrical part of the peg, next the stump, was of plain polished oak. The surgeon pressed a tiny button that appeared to be a knot in the wood itself, and immediately two panels slid back revealing a pair of mermaids, their bodies of ivory, their tails of gold, upholding a curved balcony, of exquisite workmanship, with a little gateway of filigree gold midway along it. The surgeon waited while a hidden mechanism whirred within. The gate then opened, and two little figures, dressed in the uniforms of English naval officers, came stiffly out from a sculptured niche and stood upon the balcony while a music box, likewise hidden, tinkled "Rule Britannia." The music ceased; the little figures turned about and marched to their niche; the gateway closed behind them, the wooden panels slid back into place, and the leg appeared as it had before.

Balthus was the first of the company to break silence.

"God's rabbit!" he exclaimed, bringing his fist down with a hearty thump. "I never saw the beat of that, for a peg!"

"It does well enough for an old Navy surgeon," said Dogbody, with a glance at Captain Rodd.

from Mr. Midshipman Easy
by Frederick Marryat

Joseph Conrad, Virginia Woolf and Herman Melville were fans of Frederick Marryat's (1792–1848) novel about Jack Easy's life in the British Navy. This selection from the book finds Jack in Malta. The young midshipman is in love with a noble woman whose father he has rescued from an assasination attempt. The passage begins with a letter to Jack from his own father.

My dear Son,

I have many times taken up my pen with the intention of letting you know how things went on in this country. But as I can perceive around but one dark horizon of evil, I have as often laid it down again without venturing to make you unhappy with such bad intelligence.

The account of your death, and also of your unexpectedly being yet spared to us, were duly received, and I trust, I mourned and rejoiced on each occasion with all the moderation characteristic of a philosopher. In the first instance I consoled myself with the reflection that the world you had left was in a state of slavery, and pressed down by the iron arm of despotism, and that to die was gain, not only in all the parson tells us, but also in our liberty; and, at the second intelligence, I moderated my Joy for nearly about the same reasons, resolving, notwithstanding what Dr. Middleton may say, to die as I have lived, a true philosopher.

The more I reflect the more am I convinced that there is nothing required to make this world happy but equality and the rights of man being duly observed—in short, that everything and everybody should be reduced to one level. Do we not observe that it is the law of nature—do not brooks run into rivers—rivers into seas—mountains crumble down upon the plains?—are not the seasons contented to equalise the parts of the earth? Why does the sun run round the ecliptic, instead of the equator but to give an equal share of his heat to both sides of the world? Are we not all equally born in misery? does not death level us all *æquo pede*, as the poet hath? are we not all equally hungry, thirsty, and sleepy, and thus levelled by our natural wants? And such being the case, ought we not to have our equal share of good things in this world, to which we have undoubted equal right? Can any argument be more solid or more level than this, whatever nonsense Dr. Middleton may talk?

Yes, my son, if it were not that I still hope to see the sun of Justice arise, and disperse the manifold dark clouds which obscure the land—if I did not still hope, in my time, to see an equal distribution of property—an Agrarian law passed by the House of Commons, in which all should benefit alike—I would not care how soon I left this vale of tears, created by tyranny and injustice. At present, the same system is carried on; the nation is taxed for the benefit of the few, and it groans under oppression and despotism; but I still do think that there is, if I may fortunately express myself, a bright star in the west; and signs of the times which comfort me. Already we have had a good deal of incendiarism about the country, and some of the highest aristocracy have pledged themselves to raise the people above themselves, and have advised sedition and conspiracy; have shown to the debased and unenlightened multitude that their force is physically irresistible, and recommended them to make use of it, promising that if they hold in power, they will only use that power to the abolition of our farce of a constitution, of a church, and of a king; and that if the nation is to be governed at all, it shall only be governed by the many. This is cheering. Hail, patriot lords! all hail! I am in hopes yet that the great work will be achieved, in spite of the laughs and sneers and shakes of the head, which my arguments still meet with from that obstinate fellow, Dr. Middleton.

Your mother is in a quiet way; she has given over reading and working, and even her knitting, as useless; and she now sits all day long at the chimney corner twiddling her thumbs, and waiting, as she says, for the millennium. Poor thing, she is very foolish with her ideas upon this matter, but as usual I let her have her own way in everything, copying the philosopher of old, who was tied to his Xantippe.

I trust, my dear son, that your principles have strengthened with your years and fortified with your growth, and that, if necessary, you will sacrifice all to obtain what in my opinion will prove to be the real millennium. Make all the converts you can, and believe me to be,

> Your affectionate father, and true guide,
> Nicodemus Easy.

Jack, who was alone, shook his head as he read this letter, and then laid it down with a pish! He did it involuntarily, and was surprised at himself when he found that he had so done. "I should like to argue the point," thought Jack, in spite of himself; and then he threw the letter on the table, and went into Gascoigne's room, displeased with his father and with himself. He asked Ned whether he had received any letters from England, and, it being near dinner-time, went back to dress. On his coming down into the receiving-room with Gascoigne, the governor said to them,—

"As you both speak Italian, you must take charge of a Sicilian officer, who has come here with letters of introduction to me, and who dines here to-day."

Before dinner they were introduced to the party in question, a slight-made, well-looking young man, but still there was an expression in his countenance which was not agreeable. In compliance with the wishes of the governor, Don Mathias, for so he was called, was placed between our two midshipmen, who immediately entered into conversation with him, being themselves anxious to make inquiries about their friends at Palermo.

In the course of conversation, Jack inquired of him whether he was acquainted with Don Rebiera, to which the Sicilian answered in the affirmative, and they talked about the different members of the family. Don Mathias, towards the close of the dinner, inquired of Jack by what means he had become acquainted with Don Rebiera, and Jack, in reply, narrated how he and his friend Gascoigne had saved him from being murdered by two villains; after this reply the young officer appeared to be less inclined for conversation, but before the party broke up, requested to have the acquaintance of our two midshipmen. As soon as he was gone, Gascoigne observed in a reflective way, "I have seen that face before, but where I cannot exactly say; but you know, Jack, what a memory of people I have, and I have seen him before, I am sure."

"I can't recollect that ever I have," replied our hero, "but I never knew any one who could recollect in that way as you do."

The conversation was then dropped between them, and Jack was for some time listening to the governor and Captain Wilson, for the whole party were gone away, when Gascoigne, who had been in deep thought since he had made the observation to Jack, sprang up.

"I have him at last!" cried he.

"Have who?" demanded Captain Wilson.

"That Sicilian officer—I could have sworn that I had seen him before."

"That Don Mathias?"

"No, Sir Thomas! He is not Don Mathias! He is the very Don Silvio who was murdering Don Rebiera, when we came to his assistance and saved him."

"I do believe you are right, Gascoigne."

"I'm positive of it," replied Gascoigne; "I never made a mistake in my life."

"Bring me those letters, Easy," said the governor, "and let us see what they say of him. Here it is—Don Mathias de Alayeres. You may be mistaken, Gascoigne; it is a heavy charge you are making against this young man."

"Well, Sir Thomas, if that is not Don Silvio, I'd forfeit my commission if I had it here in my hand. Besides, I observed the change in his countenance when we told him it was Easy and I who had come to Don Rebiera's assistance; and did you observe after that, Easy, that he hardly said a word."

"Very true," replied Jack.

"Well, well, we must see to this," observed the governor; "if so, this letter of introduction must be a forgery."

The party then retired to bed, and the next morning, while Easy was in Gascoigne's room talking over their suspicions, letters from Palermo were brought up to him. They were in answer to those written by Jack on his arrival at Malta: a few lines from Don Rebiera, a small note from Agnes, and a voluminous detail from his friend Don Philip, who informed him of the good health of all parties, and of their good-will towards him; of Agnes being as partial as ever; of his having spoken plainly, as he had promised Jack, to his father and mother relative to the mutual attachment; of their consent being given, and then withheld, because Father Thomas, their confessor, would not listen to the union of Agnes with a heretic; but nevertheless telling Jack that this would be got over through the medium of his brother and himself, who were determined that their sister and he should not be made unhappy about such a trifle. But the latter part of the letter contained intelligence equally important, which was, that Don Silvio had again attempted the life of their father, and would have succeeded, had not Father Thomas, who happened to be there, thrown himself between them. That Don Silvio in his rage had actually stabbed the confessor, although the wound was not dangerous. That in consequence of this, all further lenity was denied to him and the authorities were in search of him to award him the punishment due to murder and sacrilege. That up to the present they could not find him, and it was supposed that he had made his escape to Malta in one of the speronares.

Such were the contents of the letter, which were immediately communicated to the governor and Captain Wilson, upon their meeting at breakfast.

"Very well, we must see to this," observed the governor, who then made his inquiries as to the other intelligence contained in the letters.

Jack and Gascoigne were uneasy till the breakfast was over, when they made their escape: a few moments afterwards Captain Wilson rose to go on board, and sent for them, but they were not to be found.

"I understand it all, Wilson," said the governor; "leave them to me; go on board and make yourself quite easy."

In the meantime our two midshipmen had taken their hats and walked away to the parapet of the battery, where they would not he interrupted.

"Now, Gascoigne," observed Jack, "you guess what I'm about—I must shoot that rascal this very morning, and that's why I came out with you."

"But, Easy, the only difference is this, that I must shoot him, and not you; he is my property, for I found him out."

"We'll argue that point," replied Jack: "he has attempted the life of my is-to-be, please God, father-in-law, and therefore I have the best claim to him."

"I beg your pardon, Jack, he is mine, for I discovered him. Now let me put a case: suppose one man walking several yards before another, picks up a purse, what claim has the other to it? I found him, and not you."

"That's all very well, Gascoigne; but suppose the purse you picked up to be mine, then I have a right to it, although you found it; he is my bird by right, and not yours."

"But I have another observation to make, which is very important; he is a blood relation of Agnes, and if his blood is on your hands, however much he may deserve it, depend upon it, it will be raised as an obstacle to your union: think of that."

Jack paused in thought.

"And let me induce you by another remark—you will confer on me a most particular favour."

"It will be the greatest I ever could," replied Jack, "and you ought to be eternally indebted to me."

"I trust to make him *eternally* indebted to me," replied Gascoigne.

Sailors, if going into action, always begin to reckon what their share of the prize-money may be, before a shot is fired—our two midshipmen appear in this instance to be doing the same.

The point having been conceded to Gascoigne, Jack went to the inn where Don Silvio had mentioned that he had taken up his quarters, and sending up his card, followed the waiter up-stairs. The waiter opened the door, and presented the card.

"Very well," replied Don Silvio, "you can go down and show him up."

Jack hearing these words, did not wait, but walked in, where he found Don Silvio very busy removing a hone upon which he had been whetting a sharp double-edged stiletto. The Sicilian walked up to him, offering his hand with apparent cordiality; but Jack, with a look of defiance, said, "Don Silvio, we know you; my object now is to demand, on the part of my friend, the satisfaction which you do not deserve, but which our indignation at your second attempt upon Don Rebiera induces us to offer; for if you escape from him you will have to do with me. On the whole, Don Silvio, you may think yourself fortunate, for it is better to die by the hands of a gentleman than by the gibbet."

Don Silvio turned deadly pale—his hand sought his stiletto in his bosom, but it was remaining on the table; at last he replied, "Be it so— I will meet you when and where you please, in an hour from this."

Jack mentioned the place of meeting, and then walked out of the room. He and Gascoigne then hastened to the quarters of an officer they were intimate with, and having provided themselves with the necessary fire-arms, were at the spot before the time. They waited for him till the exact time, yet no Don Silvio made his appearance.

"He's off," observed Gascoigne; "the villain has escaped us."

Half an hour over the time had passed, and still there was no sign of Gascoigne's antagonist, but one of the governor's aides-de-camp was seen walking up to them.

"Here's Atkins," observed Jack; "that's unlucky, but he won't interfere."

"Gentlemen," said Atkins, taking off his hat with much solemnity, "the governor particularly wishes to speak to you both."

"We can't come just now—we'll be there in half an hour."

"You must be there in three minutes, both of you. Excuse me, my orders are positive—and to see them duly executed I have a corporal and a file of men behind that wall—of course, if you walk with me quietly there will be no occasion to send for their assistance."

"This is confounded tyranny," cried Jack. "Well may they call him 'King Tom.' "

"Yes," replied Atkins, "and he governs here in *'rey absoluto'*—so come along."

Jack and Gascoigne, having no choice, walked up to the government house, where they found Sir Thomas in the veranda, which commanded a view of the harbour and offing.

"Come here, young gentleman," said the governor, in a severe tone; "do you see that vessel about two miles clear of the port? Don Silvio is in it, going back to Sicily under a guard. And now remember what I say as a maxim through life. Fight with gentlemen, if you must fight, but not with villains and murderers. By *'consenting'* to fight with a *'blackguard,'* you as much disparage your cloth and compromise your own characters, as by refusing to give satisfaction to a *'gentleman.'*

There, go away, for I'm angry with you, and don't let me see you till dinner-time."

But before they met the governor at his table, a sloop of war arrived from the fleet with despatches from the commander-in-chief. Those to Captain Wilson required him to make all possible haste in fitting, and then to proceed and cruise off Corsica, to fall in with a Russian frigate which was on that coast; if not there, to obtain intelligence, and to follow her wherever she might be.

All was now bustle and activity on board of the *Aurora*. Captain Wilson, with our hero and Gascoigne, quitted the governor's house and repaired on board, where they remained day and night. On the third day the *Aurora* was complete and ready for sea, and about noon sailed out of Valette Harbour.

In a week the *Aurora* had gained the coast of Corsica, and there was no need of sending look-out men to the mast-head, for one of the officers or midshipmen was there from daylight to dark. She ran up the coast to the northward without seeing the object of her pursuit, or obtaining any intelligence.

Calms and light airs detained them for a few days, when a northerly breeze enabled them to run down the eastern side of the island. It was on the eighteenth day after they had quitted Malta, that a large vessel was seen ahead about eighteen miles off. The men were then at breakfast.

"A frigate, Captain Wilson, I'm sure of it," said Mr. Hawkins, the chaplain, whose anxiety induced him to go to the mast-head.

"How is she steering?"

"The same way as we are."

The *Aurora* was under all possible sail, and when the hands were piped to dinner, it was thought that they had neared the chase about two miles.

"This will be a long chase; a stern chase always is," observed Martin to Gascoigne.

"Yes, I'm afraid so—but I'm more afraid of her escaping."

"That's not unlikely either," replied the mate.

"You are one of Job's comforters, Martin," replied Gascoigne.

"Then I'm not so often disappointed," replied the mate. "There are two points to be ascertained; the first is, whether we shall come up with the vessel or lose her—the next is, if we do come up with her, whether she is the vessel we are looking for."

"You seem very indifferent about it."

"Indeed I am not: I am the oldest passed midshipman in the ship, and the taking of the frigate will, if I live, give me my promotion, and if I'm killed, I shan't want it. But I've been so often disappointed, that I now make sure of nothing until I have it."

"Well, for your sake, Martin, I will still hope that the vessel is the one we seek, that we shall not be killed, and that you will gain your promotion."

"I thank you, Easy—I wish I was one that dared hope as you do."

Poor Martin! he had long felt how bitter it was to meet disappointment upon disappointment. How true it is, that hope deferred maketh the heart sick! and his anticipations of early days, the buoyant calculations of youth, had been one by one crushed, and now, having served his time nearly three times over, the reaction had become too painful, and, as he truly said, he dared not hope: still his temper was not soured, but chastened.

"She has hauled her wind, sir," hailed the second lieutenant from the topmast cross-trees.

"What think you of that, Martin?" observed Jack.

"Either that she is an English frigate, or that she is a vessel commanded by a very brave fellow, and well-manned."

It was sunset before the *Aurora* had arrived within two miles of the vessel; the private signal had been thrown out, but had not been answered, either because it was too dark to make out the colours of the flags, or that these were unknown to an enemy. The stranger had hoisted the English colours, but that was no satisfactory proof of her being a friend; and just before dark she had put her head towards the

Aurora, who had now come stem down to her. The ship's company of the *Aurora* were all at their quarters, as a few minutes would now decide whether they had to deal with a friend or foe.

There is no situation perhaps more difficult, and demanding so much caution, as the occasional meeting with a doubtful ship. On the one hand, it being necessary to be fully prepared, and not allow the enemy the advantage which may be derived from your inaction; and on the other, the necessity of prudence, that you may not assault your friends and countrymen. Captain Wilson had hoisted the private night-signal, but here again it was difficult, from his sails intervening, for the other ship to make it out. Before the two frigates were within three cables' length of each other, Captain Wilson, determined that there should be no mistake from any want of precaution on his part, hauled up his courses and brailed up his driver that the night-signal might be clearly seen.

Lights were seen abaft on the quarter-deck of the other vessel, as if they were about to answer, but she continued to keep the *Aurora* to leeward at about half a cable's length, and as the foremost guns of each vessel were abreast of each other, hailed in English—

"Ship ahoy! what ship's that?"

"His Majesty's ship *Aurora*," replied Captain Wilson, who stood on the hammocks. "What ship's that?"

By this time the other frigate had passed half her length clear of the beam of the *Aurora*, and at the same time that a pretended reply of "His Majesty's ship—" was heard, a broadside from her guns, which had been trained aft on purpose, was poured into the *Aurora*, and at so short a distance, doing considerable execution. The crew of the *Aurora*, hearing the hailing in English, and the vessel passing them apparently without firing, had imagined that she had been one of their own cruisers. The captains of the guns had dropped their lanyards in disappointment, and the silence which had been maintained as the two vessels met was just breaking up in various ways of lamentation at their bad luck, when the broadside was poured in, thundering in their ears, and the ripping and tearing of the beams and planks astonished their senses. Many were carried down below, but it was difficult to say whether indignation at the enemy's ruse, or satisfaction at discovering that they were not called to quarters in vain, most predominated. At all events, it was answered by three voluntary cheers, which drowned the cries of those who were being assisted to the cockpit.

"Man the larboard guns and about ship!" cried Captain Wilson, leaping off the hammocks. "Look out, my lads, and rake her in stays! We'll pay him off for that foul play before we've done with him. Look out, my lads, and take good aim as she pays round."

The *Aurora* was put about, and her broadside poured into the stern of the Russian frigate—for such she was. It was almost dark, but the enemy, who appeared as anxious as the *Aurora* to come to action, hauled up her courses to await her coming up. In five minutes the two vessels were alongside, exchanging murderous broadsides at little more than pistol-shot—running slowly in for the land, then not more than five miles distant. The skin-clad mountaineers of Corsica were aroused by the furious cannonading, watching the incessant flashes of the guns, and listening to their reverberating roar.

After half-an-hour's fierce combat, during which the fire of both vessels was kept up with undiminished vigour, Captain Wilson went down on the main-deck, and himself separately pointed each gun after it was loaded; those amidships being direct for the main-channels of the enemy's ship, while those abaft the beam were gradually trained more and more forward, and those before the beam more and more aft, so as to throw all their shot nearly into one focus, giving directions that they were all to be fired at once, at the word of command. The enemy, not aware of the cause of the delay, imagined that the fire of the *Aurora* had slackened, and loudly cheered. At the word given, the broadside was poured in, and, dark as it was, the effects from it were evident. Two of the midship ports of the antagonist were blown into one, and her main-mast was seen to totter, and then to fall over the side. The *Aurora* then set her courses, which had been hauled up, and shooting ahead, took up a raking position, while the Russian was still hampered with her wreck, and poured in grape and cannister from her upper deck carronades to impede their labours on deck, while she continued her destructive fire upon the hull of the enemy from the main-deck battery.

The moon now burst out from a low bank of clouds, and enabled them to accomplish their work with more precision. In a quarter of an hour the Russian was totally dismasted, and Captain Wilson ordered half of his remaining ship's company to repair the damages, which had been most severe, whilst the larboard men at quarters continued the fire from the main-deck. The enemy continued to return the fire from four guns, two on each of her decks, which she could still make bear upon the *Aurora*; but after some time even these ceased, either from the men having deserted them, or from their being dismounted. Observing that the fire from her antagonist had ceased, the *Aurora* also discontinued, and the jolly-boat astern being still uninjured, the second lieutenant was deputed to pull alongside of the frigate to ascertain if she had struck.

The beams of the bright moon silvered the rippling water as the boat shoved off; and Captain Wilson and his officers, who were still unhurt, leant over the shattered sides of the *Aurora*, waiting for a reply: suddenly the silence of the night was broken upon by a loud splash from the bows of the Russian frigate, then about three cables' length distant.

"What could that be?" cried Captain Wilson. "Her anchor's down. Mr. Jones, a lead over the side, and see what water we have."

Mr. Jones had long been carried down below, severed in two with a round shot—but a man leaped into the chains, and lowering down the lead sounded in seven fathoms.

"Then I suspect he will give us more trouble yet," observed Captain Wilson; and so indeed it proved, for the Russian captain, in reply to the second lieutenant, had told him in English, "that he would answer that question with his broadside," and before the boat was dropped astern, he had warped round with the springs on his cable, and had recommenced his fire upon the *Aurora*.

Captain Wilson made sail upon his ship, and sailed round and round the anchored vessel, so as to give her two broadsides to her one, and from the slowness with which she worked at her springs upon her cables, it was evident that she must be now very weak-handed. Still the pertinacity and decided courage of the Russian captain convinced Captain Wilson, that, in all probability, he would sink at his anchor before he would haul down his colours; and not only would he lose more of the *Aurora*'s men, but also the Russian vessel, without he took a more decided step. Captain Wilson, therefore, resolved to try her by the board. Having poured in a raking fire, he stood off for a few moments, during which he called the officers and men on deck, and stated his intention. He then went about and himself conning the *Aurora*, ran her on board the Russian, pouring in his reserved broadside as the vessels came into collision, and heading his men as they leaped on the enemy's decks.

Although, as Captain Wilson had imagined, the Russian frigate had not many men to oppose to the *Aurora*'s, the deck was obstinately defended, the voice and the arm of the Russian captain were to be heard and seen everywhere, and his men, encouraged by him, were cut down by numbers where they stood.

Our hero, who had the good fortune to be still unhurt, was for a little while close to Captain Wilson when he boarded, and was about to oppose his unequal force against that of the Russian captain, when he was pulled back by the collar by Mr. Hawkins, the chaplain, who rushed in advance with a sabre in his hand. The opponents were well matched, and it may be said that, with little interruption, a hand-to-hand conflict ensued, for the moon lighted up the scene of carnage, and they were well able to distinguish each other's faces. At last, the chaplain's sword broke: he rushed in, drove the hilt into his antagonist's face, dosed with him, and they both fell down the hatchway together. After this, the deck was gained, or rather cleared, by the crew of the *Aurora*, for few could be said to have resisted, and in a minute or two the frigate was in their possession. The chaplain and the Russian captain were hoisted up, still clinging to each other, both senseless from the fall, but neither of them dead, although bleeding from several wounds.

As soon as the main deck had been cleared, Captain Wilson ordered the hatches to be put on, and left a party on board while he hastened to attend to the condition of his own ship and ship's company.

It was daylight before anything like order had been restored to the decks of the *Aurora*; the water was still smooth, and instead of letting go her own anchor, she had hung on with a hawser to the prize, but her sails had been furled, her decks cleared, guns secured, and the buckets were dashing away the blood from her planks and the carriages of the guns, when the sun rose and shone upon them. The numerous wounded had, by this time, been put into their hammocks, although there were still one or two cases of amputation to be performed.

The carpenter had repaired all shot-holes under or too near to the water-line, and then had proceeded to sound the well of the prize; but although her upper works had been dreadfully shattered, there was no reason to suppose that she had received any serious injury below, and therefore the hatches still remained on, although a few hands were put to the pumps to try if she made any water. It was not until the *Aurora* presented a more cheerful appearance that Captain Wilson went over to the other ship, whose deck, now that the light of heaven enabled them to witness all the horrors even to minuteness, presented a shocking spectacle of blood and carnage. Body after body was thrown over; the wounded were supplied with water and such assistance as could be rendered until the surgeons could attend them; the hatches were then taken off, and the remainder of her crew ordered on deck; about two hundred obeyed the summons, but the lower deck was as crowded with killed and wounded as was the upper. For the present the prisoners were handed over down into the fore-hold of the *Aurora*, which had been prepared for their reception, and the work of separation of the dead from the living then underwent. After this, such repairs as were immediately necessary were made, and a portion of the *Aurora*'s crew, under the orders of the second lieutenant, were sent on board to take charge of her. It was not till the evening of the day after this night conflict that the *Aurora* was in a situation to make sail. All hands were then sent on board of the *Trident*, for such was the name of the Russian frigate, to fit her out as soon as possible. Before morning,—for there was no relaxation from their fatigue, nor was there any wish for it,—all was completed, and the two frigates, although in a shattered condition, were prepared to meet any common conflict with the elements. The *Aurora* made sail with the *Trident* in tow; the hammocks were allowed to be taken down, and the watch below permitted to repose.

In this murderous conflict the *Trident* had more than two hundred men killed and wounded. The *Aurora's* loss had not been so great, but still it was severe, having lost sixty-five men and officers. Among the fallen there were Mr. Jones, the master, the third lieutenant Mr. Arkwright, and two midshipmen killed. Mr. Pottyfar, the first lieutenant, severely wounded at the commencement of the action. Martin the master's mate, and Gascoigne, the first mortally, and the second badly, wounded. Our hero had also received a slight cutlass wound, which obliged him to wear his arm, for a short time, in a sling.

Among the ship's company who were wounded was Mesty; he had been hurt with a splinter before the *Trident* was taken by the board, but had remained on deck, and had followed our hero, watching over him and protecting him as a father. He had done even more, for he had with Jack thrown himself before Captain Wilson, at a time that he had received such a blow with the flat of a sword as to stun him, and bring him down on his knee. And Jack had taken good care that Captain Wilson should not be ignorant, as he really would have been, of this timely service on the part of Mesty, who certainly, although with a great deal of 'sang froid' in his composition when in repose, was a fiend incarnate when his blood was up.

"But you must have been with Mesty," observed Captain Wilson, "when he did me the service."

"I was with him, sir," replied Jack, with great modesty; "but was of very little service."

"How is your friend Gascoigne this evening?"

"Oh, not very bad, sir—he wants a glass of grog."

"And Mr. Martin?"

Jack shook his head.

"Why, the surgeon thinks he will do well."

"Yes, sir, and so I told Martin; but he said that it was very well to give him hope—but that he thought otherwise."

"You must manage him, Mr. Easy; tell him he is sure of his promotion."

"I have, sir, but he won't believe it. He never will believe it till he has his commission signed. I really think that an acting order would do more than the doctor can."

"Well, Mr. Easy, he shall have one to-morrow morning. Have you seen Mr. Pottyfar? he, I am afraid, is very bad."

"Very bad, sir; and they say is worse every day, and yet his wound is healthy, and ought to be doing well."

Such was the conversation between Jack and his captain, as they sat at breakfast on the third morning after the action.

The next day Easy took down an acting order for Martin, and put it into his hands. The mate read it over as he lay bandaged in his hammock.

"It's only an acting order, Jack," said he; "it may not be confirmed."

Jack swore, by all the articles of war, that it would be; but Martin replied that he was sure it never would.

"No, no," said the mate, "I knew very well that I never should be made. If it is not confirmed, I may live; but if it is, I am sure to die."

Every one that went to Martin's hammock wished him joy of his promotion; but six days after the action, poor Martin's remains were consigned to the deep.

The next person who followed him was Mr. Pottyfar, the first lieutenant, who had contrived, wounded as he was, to reach a packet of the universal medicine, and had taken so many bottles before he was found out, that he was one morning found dead in his bed, with more than two dozen empty phials under his pillow, and by the side of his mattress. He was not buried with his hands in his pockets, but when sewed up in his hammock, they were, at all events, laid in the right position.

In three weeks the *Aurora*, with her prize in tow, arrived at Malta. The wounded were sent to the hospital, and the gallant Russian captain recovered from his wounds about the same time as Mr. Hawkins, the chaplain.

Jack, who constantly called to see the chaplain, had a great deal to do to console him. He would shake his hands as he lay in his bed, exclaiming against himself. "Oh," would he say, "the spirit is willing, but the flesh is weak. That I, a man of God, as they term me, who ought to have been down with the surgeons, whispering comfort to the desponding, should have gone on deck (but I could not help it), and have mixed in such a scene of slaughter. What will become of me?"

Jack attempted to console him by pointing out, that not only chaplains, but bishops, have been known to fight in armour from time immemorial. But Mr. Hawkins's recovery was long doubtful, from the agitation of his mind. When he was able to walk, Jack introduced to him the Russian captain, who was also just out of his bed.

"I am most happy to embrace so gallant an officer," said the Russian, who recognised his antagonist, throwing his arms round the chaplain, and giving him a kiss on both cheeks. "What is his rank?" continued he, addressing himself to Jack, who replied, very quietly, "that he was the ship's padre."

"The padre!" replied the captain, with surprise, as Hawkins turned away with confusion. "The padre—par exemple! Well, I always had a great respect for the church. Pray, sir," said he, turning to Easy, "do your padres always head your boarders?"

"Always, sir," replied Jack; "it's a rule of the service—and the duty of a padre to show the men the way to heaven. It's our ninety-ninth article of war."

"You are a fighting nation," replied the Russian, bowing to Hawkins, and continuing his walk, not exactly pleased that he had been floored by a parson.

Mr. Hawkins continued very disconsolate for some time; he then invalided, and applied himself to his duties on shore, where he would not be exposed to such temptations from his former habits.

As the *Aurora*, when she was last at Malta, had nearly exhausted the dockyard for her repairs, she was even longer fitting out this time, during which Captain Wilson's despatches had been received by the admiral, and had been acknowledged by a brig sent to Malta. The admiral, in reply, after complimenting him upon his gallantry and success, desired that, as soon as he was ready, he should proceed to Palermo with communications of importance to the authorities, and having remained there for an answer, was again to return to Malta to pick up such of his men as might be fit to leave the hospital, and then join the Toulon fleet. This intelligence was soon known to our hero, who was in ecstasies at the idea of again seeing Agnes and her brothers. Once more the *Aurora* sailed away from the high-crowned rocks of Valette, and with a fine breeze dashed through the deep blue waves.

But towards the evening the breeze increased, and they were under double-reefed topsails. On the second day they made the coast of Sicily, not far from where Easy and Gascoigne had been driven on shore; the weather was then more moderate, and the sea had, to a great degree, subsided. They therefore stood in close to the coast, as they had not a leading wind to Palermo. As they stood in, the glasses, as usual, were directed to land; observing the villas with which the hills and valleys were studded, with their white fronts embowered in orange groves.

"What is that, Gascoigne," said Easy, "under that precipice?—it looks like a vessel."

Gascoigne turned his glass in the direction—"Yes, it is a vessel on the rocks: by her prow she looks like a galley."

"It is a galley, sir—one of the row galleys—I can make out her bank of oars," observed the signal-man.

This was reported to Captain Wilson, who also examined her.

"She is on the rocks, certainly," observed he; "and I think I see people on board. Keep her away a point, quarter-master."

The *Aurora* was now steered right for the vessel, and in the course of an hour was not more than a mile from her. Their suppositions were correct—it was one of the Sicilian government galleys bilged on the rocks, and they now perceived that there were people on board of her, making signals with their shirts and pieces of linen.

"They must be the galley-slaves; for I perceive that they do not one of them change their positions: the galley must have been abandoned by their officers and seamen, and the slaves left to perish."

"That's very hard," observed Jack to Gascoigne; "they were condemned to the galleys, but not to death."

"They will not have much mercy from the waves," replied Gascoigne; "they will all be in kingdom come to-morrow morning, if the breeze comes more on the land. We have already come up two points this forenoon."

Although Captain Wilson did not join in this conversation, which he overheard as he stood on the forecastle gun, with his glass over the hammocks, it appears he was of the same opinion: but he demurred: he had to choose between allowing so many of his fellow-creatures to perish miserably, or to let loose upon society a set of miscreants, who would again enter a course of crime until they were re-captured, and, by so doing, probably displease the Sicilian authorities. After some little reflection he resolved that he would take his chance of the latter. The *Aurora* was hove-to in stays, and the two cutters ordered to be lowered down, and the boat's crew to be armed.

"Mr. Easy, do you take one cutter, and the armourers; pull on board of the galley, release those people, and land them in small divisions. Mr. Gascoigne, you will take the other to assist Mr. Easy, and when he lands them in his boat, you will pull by his side ready to act, in case of any hostile attempt on the part of the scoundrels; for we must not expect gratitude: of course, land them at the nearest safe spot for debarkation."

In pursuance of these orders, our two midshipmen pulled away to the vessel. They found her fixed hard upon the rocks, which had pierced her slight timbers, and, as they had supposed, the respectable part of her crew, with the commander, had taken to the boats, leaving the galley-slaves to their fate. She pulled fifty oars, but had only thirty-six manned. These oars were forty feet long, and ran in from the thole-pin with a loom six feet long, each manned by four slaves, who were chained to their seat before it, by a running chain made fast by a padlock in amidships. A plank, of two feet wide, ran fore and aft the vessel between the two banks of oars, for the boatswain to apply the lash to those who did not sufficiently exert themselves.

"Viva los Inglesos!" cried the galley-slaves, as Easy climbed up over the quarter of the vessel.

"I say, Ned, did you ever see such a precious set of villains?" observed Easy, as he surveyed the faces of the men who were chained.

"No," replied Gascoigne; "and I think if the captain had seen them as we have, that he would have left them where they were."

"I don't know—but, however, our orders are positive. Armourer, knock off all the padlocks, beginning aft; when we have a cargo we will land them. How many are there?—twelve dozen;—twelve dozen villains to let loose upon society. I have a great mind to go on board again and report my opinion to the captain—one hundred and forty-four villains, who all deserve hanging—for drowning is too good for them."

"Our orders are to liberate them, Jack."

"Yes; but I should like to argue this point with Captain Wilson."

"They'll send after them fast enough, Jack, and they'll all be in limbo again before long," replied Gascoigne.

"Well, I suppose we must obey orders; but it goes against my conscience to save such villainous-looking rascals. Armourer, hammer away."

The armourer, who with the seamen appeared very much of Jack's opinion, and had not commenced his work, now struck off the padlocks one by one with his sledgehammer. As soon as they were released the slaves were ordered into the cutter, and when it was sufficiently loaded Jack shoved off, followed by Gascoigne as guard, and landed them at the point about a cable's length distant. It required six trips before they were all landed; the last cargo were on shore, and Easy was desiring the men to shove off, when one of the galleriens turned round, and cried out to Jack in a mocking tone, "Addio, signor, a reveder la." Jack started, stared, and, in the squalid, naked wretch who addressed him, he recognised Don Silvio!

"I will acquaint Don Rebiera of your arrival, signor," said the miscreant, springing up the rocks, and mixing with the rest, who now commenced hooting and laughing at their preservers.

"Ned," observed Easy to Gascoigne, "we have let that rascal loose."

"More's the pity," replied Gascoigne; "but we have only obeyed orders."

"It can't be helped, but I've a notion there will be some mischief out of this."

"We obeyed orders," replied Gascoigne.

"We've let the rascals loose not ten miles from Don Rebiera's."

"Obeyed orders, Jack."

"With a whole gang to back him, if he goes there."

"Orders, Jack."

"Agnes at his mercy."

"Captain's orders, Jack."

"I shall argue this point when I go on board," replied Jack.

"Too late, Jack."

"Yes," replied Easy, sinking down on the stern sheets with a look of despair.

"Give way, my lads, give way."

Jack returned on board, and reported what he had done: also that Don Silvio was among those liberated; and he ventured to mention his fears of what might take place from their contiguity to the house of Don Rebiera. Captain Wilson bit his lips: he felt that his philanthropy had induced him to act without his usual prudence.

"I have done a rash thing, Mr. Easy, I am afraid. I should have taken them all on board and delivered them up to the authorities. I wish I had thought of that before. We must get to Palermo as fast as we can, and have the troops sent after these miscreants. Hands 'bout ship, fill the main yard."

The wind had veered round, and the *Aurora* was now able to lay up clear of the island of Maritimo. The next morning she anchored in Palermo Roads—gave immediate notice to the authorities, who, wishing Captain Wilson's philanthropy at the devil, immediately despatched a large body of troops in quest of the liberated malefactors. Captain Wilson, feeling for Jack's anxiety about his friends, called him over to him on deck, and gave him and Gascoigne permission to go on shore.

"Will you allow me to take Mesty with me, sir, if you please?" said Jack.

"Yes, Mr. Easy; but recollect that, even with Mesty, you are no match

for one hundred and fifty men; so be prudent. I send you to relieve
your anxiety, not to run into danger."

"Of course, sir," replied Jack, touching his hat, and walking away
quietly till he came to the hatchway, when he darted down like a shot,
and was immediately occupied with his preparations.

In half an hour our two midshipmen, with Mesty, had landed, and
proceeded to the inn where they had put up before: they were armed
up to the teeth. Their first inquiries were for Don Philip and his
brother.

"Both on leave of absence," replied the landlord, "and staying with
Don Rebiera."

"That's some comfort," thought Jack. "Now we must get horses as
fast as we can.—Mesty, can you ride?"

"By all de power, can I ride, Massa Easy; suppose you ride Kentucky
horse, you ride anyting."

In half an hour four horses and a guide were procured, and at eight
o'clock in the morning the party set off in the direction of Don
Rebiera's country seat.

They had not ridden more than six miles when they came up with
one of the detachments sent out in pursuit of the liberated criminals.
Our hero recognised the commanding officer as an old acquaintance,
and imparting to him the release of Don Silvio, and his fears upon
Don Rebiera's account, begged him to direct his attention that way.

"Corpo di Bacco—you are right, Signor Mid," replied the officer, "but
Don Philip is there, and his brother too, I believe. I will be there by ten
o'clock to-morrow morning; we will march almost the whole night."

"They have no arms," observed Easy.

"No, but they will soon get them: they will go to some small town
in a body, plunder it, and then seek the protection of the mountains.
Your captain has given us a pretty job."

Jack exchanged a few more words, and then, excusing himself on
account of his haste, put the spurs to his horse and regained his own
party, who now proceeded at a rapid pace.

"O signor!" said the guide, "we shall kill the horses."

"I'll pay for them," said Jack.

"Yes, but we shall kill them before we get there, Jack," replied Gascoigne, "and have to walk the rest of the way."

"Very true, Ned; let's pull up, and give them their wind."

"By de holy poker, Massa Easy, but my shirt stick to my ribs," cried Mesty, whose black face was hung with dewdrops from their rapid course.

"Never mind, Mesty."

It was about five o'clock in the afternoon when they arrived at the seat of Don Rebiera. Jack threw himself off his jaded steed, and hastened into the house, followed by Gascoigne. They found the whole family collected in the large sitting-room, quite ignorant of any danger threatening them, and equally astonished and pleased at the arrival of their old friends. Jack flew to Agnes, who screamed when she saw him, and felt so giddy afterwards that he was obliged to support her. Having seated her again, he was kindly greeted by the old people and the two young officers. After a few minutes dedicated to mutual inquiries, our hero stated the cause of their expeditious arrival.

"Don Silvio with one hundred and fifty galleriens, let loose on the coast yesterday afternoon!" exclaimed Don Rebiera; "you are right, I only wonder they were not here last night. But I expect Pedro from the town; he has gone down with a load of wine: he will bring us intelligence."

"At all events, we must be prepared," said Don Philip; "the troops, you say, will be here to-morrow morning."

"Holy Virgin!" exclaimed the ladies, in a breath.

"How many can we muster?" said Gascoigne.

"We have five men here, or we shall have by the evening," replied Don Philip—"all, I think, good men—my father, my brother, and myself."

"We are three—four with the guide, whom I know nothing about."

"Twelve in all—not one too many; but I think that now we are prepared, if they attack, we can hold out till the morning."

"Had we not better send the ladies away?" said Jack.

"Who is to escort them?" replied Don Philip; "we shall only weaken our force; besides, they may fall into the miscreants' hands."

"Shall we all leave the house together? they can but plunder it," observed Don Rebiera.

"Still, we may be intercepted by them, and our whole force will be nothing against so many," observed Don Philip, "if we are without defence, whereas in the house we shall have an advantage."

"E' vero," replied Don Rebiera, thoughtfully; "then let us prepare, for depend upon it Don Silvio will not lose such an opportunity to wreak his vengeance. He will be here tonight: I only wonder he has not been here with his companions before. However, Pedro will arrive in two hours."

"We must now see what means we have of defence," said Philip. "Come, brother—will you come, sir?"

Don Rebiera and his two sons quitted the room, Gascoigne entered into conversation with the senora, while Easy took this opportunity of addressing Agnes. He had been too much occupied with the consultation to pay her much attention before. He had spoken, with his eyes fixed upon her, and had been surprised at the improvement which had taken place in less than a year. He now went to her, and asked her, in a low voice, "whether she had received his letter?"

"Oh, yes!" replied she, colouring.

"And were you angry with what I said, Agnes?" in a low tone.

"No," replied she, casting her eyes down on the floor.

"I repeat now what I said, Agnes—I have never forgotten you."

"But—"

"But what?"

"Father Thomaso."

"What of him?"

"He never will—"

"Will what?"

"You are a heretic, he says."

"Tell him to mind his own business."

"He has great influence with my father and mother."

"Your brothers are on our side."

"I know that, but there will be great difficulty. Our religion is not the same. He must talk to you—he will convert you."

"We'll argue that point, Agnes. I will convert him if he has common sense; if not, it's no use arguing with him. Where is he?"

"He will soon be at home."

"Tell me, Agnes, if you had your own will, would you marry me?

"I don't know; I have never seen any one I liked so well."

"Is that all?"

"Is it not enough for a maiden to say?" replied Agnes, raising her eyes, and looking reproachfully. "Signor, let me go, here comes my father."

Notwithstanding, Jack cast his eyes to the window where Gascoigne and the senora were in converse, and, perceiving that the old lady's back was turned, he pressed Agnes to his bosom before he released her. The gentlemen then returned with all the fire-arms and destructive weapons they could collect.

"We have enough," observed Don Philip, "to arm all the people we have with us."

"And we are well armed," replied Jack, who had left Agnes standing alone. "What now are your plans?"

"Those we must now consult about. It appears"—but at this moment the conversation was interrupted by the sudden entrance of Pedro, who had been despatched to the town with the load of wine. He rushed in, flurried and heated, with his red cap in his hand.

"How now, Pedro, back so early!"

"O signor!" exclaimed the man—"they have taken the cart and the wine, and have drawn it away, up to the mountains."

"Who?" inquired Don Rebiera.

"The galley-slaves who have been let loose—and by the body of our blessed saint, they have done pretty mischief—they have broken into the houses, robbed everything—murdered many—clothed themselves with the best—collected all the arms, provisions, and wine they could lay their hands on, and have marched away into the mountains. This took place last night. As I was coming down within a mile of the town, they met me with my loaded cart, and they turned the bullocks round and drove them away along with the rest. By the blessed Virgin! but they are stained with blood, but not altogether of men, for they have cut up some of the oxen. I heard this from one of the herdsmen, but he too fled, and could not tell me more. But, signor, I heard them mention your name."

"I have no doubt of it," replied Don Rebiera. "As for the wine, I only hope they will drink too much of it tonight. But, Pedro, they will be here, and we must defend ourselves—so call the men together; I must speak to them."

"We shall never see the bullocks again," observed Pedro, mournfully.

"No: but we shall never see one another again, if we do not take care. I have information they come here to-night."

"Holy Saint Francis! and they say there are a thousand of them."

"Not quite so many, to my knowledge," observed Jack. "They told me that a great many were killed in their attack upon the town, before they mastered it."

"So much the better. Go now, Pedro, drink a cup of wine, and then call the other men."

The house was barricaded as well as circumstances would permit; the first story was also made a fortress by loading the landing-place with armoires and chests of drawers. The upper story, or attic, if it might be so called, was defended in the same way, that they might retreat from one to the other if the doors were forced.

It was eight o'clock in the evening before all was ready, and they were still occupied with the last defence, under the superintendence of Mesty, who showed himself an able engineer, when they heard the sound of an approaching multitude. They looked out of one of the windows, and perceived the house surrounded by the galley-slaves, in number apparently about a hundred. They were all dressed in a most fantastic manner with whatever they could pick up: some had fire-arms, but the most of them were supplied with only swords or knives. With them came also their cortege of plunder: carts of various descriptions, loaded with provisions of all sorts, and wine; women lashed down with ropes, sails from the vessels and boats to supply them with covering in the mountains, hay and straw, and mattresses. Their plunder appeared to be well chosen for their exigencies. To the carts were tied a variety of cattle, intended to accompany them to their retreat. They all appeared to be under a leader, who was issuing directions—that leader was soon recognised by those in the house to be Don Silvio.

"Massa Easy, you show me dat man," said Mesty, when he heard the conversation between Easy and the Rebieras; "only let me know him."

"Do you see him there, Mesty, walking down in front of those men? He has a musket in his hand, a jacket with silver buttons, and white trousers."

"Yes, Massa Easy, me see him well—let me look little more—dat enough."

The galley-slaves appeared to be very anxious to surround the house that no one should escape, and Don Silvio was arranging the men.

"Ned," said Jack, "let us show him that we are here. He said that he would acquaint Don Rebiera with our arrival—let us prove to him that he is too late."

"It would not be a bad plan," replied Gascoigne; "if it were possible that these fellows had any gratitude among them, some of them might relent at the idea of attacking those who saved them."

"Not a bit; but it will prove to them that there are more in the house than they think for; and we can frighten some of them by telling them that the soldiers are near at hand."

Jack immediately threw up the casement, and called out in a loud voice, "Don Silvio! galley-slave! Don Silvio!"

The party hailed turned round, and beheld Jack, Gascoigne, and Mesty, standing at the window of the upper floor.

"We have saved you the trouble of announcing us," called out Gascoigne. "We are here to receive you."

"And in three hours the troops will be here, so you must be quick, Don Silvio," continued Jack.

"*A reveder la,*" continued Gascoigne, letting fly his pistol at Don Silvio.

The window was then immediately closed. The appearance of our heroes, and their communication of the speedy arrival of the troops, was not without effect. The criminals trembled at the idea; Don Silvio was mad with rage—he pointed out to the men the necessity of immediate attack—the improbability of the troops arriving so soon, and the wealth which he expected was locked up by Don Rebiera in his mansion. This rallied them, and they advanced to the doors, which they attempted to force without success, losing several men by the occasional fire from those within the house. Finding their efforts, after half an hour's repeated attempts, to be useless, they retreated, and then bringing up a long piece of timber, which required sixty men to carry it, they ran with it against the door, and the weight and impetus of the timber drove it off its hinges, and an entrance was obtained; by this time it was dark, the lower story had been abandoned, but the barricade at the head of the stairs opposed their progress. Convenient loop-holes had been prepared by the defenders, who now opened a smart fire upon the assailants, the latter having no means of returning it effectually, had they had ammunition for their muskets, which fortunately they had not been able to procure. The combat now became fierce, and the galley-slaves were several times repulsed with great loss during a contest of two hours; but, encouraged by Don Silvio, and refreshed by repeated draughts of wine, they continued by degrees removing the barriers opposed to them.

"We shall have to retreat," exclaimed Don Rebiero; "very soon they will have torn down all. What do you think, Signor Easy?"

"Hold this as long as we can. How are we off for ammunition?"

"Plenty as yet—plenty to last for six hours, I think."

"What do you say, Mesty?"

"By holy St. Patrig, I say hold out here—they got no fire-arms—and we ab um at arm-length."

This decision was the occasion of the first defence being held for two hours more, an occasional relief being afforded by the retreat of the convicts to the covered carts.

At last it was evident that the barricade was no longer tenable, for the heavy pieces of furniture they had heaped up to oppose entrance, were completely hammered to fragments by poles brought up by the assailants, and used as battering-rams. The retreat was sounded; they all hastened to the other story, where the ladies were already placed, and the galley-slaves were soon in possession of the first floor—exasperated by the defence, mad with wine and victory, but finding nothing.

Again was the attack made upon the second landing, but, as the stairs were now narrower, and their defences stronger in proportion, they, for a long while, gained no advantage. On the contrary, many of their men were wounded, and taken down below.

The darkness of the night prevented both parties from seeing distinctly, which was rather in favour of the assailants. Many climbed over the fortress of piled-up furniture, and were killed as soon as they appeared on the other side, and, at last, the only ammunition used was against those who made this rash attempt. For four long hours did this assault and defence continue, until daylight came, and then the plan of assault was altered: they again brought up the poles, hammered the pieces of furniture into fragments, and gained ground. The defenders were worn out with fatigue, but flinched not; they knew that their lives, and the lives of those dearest to them, were at stake, and they never relaxed their exertions; still the criminals, with Silvio at their head, progressed, the distance between the parties gradually decreased, and there was but one massive chest of drawers now defending the landing-place, and over which there was a constant succession of blows from long poles and cutlasses, returned with the bullets from their pistols.

"We must now fight for our lives," exclaimed Gascoigne to Easy, "for what else can we do?"

"Do?—get on the roof and fight there, then," replied Jack.

"By-the-bye, that's well thought of, Jack," said Gascoigne. "Mesty, up and see if there is any place we can retreat to in case of need."

Mesty hastened to obey, and soon returned with a report that there was a trap-door leading into the loft under the roof, and that they could draw the ladder up after them.

"Then we may laugh at them," cried Jack. "Mesty, stay here while I and Gascoigne assist the ladies up," explaining to the Rebieras and to their domestics why they went.

Easy and Gascoigne hastened to the signora and Agnes, conducted them up the ladder into the loft, and requested them to have no fear; they then returned to the defences on the stairs, and joined their companions. They found them hard pressed, and that there was little chance of holding out much longer; but the stairs were narrow, and the assailants could not bring their force against them. But now, as the defences were nearly destroyed, although the convicts could not reach them with their knives, they brought up a large supply of heavy stones, which they threw with great force and execution. Two of Don Rebiera's men and Don Martin were struck down, and this new weapon proved most fatal.

"We must retreat, Jack," said Gascoigne; "the stones can do no harm where we are going to. What think you, Don Philip?"

"I agree with you; let those who are wounded be first carried up, and then we will follow."

This was effected, and as soon as the wounded men were carried up the ladder, and the arms taken up to prevent their falling into the hands of the assailants, for they were now of little use to them, the ammunition being exhausted, the whole body went into the large room which contained the trap-door of the loft, and, as soon as they were up, they drew the ladder after them. They had hardly effected this, when they were followed with the yells and shoutings of the galley-slaves, who had passed the last barriers, and thought themselves sure of their prey: but they were disappointed—they found them more secure than ever.

Nothing could exceed the rage of Don Silvio at the protracted resistance of the party, and the security of their retreat. To get at them was impossible, so he determined to set fire to the room, and suffocate them, if he could do no otherwise. He gave his directions to his men, who rushed down for straw, but in so doing, he carelessly passed under the trap-door, and Mesty, who had carried up with him two or three of the stones, dashed one down on the head of Don Silvio, who fell immediately. He was carried away, but his orders were put in execution; the room was filled with straw and fodder, and lighted. The effects were soon felt: the trap-door had been shut, but the heat and smoke burst through; after a time, the planks and rafters took the fire and their situation was terrible. A small trap-window in the roof, on the side of the house, was knocked open, and gave them a temporary relief; but now the rafters burned and crackled, and the smoke burst on them in thick columns. They could not see, and with difficulty could breathe. Fortunately the room below that which had been fired was but one out of four on the attics, and, as the loft they were in spread over the whole of the roof, they were able to remove far from it. The house was slated with massive slate of some hundredweights each, and it was not found possible to remove them so as to give air although frequent attempts were made. Donna Rebiera sank exhausted in the arms of her husband, and Agnes fell into those of our hero, who, enveloped in the smoke, kissed her again and again; and she, poor girl, thinking that they must all inevitably perish, made no scruple, in what she supposed her last moment, of returning these proofs of her ardent attachment.

"Massy Easy, help me here,—Massa Gascoigne come here. Now heab wid all your might: when we get one off we get plenty."

Summoned by Mesty, Jack and Gascoigne put their shoulders to one of the lower slates; it yielded, was disengaged, and slid down with a loud rattling below. The ladies were brought to it, and their heads put outside; they soon recovered; and now that they had removed one they found no difficulty in removing others. In a few minutes they were all with their heads in the open air, but still the house was on fire below, and they had no chance of escape. It was while they were debating upon that point, and consulting as to their chance of safety, that a breeze of wind wafted the smoke that issued from the roof away from them, and they beheld the detachment of troops making up to the house; a loud cheer was given, and attracted the notice of the soldiers. They perceived Easy and his companions; the house was surrounded and entered in an instant.

The galley-slaves who were in the house, searching for the treasure reported by Don Silvio to be concealed, were captured or killed, and in five minutes the troops had possession. But how to assist those above was the difficulty. The room below was in flames, and burning fiercely. There were no ladders that could reach so high, and there were no means of getting to them. The commandant made signs from below, as if to ask what he was to do.

"I see no chance," observed Don Philip, mournfully. "Easy, my dear fellow, and you, Gascoigne, I am sorry that the feuds of our family should have brought you to such a dreadful death; but what can be done?"

"I don't know," replied Jack, "unless we could get ropes."

"You quite sure, Massy Easy, that all galley rascals below gone?" asked Mesty.

"Yes," replied Easy, "you may see that; look at some of them bound there, under charge of the soldiers."

"Den, sar, I tink it high time we go too."

"So do I, Mesty; but how?"

"How? stop a little. Come, help me, Massy Easy; dis board" (for the loft was floored) "is loose; come help, all of you."

They all went, and with united strength pulled up the board.

"Now strike like hell!—and drive down de plaster," said Mesty, commencing the operation.

In a few minutes they had beaten an opening into one of the rooms below not on fire, pulled up another board, and Mesty having fetched the ladder, they all descended in safety, and, to the astonishment of the commandant of the troops, walked out of the door of the house, those who had been stunned with the stones having so far recovered as to require little assistance.

The soldiers shouted as they saw them appear, supporting the females. The commanding officer, who was an intimate friend of Don Philip, flew to his arms. The prisoners were carefully examined by Mesty, and Don Silvio was not among them. He might, however, be among the dead who were left in the house, which now began to burn furiously. The galley-slaves who were captured amounted in number to forty-seven. Their dead they could not count. The major part of the plunder, and the carts, were still where they had been drawn up.

As soon as the culprits had been secured, the attention of the troops was directed to putting out the flames, but their attempts were ineffectual; the mansion was burned to the bare walls, and but little of the furniture saved; indeed, the major part of it had been destroyed in the attack made by Don Silvio and his adherents.

Leaving directions with Pedro and his people, that the property collected by the miscreants should be restored to the owners, Don Rebiera ordered the horses, and with the whole party put himself under the protection of the troops, who, as soon as they had been refreshed, and taken some repose, bent their way back to Palermo with the galley-slaves, bound and linked together in a long double row.

They halted when they had gone half-way, and remained for the night. The next day at noon, Don Rebiera and his family were once more in their palazzo, and our two midshipmen and Mesty took their leave, and repaired on board to make themselves a little less like chimney-sweepers.

Captain Wilson was not out of the ship. Jack made his report, and then went down below, very much pleased at what had passed, especially as he would have another long yarn for the governor on his return to Malta.

A Pressed Man

by Robert Hay

Impressment was a fact of life for many Englishmen during the 19th century. Robert Hay's 1811 narrative describes his experience with the press gang, which seized him when he was 22 years old.

I was when crossing Towerhill* accosted by a person in seamen's dress who tapped me on the shoulder enquiring in a familiar and technical strain "what ship?" I assumed an air of gravity and surprise and told him I presumed he was under some mistake as I was not connected with shipping. The fellow, however, was too well acquainted with his business to be thus easily put off. He gave a whistle and in a moment I was in the hands of six or eight ruffians who I immediately dreaded and soon found to be a press gang. They dragged me hurriedly along through several streets amid bitter execrations bestowed on them, expressions of sympathy directed towards me and landed me in one of their houses of rendezvous. I was immediately carried into the presence of the Lieutenant of the gang, who questioned me as to my profession, whither I had ever been to sea, and

---

* In London.

what business had taken me to Towerhill. I made some evasive answers to these interrogations and did not acknowledge having been at sea: but my hands being examined and found hard with work, and perhaps a little discoloured with tar, overset all my hesitating affirmations and I was remanded for further examination.

Some of the gang then offered me Spirits and attempted to comfort me under my misfortune, but like the friends of Job, miserable comforters were they all. The very scoundrel who first laid hold of me put on a sympathising look and observed what a pity it was to be pressed when almost within sight of the mast of the Scotch Smacks. Such sympathy from such a source was well calculated to exasperate my feelings, but to think of revenge was folly and I had patiently to listen to their mock pity.

I trembled exceedingly in the fear that they would inspect my small bundle, for in it there were a pair of numbered stockings, which would not only have made them suppose I had been at sea, but would have given them good reason to think I had been in a war ship. I contrived, however, to slip them out unobserved and concealed them behind one of the benches and thus had my fears a little moderated.

In a short time I was reconducted for further examination before the Lieutenant, who told me as I was in his hands and would assuredly be kept I might as well make a frank confession of my circumstances, it would save time and insure me better treatment. What could I do? I might indeed have continued sullen and silent, but whither such procedure might or might not have procured me worse treatment, one thing I knew it would not restore me to liberty. I therefore acknowledged that I had been a voyage to the West Indies and had come home Carpenter of a ship. His eye seemed to brighten at this intelligence. "I am glad of that, my lad," said he, "we are very much in want of Carpenters. Step along with these men and they will give you a passage on board." I was then led back the way I came by the fellow who first seized me, put aboard of a pinnace at Tower Wharf and by midday was securely lodged on board the *Enterprise*.

As soon as the boat reached the ship I was sent down into the great cabin, in various parts of which tables were placed covered with green cloth, loaded with papers and surrounded with men well dressed and powdered. Such silence prevailed and such solemn gravity was displayed in every countenance that I was struck with awe and dread. The tables were so placed as to give the whole of those seated at them a fair opportunity of narrowly scrutinizing every unhappy wretch that was brought in. No sooner did I enter the cabin door than every eye was darted on me. Mine were cast down and fearing there might be some of the inquisitors who knew me I scarcely dared to raise them all the time I remained in the cabin.

A short sketch of what had passed between the press officer and myself had been communicated to the examining officer, for when I was ushered into his presence he thus addressed me:

"Well, young man, I understand you are a carpenter by trade."

"Yes, sir."

"And you have been at sea?"

"One voyage, sir."

"Are you willing to join the King's Service?"

"No, sir."

"Why?"

"Because I get much better wages in the merchant service and should I be unable to agree with the Captain I am at Liberty to leave him at the end of the voyage."

"As to wages," said he, "the chance of prize money is quite an equivalent and obedience and respect shown to your officers are all that is necessary to insure you good treatment. Besides," continued he, "you may in time be promoted to be carpenter of a line of Battle ship when your wages will be higher than in the merchant service, and should any accident happen to you, you will be provided for."

I argued under great disadvantage. My interrogator was like a judge on the bench; I like a criminal at the bar, and I had not fortitude to make any reply.

"Take my advice, my lad," continued he, "and enter the service cheerfully, you will then have a bounty, and be in a fair way for promotion. If you continue to refuse, remember you are aboard (cogent reasoning), you will be kept as a pressed man and treated accordingly."

I falteringly replied that I could not think of engaging in any service voluntarily when I knew of a better situation elsewhere. He said no more, but making a motion with his hand I was seized by two marines, hurried along towards the main hatchway with these words thundered in my ears, "A pressed man to go below." What injustice and mockery, thought I, first to have that best of blessings, liberty, snatched from me and then insulted by a seeming offer of allowing me to act with freedom! But my doom was fixed and I was thrust down among five or six score of miserable beings, who like myself had been kidnapped, and immured in the confined and unwholesome dungeon of a press room.

Here I had full leisure for reflection, but my reflection was very far from being of the agreeable kind. A few hours before I had entered London possessed of Liberty and buoyed up with animating hope. Now, I was a slave immured in a dungeon and surrounded by despair. I had proceeded from Hyde Park Corner in as direct a line as lanes and alleys would admit and had just fallen directly into those merciless hands I so anxiously wished to avoid. Such is the blindness of human nature! We are often on the very brink of a precipice when we think ourselves in the utmost safety and dream not of impending danger.

By some mismanagement on the part of the pursers stewart, I was left all that day without food and would have been so the seccond day also, for I had not yet assumed courage to make application, but that two or three of the most humane of the seamen, noticing me, took me into their mess, and applied for my allowance of provisions. With the exception of these few I was generally treated with ridicule and contempt. Seamen who have been pressed together into one ship have usually a great affection for one another. Their trade, their habits, their misfortunes are the same and they become endeared to each other by a similarity of sufferings; but my landward appearance placed me in some measure beyond the pale of sympathy. I was styled by way of distinction and ridicule "the Gentleman", and was considered a priviledged butt for the shafts of nautical witt and banter to be levelled at. I must allow this did not affect me greatly. I knew that I myself had often joined in the same strain of Irony against those who had been brought on board the *Salvador* in landsmans' clothing, and I was now merely getting paid in my own coin. Hence, however, I resolved never again to mock at the sufferings more especially when I had no other reason for such conduct than a difference of occupation or professional habits. I soon became accustomed to the jokes and when any of these nautical punsters brandished their knife and threatened to unbend my ringtail and water sail (the name of the sails set abaft the spanker and below the spanker boom), I calmly tucked up my skirts and tucking them up behind buttoned my coat closely so that they could not accomplish their purpose without coming in front to disengage the button, by which I would have been put upon my guard. I was forced to observe this precaution every night otherwise I would soon have been stumped.

Once or twice a day a limited number were permitted to go on deck to breath the fresh air, but from the surly manner in which we were treated it was easy to observe that it was not for our pleasure this indulgence was granted, but to preserve our healths, which would have soon been greatly endangered had not a little fresh air been occasionally mixed with the pestiferous breaths and pestilential vapours of the press room. I remained in this ship something more than a week, when she became so crowded as to render the removal of a considerable number a measure of necessity. I, among a considerable number of others, was put aboard of a cutter when we were very closely confined, never seeing anything on our passage down the river but the sky divided into minute squares by the gratings which covered our dungeon.

We arrived at the Nore shortly after dusk and were immediately put on board the *Ceres*, guardship. I rejoiced at its being dark when we were taken aboard because I thus escaped the prying observation of four or five hundred gazers among whom I thought it probable that some one or other would know me. The following day I got blended with a motley crowd and was less taken notice of than I would have been at my first entrance.

Here I considered it folly to dress any longer in my landsmans habillements. I therefore purchased a seccondhand jacket, trowsers and check shirt, in which I equipped myself and packed up my long coat, breeches, vest, white neckcloth, etc., lest I should on some future occasion require their services. What became of them will be seen in the sequel.

Next morning my acquaintances were greatly surprised to see how completely I had been metamorphosed. Not only was my external appearance greatly changed, but my manners were still more so. Hitherto I had preserved the greatest taciturnity. I knew that had I talked much sea phrases would have slipped and I thought it as well that my behaviour and my discourse should correspond with my appearance. Hence credit was given me for far more wisdom, learning and politeness than I possessed. How easy then is it to be thought wise? It is merely to preserve silence and though we may not thereby give an opportunity of displaying our wisdom and wit we with great ease can conceal our ignorance and folly.

I now became somewhat loquacious, probably in order to make up former lee way, and as I could with great volubility string together the technical terms of seamanship, I was soon on a footing with the rest. Next day my shipmates being in a humorous mood, I flourished my knife over my head, offered a quart of grog to any one who would point me out the gentleman as I was determined to close reef him. This was as good to them as if it had been sterling wit. They all burst out a laughing, considered me a shrewd fellow and henceforth rated my nautical abilities as much too high as they before had my learning and politeness. Not one of my shipmates knew my name, except one that was pressed shortly after myself who called me by name as soon as he came aboard, and who was no other than one of my shipmates in the *Edward*. One of those who seized the boat and pulled ashore in spite of the Captain's remonstrances and threats. Bill, Tom, Dick, Bob, Jack came all alike familiar to me and when I knew I was spoken to I answered to all of them promiscuously.

In this ship we had liberty to go on deck at all hours and were therefore much more comfortable than when on board the *Enterprise* or cutter. Our distance from the shore being only about 6 or 8 miles, the land was seen very clearly and many an anxious, earnest look did I take of it. Frequently would I feast my eyes for hours together gazing on it, and my imagination in forming schemes how to gain it. No hopes or at least very distant ones could be entertained of success. The distance from the shore was in itself no small barrier, but what made the attempt most hazardous, there was only one point of land where there was any probability of making a landing at all. This was on a small Island, I think called Grain. But how was this point to be gained in the dark? If I went to the right I would be taken up the Thames and carried to sea at the return of the tide. If I went to the left I would be carried in amongst the ships in Sheerness, where I would be sure to be observed, and either picked up by some of the war boats, or shot by some of the centinels on duty.

But even suppose the point gained. Still insuperable difficulties seemed to present themselves. How could I escape observation in my wet seamans clothes? How could I pass from that Island to the main? How could I travel anywhere without being intercepted? But were even all these obstacles surmountable, how was it possible to escape from the ship guarded as she was by Midshipmen, quartermasters, ships corporals and marines? On a review of all these circumstances any attempt to escape seemed impracticable, but as the thoughts of it were easily enough indulged in I was constantly meditating on the subject.

Amongst those who were pressed about the same time as myself was a man a few years older than I, a native of Hartley, by the name of John Patterson. I often observed him casting many a wishfull look to the shore, and often heard him utter a half suppressed sigh as he turned his eyes from it. He doubtless had observed my conduct also, for he frequently looked very earnestly at me as we had occasion to pass each other. We soon came on speaking terms, and from that time forth seemed to enjoy much pleasure in each other's company. Still, however, we abstained from introducing a subject in which it was evident enough both of us had very closely at heart. It was not till after a good many days acquaintanceship had elapsed and many conversations on indifferent topics held that we ventured to open our minds to each other. This was done slowly and with great precaution at first, but soon finding how much our sentiments were in unison we dismissed reserve and became inseperable. From this time almost the whole subject of our thoughts and conversation was the means of escape. All the various ways in which there was the least probability of success were calmly and diliberately discussed, and the arguments for and against them, duly weighed. Whatever view we took of the matter, obstacles seemingly insurmountable presented themselves to our view, and had the prize been anything less than the recovery of our liberty, we would have dispaired of success.

"He," says the proverb, "who thinks an object unattainable makes it so." So we resolved to think our escape within the bounds of possibility. Our first consideration was, How were we to get clear of the ship and reach the shore? We at length confined our attention solely to these points, resolved to make the attempt and leave the rest to providence.

Our first step was to procure some bladders which we easily prevailed with one of the men belonging to the ships boats to purchase. We then tore up some old shirts and made them into long narrow bags, large enough to hold a bladder when full blown, and of sufficient length to go round the body below the arm pits. Straps were attached to pass over each shoulder, and one to pass between the legs in order to keep all in a proper position. We had seven bladders in whole, of which Patterson had three large and I four small—our quantity of wind would be about the same, but my four distributing the wind more regularly round the body afterwards proved the most comodious.

At this time the ship was very full of hands insomuch that there were not room for all hands to sleep below. A considerable number therefore slept in the waist hammock nettings. A place on the upper deck projecting a small bit beyond the ship's side, where the greater number of beds and hammocks were stowed during the day. As both the sides and top of this place were covered with tarpaulins, we slept in it comfortable enough.

In this station did Patterson and I nightly place ourselves to watch a favourable opportunity of escape. We left our beds to the care of our messmates below, tied our bags of bladders in our coverlets to resemble a bed and free of all suspicion repaired to the hammock netting. Many nights passed away after our resolutions were taken and our preparations made before we were enabled to make the attempt. Some nights the tide did not suit, some it was too light, and some a very strict sentinel was on duty. Still, however, we adhered to our resolutions and our perseverance, as will be seen in the sequel, was crowned with success.

About the tenth or twelfth of October 1811, for I do not remember the precise date, conditions seemed to bid fair for our purpose. The weather was dark and lowering, the wind blew pretty fresh and to all appearance promised a wet night. What was of still greater consequence the tide exactly suited us. As the unfavourable, or I should rather say favourable, state of the weather continued till nightfall we resolved to attempt our project. Before dusk, we purchased and drank two or three glasses of rum each that we might stand the cold, bade adieu to a couple of our bosom confidants and then repaired to our station in the hammock netting.

When the evening drum beat a little before eight o'clock everything seemed favourable. The drum and the storm made noise enough to prevent our movements being heard, and the sentinel who paced the gangway was muffled closely up in his great coat.

When it came to the point my friend Patterson felt strongly inclined to draw back. All the dangers which we had before so amply discussed were again enumerated and amplified. With the same earnestness did I expatiate on the evils of slavery and enumerate the advantages that would result from our success. And how was success to be gained without exertion! My reasoning at last succeeded, and, fearing his resolution might forsake him after I was in the water, I prevailed on him to descend first.

When he gained the water the end of the rope got entangled about his foot and he gave a plunge to clear it. I trembled. The sound, increased as it was by my fears, seemed like the plunging of a grampus, but the noise was drowned by the surrounding storm. As soon as he was clear of the rope I slid softly down and slipped into the water without the smallest noise. I glided smoothly along close by the ship's side not daring to strike out lest my motion should be observed. I kept touching the ship's side with my hands as I floated along, and had thus an idea about how fast the tide carried me along. After I thought myself clear enough of the ship, I struck out and in a minute or two regained my companion. I found him very ill. In his strugle to clear himself of the rope he had swallowed some salt water which made him sick and when I overtook him I found him vomiting. I felt very unhappy on his account and soothed and encouraged him by all the means in my power. After his vomiting had ceased he grew better, and side by side we proceeded cheerily along. I had practised the art of swimming much more than my companion and could therefore proceed with much more ease and expedition. I amused myself with swimming round him relating anecdotes, chaunting in a low voice a verse or two of a song, etc., in encouraging him to put forth his strength. When he became fatigued we took each other by the hand and drifted slowly along untill we recovered strength to put forth farther exertion.

When two or three miles from the ship we were excessively alarmed by the sound of human voices, apparently near at hand and almost immediately observed a boat from the shore standing toward the ship we had quitted. From our relative position we saw she must pass us within a few fathoms. We were overwhelmed with dread and terror. We expected nothing else than to be picked up and taken back where we would have met with the most rigorous punishment and would probably have been put in iron besides as long as we remained in harbour. We dared not to swim out of her way lest the motion should have betrayed us, so that we had no other resource but remain motionless and trust to providence. As she approached our alarm increased. We strove to sink beneath the surface, but were prevented by the buoyancy of our bladders. Fortunately she was rather to windward and the belly of the sail hanging over the lee gunnel in some measure sheltered us from the observation of those on board. What was also in our favour the crew seemed intent on some subject of debate as a continued and indistinct sound proceeded from the boat as long as she was distinguishable. It may here be asked, had we no apprehension of steering a wrong course? We had none. We possessed a most excellent compass. This was no other than the large comet of 1811. We had frequently observed that it lay precisely over the point of land we wished to gain. We therefore shaped our course direct for it and it proved a faithful guide.

After many a trial to feel ground, Patterson exclaimed with the joy and in the words of Archimedes, "I have found it, I have found it!" I was almost afraid to try lest I should be disappointed, but seeing him at rest I let down my feet and found ground at little more than half a fathom. We found the shore very shelving, for when we first felt the ground we could scarcely observe any traces of the land. I think we had to walk about three quarters of a mile before we gained the beach and fatiguing walking we found it. On reaching the beach we threw ourselves on our knees to return our united thanks to that being who had brought us deliverance from the mighty waters, and to implore future guidance, strength and fortitude to support us under whatever trials we might still have to endure.

When we had advanced a few paces, we saw a light and by crossing a field or two soon gained it. It proceeded from a pretty large house standing alone. A board resembling a sign was fixed over the door, but we could not see whither it bore any inscription. On knocking at the door a person appeared at the window from which the light proceeded and demanded our business. We dared not tell him our true circumstances, but feigned a story of distress. It however made no impression on him. He told us in a surly tone to be gone, that it was past midnight and that he was determined not to open his door at such an unseasonable hour for any person whatever. We then tried another house whence a light issued, but with no better success. How comfortable would a glass or two of rum have been to us shivering as we were with cold and wetness? but a glass of rum we could not obtain.

We left these houses to retrace our steps to where we landed, but missed our way. We soon however gained the beach at a different and at a much better place. It seemed to be a snug little cove in which a considerable number of small boats were lying. The project on which we mainly depended previous to leaving the ship was to seize a boat and pull over to the Essex shore whence we could go to Maldon by land. Patterson had been at Maldon and knew several of the captains of coal vessels belonging to the North of England, which traded there, so that we expected if we could reach that place in safety it would not be dificult to procure a passage to the Northward. When we saw so many boats lying so oportunely, we were overjoyed and already anticipated the completion of our projects. After searching through a great number of them we found one seemingly Dutch built that had a small sail and a couple of oars aboard. This was just what we wanted. We slipped her painter and as the wind was southerly we set sail and stood as near as we could guess North East. From being so long wet we were very cold, but getting our oars out and pulling vigorously we soon brought ourselves into a state of agreeable warmth.

About an hour before day break we touched ground with our oars, on which we hauled a little more to the eastward resolving to get as far along shore as possible before dawn. We heard the *Ceres* fire her morning gun and had the happiness of seeing her hull down. It was our intention to land before sun rise and we made several attempts at this, but the shore was so shelving that we could no where get within half a mile of the shore. We therefore continued edging along shore as near as the depth of water would admit. We saw a good many vessels resembling light colliers bound to the Northwards, but we could not think of venturing to pull out to any of them lest they should betray us. We could easily have coasted it along to Blackwater river and have got in to Maldon with our boat, but we were detterred from this by considering that our appearance would have rendered us suspected, besides when day broke we saw our sail was merely a man of war's hammock, and this made our appearance still more suspicious. After a great many attempts during the morning and forenoon made to land, we, about midday, were fortunate enough to discover a small creek just wide enough to receive our boat. The water in it, being pretty deep, she did not ground untill her stern took the land, so that we were enabled to land without wetting our shoes. What became of the boat we never heard, but as we left her in a very snug berth and well moored, and as her owner's name was painted on the inside of her stern, we hoped, and doubted not, that the owner would ultimately recover her.

After passing a small earthen mound erected to keep the sea from breaking into the adjoining fields, we found ourselves on a delightful meadow. The sun was shining in meridian splendour, scarcely a cloud was to be seen in the wide expanse, the mild Zephyrs, as they skimmed along the fragrant meadow or over those fields which showed they had recently richly contributed to the support of man, seemed to whisper congratulations in our ear. We had just escaped from thralldom and were begining to taste the dawning sweets of that blessing so highly valued by Britons. Everything around us tended to exhilerate our spirits and we gave unrestrained scope to our feelings. Had any sober man seen us he would have undoubtedly questioned the soundness of our intellects. We leapt, we ran, we rolled, we tumbled, we shouted, we gambolled in all the excess of joy and exultation, and it was not till several minutes elapsed that we could so far restrain the ebulitions of our joy as to permit us to set out on our journey. Observing a farm house at some distance we made up to it and found only one woman at home. The truth cannot always be told, nor could it be told here. We were compelled to fabricate a story of our shipwreck which we did with as few falsehoods as the case would admit. But sh! how much more difficult is it to scramble along the mazy paths of falsehood and prevarication than in the broad plain and open way of integrity and truth. With whatever care a falsehood may be fabricated it is supported with the utmost difficulty. A thousand questions may be put which the utmost human ingenuity could not have anticipated and a thousand falsehoods have to be uttered in support and confirmation of the first. The higher we rear the baseless structure, the more tottering it becomes, till at length it falls with a mighty crash and entombs its shuffling fabricators beneath its massy ruins.

The woman into whose house we went was of a mild and kindly disposition, more inclined to pity and releive than to doubt and question. She herself had a son who followed the seafaring business and who had been several times wrecked, so that she felt towards all those who suffered the same misfortune a kind of maternal sympathy. She set before us what a well stored pantry and dairy could afford, pressed us to partake heartily, which we were both able and willing to do, and at parting she would accept of no payment. "Keep your money, my lads," said she, beaming a look of kindness on us, "you have yet a long way to go (we had told her we were for the North) and you know not what you may yet need. May God bless you and deliver you from all your dangers, as he has from this last one." The gratitude excited in our breasts by this genuine treat of English hospitality, blended with the joy we felt at the recovery of our liberty, excited in us the most delightful emotions. Emotions which the greatest monarch on earth, possessed of unlimited power, abounding in riches, surrounded by flatterers, and wallowing in sensual pleasure, might well envy. We learned at this house that we were about 12 miles from Maldon, for which place, after taking an affectionate leave of our kind hostess, we set out. A luxuriant store of bramble berries by the roadside and a desire to avoid entering Maldon with day light induced us to linger a little by the way so that we did not reach Maldon till after dusk. We readily procured a bed to which after supper we immediately retired and soon made up for last night's lee way.

from Cochrane: The Life and
Exploits of a Fighting Captain
by Robert Harvey

Thomas Cochrane's intolerance of corrupt or inept superiors earned him many political ene-mies. Despite his adversaries' best efforts, Cochrane ended his career as admiral of the fleet. Biographer Robert Harvey's (born 1953) description of the battle of Aix Roads illustrates the captain's fighting qualities.

Cochrane now entered the defining moment of his career: a naval battle which was only less decisive than Trafalgar because of the actions of other men, but which ended by almost destroying him. The drama that follows is one of the epics of British naval history—and is still barely known, even less understood.

The Admiralty disliked Cochrane, yet it could hardly dispense with his services. There were few able commanders at this time, still fewer like Cochrane who had the confidence of their men, were widely pop-ular, and were prepared to take huge risks. The French fleet had escaped in a gale from the British blockade of Brest, when the British ships had been blown out to sea. On 21 February 1809 the enemy had seized their chance. Eight battleships under Admiral Willaumez and several frigates had escaped into the Atlantic.

When Rear-Admiral Stopford, with seven ships, encountered the French fleet in the Bay of Biscay, they withdrew to the Aix Roads.

The anchorage there seemed impregnable and the British commander who had presided over the fiasco at Brest, Admiral Lord Gambier, on being advised by the Admiralty that he should attack the French with fireships as the only means of getting at them, was deeply equivocal:

> A trial was made six years ago, when a Spanish squadron lay at the same anchorage, but without effect. The report of it you will find in the Admiralty . . . The enemy's ships lie much exposed to the operation of fireships, it is a horrible mode of warfare, and the attempt hazardous, if not desperate; but we should have plenty of volunteers in the service. If you mean to do anything of the kind, it should be done with secrecy and quickly, and the ships used should be not less than those built for the purpose—at least a dozen, and some smaller ones.

The danger was that the French fleet, reinforced by the ships already at Aix Roads, might slip away and attack the British in the West Indies.

It was vital to stop them, but Gambier was a cautious man. An Admiralty bureaucrat of the kind that Cochrane most despised, he had spent seventeen of his twenty-two years in the navy behind a desk, his connections with the Pitt family ensuring his promotion. He had been commander of the seventeen-strong fleet when the British had bombarded Copenhagen in 1807 with appalling results for that beautiful city (which Nelson had spared in his famous 1801 battle). Although the attack was not well executed nor even particularly necessary, the Danish fleet had surrendered after this punishment, which had earned him command of the Channel fleet as well as his title.

Gambier was a dedicated tractarian Christian who distributed fundamentalist pamphlets to his crew, fiercely opposed alcohol, and refused the common practice of allowing women on board in port. He was known as 'dismal Jimmie' by his men. He was fully in the tradition of St. Vincent, a new type of Admiralty bureaucrat, determined to bring greater morality on board ship, espousing middle-class values and despising old-style aristocratic pretensions, the kind Cochrane personified. Gambier's religious concerns seemed doomed from the start. As one contemporary chaplain wrote:

> Nothing can possibly be more unsuitably or more awkwardly situated than a clergyman in a ship of war; every object around him is at variance with the sensibilities of a rational and enlightened mind . . . The entrance of a clergyman is, to a poor seaman, often a fatal signal . . . To convert a man-of-war's crew into Christians would be a task to which the courage of Loyola, the philanthropy of Howard, and the eloquence of St. Paul united, would prove inadequate.

Cochrane observed:

> The fact was, that the fleet was divided into two factions, as bitter against each other as were the Cavaliers and Roundheads in the days of Charles I . . . The tractarian faction, consisting for the most part of officers appointed by Tory influence or favour of the Admiral, and knowing my connection with Burdett and Cobbett, avoided me; whilst the opposite faction, believing that from the affair of the tracts I should incur the irreconcilable displeasure of Lord Gambier, lost no opportunity of denouncing me as a concocter of novel devices to advance my own interests at the expense of my seniors in the service.

Gambier's religion made him a close friend of the great antislavery campaigner, William Wilberforce, also a zealous Christian. The poet Thomas Hood mocked him:

> Oh! Admiral Gam—I dare not mention bier,
> In such a temperate ear;

Oh! Admiral Gam—an Admiral of the Blue,
Of course, to read the Navy List aright,
For strictly shunning wine of either hue,
You can't be Admiral of the Red or White.

Gambier's intense religious beliefs did not of course prevent him being a good commander, but as he so patently was not—he was cautious and indecisive, the legacy of his long years away from action—they merely grated on the officers beneath him, none more so than Admiral Eliab Harvey, the celebrated captain of the *Fighting Témeraire* at Trafalgar. Harvey detested his superior. The bad blood between these two senior commanders of the fleet further demoralized it.

With Gambier in a mire of uncertainty off Aix Roads, the Admiralty, which so disliked Cochrane, conceived of an extraordinary idea. It was vital that the French fleet not be allowed to escape again, yet it seemed equally likely that they would. The one officer with close knowledge of Aix Roads from his tour of duty three years before was Thomas Cochrane, who had long suggested invading the anchorage with fireships. Here at last was a use for this tiresome but fearless seaman. If Cochrane perished the Admiralty would be well rid of him, if he succeeded, they could claim the credit.

Cochrane had no sooner arrived in Plymouth than he was ordered immediately to report to Whitehall. Where once Cochrane had striven desperately to gain an audience with St. Vincent, he was now received warmly, even effusively, by the new First Sea Lord, Lord Mulgrave, a red-faced Tory just appointed to office, who was a connoisseur of the arts and displayed an enviable unflappability towards all events, good and bad. Mulgrave was to the point, welcoming him and informing him that in spite of Gambier's reservations, twelve transports were being converted for use as fireships:

You were some years ago employed on the Rochefort station and must to a great extent be acquainted with the difficulties to be surmounted. Besides which, I am told that

you then pointed out to Admiral Thornburgh some plan of
attack, which would in your estimation be successful. Will
you be good enough to detail that or any other plan
which your further experience may suggest?

Cochrane was immediately interested, and launched into his own pet
project for building 'explosion ships' to add to the fireships. Even
Cochrane was taken aback by how seriously, he, a mere captain, was
being taken by the First Sea Lord. Now came the shock: Mulgrave told
Cochrane that he was to command the expedition.

At this Cochrane was aghast: he knew the fury that giving command
of so major a venture to so junior a captain would arouse not just in
Gambier, but all the senior captains serving with him. He was deeply
cynical of the Admiralty's motives:

> It was now clear to me why I had been sent for to the Admi-
> ralty, where not a word of approbation of my previous ser-
> vices was uttered. The Channel fleet had been doing worse
> than nothing. The nation was dissatisfied, and even the exis-
> tence of the ministry was at stake. They wanted a victory,
> and the admiral commanding plainly told them he would
> not willingly risk a defeat. Other naval officers had been
> consulted, who had disapproved of the use of fireships, and,
> as a last resource, I had been sent for, in the hope that I
> would undertake the enterprise. If this were successful, the
> fleet would get the credit, which would be thus reflected on
> the ministry; and if it failed, the consequence would be the
> loss of my individual reputation, as both ministry and
> commander-in-chief would lay the blame on me.

Mulgrave brushed aside his objections:

> The present is no time for professional etiquette. All the

officers who have been consulted deem an attack with fireships impracticable, and after such an expression of opinion, it is not likely they would be offended by the conduct of fireships being given to another officer who approved of their use.

Cochrane argued that any senior officer could command the expedition as effectively as he:

The plan submitted to your Lordship was not an attack with fireships alone, and when the details become known to the service, it will be seen that there is no risk of failure whatever, if made with a fair wind and flowing tide. On the contrary, its success on inspection must be evident to any experienced officer, who would see that as the enemy's squadron could not escape up the Charente, their destruction would not only be certain but in fact easy.

Mulgrave promised to think the matter over. The following day he summoned Cochrane:

My Lord, you must go. The Board cannot listen to further refusal or delay. Rejoin your frigate at once. I will make you all right with Lord Gambier. Your confidence in the result has, I must confess, taken me by surprise, but it has increased my belief that all you anticipate will be accomplished. Make yourself easy about the jealous feeling of senior officers. I will so manage it with Lord Gambier that the amour propre of the fleet shall be satisfied.

To Gambier and the officers of the fleet, a single instruction was sent selecting Lord Cochrane 'under your Lordship's direction to conduct the fireships to be employed in the projected attack'. For once, operational considerations had overridden political ones in the Admiralty.

Cochrane's head was swimming with the opportunity offered as his carriage galloped back with all speed to Plymouth to join the twelve transports and to meet up with William Congreve, the inventor of a new type of explosive rocket, who was to take part in the attack. They set off to join the Channel fleet where Cochrane went aboard Gambier's flagship to witness an extraordinary scene.

Harvey, incensed by news of Cochrane's appointment, was giving vent to his spite. As the embarrassed young Cochrane stood by, the veteran seaman hurled a stream of invective upon the self-righteous admiral. Cochrane recalled that Harvey's:

> abuse of Lord Gambier to his face was such as I had never before witnessed from a subordinate. I should even now hesitate to record it as incredible, were it not officially known by the minutes of the court-martial in which it sometime afterwards resulted.

The young captain stood by in embarrassment and afterwards sought out Harvey to apologise to him:

> Harvey broke out into invectives of a most extraordinary kind, openly avowing that 'he never saw a man so unfit for the command of the fleet as Lord Gambier, who instead of sending boats to sound the channels, which he [Admiral Harvey] considered the best preparation for an attack on the enemy, he had been employing, or rather amusing himself with mustering the ships' companies, and had not even taken the pain to ascertain whether the enemy had placed any mortars in front of their lines; concluding by saying, that had Lord Nelson been there, he would not have anchored in Basque Roads at all, but would have dashed at the enemy at once.

Admiral Harvey then came into Sir Harry Neale's cabin, and shook hands with me, assuring me that 'he should have been very happy to see me on any other occasion' than the present. He begged me to consider that nothing personal to myself was intended, for he had a high opinion of me; but that my having been ordered to execute such a service, could only be regarded as an insult to the fleet, and that on this account he would strike his flag so soon as the service was executed'. Admiral Harvey further assured me that 'he had volunteered his services, which had been refused.'

That provoked this exchange. Cochrane began:

The service on which the Admiralty has sent me was none of my seeking. I went to Whitehall in obedience to a summons from Lord Mulgrave, and at his Lordship's request gave the board a plan of attack, the execution of which has been thrust upon me contrary to my inclination, as well knowing the invidious position in which I should be placed.

Harvey replied:

Well, this is not the first time I have been lightly treated, and that my services have not been attended to in the way they deserved; because I am no canting Methodist, no hypocrite, nor a psalm singer. I do not cheat old women out of their estates by hypocrisy and canting. I have volunteered to perform the service you came on, and should have been happy to see you on any other occasion, but am very sorry to have a junior officer placed over my head.

Harvey was soon afterwards removed from command for using 'grossly insubordinate language' towards Gambier. He was court-martialled and dismissed from the service. But he was an immensely popular figure, one of Nelson's most famous commanders and was reinstated the following year, although he was never given a command again.

Cochrane, assured by Harvey that he had no personal grudge against him, went off to the *Imperieuse* to make preparations. He wrote directly to Mulgrave in response to his request to detail his original plan of attack, dating from Thornburgh's time:

> My Lord—Having been very close the Isle d'Aix, I find that the western wall has been pulled down to build a better. At present the fort is quite open, and may be taken as soon as the French fleet is driven on shore or burned, which will be as soon as the fireships arrive. The wind continues favourable for the attack. If your Lordship can prevail on the ministry to send a military force here, you will do great and lasting good to our country.
>
> Could ministers see things with their own eyes, how differently would they act; but they cannot be everywhere present, and on their opinion of the judgement of others must depend the success of war—possibly the fate of England and all Europe.
>
> No diversion which the whole force of Great Britain is capable of making in Portugal or Spain would so much shake the French government as the capture of the islands on this coast. A few men would take Oléron; but to render the capture effective, send twenty thousand men who, without risk, would find occupation for the French army of a hundred thousand.

The Admiralty took no notice.

Cochrane supervised the conversion of the transports into fireships as they arrived from England. The construction of fireships was an old technique. Five large trails of gunpowder were laid criss-cross on the deck. Wood and canvas were stretched between them. Up above, tarred ropes dangled down from sails also covered in tar. Chains were fixed to the sides with grappling hooks so that it would be difficult for a ship which a fireship drifted against to detach itself. Resin and turpentine were poured all over the fireship to help it to burn. Finally huge holes were made in the hull so as to help suck in air and feed the flames after the ship began to burn.

With the arrival of a further nine fireships from England, Cochrane now had twenty-one under his command. But he was busier still on his own invention: explosion ships. The French would be prepared for fireships, but they would have no understanding of his new secret weapon, just approved by the Admiralty. The preparations for these were more elaborate still:

> The floor was rendered as firm as possible by means of logs placed in close contact, into every crevice of which other substances were firmly wedged so as to afford the greatest amount of resistance to the explosion. On this foundation were placed a large number of spirit and water casks, into which 1500 barrels of powder casks were placed, several hundred shells, and over these again nearly three thousand hand grenades; the whole, by means of wedges and sand, being compressed as nearly as possible into a solid mass.

Admiral Willaumez had been replaced by Vice-Admiral Allemand, who had anchored his ships in an apparently impregnable position. They were drawn up in two lines, between two small islands, the Ile d'Aix and the Ile Madame, which dominated the approaches to the river Charente. There were gun batteries on the Ile d'Aix and the Ile d'Oléron, a large spur of land to the west, as well as on the mainland.

Cochrane had already personally observed that the battery on Aix was in a poor state of repair, and its firepower grossly exaggerated. Moreover his earlier reconnaissance had led him to discover a remarkable thing. The only clear line of attack upon the French would have to be between a large reef, around 3 miles wide, called the Boyart Shoal, which was uncovered at low tide, and the Ile d'Aix. Cochrane, crucially, had found out that:

> From previous employment on the spot on several occasions I well knew there was room in the channel to keep out of the way of red-hot shot from the Aix batteries even if, by means of blue lights [flares] or other devices, they had discovered us. The officers and crews of the line-of-battle ships would be impressed with the idea that every fireship was an explosion vessel, and that in place of offering opposition they would, in all probability, be driven ashore in their attempt to escape from such diabolical engines of warfare, and thus become an easy prey.

In other words, the fort providing protection for the French fleet was no use at all. Even if the Admiralty ignored his recommendation that they seize the bases on Aix and Oléron, the 'lethal' fire of their guns could not reach the British ships if the latter stuck to the right-hand side of the channel. The Aix guns were 36-pounders manned by 2000 men, but these were raw recruits and the guns themselves were in a state of disrepair. There was no threat from this quarter, which Gambier persisted in regarding as extremely dangerous. 'Dismal Jimmie' had written to the Admiralty just a few days before:

> The enemy's ships are anchored in two lines, very near each other, in a direction due south from the Isle d'Aix, and the ships in each line not farther apart than their own length; by which it appears, as I imagined, that the space for their anchorage is so confined by the shoaliness of the water, as not to admit of ships to run in and anchor clear of each other. The most distant ships of their two lines are within point-blank shot of the works on the isle d'Aix; such ships,

therefore, as might attack the enemy would be exposed to be raked by red-hot shot, etc., from the island, and should the ships be disabled in their masts, they must remain within range of the enemy's fire until they are destroyed— there not being sufficient depth of water to allow them to move to the southward out of distance.

Having thus set out the dangers of an attack in alarmist tones, Gambier then typically reached an ingratiatingly ambiguous conclusion:

I beg leave to add that, if their Lordships are of the opinion that an attack on the enemy's ships by those of the fleet under my command is practicable, I am ready to obey any orders they may be pleased to honour me with, however great the risk may be of the loss of men and ships.

What neither Gambier nor Cochrane knew was that the French had their own secret defence—a 900-feet-long boom made of wooden trunks held together by chains and anchored to the sea floor. Allemand had also taken other precautions: he had stationed four frigates along the boom, as well as some seventy smaller boats whose purpose was to tow the fireships away from the main fleet should they succeed—which seemed unlikely—in breaking through the boom. The ten French battleships in the front line had lowered their sails in order to lessen their chances of catching fire.

On the morning of 10 April Cochrane went to Gambier to seek formal authorization to put his plan into action. To his astonishment, Gambier refused, citing the danger to the crews of the fireships: 'If you choose to rush on to self-destruction that is your own affair, but it is my duty to take care of the lives of others, and I will not place the crews of the fireships in palpable danger.' Depressed and frustrated, Cochrane returned to the *Imperieuse*. The following day the wind got up from the west and a heavy sea began to run. Far from being deterred by this, Cochrane saw that it presented an opportunity: the sea would favour the British, especially as the tide came in, and the French would be less on their guard, thinking the conditions too dangerous for an attack. Of course, the swell would make navigation much trickier in the treacherous channel.

Gambier, meanwhile, had had time to reflect. His explicit orders were to allow Cochrane to make the attack. He could not continue to refuse him authority without risking injury to his own reputation. Cochrane returned on board the flagship to ask for permission. This time it was grudgingly given.

His ships would attack in three waves. The first would be his three explosion ships, the foremost of which he, never reluctant to place himself in intense danger at the front of the fighting, would command. The second wave would consist of the twenty-one fireships. Behind them were three frigates, the *Pallas*, the *Aigle* and the *Unicorn*— accompanied by HMS *Caesar* to pick up the returning crews of the explosion vessels and fireships, although they would not come close to the action at this stage.

There were two sobering thoughts. First, the French understandably regarded fireships as a barbaric instrument of war, and would execute anyone they caught that could be identified as crewing them. The sailors were instructed to say, if caught, that they belonged to victualling ships nearby. Second, although the flood-tide to shore in this heavy swell favoured the fireships' approach, it would make it very difficult for their crews, now in shall boats, to go out against the flow and regain the safety of the rescue ships. Of Gambier's great fear, Cochrane had nothing but contempt:

> A more striking comment on the 'red-hot shot', etc., of which Lord Gambier made so much in one of his letters to the Admiralty, could scarcely be found. Of course, had a red-hot shot from the batteries on Aix reached us [in his explosion ship]—and they were not half-a-mile distant— nothing could have prevented our being 'hoist with our

own petard'. I can, however, safely say, that such a catastrophe never entered into my calculations.

Gambier, astonishingly, anchored his fleet 9 miles away. It was such a
distance that it could only be supposed he wanted to be able to make
a break for it and escape if the French fleet came out after him—the
reverse of virtually all British naval tactics for a century or more, which
were based on carrying the fight to the French. The fleet would be too
far to exercise the slightest influence on the initial action and, worse, it
was impossible for him to see what was really going on; even signals
were liable to be misinterpreted at that distance.

Cochrane floated in on the flood-tide aboard the foremost explosion
vessel—itself a desperately dangerous venture, as he and his men were
sitting on top of tons of explosive; one lucky shot from the French and
they would be annihilated. Besides Cochrane and Lieutenant Bissel of
the *Imperieuse* were four seamen. Behind him a second explosion ship
followed with Midshipman Marryat on board, commanded by a lieutenant. Cochrane had no idea there was a boom but his ship navigated
successfully down the channel at dead of night, in spite of the heavy
swell, approaching as close to the distant huddle of the French fleet as he
dared. Then he lit the 15-minute fuse of the explosives aboard. He was
certainly very close to the boom when he did so; his men had already
climbed aboard the getaway gig.

As soon as he jumped aboard, they rowed for all they were worth
away from the explosion ship in the pitch darkness. According to
press accounts Cochrane, hearing barking, saw a dog aboard—the
ship's mascot—and rowed back to fetch it. Certainly something delayed
his departure, and the fuse, for some reason, went off after only 9 minutes. Cochrane's boat had barely managed to get clear of the ship again
when it went up. He was saved by his failure to get further. If he had not
gone back he would have been on the receiving end of the shower of
debris that soared overhead and landed in an arc in the sea just beyond.
The explosion was awesome. Cochrane vividly described the scene:

For a moment, the sky was red with the lurid glare arising from the simultaneous ignition of 1500 barrels of powder. On this gigantic flash subsiding, the air seemed alive with shells, grenades, rockets, and masses of timber, the wreck of the shattered vessel; whilst the water was strewn with spars shaken out of the enormous boom, on which, on the subsequent testimony of Captain Proteau, whose frigate lay just within the boom, the vessel had brought up before she exploded. The sea was convulsed as by an earthquake, rising in a huge wave on whose crest our boat was lifted like a cork and as suddenly dropped into a vast trough, out of which, as it closed on us with a rush of a whirlpool, none expected to emerge. The skill of the boat's crew however overcame the threatened danger, which passed away as suddenly as it had arisen, and in a few minutes nothing but a heavy rolling sea had to be encountered, all having become silence and darkness.

The boom now lay shattered. The second ship passed through its broken fragments some 10 minutes later, and the decision was taken to detonate it and abandon ship in the same way. Another tremendous explosion shattered the peace of the night sky. The third explosion ship had, however, been pushed away from the scene by the *Imperieuse* because a fireship had come too close, and there was a risk of all three blowing up together. Marryat was ordered to go aboard the fireship and steer it away, a heroic action—after which Cochrane asked him laconically whether he had felt warm.

To Cochrane's disappointment the fireships were badly handled. As he rowed back to the *Imperieuse*, three or four passed him, being towed by small rowing boats towards their destination. But the towing boats of some seventeen others had abandoned them about 4 miles out to sea, judging the risk too great, and most drifted harmlessly ashore.

The whole spectacle had been enough to cause havoc among the

French fleet. Their first experience of the attack had been the ear-shattering explosion and conflagration aboard Cochrane's ship, followed by another even closer to hand. Then the night sky had been lit up by the spectacle of twenty blazing vessels, some close, others out to sea, in a massive attack to destroy the French fleet.

Their first assumption was that the fireships coming towards them were also explosion vessels, and in the small space of water of the Aix anchorage, the French ships of the line manoeuvred desperately to avoid them, while both wind and tide drove them relentlessly towards the shore. The flagship *Ocean* was the first to run aground. According to one of its officers:

> At 10.0 we grounded, and immediately after a fireship in the height of her combustion grappled us athwart our stern; for ten minutes she remained in this situation while we employed every means in our power to prevent the fire from catching the ship; our fire engines and pumps played upon the poop enough to prevent it from catching fire; with spars we hove off the fireship, with axes we cut the chains of the grapplings lashed to her yards, but a chevaux de frise on her sides held her firmly to us. In this deplorable situation we thought we must have been burned, as the flames of the fireship covered all our poop.
>
> Two of our line-of-battle ships, the *Tonnerre* and *Patriote*, at this time fell on board of us; the first broke our bowsprit and destroyed our main chains. Providence afforded us assistance on this occasion. At the moment the fireship was athwart our stern, and began to draw forward along the starboard side, the *Tonnerre* separated herself from us, and unless this had happened the fireship would have fallen into the angle formed by two ships and would infallibly have burnt them. The fireship having got so far forward as to be under our bowsprit, we left it there

some time to afford the two ships above mentioned time to get far enough away to avoid being boarded by this fireship. While this fireship was on board of us we let the cocks run in order to wet the powder, but they were so feeble that we could not do that.

Some fifty of the *Ocean*'s men fell into the water and drowned. In the confusion the French ships made towards the coastal mud-flats and the Palles Shoal off the Ile Madame; they got too close. The tide was on the turn and now ebbing fast. The *Ocean* was joined ashore by the *Aquilon*, *Tonnerre*, *Ville de Varsovie* and *Calcutta*; soon there were seven, with their hulls stranded like ducks' bottoms out of the water.

As the first streaks of light illuminated the morning sky, Cochrane looked on the scene with deep satisfaction. His victory had been far from perfect. He had been forced to blow up the explosion ships before they could reach the fleet but they had destroyed the boom that protected the French. The fireship attack had almost been a disaster, but the confusion sown by the first two explosion ships and the four fireships that had reached the French had been enough effectively to disperse the fleet, run most of it aground, and place it at the mercy of the British. Complete victory lay in the offing, thanks to his imagination, and the bravery of his crews.

At 5.48 a.m., at first light, he signalled triumphantly to the flag-ship, the *Caledonia*, some 9 miles away: 'Half the fleet to destroy the enemy. Seven on shore.' Gambier signalled back with the 'answering pennant'—a bare acknowledgment. Cochrane, just outside the Aix channel, watching the floundering French fleet, waited for Gambier's ships to approach and give him the signal to attack with his small flotilla of frigates. He wondered why there was no movement by Gambier's ships, but watched delightedly through his telescope as four more French ships were beached.

At 6.40 he reported this to the *Caledonia*. The answering pennant was hoisted and Gambier made no move. Cochrane's notoriously short fuse was now burning to explosion point. He had just taken in a ship laden with explosives at enormous personal risk to himself, narrowly escaped with his life, rowed back against a surging flood-tide and taken action to save his ship from a rogue fireship. He had seen his attack effectively incapacitate the entire French fleet. It was impossible for beached ships to fire broadside, indeed any guns at all. Now that they could be picked off at will, Gambier and his huge fleet were still hesitant to come in and finish them off.

An hour later, at 7.40, Cochrane sent off another signal: 'Only two afloat.' The reply was the answering pennant again and the fleet made no move. Whatever the explanation he gave at the subsequent court martial, Gambier's motives in refusing to attack the beached French fleet were probably mixed. He had been witness to the amazing fireworks of the night before. He heartily disapproved of the whole tactic of sending in explosion ships and fireships, and disliked the impulsive and reckless Cochrane. His captains had been almost mutinous about Cochrane's appointment.

How could the commander-in-chief even be sure that Cochrane was telling the truth and not seeking to entice the fleet into a dangerous engagement from which it might emerge badly damaged? His duty was the protection of the fleet, and he could not put it at risk on the word of an impertinent young captain. He decided, first, not to risk his ships in the confined waters of the Aix-Boyart channel under the guns of enemy batteries; and, second, to teach Cochrane a lesson and show who was in command. The Admiralty had ordered him to support Cochrane's flagship attack. It had not insisted that he risk any of his own ships.

This was to be one of the most contemptible acts of any commander-in-chief in British naval history, far eclipsing Admiral Byng's realistic decision to surrender Minorca only half a century before—for which he had been shot. The ideal chance to move in and destroy the beached French fleet would be short-lived. The British ships would have the perfect chance to come in on the flood before the French ships floated once again. It was a small window of opportunity.

Cochrane fumed in an agony of frustration and impotence. He signalled at 9.30: 'Enemy preparing to move.' Gambier was later to claim that 'as the enemy was on shore, [I] did not think it necessary to run any unnecessary risk of the fleet, when the object of their destruction seemed to be already obtained'. There is a small possibility that he was telling the truth—in other words that he believed the French ships to have been incapacitated by their grounding—although any sailor with more experience than Gambier would have realized that a ship beached by a tide was perfectly capable of floating off with little damage done.

But if so this misreading of Cochrane's signals was a terrible mistake. It is true that there was a slight element of ambiguity in the first three signals—but only to the most obtuse commander. Cochrane claimed later that he then sent another signal 'the frigates alone can destroy the enemy'—which allowed of no ambiguity, but was clearly impertinent. It was not, however, logged aboard the flagship. But after his 9.30 signal even Gambier could have harboured no illusions that the enemy was destroyed.

At 11.00 a.m. the admiral ordered his captains aboard to confer—itself a time-wasting procedure. He at last ordered his ships inshore—and then, to Cochrane's astonishment, the fleet stopped some 4 miles out. Cochrane watched in utter disbelief: victory was ebbing away with the incoming tide. As he wrote:

> There was no mistaking the admiral's intention in again bringing the fleet to an anchor. Notwithstanding that the enemy had been four hours at our mercy, and to a considerable extent was still so, it was now evident that no attack was intended, and that every enemy's ship would be permitted to float away unmolested and unassailed! I frankly admit that this was too much to be endured. The words of Lord Mulgrave rang in my ears, 'The Admiralty is bent on destroying that fleet before it can get out to the West Indies.'

• • •

Having displayed so much courage the previous night, he now took what is said to have been the bravest decision of his entire career, because it involved both defying his commander-in-chief and taking on alone the French fleet—although to him the risk may have seemed small as the ships were at his mercy. But they were floating off, and Gambier's prevarications had left it almost too late even for him to attack successfully.

He decided to raise anchor aboard the *Imperieuse* and drift, stern foremost, down the perilous Aix channel—that is, with his vulnerable rear exposed to enemy fire—straight into the midst of a dozen warships. This required superb seamanship. The idea was not to let Gambier see what he was doing until the last moment, and to be able to claim that he had floated accidentally with the tide. The shore batteries on the Ile d'Oléron opened up, but the shells fell reassuringly far from the ship— as Cochrane had always predicted they would. The ones on the Ile d'Aix were so ineffectual that, according to a British gunner, 'we could not find above thirteen guns that could be directed against us in passing; and these we thought so little of that we did not return their fire'.

However, the huge flagship *Ocean* was now afloat again, as were four other ships, which immediately turned tail and made for the safety of the Charente estuary upon the *Imperieuse*'s backwards approach. The French were now so demoralized they were not pre- pared to take on even Cochrane's single ship. Cochrane wrote later, 'Better to risk the frigates or even my commission than to suffer such a disgraceful termination [of the engagement]'. At last, when he had safely emerged from the channel, he unfurled his sails, signalling at the same time to Gambier:

> 1.30 p.m. The enemy's ships are getting under sail.
> 1.40 p.m. The enemy is superior to the chasing ship.
> 1.45 p.m. The ship is in distress, and required to be assisted immediately.

Thus he had cleverly outwitted his admiral. He could claim that he had not been responsible for the *Imperieuse*'s approach to the French fleet, and it was unheard of for a commander not to come to the help of one of his ships in distress, thus forcing Gambier's hand.

By two o'clock the *Imperieuse* was close enough to deliver a broadside into the 50-gun French magazine ship, the *Calcutta*, while her forecastle guns fired upon the *Aquilon* and her bow guns fired on the *Ville de Varsovie*—three ships at the same time. Captain Lafon of the *Calcutta*, fearing that his explosive-laden ship would blow up, climbed understandably but ignominiously out of his stern cabin window and ran away across the mud—for which he was later shot by the French.

The *Imperieuse* itself came under fire. Marryat recalled graphically how a seaman in the forecastle was decapitated by a cannonball, and how another was blown in two while the spine still attached the two parts: the corpse, its reflexes still working, jumped to its feet, stared at him 'horribly in the face', and fell down. In fact only three members of the crew were killed and eleven wounded throughout the whole engagement—another example of this 'reckless' man's meticulous care for the safety of his men. The *Calcutta* surrendered at 3.20 and Cochrane's men took possession.

Behind him, Gambier had at last been goaded into action. He sent in two battleships, the *Valiant* and *Revenge*, along with the 44-gun *Indefatigable*, described by Marryat:

> She was a beautiful ship, in what we call 'high kelter'; she seemed a living body, conscious of her own superior power over her opponents, whose shot she despised as they fell thick and fast about her, while she deliberately took up an admirable position for battle. And having furled her sails, and squared her yards, as if she had been at Spithead, her men came down from aloft, went to their guns, and opened such a fire on the enemy's ships as would have delighted the great Nelson himself.

• • •

The *Revenge* fired at the *Calcutta* before realising she had already been occupied by Cochrane's sailors. The *Aquilon* and the *Ville de Varsovie* surrendered at 5.30. The *Caesar*, under Rear-Admiral Stopford, had also joined the battle by then. At 6 p.m. the crew of the *Tonnerre* abandoned ship and set fire to her; it blew up an hour later, as did the *Calcutta*, which had been set alight by Cochrane's men, at about 9 p.m. Six of the French ships, however, had escaped up the Charente. Stopford sent in hastily converted fireships after them, but these were unable to prevail against the wind, and he used them instead against other, lesser vessels.

The fighting raged on through the following night. At 4 a.m., however, Gambier hoisted three lights aboard his flagship as a signal for the recall of the British ships. The two ships Cochrane had captured, the *Aquilon* and the *Ville de Varsovie*, were set alight by Stopford—although Cochrane had hoped to bring them back as prizes. As the *Indefatigable* sailed past, Cochrane tried to persuade her captain to join him in a final attack on the French flagship, the *Ocean*, but he refused. So Cochrane set off in pursuit, accompanied by a flotilla of small boats. Gambier thereupon sent him an astonishing letter, which had to be rowed all the way to his ship:

> You have done your part so admirably that I will not suffer you to tarnish it by attempting impossibilities, which I think, as well as those captains who have come from you, any further effort to destroy those ships would be. You must, therefore, join as soon as you can, with the bombs, etc., as I wish for some information, which you allude to, before I close my despatches.
>
> PS: I have ordered three brigs and two rocket vessels to join you, with which, and the bomb, you may make an attempt on the ship that is aground on the Palles, or towards Ile Madame, but I do not think you will succeed; and I am anxious that you should come to me, as I wish to

send you to England as soon as possible. You must, therefore, come as soon as the tide turns.

Cochrane replied curtly:

I have just had the honour to receive your Lordship's letter.
We can destroy the ships that are on shore, which I hope
your Lordship will approve of.

For four hours now Cochrane and his little boats had engaged the
mighty *Ocean*, convinced that further successes could be obtained. But
at 5 a.m. a further letter arrived from Gambier unambiguously
relieving Cochrane of his command:

It is necessary I should have some communication with you
before I close my despatches to the Admiralty. I have, therefore, ordered Captain Wolfe to relieve you in the services you
are engaged in. I wish you to join me as soon as possible,
that you may convey Sir Harry Neale to England, who will
be charged with my despatches, or you may return to carry
on the service where you are. I expect two bombs to arrive
every moment, they will be useful in it.

At last, after nearly 36 hours of exhausting battle, Cochrane obeyed
orders and returned to the flagship. The battle-stained and exhausted
young captain confronted the impeccably dressed and pompous noncombatant admiral who had done so little to help him, and had
turned what should have been an overwhelming victory into half of
one. Cochrane:

begged his lordship, by way of preventing the ill-feeling of
the fleet from becoming detrimental to the honour of the
service, to set me aside altogether and send in Admiral
Stopford, with the frigates or other vessels, as with regard to

him there could be no ill-feeling: further declaring my confidence that from Admiral Stopford's zeal for the service, he
would, being backed by his officers, accomplish results
more creditable than anything that had yet been done. I
apologised for the freedom I used, stating that I took the
liberty as a friend, for it would be impossible, as matters
stood, to prevent a noise being made in England.

Gambier replied huffily, 'If you throw blame upon what has been
done, it will appear like arrogantly claiming all the merit to yourself.'
Cochrane retorted: 'I have no wish to carry the despatches, or to go to
London with Sir Harry Neale on the occasion. My object is alone that
which has been entrusted to me by the Admiralty—to destroy the vessels of the enemy!'

Cochrane was peremptorily ordered to depart for England the following morning, arriving at Spithead six days later. Even the French
acknowledged the magnitude of the victory:

> This day of the 12th was a very disastrous one: four of our
> ships were destroyed, many brave people lost their lives by
> the disgraceful means the enemy made use of to destroy
> our lines of defence.

The planned French expedition to Martinique had been completely
destroyed.

Youth
by Joseph Conrad

Joseph Conrad (1857–1924) learned seaman-ship after moving from Poland to France in 1874. He joined the British merchant marine in 1878. A back injury curtailed Conrad's sea-going career in 1889, and he turned to writing.

This could have occurred nowhere but in England, where men and sea interpenetrate, so to speak—the sea entering into the life of most men, and the men knowing something or everything about the sea, in the way of amusement, of travel, or of breadwinning.

We were sitting round a mahogany table that reflected the bottle, the claret glasses, and our faces as we leaned on our elbows. There was a director of companies, an accountant, a lawyer, Marlow, and myself. The director had been a Conway boy, the accountant had served four years at sea, the lawyer—a fine crusted Tory, High Churchman, the best of old fellows, the soul of honor—had been chief officer in the P. & O. service in the good old days when mailboats were square-rigged at least on two masts, and used to come down the China Sea before a fair monsoon with stun'sails set alow and aloft. We all began life in the merchant service. Between the five of us there was the strong bond of the sea, and also the fellowship of the craft, which no amount of enthusiasm for yachting, cruising, and so on can give, since one is only the amusement of life and the other is life itself.

Marlow (at least I think that is how he spelt his name) told the story, or rather the chronicle, of a voyage:

"Yes, I have seen a little of the Eastern seas; but what I remember best is my first voyage there. You fellows know there are those voyages that seem ordered for the illustration of life, that might stand for a symbol of existence. You fight, work, sweat, nearly kill yourself, sometimes do kill yourself, trying to accomplish something—and you can't. Not from any fault of yours. You simply can do nothing, neither great nor little—not a thing in the world—not even marry an old maid, or get a wretched 600-ton cargo of coal to its port of destination.

"It was altogether a memorable affair. It was my first voyage to the East, and my first voyage as second mate; it was also my skipper's first command. You'll admit it was time. He was sixty if a day; a little man, with a broad, not very straight back, with bowed shoulders and one leg more bandy than the other, he had that queer twisted-about appearance you see so often in men who work in the fields. He had a nutcracker face—chin and nose trying to come together over a sunken mouth—and it was framed in iron-gray fluffy hair, that looked like a chinstrap of cotton-wool sprinkled with coaldust. And he had blue eyes in that old face of his, which were amazingly like a boy's, with that candid expression some quite common men preserve to the end of their days by a rare internal gift of simplicity of heart and rectitude of soul. What induced him to accept me was a wonder. I had come out of a crack Australian clipper, where I had been third officer, and he seemed to have a prejudice against crack clippers as aristocratic and high-toned. He said to me, 'You know, in this ship you will have to work.' I said I had to work in every ship I had ever been in. 'Ah, but this is different, and you gentlemen out of them big ships; . . . but there! I dare say you will do. Join tomorrow.'

"I joined tomorrow. It was twenty-two years ago; and I was just twenty. How time passes! It was one of the happiest days of my life. Fancy! Second mate for the first time—a really responsible officer! I wouldn't have thrown up my new billet for a fortune. The mate looked me over carefully. He was also an old chap, but of another stamp. He had a Roman nose, a snow-white, long beard, and his name was Mahon, but he insisted that it should be pronounced Mann. He was well connected; yet there was something wrong with his luck, and he had never got on.

"As to the captain, he had been for years in coasters, then in the Mediterranean, and last in the West Indian trade. He had never been round the Capes. He could just write a kind of sketchy hand, and didn't care for writing at all. Both were thorough good seamen of course, and between those two old chaps I felt like a small boy between two grandfathers.

"The ship also was old. Her name was the *Judea*. Queer name, isn't it? She belonged to a man Wilmer, Wilcox—some name like that; but he has been bankrupt and dead these twenty years or more, and his name don't matter. She had been laid up in Shadwell basin for ever so long. You may imagine her state. She was all rust, dust, grime—soot aloft, dirt on deck. To me it was like coming out of a palace into a ruined cottage. She was about 400 tons, had a primitive windlass, wooden latches to the doors, not a bit of brass about her, and a big square stern. There was on it, below her name in big letters, a lot of scrollwork, with the gilt off, and some sort of a coat of arms, with the motto 'Do or Die' underneath. I remember it took my fancy immensely. There was a touch of romance in it, something that made me love the old thing—something that appealed to my youth!

"We left London in ballast—sand ballast—to load a cargo of coal in a northern port for Bangkok. Bangkok! I thrilled. I had been six years at sea, but had only seen Melbourne and Sydney, very good places, charming places in their way—but Bangkok!

"We worked out of the Thames under canvas, with a North Sea pilot on board. His name was Jermyn, and he dodged all day long about the galley drying his handkerchief before the stove. Apparently he never slept. He was a dismal man, with a perpetual tear sparkling at the end of his nose, who either had been in trouble, or was in trouble, or

expected to be in trouble—couldn't be happy unless something went
wrong. He mistrusted my youth, my common sense, and my seamanship, and made a point of showing it in a hundred little ways. I dare
say he was right. It seems to me I knew very little then, and I know not
much more now; but I cherish a hate for that Jermyn to this day.

"We were a week working up as far as Yarmouth Roads, and then we
got into a gale—the famous October gale of twenty-two years ago. It
was wind, lightning, sleet, snow, and a terrific sea. We were flying light,
and you may imagine how bad it was when I tell you we had smashed
bulwarks and a flooded deck. On the second night she shifted her ballast into the lee bow, and by that time we had been blown off somewhere on the Dogger Bank. There was nothing for it but go below with
shovels and try to right her, and there we were in that vast hold,
gloomy like a cavern, the tallow dips stuck and flickering on the
beams, the gale howling above, the ship tossing about like mad on her
side; there we all were, Jermyn, the captain, everyone, hardly able to
keep our feet, engaged on that gravedigger's work, and trying to toss
shovelfuls of wet sand up to windward. At every tumble of the ship you
could see vaguely in the dim light men falling down with a great
flourish of shovels. One of the ship's boys (we had two), impressed by
the weirdness of the scene, wept as if his heart would break. We could
hear him blubbering somewhere in the shadows.

"On the third day the gale died out, and by and by a north-country
tug picked us up. We took sixteen days in all to get from London to
the Tyne! When we got into dock we had lost our turn for loading,
and they hauled us off to a pier where we remained for a month. Mrs.
Beard (the captain's name was Beard) came from Colchester to see the
old man. She lived on board. The crew of runners had left, and there
remained only the officers, one boy and the steward, a mulatto who
answered to the name of Abraham. Mrs. Beard was an old woman,
with a face all wrinkled and ruddy like a winter apple, and the figure
of a young girl. She caught sight of me once, sewing on a button, and
insisted on having my shirts to repair. This was something different
from the captains' wives I had known on board crack clippers. When I

brought her the shirts, she said: 'And the socks? They want mending, I am sure, and John's—Captain Beard's—things are all in order now. I would be glad of something to do.' Bless the old woman. She over-hauled my outfit for me, and meantime I read for the first time *Sartor Resartus* and Burnaby's *Ride to Khiva*. I didn't understand much of the first then; but I remember I preferred the soldier to the philosopher at the time; a preference which life has only confirmed. One was a man, and the other was either more—or less. However, they are both dead and Mrs. Beard is dead, and youth, strength, genius, thoughts, achieve-ments, simple hearts—all dies. . . . No matter.

"They loaded us at last. We shipped a crew. Eight able seamen and two boys. We hauled off one evening to the buoys at the dock gates, ready to go out, and with a fair prospect of beginning the voyage next day. Mrs. Beard was to start for home by a late train. When the ship was fast we went to tea. We sat rather silent through the meal—Mahon, the old couple, and I. I finished first, and slipped away for a smoke, my cabin being in a deckhouse just against the poop. It was high water, blowing fresh with a drizzle; the double dock gates were opened, and the steam colliers were going in and out in the darkness with their lights burning bright, a great plashing of propellers, rattling of winches, and a lot of hailing on the pier-heads. I watched the proces-sion of headlights gliding high and of green lights gliding low in the night, when suddenly a red gleam flashed at me, vanished, came into view again, and remained. The fore end of a steamer loomed up close. I shouted down the cabin, 'Come up, quick!' and then heard a startled voice saying afar in the dark, 'Stop her, sir.' A bell jingled. Another voice cried warningly, 'We are going right into that bark, sir.' The answer to this was a gruff 'All right,' and the next thing was a heavy crash as the steamer struck a glancing blow with the bluff of her bow about our forerigging. There was a moment of confusion, yelling, and running about. Steam roared. Then somebody was heard saying, "All clear, sir.' . . . 'Are you all right?' asked the gruff voice. I had jumped forward to see the damage, and hailed back, 'I think so.' 'Easy astern,' said the gruff voice. A bell jingled. 'What steamer is that?' screamed Mahon. By that

time she was no more to us than a bulky shadow maneuvering a little
way off. They shouted at us some name—a woman's name, Miranda or
Melissa—or some such thing. 'This means another month in this
beastly hole,' said Mahon to me, as we peered with lamps about the
splintered bulwarks and broken braces. 'But where's the captain?'

"We had not heard or seen anything of him all that time. We went
aft to look. A doleful voice arose hailing somewhere in the middle of
the dock, '*Judea* ahoy!' . . . How the devil did he get there? . . . 'Hallo!'
we shouted. 'I am adrift in our boat without oars,' he cried. A belated
water-man offered his services, and Mahon struck a bargain with him
for a half crown to tow our skipper alongside; but it was Mrs. Beard
that came up the ladder first. They had been floating about the dock
in that mizzly cold rain for nearly an hour. I was never so surprised in
my life.

"It appears that when he heard my shout 'Come up' he understood at once what was the matter, caught up his wife, ran on deck,
and across, and down into our boat, which was fast to the ladder.
Not bad for a sixty-year-old. Just imagine that old fellow saving hero-
ically in his arms that old woman—the woman of his life. He set her
down on a thwart, and was ready to climb back on board when the
painter came adrift somehow, and away they went together. Of course
in the confusion we did not hear him shouting. He looked abashed.
She said cheerfully, 'I suppose it does not matter my losing the train
now?' 'No, Jenny—you go below and get warm,' he growled. Then to
us: 'A sailor has no business with a wife—I say. There I was, out of the
ship. Well, no harm done this time. Let's go and look at what that fool
of a steamer smashed.'

"It wasn't much, but it delayed us three weeks. At the end of that
time, the captain being engaged with his agents, I carried Mrs. Beard's
bag to the railway station and put her all comfy into a third-class carriage. She lowered the window to say, 'You are a good young man. If
you see John—Captain Beard—without his muffler at night, just
remind him from me to keep his throat well wrapped up.' 'Certainly,
Mrs. Beard,' I said. 'You are a good young man; I noticed how attentive

you are to John—to Captain—' The train pulled out suddenly; I took my cap off to the old woman: I never saw her again. . . . Pass the bottle.

"We went to sea next day. When we made that start for Bangkok we had been already three months out of London. We had expected to be a fortnight or so—at the outside.

"It was January, and the weather was beautiful—the beautiful sunny winter weather that has more charm than in the summertime, because it is unexpected, and crisp, and you know it won't, it can't, last long. It's like a windfall, like a godsend, like an unexpected piece of luck.

"It lasted all down the North Sea, all down Channel; and it lasted till we were three hundred miles or so to the westward of the Lizards; then the wind went round to the sou'west and began to pipe up. In two days it blew a gale. The *Judea*, hove to, wallowed on the Atlantic like an old candle-box. It blew day after day: it blew with spite, without interval, without mercy, without rest. The world was nothing but an immensity of great foaming waves rushing at us, under a sky low enough to touch with the hand and dirty like a smoked ceiling. In the stormy space surrounding us there was as much flying spray as air. Day after day and night after night there was nothing round the ship but the howl of the wind, the tumult of the sea, the noise of water pouring over her deck. There was no rest for her and no rest for us. She tossed, she pitched, she stood on her head, she sat on her tail, she rolled, she groaned, and we had to hold on while on deck and cling to our bunks when below, in a constant effort of body and worry of mind.

"One night Mahon spoke through the small window of my berth. It opened right into my very bed, and I was lying there sleepless, in my boots, feeling as though I had not slept for years, and could not if I tried. He said excitedly:

" 'You got the sounding rod in here, Marlow? I can't get the pumps to suck. By God! It's no child's play.'

"I gave him the sounding rod and lay down again, trying to think of various things—but I thought only of the pumps. When I came on deck they were still at it, and my watch relieved at the pumps. By the light of the lantern brought on deck to examine the sounding rod I caught a glimpse of their weary, serious faces. We pumped all the four hours. We pumped all night, all day, all the week—watch and watch. She was working herself loose, and leaked badly—not enough to drown us at once, but enough to kill us with the work at the pumps. And while we pumped the ship was going from us piecemeal: the bulwarks went, the stanchions were torn out, the ventilators smashed, the cabin door burst in. There was not a dry spot in the ship. She was being gutted bit by bit. The longboat changed, as if by magic, into matchwood where she stood in her gripes. I had lashed her myself, and was rather proud of my handiwork, which had withstood so long the malice of the sea. And we pumped. And there was no break in the weather. The sea was white like a sheet of foam, like a caldron of boiling milk; there was not a break in the clouds, no—not the size of a man's hand—no, not for so much as ten seconds. There was for us no sky, there were for us no stars, no sun, no universe—nothing but angry clouds and an infuriated sea. We pumped watch and watch, for dear life; and it seemed to last for months, for years, for all eternity, as though we had been dead and gone to a hell for sailors. We forgot the day of the week, the name of the month, what year it was, and whether we had ever been ashore. The sails blew away, she lay broadside on under a weather cloth, the ocean poured over her, and we did not care. We turned those handles, and had the eyes of idiots. As soon as we had crawled on deck I used to take a round turn with a rope about the men, the pumps, and the mainmast, and we turned, we turned incessantly, with the water to our waists, to our necks, over our heads. It was all one. We had forgotten how it felt to be dry.

"And there was somewhere in me the thought: By Jove! This is the deuce of an adventure—something you read about; and it is my first voyage as second mate—and I am only twenty—and here I am lasting it out as well as any of these men, and keeping my chaps up to the mark. I was pleased. I would not have given up the experience for worlds. I had moments of exultation. Whenever the old dismantled craft pitched heavily with her counter high in the air, she seemed to me to throw up, like an appeal, like a defiance, like a cry to the clouds without mercy, the words written on her stern: '*Judea*, London. Do or Die.'

"O youth! The strength of it, the faith of it, the imagination of it! To me she was not an old rattletrap carting about the world a lot of coal for a freight—to me she was the endeavor, the test, the trial of life. I think of her with pleasure, with affection, with regret—as you would think of someone dead you have loved. I shall never forget her. . . . Pass the bottle.

"One night when tied to the mast, as I explained, we were pumping on, deafened with the wind, and without spirit enough in us to wish ourselves dead, a heavy sea crashed aboard and swept clean over us. As soon as I got my breath I shouted, as in duty bound, 'Keep on, boys!' when suddenly I felt something hard floating on deck strike the calf of my leg. I made a grab at it and missed. It was so dark we could not see each other's faces within a foot—you understand.

"After that thump the ship kept quiet for a while, and the thing, whatever it was struck my leg again. This time I caught it—and it was a saucepan. At first, being stupid with fatigue and thinking of nothing but the pumps, I did not understand what I had in my hand. Suddenly it dawned upon me, and I shouted, 'Boys, the house on deck is gone. Leave this, and let's look for the cook.'

"There was a deckhouse forward, which contained the galley, the cook's berth, and the quarters of the crew. As we had expected for days to see it swept away, the hands had been ordered to sleep in the cabin—the only safe place in the ship. The steward, Abraham, however, persisted in clinging to his berth, stupidly, like a mule—from sheer fright I believe, like an animal that won't leave a stable falling in an earthquake. So we went to look for him. It was chancing death, since once out of our lashings we were as exposed as if on a raft. But we went. The house was shattered as if a shell had exploded inside. Most of it had gone overboard—stove, men's quarters, and their property, all was gone; but two posts, holding a portion of the bulkhead to which Abraham's bunk was attached, remained as if by a miracle. We groped in the ruins and came upon this, and there he was, sitting in his bunk, surrounded by foam and wreckage, jabbering cheerfully to himself. He was out of his mind; completely and forever mad, with this sudden shock coming upon the fag-end of his endurance. We snatched him up, lugged him aft, and pitched him headfirst down the cabin companion. You understand there was no time to carry him down with infinite precautions and wait to see how he got on. Those below would pick him up at the bottom of the stairs all right. We were in a hurry to go back to the pumps. That business could not wait. A bad leak is an inhuman thing.

"One would think that the sole purpose of that fiendish gale had been to make a lunatic of that poor devil of a mulatto. It eased before morning, and next day the sky cleared, and as the sea went down the leak took up. When it came to bending a fresh set of sails the crew demanded to put back—and really there was nothing else to do. Boats gone, decks swept clean, cabin gutted, men without a stitch but what they stood in, stores spoiled, ship strained. We put her head for home, and—would you believe it? The wind came east right in our teeth. It blew fresh, it blew continuously. We had to beat up every inch of the way, but she did not leak so badly, the water keeping comparatively smooth. Two hours' pumping in every four is no joke but it kept her afloat as far as Falmouth.

"The good people there live on casualties of the sea, and no doubt were glad to see us. A hungry crowd of shipwrights sharpened their chisels at the sight of that carcass of a ship. And, by Jove! they had pretty pickings off us before they were done. I fancy the owner was already in a tight place. There were delays. Then it was decided to take part of the cargo out and calk her topsides. This was done, the repairs finished, cargo reshipped; a new crew came on board, and we went out—for Bangkok. At the end of a week we were back again. The crew said they weren't going to Bangkok—a hundred and fifty days' passage—in a something hooker that wanted pumping eight hours out of the twenty-four; and the nautical papers inserted again the little paragraph: '*Judea*. Bark. Tyne to Bangkok; coals; put back to Falmouth leaky and with crew refusing duty.'

"There were more delays—more tinkering. The owner came down for a day, and said she was as right as a little fiddle. Poor old Captain Beard looked like the ghost of a Geordie skipper—through the worry and humiliation of it. Remember he was sixty, and it was his first command. Mahon said it was a foolish business, and would end badly. I loved the ship more than ever, and wanted awfully to get to Bangkok. To Bangkok! Magic name, blessed name. Mesopotamia wasn't a patch on it. Remember I was twenty, and it was my first second-mate's billet, and the East was waiting for me.

"We went out and anchored in the outer roads with a fresh crew—the third. She leaked worse than ever. It was as if those confounded shipwrights had actually made a hole in her. This time we did not even go outside. The crew simply refused to man the windlass.

"They towed us back to the inner harbor, and we became a fixture, a feature, an institution of the place. People pointed us out to visitors as 'That 'ere bark that's going to Bangkok—has been here six months—put back three times.' On holidays the small boys pulling about in boats would hail, 'Judea, ahoy!' and if a head showed above the rail shouted, 'Where you bound to?—Bangkok?' and jeered. We were only three on board. The poor old skipper mooned in the cabin. Mahon undertook the cooking, and unexpectedly developed all a Frenchman's genius for preparing nice little messes. I looked languidly after the rigging. We became citizens of Falmouth. Every shopkeeper knew us. At the barber's or tobacconist's they asked familiarly, 'Do you think you will ever get to Bangkok?' Meantime the owner, the underwriters, and the charterers squabbled amongst themselves in London, and our pay went on. . . . Pass the bottle.

"It was horrid. Morally it was worse than pumping for life. It seemed as though we had been forgotten by the world, belonged to nobody, would get nowhere; it seemed that, as if bewitched, we would have to live for ever and ever in that inner harbor, a derision and a by-word to generations of long-shore loafers and dishonest boatmen. I obtained three months' pay and a five days' leave, and made a rush for London. It took me a day to get there and pretty well another to come back—but three months' pay went all the same. I don't know what I did with it. I went to a music hall, I believe, lunched, dined, and supped in a swell place in Regent Street, and was back on time, with nothing but a complete set of Byron's works and a new railway rug to show for three months' work. The boatman who pulled me off to the ship said: 'Hallo! I thought you had left the old thing. *She* will never get to Bangkok.' 'That's all *you* know about it,' I said, scornfully—but I didn't like that prophecy at all.

"Suddenly a man, some kind of agent to somebody, appeared with full powers. He had grog-blossoms all over his face, an indomitable energy, and was a jolly soul. We leaped into life again. A hulk came alongside, took our cargo, and then we went into dry dock to get our copper stripped. No wonder she leaked. The poor thing, strained beyond endurance by the gale, had, as if in disgust, spat out all the oakum of her lower seams. She was recalked, new-coppered, and made as tight as a bottle. We went back to the hulk and reshipped our cargo.

"Then, on a fine moonlight night, all the rats left the ship.

"We had been infested with them. They had destroyed our sails, consumed more stores than the crew, affably shared our beds and our dangers, and now, when the ship was made seaworthy, concluded to clear out. I called Mahon to enjoy the spectacle. Rat after rat appeared on our rail, took a last look over his shoulder, and leaped with a hollow thud into the empty hulk. We tried to count them, but soon lost the tale. Mahon said: 'Well, well! don't talk to me about the intelligence of rats. They ought to have left before, when we had that narrow squeak from foundering. There you have the proof how silly is the superstition about them. They leave a good ship for an old rotten hulk, where there is nothing to eat, too, the fools! . . . I don't believe they know what is safe or what is good for them, any more than you or I.'

"And after some more talk we agreed that the wisdom of rats had been grossly overrated, being in fact no greater than that of men.

"The story of the ship was known, by this, all up the Channel from Land's End to the Forelands, and we could get no crew on the south coast. They sent us one all complete from Liverpool, and we left once more—for Bangkok.

"We had fair breezes, smooth water right into the tropics, and the old *Judea* lumbered along in the sunshine. When she went eight knots everything cracked aloft, and we tied our caps to our heads; but mostly she strolled on at the rate of three miles an hour. What could you expect? She was tired—that old ship. Her youth was where mine is— where yours is—you fellows who listen to this yarn; and what friend would throw your years and your weariness in your face? We didn't grumble at her. To us aft, at least, it seemed as though we had been born in her, reared in her, had lived in her for ages, had never known any other ship. I would just as soon have abused the old village church at home for not being a cathedral.

"And for me there was also my youth to make me patient. There was all the East before me, and all life, and the thought that I had been tried in that ship and had come out pretty well. And I thought of men of old who, centuries ago, went that road in ships that sailed no better, to the land of palms, and spices, and yellow sands, and of brown nations ruled by kings more cruel than Nero the Roman, and more splendid than Solomon the Jew. The old bark lumbered on, heavy with her age and the burden of her cargo, while I lived the life of youth in ignorance and hope. She lumbered on through an interminable procession of days; and the fresh gilding flashed back at the setting sun, seemed to cry out over the darkening sea the words painted on her stern, '*Judea*, London. Do or Die.'

"Then we entered the Indian Ocean and steered northerly for Java Head. The winds were light. Weeks slipped by. She crawled on, do or die, and people at home began to think of posting us as overdue.

"One Saturday evening, I being off duty, the men asked me to give them an extra bucket of water or so—for washing clothes. As I did not wish to screw on the fresh-water pump so late, I went forward whistling, and with a key in my hand to unlock the forepeak scuttle, intending to serve the water out of a spare tank we kept there.

"The smell down below was as unexpected as it was frightful. One would have thought hundreds of paraffin lamps had been flaring and smoking in that hole for days. I was glad to get out. The man with me coughed and said, 'Funny smell, sir.' I answered negligently, 'It's good for the health, they say,' and walked aft.

"The first thing I did was to put my head down the square of the midship ventilator. As I lifted the lid a visible breath, something like a thin fog, a puff of faint haze, rose from the opening. The ascending air was hot, and had a heavy, sooty, paraffiny smell. I gave one sniff, and put down the lid gently. It was no use choking myself. The cargo was on fire.

"Next day she began to smoke in earnest. You see it was to be expected, for though the coal was of a safe kind, that cargo had been so handled, so broken up with handling, that it looked more like smithy coal than anything else. Then it had been wetted—more than once. It rained all the time we were taking it back from the hulk, and now with this long passage it got heated, and there was another case of spontaneous combustion.

"The captain called us into the cabin. He had a chart spread on the table, and looked unhappy. He said, 'The coast of West Australia is near, but I mean to proceed to our destination. It is the hurricane month, too; but we will just keep her head for Bangkok, and fight the fire. No more putting back anywhere, if we all get roasted. We will try first to stifle this 'ere damned combustion by want of air.'

"We tried. We battened down everything, and still she smoked. The smoke kept coming out through imperceptible crevices; it forced itself through bulkheads and covers; it oozed here and there and everywhere in slender threads, in an invisible film, in an incomprehensible manner. It made its way into the cabin, into the forecastle; it poisoned the sheltered places on the deck; it could be sniffed as high as the mainyard. It was clear that if the smoke came out the air came in. This was disheartening. This combustion refused to be stifled.

"We resolved to try water, and took the hatches off. Enormous volumes of smoke, whitish, yellowish, thick, greasy, misty, choking, ascended as high as the trucks. All hands cleared out aft. Then the poisonous cloud blew away, and we went back to work in a smoke that was no thicker now than that of an ordinary factory chimney.

"We rigged the force pump, got the hose along, and by and by it burst. Well, it was as old as the ship—a prehistoric hose, and past repair. Then we pumped with the feeble head pump, drew water with buckets, and in this way managed in time to pour lots of Indian Ocean into the main hatch. The bright stream flashed in sunshine, fell into a layer of white crawling smoke, and vanished on the black surface of coal. Steam ascended mingling with the smoke. We poured salt water as into a barrel without a bottom. It was our fate to pump in that ship, to pump out of her, to pump into her; and after keeping water out of her to save ourselves from being drowned, we frantically poured water into her to save ourselves from being burnt.

"And she crawled on, do or die, in the serene weather. The sky was a miracle of purity, a miracle of azure. The sea was polished, was blue, was pellucid, was sparkling like a precious stone, extending on all sides, all round to the horizon—as if the whole terrestrial globe had been one jewel, one colossal sapphire, a single gem fashioned into a planet. And on the luster of the great calm waters the *Judea* glided imperceptibly, enveloped in languid and unclean vapors, in a lazy cloud that drifted to leeward, light and slow, a pestiferous cloud defiling the splendor of sea and sky.

"All this time of course we saw no fire. The cargo smoldered at the bottom somewhere. Once Mahon, as we were working side by side, said to me with a queer smile: 'Now, if she only would spring a tidy leak—like that time when we first left the Channel—it would put a stopper on this fire. Wouldn't it?' I remarked irrelevantly, 'Do you remember the rats?'

"We fought the fire and sailed the ship too as carefully as though nothing had been the matter. The steward cooked and attended on us. Of the other twelve men, eight worked while four rested. Everyone took his turn, captain included. There was equality, and if not exactly fraternity, then a deal of good feeling. Sometimes a man, as he dashed a bucketful of water down the hatchway, would yell out, 'Hurrah for

Bangkok!' and the rest laughed. But generally we were taciturn and serious—and thirsty. Oh! how thirsty! And we had to be careful with the water. Strict allowance. The ship smoked, the sun blazed. . . . Pass the bottle.

"We tried everything. We even made an attempt to dig down to the fire. No good, of course. No man could remain more than a minute below. Mahon, who went first, fainted there, and the man who went to fetch him out did likewise. We lugged them out on deck. Then I leaped down to show how easily it could be done. They had learned wisdom by that time, and contented themselves by fishing for me with a chain-hook tied to a broom handle, I believe. I did not offer to go and fetch up my shovel, which was left down below.

"Things began to look bad. We put the longboat into the water. The second boat was ready to swing out. We had also another, a fourteen-foot thing, on davits aft, where it was quite safe.

"Then, behold, the smoke suddenly decreased. We redoubled our efforts to flood the bottom of the ship. In two days there was no smoke at all. Everybody was on the broad grin. This was on a Friday. On Saturday no work, but sailing the ship of course, was done. The men washed their clothes and their faces for the first time in a fortnight, and had a special dinner given them. They spoke of spontaneous combustion with contempt, and implied *they* were the boys to put out combustions. Somehow we all felt as though we each had inherited a large fortune. But a beastly smell of burning hung about the ship. Captain Beard had hollow eyes and sunken cheeks. I had never noticed so much before how twisted and bowed he was. He and Mahon prowled soberly about hatches and ventilators, sniffing. It struck me suddenly poor Mahon was a very, very old chap. As to me, I was pleased and proud as though I had helped to win a great naval battle. O youth!

"The night was fine. In the morning a homeward-bound ship passed us hull down—the first we had seen for months; but we were nearing the land at last, Java Head being about 190 miles off, and nearly due north.

"Next day it was my watch on deck from eight to twelve. At breakfast the captain observed, 'It's wonderful how that smell hangs about the cabin.' About ten, the mate being on the poop, I stepped down on the main deck for a moment. The carpenter's bench stood abaft the main-mast: I leaned against it sucking at my pipe, and the carpenter, a young chap, came to talk to me. He remarked. 'I think we have done very well, haven't we?' and then I perceived with annoyance the fool was trying to tilt the bench. I said curtly, 'Don't, Chips,' and immediately became aware of a queer sensation, of an absurd delusion—I seemed somehow to be in the air. I heard all round me like a pent-up breath released—as if a thousand giants simultaneously had said Phoo!—and felt a dull concussion which made my ribs ache suddenly. No doubt about it—I was in the air, and my body was describing a short parabola. But short as it was, I had the time to think several thoughts in, as far as I can remember, the following order: 'This can't be the carpenter—What is it?—Some accident—Submarine volcano?—Coals, gas!—By Jove! We are being blown up—Everybody's dead—I am falling into the afterhatch—I see fire in it.'

"The coaldust suspended in the air of the hold had glowed dull-red at the moment of the explosion. In the twinkling of an eye, in an infin-itesimal fraction of a second since the first tilt of the bench, I was sprawling full length on the cargo. I picked myself up and scrambled out. It was quick like a rebound. The deck was a wilderness of smashed timber, lying crosswise like trees in a wood after a hurricane; an immense curtain of solid rags waved gently before me—it was the mainsail blown to strips. I thought: the masts will be toppling over directly; and to get out of the way bolted on all fours towards the poop ladder. The first person I saw was Mahon, with eyes like saucers, his mouth open, and the long white hair standing straight on end round his head like a silver halo. He was just about to go down when the sight of the main deck stirring, heaving up, and changing into splinters before his eyes, petrified him on the top step. I stared at him in unbe-lief, and he stared at me with a queer kind of shocked curiosity. I did not know that I had no hair, no eyebrows, no eyelashes, that my young mustache was burnt off, that my face was black, one cheek laid open, my nose cut, and my chin bleeding. I had lost my cap, one of my slippers, and my shirt was torn to rags. Of all this I was not aware. I was amazed to see the ship still afloat, the poop deck whole—and, most of all, to see anybody alive. Also the peace of the sky and the serenity of the sea were distinctly surprising. I suppose I expected to see them convulsed with horror. . . . Pass the bottle.

"There was a voice hailing the ship from somewhere—in the air, in the sky—I couldn't tell. Presently I saw the captain—and he was mad. He asked me eagerly, 'Where's the cabin table?' and to hear such a question was a frightful shock. I had just been blown up, you understand, and vibrated with that experience—I wasn't quite sure whether I was alive. Mahon began to stamp with both feet and yelled at him, 'Good God! don't you see the deck's blown out of her?' I found my voice, and stammered out as if conscious of some gross neglect of duty, 'I don't know where the cabin table is.' It was like an absurd dream.

"Do you know what he wanted next? Well, he wanted to trim the yards. Very placidly, and as if lost in thought, he insisted on having the foreyard squared. 'I don't know if there's anybody alive,' said Mahon, almost tearfully. 'Surely,' he said, gently, 'there will be enough left to square the foreyard.'

"The old chap, it seems, was in his own berth winding up the chronometers, when the shock sent him spinning. Immediately it occurred to him—as he said afterwards—that the ship had struck something, and ran out into the cabin. There, he saw, the cabin table had vanished somewhere. The deck being blown up, it had fallen down into the lazarette of course. Where we had our breakfast that morning he saw only a great hole in the floor. This appeared to him so awfully mysterious, and impressed him so immensely, that what he saw and heard after he got on deck were mere trifles in comparison. And, mark, he noticed directly the wheel deserted and his bark off her course—and his only thought was to get that miserable, stripped, undecked, smoldering shell of a ship back again with her head pointing at her port of destination. Bangkok! That's what he was after. I tell you this quiet, bowed, bandy-legged, almost deformed little man was immense in the singleness of his idea and in his placid ignorance of our agitation. He motioned us forward with a commanding gesture, and went to take the wheel himself.

"Yes; that was the first thing we did—trim the yards of that wreck! No one was killed, or even disabled, but everyone was more or less hurt. You should have seen them! Some were in rags, with black faces, like coal heavers, like sweeps, and had bullet heads that seemed closely cropped, but were in fact singed to the skin. Others, of the watch below, awakened by being shot out from their collapsing bunks, shivered incessantly, and kept on groaning even as we went about our work. But they all worked. That crew of Liverpool hard cases had in them the right stuff. It's my experience they always have. It is the sea that gives it—the vastness, the loneliness surrounding their dark stolid souls. Ah! Well! We stumbled, we crept, we fell, we barked our shins on the wreckage, we hauled. The masts stood, but we did not know how much they might be charred down below. It was nearly calm, but a long swell ran from the west and made her roll. They might go at any moment. We looked at them with apprehension. One could not foresee which way they would fall.

"Then we retreated aft and looked about us. The deck was a tangle of planks on edge, of planks on end, of splinter, of ruined woodwork. The masts rose from that chaos like big trees above a matted undergrowth. The interstices of that mass of wreckage were full of something whitish, sluggish, stirring—of something that was like a greasy fog. The smoke of the invisible fire was coming up again, was trailing, like a poisonous thick mist in some valley choked with dead wood. Already lazy wisps were beginning to curl upwards amongst the mass of splinters. Here and there a piece of timber, stuck upright, resembled a post. Half of a fife rail had been shot through the foresail, and the sky made a patch of glorious blue in the ignobly soiled canvas. A portion of several boards holding together had fallen across the rail, and one end protruded overboard, like a gangway leading upon nothing, like a gangway leading over the deep sea, leading to death—as if inviting us to walk the plank at once and be done with our ridiculous troubles. And still the air, the sky—a ghost, something invisible was hailing the ship.

"Someone had the sense to look over, and there was the helmsman, who had impulsively jumped overboard, anxious to come back. He yelled and swam lustily like a merman, keeping up with the ship. We threw him a rope, and presently he stood amongst us streaming with water and very crestfallen. The captain had surrendered the wheel, and apart, elbow on rail and chin in hand, gazed at the sea wistfully. We asked ourselves, What next? I thought, Now, this is something like. This is great. I wonder what will happen. O youth!

"Suddenly Mahon sighted a steamer far astern. Captain Beard said, 'We may do something with her yet.' We hoisted two flags, which said in the international language of the sea, 'On fire. Want immediate assistance.' The steamer grew bigger rapidly, and by and by spoke with two flags on her foremast, 'I am coming to your assistance.'

"In half an hour she was abreast, to windward, within hail, and rolling slightly, with her engines stopped. We lost our composure, and yelled all together with excitement, 'We've been blown up.' A man in a white helmet, on the bridge, cried, 'Yes! All right! all right!' and he nodded his head, and smiled, and made soothing motions with his hand as though at a lot of frightened children. One of the boats dropped in the water, and walked towards us upon the sea with her long oars. Four Calashes pulled a swinging stroke. This was my first sight of Malay seamen. I've known them since, but what struck me then was their unconcern: they came alongside, and even the bowman standing up and holding to our main chains with the boathook did not deign to lift his head for a glance. I thought people who had been blown up deserved more attention.

"A little man, dry like a chip and agile like a monkey, clambered up. It was the mate of the steamer. He gave one look, and cried, 'O boys—you had better quit!'

"We were silent. He talked apart with the captain for a time—seemed to argue with him. Then they went away together to the steamer.

"When our skipper came back we learned that the steamer was the *Somerville*, Captain Nash, from West Australia to Singapore via Batavia with mails, and that the agreement was she would tow us to Anjer or Batavia, if possible, where we could extinguish the fire by scuttling, and then proceed on our voyage—to Bangkok! The old man seemed excited. 'We will do it yet,' he said to Mahon, fiercely. He shook his fist at the sky. Nobody else said a word.

"At noon the steamer began to tow. She went ahead slim and high, and what was left of the *Judea* followed at the end of seventy fathom of towrope—followed her swiftly like a cloud of smoke with mast-heads protruding above. We went aloft to furl the sails. We coughed on the yards, and were careful about the bunts. Do you see the lot of us there, putting a neat furl on the sails of that ship doomed to arrive nowhere? There was not a man who didn't think that at any moment the masts would topple over. From aloft we could not see the ship for smoke, and they worked carefully, passing the gaskets with even turns. 'Harbor furl—aloft there!' cried Mahon from below.

"You understand this? I don't think one of those chaps expected to get down in the usual way. When we did I heard them saying to each other, 'Well, I thought we would come down overboard, in a lump—sticks and all—blame me if I didn't.' 'That's what I was thinking to myself,' would answer wearily another battered and bandaged scare-crow. And, mind, these were men without the drilled-in habit of obe-dience. To an onlooker they would be a lot of profane scallywags without a redeeming point. What made them do it—what made them obey me when I, thinking consciously how fine it was, made them drop the bunt of the foresail twice to try and do it better? What? They had no professional reputation—no examples, no praise. It wasn't a sense of duty; they all knew well enough how to shirk, and laze, and dodge—when they had a mind to it—and mostly they had. Was it the two pounds ten a month that sent them there? They didn't think their pay half good enough. No; it was something in them, something inborn and subtle and everlasting. I don't say positively that the crew of a French or German merchantman wouldn't have done it, but I doubt whether it would have been done in the same way. There was a completeness in it, something solid like a principle, and masterful like an instinct—a disclosure of something secret—of that hidden something, that gift of good or evil that makes racial difference, that shapes the fate of nations.

"It was that night at ten that, for the first time since we had been fighting it, we saw the fire. The speed of the towing had fanned the smoldering destruction. A blue gleam appeared forward, shining below the wreck of the deck. It wavered in patches, it seemed to stir and creep like the light of a glowworm. I saw it first, and told Mahon. 'Then the game's up,' he said. 'We had better stop this towing, or she will burst out suddenly fore and aft before we can clear out.' We set up a yell; rang bells to attract their attention; they towed on. At last Mahon and I had to crawl forward and cut the rope with an axe. There was no time to cast off the lashings. Red tongues could be seen licking the wilderness of splinters under our feet as we made our way back to the poop.

"Of course they very soon found out in the steamer that the rope was gone. She gave a loud blast of her whistle, her lights were seen sweeping in a wide circle, she came up ranging close alongside, and stopped. We were all in a tight group on the poop looking at her. Every man had saved a little bundle or a bag. Suddenly a conical flame with a twisted top shot up forward and threw upon the black sea a circle of light, with the two vessels side by side and heaving gently in its center. Captain Beard had been sitting on the gratings still and mute for hours, but now he rose slowly and advanced in front of us, to mizzenshrouds. Captain Nash hailed: 'Come along! Look sharp. I have mailbags on board. I will take you and your boats to Singapore.'

" 'Thank you!' said our skipper. 'We must see the last of the ship.'

" 'I can't stand by any longer,' shouted the other. 'Mails—you know.'

" 'Ay! ay! We are all right.'

" 'Very well! I'll report you in Singapore. . . . Good-by!'

"He waved his hand. Our men dropped their bundles quietly. The steamer moved ahead, and passing out of the circle of light, vanished at once from our sight, dazzled by the fire which burned fiercely. And then I knew that I would see the East first as commander of a small boat. I thought it fine; and the fidelity to the old ship was fine. We should see the last of her. Oh, the glamor of youth! Oh, the fire of it, more dazzling than the flames of the burning ship, throwing a magic light on the wide earth, leaping audaciously to the sky, presently to be quenched by time, more cruel, more pitiless, more bitter than the sea—and like the flames of the burning ship surrounded by an impenetrable night.

"The old man warned us in his gentle and inflexible way that it was part of our duty to save for the underwriters as much as we could of the ship's gear. Accordingly we went to work aft, while she blazed forward to give us plenty of light. We lugged out a lot of rubbish. What didn't we save? An old barometer fixed with an absurd quantity of screws nearly cost me my life: a sudden rush of smoke came upon me, and I just got away in time. There were various stores, bolts of canvas, coils of rope; the poop looked like a marine bazaar, and the boats were lumbered to the gunwales. One would have thought the old man wanted to take as much as he could of his first command with him. He was very, very quiet, but off his balance evidently. Would you believe it? He wanted to take a length of old stream-cable and a kedge anchor with him in the longboat. We said, 'Ay, ay, sir,' deferentially, and on the quiet let the things slip overboard. The heavy medicine chest went that way, two bags of green coffee, tins of paint—fancy, paint!—a whole lot of things. Then I was ordered with two hands into the boats to make a stowage and get them ready against the time it would be proper for us to leave the ship.

"We put everything straight, stepped the longboat's mast for our skipper, who was to take charge of her, and I was not sorry to sit down for a moment. My face felt raw, every limb ached as if broken, I was aware of all my ribs, and would have sworn to a twist in the backbone. The boats, fast astern, lay in a deep shadow, and all around I could see the circle of the sea lighted by the fire. A gigantic flame arose forward straight and clear. It flared fierce, with noises like a whirr of wings, with rumbles as of thunder. There were cracks, detonations, and from the cone of flame the sparks flew upwards, as man is born to trouble, to leaky ships, and to ships that burn.

"What bothered me was that the ship, lying broadside to the swell and to such wind as there was—a mere breath—the boats would not keep astern where they were safe, but persisted, in a pigheaded way boats have, in getting under the counter and then swinging along-side. They were knocking about dangerously and coming near the flame, while the ship rolled on them, and, of course, there was always the danger of the masts going over the side at any moment. I and my two boatkeepers kept them off as best we could, with oars and boathooks; but to be constantly at it became exasperating, since there was no reason why we should not leave at once. We could not see those on board, nor could we imagine what caused the delay. The boatkeepers were swearing feebly, and I had not only my share of the work but also had to keep at it two men who showed a con-stant inclination to lay themselves down and let things slide.

"At last I hailed, 'On deck there,' and someone looked over. 'We're ready here,' I said. The head disappeared, and very soon popped up again. 'The captain says, All right, sir, and to keep the boats well clear of the ship.'

"Half an hour passed. Suddenly there was frightful racket, rattle, clanking of chain, hiss of water, and millions of sparks flew up into the shivering column of smoke that stood leaning slightly above the ship. The catheads had burned away, and the two red-hot anchors had gone to the bottom, tearing out after them two hundred fathom of red-hot chain. The ship trembled, the mass of flame swayed as if ready to col-lapse, and the fore-topgallant mast fell. It darted down like an arrow of fire, shot under, and instantly leaping up within an oar's length of the boats, floated quietly, very black on the luminous sea. I hailed the deck again. After some time a man in an unexpectedly cheerful but also muffled tone, as though he had been trying to speak with his mouth shut, informed me, 'Coming directly, sir,' and vanished. For a long time I heard nothing but the whirr and roar of the fire. There were also whistling sounds. The boats jumped, tugged at the painters, ran at each other playfully, knocked their sides together, or, do what we would, swung in a bunch against the ship's side. I couldn't stand it any longer, and swarming up a rope, clambered aboard over the stern.

"It was as bright as day. Coming up like this, the sheet of fire facing me was a terrifying sight, and the heat seemed hardly bearable at first. On a settee cushion dragged out of the cabin Captain Beard, his legs drawn up and one arm under his head, slept with the light playing on him. Do you know what the rest were busy about? They were sitting on deck right aft, round an open case, eating bread and cheese and drinking bottled stout.

"On the background of flames twisting in fierce tongues above their heads they seemed at home like salamanders, and looked like a band of desperate pirates. The fire sparkled in the whites of their eyes, gleamed on patches of white skin seen through the torn shirts. Each had the marks as of a battle about him—bandaged heads, tied-up arms, a strip of dirty rag round a knee—and each man had a bottle between his legs and a chunk of cheese in his hand. Mahon got up. With his handsome and disreputable head, his hooked profile, his long white beard, and with an uncorked bottle in his hand, he resembled one of those reckless sea robbers of old making merry amidst violence and disaster. 'The last meal on board,' he explained solemnly. 'We had nothing to eat all day, and it was no use leaving all this.' He flourished the bottle and indicated the sleeping skipper. 'He said he couldn't swallow anything, so I got him to lie down,' he went on; and as I stared, 'I don't know whether you are aware, young fellow, the man had no sleep to speak of for days—and there will be dam' little sleep in the boats.' 'There will be no boats by and by if you fool about much longer,' I said, indignantly. I walked up to the skipper and shook him by the shoulder. At last he opened his eyes, but did not move. 'Time to leave her, sir,' I said quietly.

"He got up painfully, looked at the flames, at the sea sparkling round the ship, and black, black as ink farther away; he looked at the stars shining dim through a thin veil of smoke in a sky black, black as Erebus.

" 'Youngest first,' he said.

"And the ordinary seaman, wiping his mouth with the back of his hand, got up, clambered over the taffrail and vanished. Others followed. One, on the point of going over, stopped short to drain his bottle, and with a great swing of his arm flung it at the fire. 'Take this!' he cried.

"The skipper lingered disconsolately, and we left him to commune alone for a while with his first command. Then I went up again and brought him away at last. It was time. The ironwork on the poop was hot to the touch.

"Then the painter of the longboat was cut, and the three boats, tied together, drifted clear of the ship. It was just sixteen hours after the explosion when we abandoned her. Mahon had charge of the second boat, and I had the smallest—the fourteen-foot thing. The longboat would have taken the lot of us; but the skipper said we must save as much property as we could—for the underwriters—and so I got my first command. I had two men with me, a bag of biscuits, a few tins of meat, and a breaker of water. I was ordered to keep close to the longboat, that in case of bad weather we might be taken into her.

"And do you know what I thought? I thought I would part company as soon as I could. I wanted to have my first command all to myself. I wasn't going to sail in a squadron if there were a chance for independent cruising. I would make land by myself. I would beat the other boats. Youth! All youth! The silly, charming, beautiful youth.

"But we did not make a start at once. We must see the last of the ship. And so the boats drifted about that night, heaving and setting on the swell. The men dozed, waked, sighed, groaned. I looked at the burning ship.

"Between the darkness of earth and heaven she was burning fiercely upon a disc of purple sea shot by the blood-red play of gleams; upon a disc of water glittering and sinister. A high, clear flame, an immense and lonely flame, ascended from the ocean, and from its summit the black smoke poured continuously at the sky. She burned furiously; mournful and imposing like a funeral pile kindled in the night, surrounded by the sea, watched over by the stars. A magnificent death had come like a grace, like a gift, like a reward to that old ship at the end of her laborious day. The surrender of her weary ghost to the keeper of stars and sea was stirring like the sight of a glorious triumph. The masts fell just before daybreak, and for a moment there was a burst and turmoil of sparks that seemed to fill with flying fire the night patient and watchful, the vast night lying silent upon the sea. At daylight she was only a charred shell, floating still under a cloud of smoke and bearing a glowing mass of coal within.

"Then the oars were got out, and the boats forming in a line moved round her remains as if in procession—the longboat leading. As we pulled across her stern a slim dart of fire shot out viciously at us, and suddenly she went down, head first, in a great hiss of steam. The unconsumed stern was the last to sink; but the paint had gone, had cracked, had peeled off, and there were no letters, there was no word, no stubborn device that was like her soul, to flash at the rising sun her creed and her name.

"We made our way north. A breeze sprang up, and about noon all the boats came together for the last time. I had no mast or sail in mine, but I made a mast out of a spare oar and hoisted a boat-awning for a sail, with a boathook for a yard. She was certainly over-masted, but I had the satisfaction of knowing that with the wind aft I could beat the other two. I had to wait for them. Then we all had a look at the captain's chart, and, after a sociable meal of hard bread and water, got our last instructions. These were simple: steer north, and keep together as much as possible. 'Be careful with that jury-rig, Marlow,' said the captain; and Mahon, as I sailed proudly past his boat, wrinkled his curved nose and hailed, 'You will sail that ship of yours under water, if you don't look out, young fellow.' He was a malicious old man—and may the deep sea where he sleeps now rock him gently, rock him tenderly to the end of time!

"Before sunset a thick rain-squall passed over the two boats, which were far astern, and that was the last I saw of them for a time. Next day I sat steering my cockle-shell—my first command—with nothing but water and sky round me. I did sight in the afternoon the upper sails of a ship far away, but said nothing, and my men did not notice her. You see I was afraid she might be homeward bound, and I had no mind to turn back from the portals of the East. I was steering for Java—another blessed name—like Bangkok, you know. I steered many days.

"I need not tell you what it is to be knocking about in an open boat. I remember nights and days of calm, when we pulled, we pulled, and the boat seemed to stand still, as if bewitched within the circle of the sea horizon. I remember the heat, the deluge of rain-squalls that kept us baling for dear life (but filled our water cask), and I remember sixteen hours on end with a mouth dry as a cinder and a steering oar over the stern to keep my first command head on to a breaking sea. I did not know how good a man I was till then. I remember the drawn faces, the dejected figures of my two men, and I remember my youth and the feeling that will never come back any more—the feeling that I could last forever, outlast the sea, the earth, and all men; the deceitful feeling that lures us on to joys, to perils, to love, to vain effort—to death; the triumphant conviction of strength, the heat of life in the handful of dust, the glow in the heart that with every year grows dim, grows cold, grows small, and expires—and expires, too soon, too soon—before life itself.

"And this is how I see the East. I have seen its secret places and have looked into its very soul; but now I see it always from a small boat, a high outline of mountains, blue and afar in the morning; like faint mist at noon; a jagged wall of purple at sunset. I have the feel of the oar in my hand, the vision of a scorching blue sea in my eyes. And I see a bay, a wide bay, smooth as glass and polished like ice, shimmering in the dark. A red light burns far off upon the gloom of the land, and the night is soft and warm. We drag at the oars with aching arms, and suddenly a puff of wind, a puff faint and tepid and laden with strange odors of blossoms, of aromatic wood, comes out of the still night—the first sigh of the East on my face. That I can never forget. It was impalpable and enslaving, like a charm, like a whispered promise of mysterious delight.

"We had been pulling this finishing spell for eleven hours. Two pulled, and he whose turn it was to rest sat at the tiller. We had made out the red light in that bay and steered for it, guessing it must mark some small coasting port. We passed two vessels, outlandish and high-sterned, sleeping at anchor, and, approaching the light, now very dim, ran the boat's nose against the end of a jutting wharf. We were blind with fatigue. My men dropped the oars and fell off the thwarts as if dead. I made fast to a pile. A current rippled softly. The scented obscurity of the shore was grouped into vast masses, a density of colossal clumps of vegetation, probably—mute and fantastic shapes. And at their foot the semicircle of a beach gleamed faintly, like an illusion. There was not a light, not a stir, not a sound. The mysterious East faced me, perfumed like a flower, silent like death, dark like a grave.

"And I sat weary beyond expression, exulting like a conqueror, sleepless and entranced as if before a profound, a fateful enigma.

"A splashing of oars, a measured dip reverberating on the level of water, intensified by the silence of the shore into loud claps, made me jump up. A boat, a European boat, was coming in. I invoked the name of the dead; I hailed: 'Judea ahoy!' A thin shout answered.

"It was the captain. I had beaten the flagship by three hours, and I was glad to hear the old man's voice again, tremulous and tired. 'Is it you, Marlow?' 'Mind the end of that jetty, sir,' I cried.

"He approached cautiously, and brought up with the deep-sea lead line which we had saved—for the underwriters. I eased my painter and fell alongside. He sat, a broken figure at the stern, wet with dew, his hands clasped in his lap. His men were asleep already. 'I had a terrible time of it,' he murmured. 'Mahon is behind—not very far.' We conversed in whispers, in low whispers, as if afraid to wake up the land. Guns, thunder, earthquakes would not have awakened the men just then.

"Looking round as we talked, I saw away at sea a bright light traveling in the night. 'There's a steamer passing the bay,' I said. She was not passing, she was entering, and she even came close and anchored. 'I wish,' said the old man, 'you would find out whether she is English. Perhaps they could give us a passage somewhere.' He seemed nervously anxious. So by dint of punching and kicking I started one of my men into a state of somnambulism, and giving him an oar, took another and pulled towards the lights of the steamer.

"There was a murmur of voices in her, metallic hollow clangs of the engine room, footsteps on the deck. Her ports shone, round like dilated eyes. Shapes moved about, and there was a shadowy man high up on the bridge. He heard my oars.

"And then, before I could open my lips, the East spoke to me, but it was in a Western voice. A torrent of words was poured into the enigmatical, the fateful silence; outlandish, angry words, mixed with words and even whole sentences of good English, less strange but even more surprising. The voice swore and cursed violently; it riddled the solemn peace of the bay by a volley of abuse. It began by calling me Pig, and from that went crescendo into unmentionable adjectives—in English. The man up there raged aloud in two languages, and with a sincerity in his fury that almost convinced me I had, in some way, sinned against the harmony of the universe. I could hardly see him, but began to think he would work himself into a fit.

"Suddenly he ceased, and I could hear him snorting and blowing like a porpoise. I said:

" 'What steamer is this, pray?'

" 'Eh! What's this? And who are you?'

" 'Castaway crew of an English bark burnt at sea. We came here tonight. I am the second mate. The captain is in the longboat, and wishes to know if you would give us a passage somewhere.'

" 'Oh, my goodness! I say. . . . This is the *Celestial* from Singapore on her return trip. I'll arrange with your captain in the morning, . . . and, . . . I say, . . . did you hear me just now?'

" 'I should think the whole bay heard you.'

" 'I thought you were a shoreboat. Now, look here—this infernal lazy scoundrel of a caretaker has gone to sleep again—curse him. The light is out, and I nearly ran foul of the end of this damned jetty. This is the third time he plays me this trick. Now, I ask you, can anybody stand this kind of thing? It's enough to drive a man out of his mind.

I'll report him. . . . I'll get the Assistant Resident to give him the sack, by—! See—there's no light. It's out, isn't it? I take you to witness the light's out. There should be a light, you know. A red light on the—'

" 'There was a light,' I said mildly.

" 'But it's out, man! What's the use of talking like this? You can see for yourself it's out—don't you? If you had to take a valuable steamer along this Godforsaken coast you would want a light, too. I'll kick him from end to end of his miserable wharf. You'll see if I don't. I will—'

" 'So I may tell my captain you'll take us?' I broke in.

" 'Yes, I'll take you. Good night,' he said, brusquely.

"I pulled back, made fast again to the jetty, and then went to sleep at last. I had faced the silence of the East. I had heard some of its language. But when I opened my eyes again the silence was as complete as though it had never been broken. I was lying in a flood of light, and the sky had never looked so far, so high, before. I opened my eyes and lay without moving.

"And then I saw the men of the East—they were looking at me. The whole length of the jetty was full of people. I saw brown, bronze, yellow faces, the black eyes, the glitter, the color of an Eastern crowd. And all these beings stared without a murmur, without a sigh, without a movement. They stared down at the boats, at the sleeping men who at night had come to them from the sea. Nothing moved. The fronds of palms stood still against the sky. Not a branch stirred along the shore, and the brown roofs of hidden houses peeped through the green foliage, through the big leaves that hung shining and still like leaves forged of heavy metal. This was the East of the ancient navigators, so old, so mysterious, resplendent and somber, living and unchanged, full of danger and promise. And these were the men. I sat up suddenly. A wave of movement passed through the crowd from end to end, passed along the heads, swayed the bodies, ran along the jetty like a ripple on the water, like a breath of wind on a field—and all was still again. I see it now—the wide sweep of the bay, the glittering sands, the wealth of green infinite and varied, the sea blue like the sea of a dream, the crowd of attentive faces, the blaze of vivid color—the water reflecting it all, the curve of the shore, the jetty, the high-sterned outlandish craft floating still, and the three boats with the tired men from the West sleeping, unconscious of the land and the people and of the violence of sunshine. They slept thrown across the thwarts, curled on bottom-boards, in the careless attitudes of death. The head of the old skipper, leaning back in the stern of the longboat, had fallen on his breast, and he looked as though he would never wake. Farther out old Mahon's face was upturned to the sky, with the long white beard spread out on his breast, as though he had been shot where he sat at the tiller; and a man, all in a heap in the bows of the boat, slept with both arms embracing the stemhead and with his cheek laid on the gunwhale. The East looked at them without a sound.

"I have known its fascination since; I have seen the mysterious shores, the still water, the lands of brown nations, where a stealthy Nemesis lies in wait, pursues, overtakes so many of the conquering race, who are proud of their wisdom, of their knowledge, of their strength. But for me all the East is contained in that vision of my youth. It is all in that moment when I opened my young eyes on it. I came upon it from a tussle with the sea—and I was young—and I saw it looking at me. And this is all that is left of it! Only a moment; a moment of strength, of romance, of glamor—of youth! . . . A flick of sunshine upon a strange shore, the time to remember, the time for a sigh, and—good-by!—Night—Good-by . . . !"

He drank.

"Ah! The good old time—the good old time. Youth and the sea. Glamor and the sea! The good, strong sea, the salt, bitter sea, that could whisper to you and roar at you and knock your breath out of you."

He drank again.

"By all that's wonderful it is the sea, I believe, the sea itself—or is it youth alone? Who can tell? But you here—you all had something out of life: money, love—whatever one gets on shore—and, tell me, wasn't that the best time, that time when we were young at sea; young and had nothing, on the sea that gives nothing, except hard knocks—and sometimes a chance to feel your strength—that only—that you all regret?"

And we all nodded at him: the man of finance, the man of accounts, the man of law, we all nodded at him over the polished table that like a still sheet of brown water reflected our faces, lined, wrinkled; our faces marked by toil, by deceptions, by success, by love; our weary eyes looking still, looking always, looking anxiously for something out of life, that while it is expected is already gone—has passed unseen, in a sigh, in a flash—together with the youth, with the strength, with the romance of illusions.

from Two Years Before the Mast
by Richard Henry Dana, Jr.

Richard Henry Dana, Jr.'s (1815–1882) father was one of New England's most distinguished literary figures. The younger Dana in 1834 signed on as a common seaman with the merchant ship Pilgrim, *bound for California. The ship on its return made a winter passage around Cape Horn.*

There began now to be a decided change in the appearance of things. The days became shorter and shorter; the sun running lower in its course each day, and giving less and less heat; and the nights so cold as to prevent our sleeping on deck; the Magellan Clouds in sight, of a clear night; the skies looking cold and angry; and, at times, a long, heavy, ugly sea, setting in from the southward, told us what we were coming to. Still, however, we had a fine, strong breeze, and kept on our way, under as much sail as our ship would bear. Toward the middle of the week, the wind hauled to the southward, which brought us upon a taught bow-line, made the ship meet, nearly head-on, the heavy swell which rolled from that direction; and there was something not at all encouraging in the manner in which she met it. Being so deep and heavy, she wanted the buoyancy which should have carried her over the seas, and she dropped heavily into them, the water washing over the decks; and every now and then, when an unusually large sea met her fairly upon the bows, she struck it with a sound as dead and heavy as that with which a sledge-hammer falls upon the pile, and took the whole of it in upon the forecastle, and rising, carried it aft in the scuppers, washing the rigging off the pins, and carrying along with it everything which was loose on deck. She had been acting in this way all of our forenoon watch below; as we could tell by the washing of the water over our heads, and the heavy breaking of the seas against her bows, (with a sound as though she were striking against a rock,) only the thickness of the plank from our heads, as we lay in our berths, which are directly against the bows. At eight bells, the watch was called, and we came on deck, one hand going aft to take the wheel, and another going to the galley to get the *grub* for dinner. I stood on the forecastle, looking at the seas, which were rolling high, as far as the eye could reach, their tops white with foam, and the body of them of a deep indigo blue, reflecting the bright rays of the sun. Our ship rose slowly over a few of the largest of them, until one immense fellow came rolling on, threatening to cover her, and which I was sailor enough to know, by "the feeling of her" under my feet, she would not rise over. I sprang upon the knight-heads, and seizing hold of the fore-stay with my hands, drew myself up upon it. My feet were just off the stanchion, when she struck fairly into the middle of the sea, and it washed her fore and aft, burying her in the water. As soon as she rose out of it, I looked aft, and everything forward of the main-mast, except the long-boat, which was griped and double-lashed down to the ring-bolts, was swept off clear. The galley, the pig-sty, the hen-coop, and a large sheep-pen which had been built upon the fore-hatch, were all gone, in the twinkling of an eye— leaving the deck as clean as a chin new-reaped—and not a stick left, to show where they had stood. In the scuppers lay the galley, bottom up, and a few boards floating about,—the wreck of the sheep-pen,— and half a dozen miserable sheep floating among them, wet through, and not a little frightened at the sudden change that had come upon them. As soon as the sea had washed by, all hands sprung up out of the forecastle to see what had become of the ship; and in a few moments the cook and Old Bill crawled out from under the galley, where they had been lying in the water, nearly smothered, with the galley over them. Fortunately, it rested against the bulwarks, or it would have broken some of their bones. When the water ran off, we picked the sheep up, and put them in the long-boat, got the galley back in its place, and set things a little to rights; but, had not our ship had uncommonly high bulwarks and rail, everything must have been washed overboard, not excepting Old Bill and the cook. Bill had been standing at the galley-door, with the kid of beef in his hand for the forecastle mess, when, away he went, kid, beef, and all. He held on to the kid till the last, like a good fellow, but the beef was gone, and when the water had run off, we saw it lying high and dry, like a rock at low tide—nothing could hurt *that*. We took the loss of our beef very easily, consoling ourselves with the recollection that the cabin had more to lose than we; and chuckled not a little at seeing the remains of the chicken-pie and pancakes floating in the scuppers. "This will never do!" was what some said, and every one felt. Here we were, not yet within a thousand miles of the latitude of Cape Horn, and our decks swept by a sea, not one half so high as we must expect to find there. Some blamed the captain for loading his ship so deep, when he knew what he must expect; while others said that the wind was always south-west, off the Cape, in the winter; and that, running before it, we should not mind the seas so much. When we got down into the fore-castle, Old Bill, who was somewhat of a croaker,—having met with a great many accidents at sea—said that if that was the way she was going to act, we might as well make our wills, and balance the books at once, and put on a clean shirt. " 'Vast there, you bloody old owl! you're always hanging out blue lights! You're frightened by the ducking you got in the scuppers, and can't take a joke! What's the use in being always on the look-out for Davy Jones?" "Stand by!" says another, "and we'll get an afternoon watch below, by this scrape;" but in this they were disappointed, for at two bells, all hands were called and set to work, getting lashings upon everything on deck; and the captain talked of sending down the long top-gallant masts; but, as the sea went down toward night, and the wind hauled abeam, we left them standing, and set the studding-sails.

The next day, all hands were turned-to upon unbending the old sails, and getting up the new ones; for a ship, unlike people on shore, puts on her best suit in bad weather. The old sails were sent down, and three new top-sails, and new fore and main courses, jib, and fore top-mast stay-sail, which were made on the coast, and never had been used, were bent, with a complete set of new earings, robands and reef-points; and reef-tackles were rove to the courses, and spilling-lines to the top-sails. These, with new braces and clewlines, fore and aft, gave us a good suit of running rigging.

The wind continued westerly, and the weather and sea less rough since the day on which we shipped the heavy sea, and we were making great progress under studding-sails, with our light sails all set, keeping a little to the eastward of south; for the captain, depending upon westerly winds off the Cape, had kept so far to the westward, that, though we were within about five hundred miles of the latitude of Cape Horn, we were nearly seventeen hundred miles to the westward of it. Through the rest of the week, we continued on with a fair wind, gradually, as we got more to the southward, keeping a more easterly course, and bringing the wind on our larboard quarter, until—

Sunday, June 26th; when, having a fine, clear day, the captain got a lunar observation, as well as his meridian altitude, which made us in lat. 47° 50′ S., long. 113° 49′ W.; Cape Horn bearing, according to my calculation, E. S. E. 1/2 E., and distant eighteen hundred miles.

Monday, June 27th. During the first part of this day, the wind continued fair, and, as we were going before it, it did not feel very cold, so that we kept at work on deck, in our common clothes and round jackets. Our watch had an afternoon watch below, for the first time since leaving San Diego, and having inquired of the third mate what the latitude was at noon, and made our usual guesses as to the time she would need, to be up with the Horn, we turned-in, for a nap. We were sleeping away "at the rate of knots," when three knocks on the scuttle, and "All hands, ahoy!" started us from our berths. What could be the matter? It did not appear to be blowing hard, and looking up through the scuttle, we could see that it was a clear day, overhead; yet the watch were taking in sail. We thought there must be a sail in sight, and that we were about to heave-to and speak her; and were just congratulating ourselves upon it—for we had seen neither sail nor land since we left port—when we heard the mate's voice on deck, (he turned-in "all standing," and was always on deck the moment he was called,) singing out to the men who were taking in the studding-sails, and asking where his watch were. We did not wait for a second call, but tumbled up the ladder; and there, on the starboard bow, was a bank of mist, covering sea and sky, and driving directly for us. I had seen the same before, in my passage round in the Pilgrim, and knew what it meant, and that there was no time to be lost. We had nothing on but thin clothes, yet there was not a moment to spare, and at it we went.

The boys of the other watch were in the tops, taking in the top-gallant studding-sails, and the lower and top-mast studding-sails were coming down by the run. It was nothing but "haul down and clew up," until we got all the studding-sails in, and the royals, flying-jib, and mizen top-gallant sail furled, and the ship kept off a little, to take the squall. The fore and main top-gallant sails were still on her, for the "old man" did not mean to be frightened in broad daylight, and was determined to carry sail till the last minute. We all stood waiting for its coming, when the first blast showed us that it was not to be trifled with. Rain, sleet, snow, and wind, enough to take our breath from us, and make the toughest turn his back to windward! The ship lay nearly over upon her beam-ends; the spars and rigging snapped and cracked; and her top-gallant masts bent like whip-sticks. "Clew up the fore and main top-gallant sails!" shouted the captain, and all hands sprang to the clewlines. The decks were standing nearly at an angle of forty-five degrees, and the ship going like a mad steed through the water, the whole forward part of her in a smother of foam. The halyards were let go and the yard clewed down, and the sheets started, and in a few minutes the sails smothered and kept in by clewlines and buntlines.—"Furl 'em, sir?" asked the mate.—"Let go the top-sail halyards, fore and aft!" shouted the captain, in answer, at the top of his voice. Down came the top-sail yards, the reef-tackles were manned and hauled out, and we climbed up to windward, and sprang into the weather rigging. The violence of the wind, and the hail and sleet, driving nearly horizontally across the ocean, seemed actually to pin us down to the rigging. It was hard work making head against them. One after another, we got out upon the yards. And here we had work to do; for our new sails, which had hardly been bent long enough to get the starch out of them, were as stiff as boards, and the new earings and reef-points, stiffened with the sleet, knotted like pieces of iron wire. Having only our round jackets and straw hats on, we were soon wet through, and it was every moment growing colder. Our hands were soon stiffened and numbed, which, added to the stiffness of everything else, kept us a good while on the yard. After we had got the sail hauled upon the yard, we had to wait a long time for the weather earing to be passed; but there was no fault to be found, for French John was at the earing, and a better sailor never laid out on a yard; so we leaned over the yard, and beat our hands upon the sail, to keep them from freezing. At length the word came—"Haul out to leeward,"—and we seized the reef-points and hauled the band taught for the lee earing. "Taught band—Knot away;" and we got the first reef fast, and were just going to lay down, when—"Two reefs—two reefs!" shouted the mate, and we had a second reef to take, in the same way. When this was fast, we laid down on deck, manned the halyards to leeward, nearly up to our knees in water, set the top-sail, and then laid aloft on the main top-sail yard, and reefed that sail in the same manner; for, as I have before stated, we were a good deal reduced in numbers, and, to make it worse, the carpenter, only two days before, cut his leg with an axe, so that he could not go aloft. This weakened us so that we could not well manage more than one top-sail at a time, in such weather as this, and, of course, our labor was doubled. From the main topsail yard, we went upon the main yard, and took a reef in the main-sail. No sooner had we got on deck, than—"Lay aloft there, mizzen-top-men, and close-reef the mizzen top-sail!" This called me; and being nearest to the rigging, I got first aloft, and out to the weather earing. English Ben was on the yard just after me, and took the lee earing, and the rest of our gang were soon on the yard, and began to fist the sail, when the mate considerately sent up the cook and steward, to help us. I could now account for the long time it took to pass the other earings, for, to do my best, with a strong hand to help me at the dog's ear, I could not get it passed until I heard them beginning to complain in the bunt. One reef after another we took in, until the sail was close-reefed, when we went down and hoisted away at the halyards. In the mean time, the jib had been furled and the stay-sail set, and the ship, under her reduced sail, had got more upright and was under management; but the two top-gallant sails were still hanging in the buntlines, and slatting and jerking as though they would take the masts out of her. We gave a look aloft, and knew that our work was not done yet; and sure enough, no sooner did the mate see that we were on deck, than—"Lay aloft there, four of you, and furl the top-gallant sails!" This called me again, and two of us went aloft, up the fore rigging, and two more up the main, upon the top-gallant yards. The shrouds were now iced over, the sleet having formed a crust or cake round all the standing rigging, and on the weather side of the masts and yards. When we got upon the yard, my hands were so numb that I could not have cast off the knot of the gasket to have saved my life. We both lay over the yard for a few seconds, beating our hands upon the sail, until we started the blood into our fingers' ends, and at the next moment our hands were in a burning heat. My companion on the yard was a lad, who came out in the ship a weak, puny boy, from one of the Boston schools,—"no larger than a sprit-sail sheet knot," nor "heavier than a paper of lampblack," and "not strong enough to haul a shad off a gridiron," but who, was now "as long as a spare top-mast, strong enough to knock down an ox, and hearty enough to eat him." We fisted the sail together, and after six or eight minutes of hard hauling and pulling and beating down the sail, which was as stiff as sheet iron, we managed to get it furled; and snugly furled it must be, for we knew the mate well enough to be certain that if it got adrift again, we should be called up from our watch below, at any hour of the night, to furl it.

I had been on the look-out for a moment to jump below and clap on a thick jacket and south-wester; but when we got on deck we found that eight bells had been struck, and the other watch gone below, so that there were two hours of dog watch for us, and a plenty of work to do. It had now set in for a steady gale from the south-west; but we were not yet far enough to the southward to make a fair wind of it, for we must give Terra del Fuego a wide berth. The decks were covered with snow, and there was a constant driving of sleet. In fact, Cape Horn had set in with good earnest. In the midst of all this, and before it became dark, we had all the studding-sails to make up and stow away, and then to lay aloft and rig in all the booms, fore and aft, and coil away the tacks, sheets, and halyards. This was pretty tough work for four or five hands, in the face of a gale which almost took us off the yards, and with ropes so stiff with ice that it was almost impossible to bend them. I was nearly half an hour out on the end of the fore yard, trying to coil away and stop down the top-mast studding-sail tack and lower halyards. It was after dark when we got through, and we were not a little pleased to hear four bells struck, which sent us below for two hours, and gave us each a pot of hot tea with our cold beef and bread, and, what was better yet, a suit of thick, dry clothing, fitted for the weather, in place of our thin clothes, which were wet through and now frozen stiff.

This sudden turn, for which we were so little prepared, was as unacceptable to me as to any of the rest; for I had been troubled for several days with a slight tooth-ache, and this cold weather, and wetting and freezing, were not the best things in the world for it. I soon found that it was getting strong hold, and running over all parts of my face; and before the watch was out I went aft to the mate, who had charge of the medicine-chest, to get something for it. But the chest showed like the end of a long voyage, for there was nothing that would answer but a few drops of laudanum, which must be saved for any emergency; so I had only to bear the pain as well as I could.

When we went on deck at eight bells, it had stopped snowing, and there were a few stars out, but the clouds were still black, and it was blowing a steady gale. Just before midnight, I went aloft and sent down the mizen royal yard, and had the good luck to do it to the satisfaction of the mate, who said it was done "out of hand and ship-shape." The next four hours below were but little relief to me, for I lay awake in my berth, the whole time, from the pain in my face, and heard every bell strike, and, at four o'clock, turned out with the watch, feeling little spirit for the hard duties of the day. Bad weather and hard work at sea can be borne up against very well, if one only has spirit and health; but there is nothing brings a man down, at such a time, like bodily pain and want of sleep. There was, however, too much to do to allow time to think; for the gale of yesterday, and the heavy seas we met with a few days before, while we had yet ten degrees more southing to make, had convinced the captain that we had something before us which was not to be trifled with, and orders were given to send down the long top-gallant masts. The top-gallant and royal yards were accordingly struck, the flying jib-boom rigged in, and the top-gallant masts sent down on deck, and all lashed together by the side of the long-boat. The rigging was then sent down and coiled away below, and everything made snug aloft. There was not a sailor in the ship who was not rejoiced to see these sticks come down; for, so long as the yards were aloft, on the least sign of a lull, the top-gallant sails were loosed, and then we had to furl them again in a snow-squall, and *shin* up and down single ropes caked with ice, and send royal yards down in the teeth of a gale coming right from the south pole. It was an interesting sight, too, to see our noble ship, dismantled of all her top-hamper of long tapering masts and yards, and boom pointed with spear-head, which ornamented her in port; and all that canvass, which a few days before had covered her like a cloud, from the truck to the water's edge, spreading far out beyond her hull on either side, now gone; and she, stripped, like a wrestler for the fight. It corresponded, too, with the desolate character of her situation;—alone, as she was, battling with storms, wind, and ice, at this extremity of the globe, and in almost constant night.

Friday, July 1st. We were now nearly up to the latitude of Cape Horn, and having over forty degrees of easting to make, we squared away the yards before a strong westerly gale, shook a reef out of the fore top-sail, and stood on our way, east-by-south, with the prospect of being up with the Cape in a week or ten days. As for myself, I had had no sleep for forty-eight hours; and the want of rest, together with constant wet and cold, had increased the swelling, so that my face was nearly as large as two, and I found it impossible to get my mouth open wide enough to eat. In this state, the steward applied to the captain for some rice to boil for me, but he only got a—"No! d—you! Tell him to eat salt junk and hard bread, like the rest of them." For this, of course, I was much obliged to him, and in truth it was just what I expected. However, I did not starve, for the mate, who was a man as well as a sailor, and had always been a good friend to me, smuggled a pan of rice into the galley, and told the cook to boil it for me, and not let the "old man" see it. Had it been fine weather, or in port, I should have gone below and lain by until my face got well; but in such weather as this, and short-handed as we were, it was not for me to desert my post; so I kept on deck, and stood my watch and did my duty as well as I could.

Saturday, July 2d. This day the sun rose fair, but it ran too low in the heavens to give any heat, or thaw out our sails and rigging; yet the sight of it was pleasant; and we had a steady "reef-topsail breeze" from the westward. The atmosphere, which had previously been clear and cold, for the last few hours grew damp, and had a disagreeable, wet chilliness in it; and the man who came from the wheel said he heard the captain tell "the passenger" that the thermometer had fallen several degrees since morning, which he could not account for in any other way than by supposing that there must be ice near us; though such a thing had never been heard of in this latitude, at this season of the year. At twelve o'clock we went below, and had just got through dinner, when the cook put his head down the scuttle and told us to come on deck and see the finest sight that we had ever seen. "Where away, cook?" asked the first man who was up. "On the larboard bow." And there lay, floating in the ocean, several miles off, an immense, irregular mass, its top and points covered with snow, and its centre of a deep indigo color. This was an iceberg, and of the largest size, as one of our men said who had been in the Northern ocean. As far as the eye could reach, the sea in every direction was of a deep blue color, the waves running high and fresh, and sparkling in the light, and in the midst lay this immense mountain-island, its cavities and valleys thrown into deep shade, and its points and pinnacles glittering in the sun. All hands were soon on deck, looking at it, and admiring in various ways its beauty and grandeur. But no description can give any idea of the strangeness, splendor, and, really, the sublimity, of the sight. Its great size;—for it must have been from two to three miles in circumference, and several hundred feet in height;—its slow motion, as its base rose and sank in the water, and its high points nodded against the clouds; the dashing of the waves upon it, which, breaking high with foam, lined its base with a white crust; and the thundering sound of the cracking of the mass, and the breaking and tumbling down of huge pieces; together with its nearness and approach, which added a slight element of fear,—all combined to give to it the character of true sublimity. The main body of the mass was, as I have said, of an indigo color, its base crusted with frozen foam; and as it grew thin and transparent toward the edges and top, its color shaded off from a deep blue to the whiteness of snow. It seemed to be drifting slowly toward the north, so that we kept away and avoided it. It was in sight all afternoon; and when we got to leeward of it, the wind died away, so that we lay-to quite near it for a greater part of the night. Unfortunately, there was no moon, but it was a clear night, and we could plainly mark the long, regular heaving of the stupendous mass, as its edges moved slowly against the stars. Several times in our watch loud cracks were heard, which sounded as though they must have run through the whole length of the iceberg, and several pieces fell down with a thundering crash, plunging heavily into the sea. Toward morning, a strong breeze sprang up, and we filled away, and left it astern, and at daylight it was out of sight. The next day, which was

Sunday, July 3d, the breeze continued strong, the air exceedingly chilly, and the thermometer low. In the course of the day we saw several icebergs, of different sizes, but none so near as the one which we saw the day before. Some of them, as well as we could judge, at the distance at which we were, must have been as large as that, if not larger. At noon we were in latitude 55° 12' south, and supposed longitude 89° 5' west. Toward night the wind hauled to the southward, and headed us off our course a little, and blew a tremendous gale; but this we did not mind, as there was no rain nor snow, and we were already under close sail.

Monday, July 4th. This was "independent day" in Boston. What firing of guns, and ringing of bells, and rejoicings of all sorts, in every part of our country! The ladies (who have not gone down to Nahant, for a breath of cool air, and sight of the ocean) walking the streets with parasols over their heads, and the dandies in their white pantaloons and silk stockings! What quantities of ice-cream have been eaten, and what quantities of ice brought into the city from a distance, and sold out by the lump and the pound! The smallest of the islands which we saw to-day would have made the fortune of poor Jack, if he had had it in Boston; and I dare say he would have had no objection to being there with it. This, to be sure, was no place to keep the fourth of July. To keep ourselves warm, and the ship out of the ice, was as much as we could do. Yet no one forgot the day; and many were the wishes, and conjectures, and comparisons, both serious and ludicrous, which were made among all hands. The sun shone bright as long as it was up, only that a scud of black clouds was ever and anon driving across it. At noon we were in lat. 54° 27' S., and long. 85° 5' W., having made a good deal of easting, but having lost in our latitude by the heading of the wind. Between daylight and dark—that is, between nine o'clock and three—we saw thirty-four ice islands, of various sizes; some no bigger than the hull of our vessel, and others apparently nearly as large as the one that we first saw; though, as we went on, the islands became smaller and more numerous; and, at sundown of this day, a man at the mast-head saw large fields of floating ice, called "field-ice," at the south-east. This kind of ice is much more dangerous than the large islands, for those can be seen at a distance, and kept away from; but the field-ice, floating in great quantities, and covering the ocean for miles and miles, in pieces of every size—large, flat, and broken cakes, with here and there an island rising twenty and thirty feet, and as large as the ship's hull;— this, it is very difficult to sheer clear of. A constant look-out was necessary; for any of these pieces, coming with the heave of the sea, were large enough to have knocked a hole in the ship, and that would have been the end of us; for no boat (even if we could have got one out) could have lived in such a sea; and no man could have lived in a boat in such weather. To make our condition still worse, the wind came out due east, just after sundown, and it blew a gale dead ahead, with hail and sleet, and a thick fog, so that we could not see half the length of the ship. Our chief reliance, the prevailing westerly gales, was thus cut off; and here we were, nearly seven hundred miles to the westward of the Cape, with a gale dead from the eastward, and the weather so thick that we could not see the ice with which we were surrounded, until it was directly under our bows. At four p.m. (it was then quite dark) all hands were called, and sent aloft in a violent squall of hail and rain, to take in sail. We had now all got on our "Cape Horn rig"—thick boots, south-westers coming down over our neck and ears, thick trowsers and jackets, and some with oil-cloth suits over all. Mittens, too, we wore on deck, but it would not do to go aloft with them on, for it was impossible to work with them, and, being wet and stiff, they might let a man slip overboard, for all the hold he could get upon a rope; so, we were obliged to work with bare hands, which, as well as our faces, were often cut with the hail-stones, which fell thick and large. Our ship was now all cased with ice,—hull, spars, and standing rigging;— and the running rigging so stiff that we could hardly bend it so as to belay it, or, still worse, take a knot with it; and the sails nearly as stiff as sheet iron. One at a time, (for it was a long piece of work and required many hands,) we furled the courses, mizen top-sail, and fore top-mast stay-sail, and close-reefed the fore and main top-sails, and hove the ship to under the fore, with the main hauled up by the clewlines and buntlines, and ready to be sheeted home, if we found it necessary to make sail to get to windward of an island. A regular look-out was then set, and kept by each watch in turn, until the morning. It was a tedious and anxious night. It blew hard the whole time, and there was an almost constant driving of either rain, hail, or snow. In addition to this, it was "as thick as muck," and the ice was all about us. The captain was on deck nearly the whole night, and kept the cook in the galley, with a roaring fire, to make coffee for him, which he took every few hours, and once or twice gave a little to his officers; but not a drop of anything was there for the crew. The captain, who sleeps all the daytime, and comes and goes at night as he chooses, can have his brandy and water in the cabin, and his hot coffee at the galley; while Jack, who has to stand through everything, and work in wet and cold, can have nothing to wet his lips or warm his stomach. This was a "temperance ship," and, like too many such ships, the temperance was all in the forecastle. The sailor, who only takes his one glass as it is dealt out to him, is in danger of being drunk; while the captain, who has all under his hand, and can drink as much as he chooses, and upon whose self-possession and cool judgment the lives of all depend, may be trusted with any amount, to drink at his will. Sailors will never be convinced that rum is a dangerous thing, by taking it away from them, and giving it to the officers; nor that, that temperance is their friend, which takes from them what they have always had, and gives them nothing in the place of it. By seeing it allowed to their officers, they will not be convinced that it is taken from them for their good; and by receiving nothing in its place, they will not believe that it is done in kindness. On the contrary, many of them look upon the change as a new instrument of tyranny. Not that they prefer rum. I never knew a sailor, in my life, who would not prefer a pot of hot coffee or chocolate, in a cold night, to all the rum afloat. They all say that rum only warms them for a time; yet, if they can get nothing better, they will miss what they have lost. The momentary warmth and glow from drinking it; the break and change which is made in a long, dreary watch by the mere calling all hands aft and serving of it out; and the simply having some event to look forward to, and to talk about; give it an importance and a use which no one can appreciate who has not stood his watch before the mast. On my passage round Cape Horn before, the vessel that I was in was not under temperance articles, and grog was served out every middle and morning watch, and after every reefing of top-sails; and though I had never drank rum before, and never intend to again, I took my allowance then at the capstan, as the rest did, merely for the momentary warmth it gave the system, and the change in our feelings and aspect of our duties on the watch. At the same time, as I have stated, there was not a man on board who would not have pitched the rum to the dogs, (I have heard them say so, a dozen times) for a pot of coffee or chocolate; or even for our common beverage—"water bewitched, and tea begrudged," as it was.[*] The temperance reform is the best thing that ever was undertaken for the sailor; but when the grog is taken from him, he ought to have something in its place. As it is now, in most vessels, it is a mere saving to the owners; and this accounts for the sudden increase of temperance ships, which surprised even the best friends of the cause. If every merchant, when he struck grog from the list of the expenses of his ship, had been obliged to

[*] The proportions of the ingredients of the tea that was made for us, (and ours, as I have before stated, was a favorable specimen of American merchantmen) were, a pint of tea, and a pint and a half of molasses, to about three gallons of water. These are all boiled down together in the "coppers," and before serving it out, the mess is stirred up with a stick, so as to give each man his fair share of sweetening and tea-leaves. The tea for the cabin is, of course, made in the usual way, in a tea-pot, and drank with sugar.

substitute as much coffee, or chocolate, as would give each man a pot-full when he came off the top-sail yard, on a stormy night;—I fear Jack might have gone to ruin on the old road.*

But this is not doubling Cape Horn. Eight hours of the night, our watch was on deck, and during the whole of that time we kept a bright look-out: one man on each bow, another in the bunt of the fore yard, the third mate on the scuttle, one on each quarter, and a man always standing by the wheel. The chief mate was everywhere, and com-manded the ship when the captain was below. When a large piece of ice was seen in our way, or drifting near us, the word was passed along, and the ship's head turned one way and another; and sometimes the yards squared or braced up. There was little else to do than to look out; and we had the sharpest eyes in the ship on the forecastle. The only variety was the monotonous voice of the look-out forward—"Another island!"—"Ice ahead!"—"Ice on the lee bow!"—"Hard up the helm!"—"Keep her off a little!"—"Stead-y!"

In the mean time, the wet and cold had brought my face into such a state that I could neither eat nor sleep; and though I stood it out all night, yet, when it became light, I was in such a state, that all hands told me I must go below, and lie-by for a day or two, or I should be laid up for a long time, and perhaps have the lock-jaw. When the watch was changed I went into the steerage, and took off my hat and comforter, and showed my face to the mate, who told me to go below at once, and stay in my berth until the swelling went down, and gave the cook orders to make a poultice for me, and said he would speak to the captain.

---

* I do not wish these remarks, so far as they relate to the saving of expense in the outfit, to be applied to the owners of our ship, for she was supplied with an abundance of stores, of the best kind that are given to seamen; though the dispensing of them is necessarily left to the captain. Indeed, so high was the reputation of "the employ" among men and officers, for the character and outfit of their vessels, and for their liberality in conducting their voyages, that when it was known that they had a ship fitting out for a long voyage, and that hands were to be shipped at a certain time,—a half hour before the time, as one of the crew told me, numbers of sailors were steering down the wharf, hopping over the barrels, like flocks of sheep.

I went below and turned-in, covering myself over with blankets and jackets, and lay in my berth nearly twenty-four hours, half asleep and half awake, stupid, from the dull pain. I heard the watch called, and the men going up and down, and sometimes a noise on deck, and a cry of "ice," but I gave little attention to anything. At the end of twenty-four hours the pain went down, and I had a long sleep; which brought me back to my proper state, yet my face was so swollen and tender, that I was obliged to keep to my berth for two or three days longer. During the two days I had been below, the weather was much the same that it had been, head winds, and snow and rain; or, if the wind came fair, too foggy, and the ice too thick, to run. At the end of the third day the ice was very thick; a complete fog-bank covered the ship. It blew a tremendous gale from the eastward, with sleet and snow, and there was every promise of a dangerous and fatiguing night. At dark, the captain called all hands aft, and told them that not a man was to leave the deck that night; that the ship was in the greatest danger; any cake of ice might knock a hole in her, or she might run on an island and go to pieces. No one could tell whether she would be a ship the next morning. The look-outs were then set, and every man was put in his station. When I heard what was the state of things, I began to put on my clothes to stand it out with the rest of them, when the mate came below, and looking at my face, ordered me back to my berth, saying that if we went down, we should all go down together, but if I went on deck I might lay myself up for life. This was the first word I had heard from aft; for the captain had done nothing, nor inquired how I was, since I went below.

In obedience to the mate's orders, I went back to my berth; but a more miserable night I never wish to spend. I never felt the curse of sickness so keenly in my life. If I could only have been on deck with the rest, where something was to be done, and seen, and heard; where there were fellow-beings for companions in duty and danger—but to be cooped up alone in a black hole, in equal danger, but without the power to do, was the hardest trial. Several times, in the course of the night, I got up, determined to go on deck; but the silence which showed that there was nothing doing, and the knowledge that I might make myself seriously ill, for nothing, kept me back. It was not easy to sleep, lying, as I did, with my head directly against the bows, which might be dashed in by an island of ice, brought down by the very next sea that struck her. This was the only time I had been ill since I left Boston, and it was the worst time it could have happened. I felt almost willing to bear the plagues of Egypt for the rest of the voyage, if I could but be well and strong for that one night. Yet it was a dreadful night for those on deck. A watch of eighteen hours, with wet, and cold, and constant anxiety, nearly wore them out; and when they came below at nine o'clock for breakfast, they almost dropped asleep on their chests, and some of them were so stiff that they could with difficulty sit down. Not a drop of anything had been given them during the whole time, (though the captain, as on the night that I was on deck, had his coffee every four hours,) except that the mate stole a pot-full of coffee for two men to drink behind the galley, while he kept a look-out for the captain. Every man had his station, and was not allowed to leave it; and nothing happened to break the monotony of the night, except once setting the main top-sails to run clear of a large island to leeward, which they were drifting fast upon. Some of the boys got so sleepy and stupified, that they actually fell asleep at their posts; and the young third mate, whose station was the exposed one of standing on the fore scuttle, was so stiff, when he was relieved, that he could not bend his knees to get down. By a constant look-out, and a quick shifting of the helm, as the islands and pieces came in sight, the ship went clear of everything but a few small pieces, though daylight showed the ocean covered for miles. At daybreak it fell a dead calm, and with the sun, the fog cleared a little, and a breeze sprung up from the westward, which soon grew into a gale. We had now a fair wind, daylight, and comparatively clear weather; yet, to the surprise of every one, the ship continued hove-to. Why does not he run? What is the captain about? was asked by every one; and from questions, it soon grew into complaints and murmurings. When the daylight was so short, it was too bad to lose it, and a fair wind, too, which every one had been praying for. As hour followed hour, and the captain showed no sign of making sail, the crew became impatient, and there was a good deal of talking and consultation together, on the forecastle. They had been beaten out with the exposure and hardship, and impatient to get out of it, and this unaccountable delay was more than they could bear in quietness, in their excited and restless state. Some said that the captain was frightened,—completely cowed, by the dangers and difficulties that surrounded us, and was afraid to make sail; while others said that in his anxiety and suspense he had made a free use of brandy and opium, and was unfit for his duty. The carpenter, who was an intelligent man, and a thorough seaman, and had great influence with the crew, came down into the forecastle, and tried to induce the crew to go aft and ask the captain why he did not run, or request him, in the name of all hands, to make sail. This appeared to be a very reasonable request, and the crew agreed that if he did not make sail before noon, they would go aft. Noon came, and no sail was made. A consultation was held again, and it was proposed to take the ship from the captain and give the command of her to the mate, who had been heard to say that, if he could have his way, the ship would have been half the distance to the Cape before night,—ice or no ice. And so irritated and impatient had the crew become, that even this proposition, which was open mutiny, punishable with state prison, was entertained, and the carpenter went to his berth, leaving it tacitly understood that something serious would be done, if things remained as they were many hours longer. When the carpenter left, we talked it all over, and I gave my advice strongly against it. Another of the men, too, who had known something of the kind attempted in another ship by a crew who were dissatisfied with their captain, and which was followed with serious consequences, was opposed to it. Stimson, who soon came down, joined us, and we determined to have nothing to do with it. By these means, they were soon induced to give it up, for the present, though they said they would not lie where they were much longer without knowing the reason.

The affair remained in this state until four o'clock, when an order came forward for all hands to come aft upon the quarter-deck. In about ten minutes they came forward again, and the whole affair had been blown. The carpenter, very prematurely, and without any authority from the crew, had sounded the mate as to whether he would take command of the ship, and intimated an intention to displace the captain; and the mate, as in duty bound, had told the whole to the captain, who immediately sent for all hands aft. Instead of violent measures, or, at least, an outbreak of quarter-deck bravado, threats, and abuse, which they had every reason to expect, a sense of common danger and common suffering seemed to have tamed his spirit, and begotten something like a humane fellow-feeling; for he received the crew in a manner quiet, and even almost kind. He told them what he had heard, and said that he did not believe that they would try to do any such thing as was intimated; that they had always been good men,—obedient, and knew their duty, and he had no fault to find with them; and asked them what they had to complain of—said that no one could say that he was slow to carry sail, (which was true enough;) and that, as soon as he thought it was safe and proper, he should make sail. He added a few words about their duty in their present situation, and sent them forward, saying that he should take no further notice of the matter; but, at the same time, told the carpenter to recollect whose power he was in, and that if he heard another word from him he would have cause to remember him to the day of his death.

This language of the captain had a very good effect upon the crew, and they returned quietly to their duty.

For two days more the wind blew from the southward and eastward; or in the short intervals when it was fair, the ice was too thick to run; yet the weather was not so dreadfully bad, and the crew had watch and watch. I still remained in my berth, fast recovering, yet still not well enough to go safely on deck. And I should have been perfectly useless; for, from having eaten nothing for nearly a week, except a little rice which I forced into my mouth the last day or two, I was as weak as an infant. To be sick in a forecastle is miserable indeed. It is the worst part of a dog's life; especially in bad weather. The forecastle, shut up tight to keep out the water and cold air;—the watch either on deck, or asleep in their berths;—no one to speak to;—the pale light of the single lamp, swinging to and fro from the beam, so dim that one can scarcely see, much less read by it;—the water dropping from the beams and car- lines, and running down the sides; and the forecastle so wet, and dark, and cheerless, and so lumbered up with chests and wet clothes, that sitting up is worse than lying in the berth! These are some of the evils. Fortunately, I needed no help from any one, and no medicine; and if I had needed help, I don't know where I should have found it. Sailors are willing enough, but it is true, as is often said—No one ships for nurse on board a vessel. Our merchant ships are always under- manned, and if one man is lost by sickness, they cannot spare another to take care of him. A sailor is always presumed to be well, and if he's sick, he's a poor dog. One has to stand his wheel, and another his look-out, and the sooner he gets on deck again, the better.

Accordingly, as soon as I could possibly go back to my duty, I put on my thick clothes and boots and south-wester, and made my appear- ance on deck. Though I had been but a few days below, yet everything looked strangely enough. The ship was cased in ice,—decks, sides, masts, yards, and rigging. Two close-reefed top-sails were all the sail she had on, and every sail and rope was frozen so stiff in its place, that it seemed as though it would be impossible to start anything. Reduced, too, to her topmasts, she had altogether a most forlorn and crippled appearance. The sun had come up brightly; the snow was swept off the decks, and ashes thrown upon them, so that we could walk, for they had been as slippery as glass. It was, of course, too cold to carry on any ship's work, and we had only to walk the deck and keep ourselves warm. The wind was still ahead, and the whole ocean, to the eastward, covered with islands and field-ice. At four bells the order was given to square away the yards; and the man who came from the helm said that the captain had kept her off to N. N. E. What could this mean? Some said that he was going to put into Valparaiso, and winter, and others that he was going to run out of the ice and cross the Pacific, and go home round the Cape of Good Hope. Soon, however, it leaked out, and we found that we were running for the straits of Magellan. The news soon spread through the ship, and all tongues were at work, talking about it. No one on board had been through the straits, but I had in my chest an account of the passage of the ship *A.J. Donelson*, of New York, through those straits, a few years before. The account was given by the captain, and the representation was as favorable as possible. It was soon read by every one on board, and various opinions pronounced. The determination of our captain had at least this good effect; it gave every one something to think and talk about, made a break in our life, and diverted our minds from the monotonous dreariness of the prospect before us. Having made a fair wind of it, we were going off at a good rate, and leaving the thickest of the ice behind us. This, at least, was something.

Having been long enough below to get my hands well warmed and softened, the first handling of the ropes was rather tough; but a few days hardened them, and as soon as I got my mouth open wide enough to take in a piece of salt beef and hard bread, I was all right again.

Sunday, July 10th. Lat. 54° 10′, long. 79° 07′. This was our position at noon. The sun was out bright; the ice was all left behind, and things had quite a cheering appearance. We brought our wet pea-jackets and trowsers on deck, and hung them up in the rigging, that the breeze and the few hours of sun might dry them a little; and, by the permission of the cook, the galley was nearly filled with stockings and mittens, hung round to be dried. Boots, too, were brought up; and having got a little tar and slush from below, we gave them a thick coat. After dinner, all hands were turned-to, to get the anchors over the bows, bend on the chains, &c. The fish-tackle was got up, fish-davit rigged out, and after two or three hours of hard and cold work, both the anchors were ready for instant use, a couple of kedges got up, a hawser coiled away upon the fore-hatch, and the deep-sea-lead-line overhauled and got ready. Our spirits returned with having something to do; and when the tackle was manned to bowse the anchor home, notwithstanding the desolation of the scene, we struck up "Cheerily ho!" in full chorus. This pleased the mate, who rubbed his hands and cried out—"That's right, my boys; never say die! That sounds like the old crew!" and the captain came up, on hearing the song, and said to the passenger, within hearing of the man at the wheel,—"That sounds like a lively crew. They'll have their song so long as there're enough left for a chorus!"

This preparation of the cable and anchors was for the passage of the straits; for, being very crooked, and with a variety of currents, it is necessary to come frequently to anchor. This was not, by any means, a pleasant prospect, for, of all the work that a sailor is called upon to do in cold weather, there is none so bad as working the ground-tackle. The heavy chain cables to be hauled and pulled about decks with bare hands; wet hawsers, slip-ropes, and buoy-ropes to be hauled aboard, dripping in water, which is running up your sleeves, and freezing; clearing hawse under the bows; getting under weigh and coming-to, at all hours of the night and day, and a constant look-out for rocks and sands and turns of tides;—these are some of the disagreeables of such a navigation to a common sailor. Fair or foul, he wants to have nothing to do with the ground-tackle between port and port. One of our hands, too, had unluckily fallen upon a half of an old newspaper which contained an account of the passage, through the straits, of a Boston brig, called, I think, the Peruvian, in which she lost every cable and anchor she had, got aground twice, and arrived at Valparaiso in distress. This was set off against the account of the *A.J. Donelson*, and led us to look forward with less confidence to the passage, especially as no one on board had ever been through, and the captain had no very perfect charts. However, we were spared any further experience on the point; for the next day, when we must have been near the Cape of Pillars, which is the south-west point of the mouth of the straits, a gale set in from the eastward, with a heavy fog, so that we could not see half of the ship's length ahead. This, of course, put an end to the project, for the present; for a thick fog and a gale blowing dead ahead are not the most favorable circumstances for the passage of difficult and dangerous straits. This weather, too, seemed likely to last for some time, and we could not think of beating about the mouth of the straits for a week or two, waiting for a favorable opportunity; so we braced up on the larboard tack, put the ship's head due south, and struck her off for Cape Horn again.

In our first attempt to double the Cape, when we came up to the latitude of it, we were nearly seventeen hundred miles to the westward, but, in running for the straits of Magellan, we stood so far to the eastward, that we made our second attempt at a distance of not more than four or five hundred miles; and we had great hopes, by this means, to run clear of the ice; thinking that the easterly gales, which had prevailed for a long time, would have driven it to the westward. With the wind about two points free, the yards braced in a little, and two close-reefed top-sails and a reefed fore-sail on the ship, we made great way toward the southward; and, almost every watch, when we came on deck, the air seemed to grow colder, and the sea to run higher. Still, we saw no ice, and had great hopes of going clear of it altogether, when, one afternoon, about three o'clock, while we were taking a *siesta* during our watch below, "All hands!" was called in a loud and fearful voice. "Tumble up here, men!—tumble up!—don't stop for your clothes—before we're upon it!" We sprang out of our berths and hurried upon deck. The loud, sharp voice of the captain was heard giving orders, as though for life or death, and we ran aft to the braces, not waiting to look ahead, for not a moment was to be lost. The helm was hard up, the after yards shaking, and the ship in the act of wearing. Slowly, with the stiff ropes and iced rigging, we swung the yards round, everything coming hard and with a creaking and rending sound, like pulling up a plank which has been frozen into the ice. The ship wore round fairly, the yards were steadied, and we stood off on the other tack, leaving behind us, directly under our larboard quarter, a large ice island, peering out of the mist, and reaching high above our tops, while astern; and on either side of the island, large tracts of field-ice were dimly seen, heaving and rolling in the sea. We were now safe, and standing to the northward; but, in a few minutes more, had it not been for the sharp look-out of the watch, we should have been fairly upon the ice, and left our ship's old bones adrift in the Southern ocean. After standing to the northward a few hours, we wore ship, and, the wind having hauled, we stood to the southward and eastward. All night long, a bright look-out was kept from every part of the deck; and whenever ice was seen on the one bow or the other, the helm was shifted and the yards braced, and by quick working of the ship she was kept clear. The accustomed cry of "Ice ahead!"—"Ice on the lee bow!"—"Another island!" in the same tones, and with the same orders following them, seemed to bring us directly back to our old position of the week before. During our watch on deck, which was from twelve to four, the wind came out ahead, with a pelting storm of hail and sleet, and we lay hove-to, under a close-reefed main top-sail, the whole watch. During the next watch it fell calm, with a drenching rain, until daybreak, when the wind came out to the westward, and the weather cleared up, and showed us the whole ocean, in the course which we should have steered, had it not been for the head wind and calm, completely blocked up with ice. Here then our progress was stopped, and we wore ship, and once more stood to the northward and eastward; not for the straits of Magellan, but to make another attempt to double the Cape, still farther to the eastward; for the captain was determined to get round if perseverance could do it, and the third time, he said, never failed.

With a fair wind we soon ran clear of the field-ice, and by noon had only the stray islands floating far and near upon the ocean. The sun was out bright, the sea of a deep blue, fringed with the white foam of the waves which ran high before a strong south-wester; our solitary ship tore on through the water as though glad to be out of her confinement; and the ice islands lay scattered upon the ocean here and there, of various sizes and shapes, reflecting the bright rays of the sun, and drifting slowly northward before the gale. It was a contrast to much that we had lately seen, and a spectacle not only of beauty, but of life; for it required but little fancy to imagine these islands to be animate masses which had broken loose from the "thrilling regions of thick-ribbed ice," and were working their way, by wind and current, some alone, and some in fleets, to milder climes. No pencil has ever yet given anything like the true effect of an iceberg. In a picture, they are huge, uncouth masses, stuck in the sea, while their chief beauty and grandeur,—their slow, stately motion; the whirling of the snow about their summits, and the fearful groaning and cracking of their parts,— the picture cannot give. This is the large iceberg; while the small and distant islands, floating on the smooth sea, in the light of a clear day, look like little floating fairy isles of sapphire.

From a north-east course we gradually hauled to the eastward, and after sailing about two hundred miles, which brought us as near to the western coast of Terra del Fuego as was safe, and having lost sight of the ice altogether,—for the third time we put the ship's head to the southward, to try the passage of the Cape. The weather continued clear and cold, with a strong gale from the westward, and we were fast getting up with the latitude of the Cape, with a prospect of soon being round. One fine afternoon, a man who had gone into the fore-top to shift the rolling tackles, sung out, at the top of his voice, and with evident glee,—"Sail ho!" Neither land nor sail had we seen since leaving San Diego; and any one who has traversed the length of a whole ocean alone, can imagine what an excitement such an announcement produced on board. "Sail ho!" shouted the cook, jumping out of his galley; "Sail ho!" shouted a man, throwing back the slide of the scuttle, to the watch below, who were soon out of their berths and on deck; and "Sail ho!" shouted the captain down the companion-way to the passenger in the cabin. Beside the pleasure of seeing a ship and human beings in so desolate a place, it was important for us to speak a vessel, to learn whether there was ice to the eastward, and to ascertain the longitude; for we had no chronometer, and had been drifting about so long that we had nearly lost our reckoning, and opportunities for lunar observations are not frequent or sure in such a place as Cape Horn. For these various reasons, the excitement in our little community was running high, and conjectures were made, and everything thought of for which the captain would hail, when the man aloft sung out—"Another sail, large on the weather bow!" This was a little odd, but so much the better, and did not shake our faith in their being sails. At length the man in the top hailed, and said he believed it was land, after all. "Land in your eye!" said the mate, who was looking through the telescope; "they are ice islands, if I can see a hole through a ladder;" and a few moments showed the mate to be right; and all our expectations fled; and instead of what we most wished to see, we had what we most dreaded, and what we hoped we had seen the last of. We soon, however, left these astern, having passed within about two miles of them; and at sundown the horizon was clear in all directions.

Having a fine wind, we were soon up with and passed the latitude of the Cape, and having stood far enough to the southward to give it a wide berth, we began to stand to the eastward, with a good prospect of being round and steering to the northward on the other side, in a very few days. But ill luck seemed to have lighted upon us. Not four hours had we been standing on in this course, before it fell dead calm; and in half an hour it clouded up; a few straggling blasts, with spits of snow and sleet, came from the eastward; and in an hour more, we lay hove-to under a close-reefed main top-sail, drifting bodily off to leeward before the fiercest storm that we had yet felt, blowing dead ahead, from the eastward. It seemed as though the genius of the place had been roused at finding that we had nearly slipped through his fingers, and had come down upon us with tenfold fury. The sailors said that every blast, as it shook the shrouds, and whistled through the rigging, said to the old ship, "No, you don't!"—"No, you don't!"

For eight days we lay drifting about in this manner. Sometimes,—generally towards noon,—it fell calm; once or twice a round copper ball showed itself for a few moments in the place where the sun ought to have been; and a puff or two came from the westward, giving some hope that a fair wind had come at last. During the first two days, we made sail for these puffs, shaking the reefs out of the top-sails and boarding the tacks of the courses; but finding that it only made work for us when the gale set in again, it was soon given up, and we lay-to under our close-reefs. We had less snow and hail than when we were farther to the westward, but we had an abundance of what is worse to a sailor in cold weather—drenching rain. Snow is blinding, and very bad when coming upon a coast, but, for genuine discomfort, give me rain with freezing weather. A snow-storm is exciting, and it does not wet through the clothes (which is important to a sailor); but a constant rain there is no escaping from. It wets to the skin, and makes all protection vain. We had long ago run through all our dry clothes, and as sailors have no other way of drying them than by the sun, we had nothing to do but to put on those which were the least wet. At the end of each watch, when we came below, we took off our clothes and wrung them out; two taking hold of a pair of trowsers,—one at each end,— and jackets in the same way. Stockings, mittens, and all, were wrung out also, and then hung up to drain and chafe dry against the bulkheads. Then, feeling of all our clothes, we picked out those which were the least wet, and put them on, so as to be ready for a call, and turned-in, covered ourselves up with blankets, and slept until three knocks on the scuttle and the dismal sound of "All starbowlines ahoy! Eight bells, there below! Do you hear the news?" drawled out from on deck, and the sulky answer of "Aye, aye!" from below, sent us up again.

On deck, all was as dark as a pocket, and either a dead calm, with the rain pouring steadily down, or, more generally, a violent gale dead ahead, with rain pelting horizontally, and occasional variations of hail and sleet;—decks afloat with water swashing from side to side, and constantly wet feet; for boots could not be wrung out like drawers, and no composition could stand the constant soaking. In fact, wet and cold feet are inevitable in such weather, and are not the least of those little items which go to make up the grand total of the discomforts of a winter passage round the Cape. Few words were spoken between the watches as they shifted, the wheel was relieved, the mate took his place on the quarter-deck, the look-outs in the bows; and each man had his narrow space to walk fore and aft in, or, rather, to swing himself forward and back in, from one belaying pin to another,—for the decks were too slippery with ice and water to allow of much walking. To make a walk, which is absolutely necessary to pass away the time, one of us hit upon the expedient of sanding the deck; and afterwards, whenever the rain was not so violent as to wash it off, the weather-side of the quarter-deck, and a part of the waist and forecastle were sprinkled with the sand which we had on board for holystoning; and thus we made a good promenade, where we walked fore and aft, two and two, hour after hour, in our long, dull, and comfortless watches. The bells seemed to be an hour or two apart, instead of half an hour, and an age to elapse before the welcome sound of eight bells. The sole object was to make the time pass on. Any change was sought for, which would break the monotony of the time; and even the two hours' trick at the wheel, which came round to each of us, in turn, once in every other watch, was looked upon as a relief. Even the never-failing resource of long yarns, which eke out many a watch, seemed to have failed us now; for we had been so long together that we had heard each other's stories told over and over again, till we had them by heart; each one knew the whole history of each of the others, and we were fairly and literally talked out. Singing and joking, we were in no humor for, and, in fact, any sound of mirth or laughter would have struck strangely upon our ears, and would not have been tolerated, any more than whistling, or a wind instrument. The last resort, that of speculating upon the future, seemed now to fail us, for our discouraging situation, and the danger we were really in, (as we expected every day to find ourselves drifted back among the ice) "clapped a stopper" upon all that. From saying—"*when* we get home"—we began insensibly to alter it to—"*if* we get home"—and at last the subject was dropped by a tacit consent.

In this state of things, a new light was struck out, and a new field opened, by a change in the watch. One of our watch was laid up for two or three days by a bad hand, (for in cold weather the least cut or bruise ripens into a sore,) and his place was supplied by the carpenter. This

was a windfall, and there was quite a contest, who should have the carpenter to walk with him. As "Chips" was a man of some little education, and he and I had had a good deal of intercourse with each other,
he fell in with me in my walk. He was a Fin, but spoke English very well,
and gave me long accounts of his country;—the customs, the trade, the
towns, what little he knew of the government, (I found he was no friend
of Russia,) his voyages, his first arrival in America, his marriage and
courtship;—he had married a countrywoman of his, a dressmaker,
whom he met with in Boston. I had very little to tell him of my quiet,
sedentary life at home; and in spite of our best efforts, which had protracted these yarns through five or six watches, we fairly talked one
another out, and I turned him over to another man in the watch, and
put myself upon my own resources.

I commenced a deliberate system of time-killing, which united
some profit with a cheering up of the heavy hours. As soon as I came
on deck, and took my place and regular walk, I began with repeating
over to myself a string of matters which I had in my memory, in regular order. First, the multiplication table and the tables of weights and
measures; then the states of the Union, with their capitals; the coun-
ties of England, with their shire towns; the kings of England in their
order; and a large part of the peerage, which I committed from an
almanac that we had on board; and then the Kanaka numerals. This
carried me through my facts, and being repeated deliberately, with
long intervals, often eked out the two first bells. Then came the ten
commandments; the thirty-ninth chapter of Job, and a few other pas-
sages from Scripture. The next in the order, that I never varied from,
came Cowper's Castaway, which was a great favorite with me; the
solemn measure and gloomy character of which, as well as the incident that it was founded upon, made it well suited to a lonely watch
at sea. Then his lines to Mary, his address to the jackdaw, and a short
extract from Table Talk; (I abounded in Cowper, for I happened to
have a volume of his poems in my chest;) "Ille et nefasto" from
Horace, and Goethe's Erl King. After I had got through these, I allowed

myself a more general range among everything that I could remember, both in prose and verse. In this way, with an occasional break by relieving the wheel, heaving the log, and going to the scuttle-butt for a drink of water, the longest watch was passed away; and I was so regular in my silent recitations, that if there was no interruption by ship's duty, I could tell very nearly the number of bells by my progress.

Our watches below were no more varied than the watch on deck. All washing, sewing, and reading was given up; and we did nothing but eat, sleep, and stand our watch, leading what might be called a Cape Horn life. The forecastle was too uncomfortable to sit up in; and whenever we were below, we were in our berths. To prevent the rain, and the sea-water which broke over the bows, from washing down, we were obliged to keep the scuttle closed, so that the forecastle was nearly airtight. In this little, wet, leaky hole, we were all quartered, in an atmosphere so bad that our lamp, which swung in the middle from the beams, sometimes actually burned blue, with a large circle of foul air about it. Still, I was never in better health than after three weeks of this life. I gained a great deal of flesh, and we all ate like horses. At every watch, when we came below, before turning-in, the bread barge and beef kid were overhauled. Each man drank his quart of hot tea night and morning; and glad enough we were to get it, for no nectar and ambrosia were sweeter to the lazy immortals, than was a pot of hot tea, a hard biscuit, and a slice of cold salt beef, to us after a watch on deck. To be sure, we were mere animals, and had this life lasted a year instead of a month, we should have been little better than the ropes in the ship. Not a razor, nor a brush, nor a drop of water, except the rain and the spray, had come near us all the time; for we were on an allowance of fresh water; and who would strip and wash himself in salt water on deck, in the snow and ice, with the thermometer at zero?

After about eight days of constant easterly gales, the wind hauled occasionally a little to the southward, and blew hard, which, as we were well to the southward, allowed us to brace in a little and stand on, under all the sail we could carry. These turns lasted but a short while, and sooner or later it set in again from the old quarter; yet at each time we made something, and were gradually edging along to the eastward. One night, after one of these shifts of the wind, and when all hands had been up a great part of the time, our watch was left on deck, with the main-sail hanging in the buntlines, ready to be set if necessary. It came on to blow worse and worse, with hail and snow beating like so many furies upon the ship, it being as dark and thick as night could make it. The main-sail was blowing and slatting with a noise like thunder, when the captain came on deck, and ordered it to be furled. The mate was about to call all hands, when the captain stopped him, and said that the men would be beaten out if they were called up so often; that as our watch must stay on deck, it might as well be doing that as anything else. Accordingly, we went upon the yard; and never shall I forget that piece of work. Our watch had been so reduced by sickness, and by some having been left in California, that, with one man at the wheel, we had only the third mate and three beside myself to go aloft; so that, at most, we could only attempt to furl one yard-arm at a time. We manned the weather yard-arm, and set to work to make a furl of it. Our lower masts being short, and our yards very square, the sail had a head of nearly fifty feet, and a short leach, made still shorter by the deep reef which was in it, which brought the clue away out on the quarters of the yard, and made a bunt nearly as square as the mizen royal-yard. Beside this difficulty, the yard over which we lay was cased with ice, the gaskets and rope of the foot and leach of the sail as stiff and hard as a piece of suction-hose, and the sail itself about as pliable as though it had been made of sheets of sheathing copper. It blew a perfect hurricane, with alternate blasts of snow, hail, and rain. We had to *fist* the sail with bare hands. No one could trust himself to mittens, for if he slipped, he was a gone man. All the boats were hoisted in on deck, and there was nothing to be lowered for him. We had need of every finger God had given us. Several times we got the sail upon the yard, but it blew away again before we could secure it. It required men to lie over the yard to pass each turn of the gaskets, and when they were passed, it was almost impossible to knot them so that they would hold. Frequently we were obliged to leave off altogether and take to beating our hands upon the sail, to keep them from freezing. After some time,—which seemed forever,—we got the weather side stowed after a fashion, and went over to leeward for another trial. This was still worse, for the body of the sail had been blown over to leeward, and as the yard was a-cock-bill by the lying over of the vessel, we had to light it all up to windward. When the yard-arms were furled, the bunt was all adrift again, which made more work for us. We got all secure at last, but we had been nearly an hour and a half upon the yard, and it seemed an age. It had just struck five bells when we went up, and eight were struck soon after we came down. This may seem slow work; but considering the state of everything, and that we had only five men to a sail with just half as many square yards of canvass in it as the main-sail of the Independence, sixty-gun ship, which musters seven hundred men at her quarters, it is not wonderful that we were no quicker about it. We were glad enough to get on deck, and still more, to go below. The oldest sailor in the watch said, as he went down,—"I shall never forget that main yard;—it beats all my going a fishing. Fun is fun, but furling one yard-arm of a course, at a time, off Cape Horn, is no better than man-killing."

During the greater part of the next two days, the wind was pretty steady from the southward. We had evidently made great progress, and had good hope of being soon up with the Cape, if we were not there already. We could put but little confidence in our reckoning, as there had been no opportunities for an observation, and we had drifted too much to allow of our dead reckoning being anywhere near the mark. If it would clear off enough to give a chance for an observation, or if we could make land, we should know where we were; and upon these, and the chances of falling in with a sail from the eastward, we depended almost entirely.

Friday, July 22d. This day we had a steady gale from the southward, and stood on under close sail, with the yards eased a little by the weather braces, the clouds lifting a little, and showing signs of breaking away. In the afternoon, I was below with Mr. Hatch, the third mate, and two others, filling the bread locker in the steerage from the casks, when a bright gleam of sunshine broke out and shone down the companion-way and through the sky-light, lighting up everything below, and sending a warm glow through the heart of every one. It was a sight we had not seen for weeks,—an omen, a god-send. Even the roughest and hardest face acknowledged its influence. Just at that moment we heard a loud shout from all parts of the deck, and the mate called out down the companion-way to the captain, who was sitting in the cabin. What he said, we could not distinguish, but the captain kicked over his chair, and was on deck at one jump. We could not tell what it was; and, anxious as we were to know, the discipline of the ship would not allow of our leaving our places. Yet, as we were not called, we knew there was no danger. We hurried to get through with our job, when, seeing the steward's black face peering out of the pantry, Mr. Hatch hailed him, to know what was the matter. "Lan' o, to be sure, sir! No you hear 'em sing out, 'Lan' o'? De cap'em say 'im Cape Horn!"

This gave us a new start, and we were soon through our work, and on deck; and there lay the land, fair upon the larboard beam, and slowly edging away upon the quarter. All hands were busy looking at it,—the captain and mates from the quarter-deck, the cook from his galley, and the sailors from the forecastle; and even Mr. Nuttall, the passenger, who had kept in his shell for nearly a month, and hardly been seen by anybody, and who we had almost forgotten was on board, came out like a butterfly, and was hopping round as bright as a bird.

The land was the island of Staten Land, just to the eastward of Cape Horn; and a more desolate-looking spot I never wish to set eyes upon; bare, broken, and girt with rocks and ice, with here and there, between the rocks and broken hillocks, a little stunted vegetation of shrubs. It was a place well suited to stand at the junction of the two oceans, beyond the reach of human cultivation, and encounter the blasts and snows of a perpetual winter. Yet, dismal as it was, it was a pleasant sight to us; not only as being the first land we had seen, but because it told us that we had passed the Cape,—were in the Atlantic,—and that, with twenty-four hours of this breeze, might bid defiance to the

Southern ocean. It told us, too, our latitude and longitude better than any observation; and the captain now knew where we were, as well as if we were off the end of Long wharf.

In the general joy, Mr. Nuttall said he should like to go ashore upon the island and examine a spot which probably no human being had ever set foot upon; but the captain intimated that he would see the island—specimens and all,—in—another place, before he would get out a boat or delay the ship one moment for him.

We left the land gradually astern; and at sundown had the Atlantic ocean clear before us.

from Billy Budd, Sailor
by Herman Melville

Herman Melville (1819–1891) wrote his novella about "the handsome sailor" between 1885 and 1891. The story was not published until 1924, when Melville's work was enjoying a popular revival. Billy is admired by all of his shipmates on H.M.S. Bellipotent, with one exception: the jealous master-at-arms Claggart.

E lsewhere it has been said that in the lack of frigates (of course better sailers than line-of-battle ships) in the English squadron up the Straits at that period, the *Bellipotent* 74 was occasionally employed not only as an available substitute for a scout, but at times on detached service of more important kind. This was not alone because of her sailing qualities, not common in a ship of her rate, but quite as much, probably, that the character of her commander, it was thought, specially adapted him for any duty where under unforeseen difficulties a prompt initiative might have to be taken in some matter demanding knowledge and ability in addition to those qualities implied in good seamanship. It was on an expedition of the latter sort, a somewhat distant one, and when the *Bellipotent* was almost at her furthest remove from the fleet, that in the latter part of an afternoon watch she unexpectedly came in sight of a ship of the enemy. It proved to be a frigate. The latter, perceiving through the glass that the weight of men and metal would be heavily against her, invoking her light heels crowded sail to get away. After a chase urged almost against hope and lasting until about the middle of the first dogwatch, she signally succeeded in effecting her escape.

Not long after the pursuit had been given up, and ere the excitement incident thereto had altogether waned away, the master-at-arms, ascending from his cavernous sphere, made his appearance cap in hand by the mainmast respectfully waiting the notice of Captain Vere, then solitary walking the weather side of the quarter-deck, doubtless somewhat chafed at the failure of the pursuit. The spot where Claggart stood was the place allotted to men of lesser grades seeking some more particular interview either with the officer of the deck or the captain himself. But from the latter it was not often that a sailor or petty officer of those days would seek a hearing; only some exceptional cause would, according to established custom, have warranted that.

Presently, just as the commander, absorbed in his reflections, was on the point of turning aft in his promenade, he became sensible of Claggart's presence, and saw the doffed cap held in deferential expectancy. Here be it said that Captain Vere's personal knowledge of this petty officer had only begun at the time of the ship's last sailing from home, Claggart then for the first, in transfer from a ship detained for repairs, supplying on board the *Bellipotent* the place of a previous master-at-arms disabled and ashore.

No sooner did the commander observe who it was that now deferentially stood awaiting his notice than a peculiar expression came over him. It was not unlike that which uncontrollably will flit across the countenance of one at unawares encountering a person who, though known to him indeed, has hardly been long enough known for thorough knowledge, but something in whose aspect nevertheless now for the first provokes a vaguely repellent distaste. But coming to a stand and resuming much of his wonted official manner, save that a sort of impatience lurked in the intonation of the opening word, he said "Well? What is it, Master-at-arms?"

With the air of a subordinate grieved at the necessity of being a messenger of ill tidings, and while conscientiously determined to be frank yet equally resolved upon shunning overstatement, Claggart at this invitation, or rather summons to disburden, spoke up. What he said, conveyed in the language of no uneducated man, was to the effect following, if not altogether in these words, namely, that during the chase and preparations for the possible encounter he had seen enough to convince him that at least one sailor aboard was a dangerous character in a ship mustering some who not only had taken a guilty part in the late serious troubles, but others also who, like the man in question, had entered His Majesty's service under another form than enlistment.

At this point Captain Vere with some impatience interrupted him: "Be direct, man; say *impressed men.*"

Claggart made a gesture of subservience, and proceeded. Quite lately he (Claggart) had begun to suspect that on the gun decks some sort of movement prompted by the sailor in question was covertly going on, but he had not thought himself warranted in reporting the suspicion so long as it remained indistinct. But from what he had that afternoon observed in the man referred to, the suspicion of something clandestine going on had advanced to a point less removed from certainty. He deeply felt, he added, the serious responsibility assumed in making a report involving such possible consequences to the individual mainly concerned, besides tending to augment those natural anxieties which every naval commander must feel in view of extraordinary outbreaks so recent as those which, he sorrowfully said it, it needed not to name.

Now at the first broaching of the matter Captain Vere, taken by surprise, could not wholly dissemble his disquietude. But as Claggart went on, the former's aspect changed into restiveness under something in the testifier's manner in giving his testimony. However, he refrained from interrupting him. And Claggart, continuing, concluded with this: "God forbid, your honor, that the *Bellipotent's* should be the experience of the—"

"Never mind that!" here peremptorily broke in the superior, his face altering with anger, instinctively divining the ship that the other was about to name, one in which the Nore Mutiny had assumed a singularly tragical character that for a time jeopardized the life of its commander. Under the circumstances he was indignant at the purposed allusion. When the commissioned officers themselves were on all occasions very heedful how they referred to the recent events in the fleet, for a petty officer unnecessarily to allude to them in the presence of his captain, this struck him as a most immodest presumption. Besides, to his quick sense of self-respect it even looked under the circumstances something like an attempt to alarm him. Nor at first was he without some surprise that one who so far as he had hitherto come under his notice had shown considerable tact in his function should in this particular evince such lack of it.

But these thoughts and kindred dubious ones flitting across his mind were suddenly replaced by an intuitional surmise which, though as yet obscure in form, served practically to affect his reception of the ill tidings. Certain it is that, long versed in everything pertaining to the complicated gun-deck life, which like every other form of life has its secret mines and dubious side, the side popularly disclaimed, Captain Vere did not permit himself to be unduly disturbed by the general tenor of his subordinate's report.

Furthermore, if in view of recent events prompt action should be taken at the first palpable sign of recurring insubordination, for all that, not judicious would it be, he thought, to keep the idea of lingering disaffection alive by undue forwardness in crediting an informer, even if his own subordinate and charged among other things with police surveillance of the crew. This feeling would not perhaps have so prevailed with him were it not that upon a prior occasion the patriotic zeal officially evinced by Claggart had somewhat irritated him as appearing rather supersensible and strained. Furthermore, something even in the official's self-possessed and somewhat ostentatious manner in making his specifications strangely reminded him of a bandsman, a perjurous witness in a capital case before a court-martial ashore of which when a lieutenant he (Captain Vere) had been a member.

Now the peremptory check given to Claggart in the matter of the arrested allusion was quickly followed up by this: "You say that there is at least one dangerous man aboard. Name him."

"William Budd, a foretopman, your honor."

"William Budd!" repeated Captain Vere with unfeigned astonishment. "And mean you the man that Lieutenant Ratcliffe took from the merchantman not very long ago, the young fellow who seems to be so popular with the men—Billy, the Handsome Sailor, as they call him?"

"The same, your honor; but for all his youth and good looks, a deep one. Not for nothing does he insinuate himself into the good will of his shipmates, since at the least they will at a pinch say—all hands will—a good word for him, and at all hazards. Did Lieutenant Ratcliffe happen to tell your honor of that adroit fling of Budd's, jumping up in the cutter's bow under the merchantman's stern when he was being taken off? It is even masked by that sort of good-humored air that at heart he resents his impressment. You have but noted his fair cheek. A mantrap may be under the ruddy-tipped daisies."

Now the Handsome Sailor as a signal figure among the crew had naturally enough attracted the captain's attention from the first. Though in general not very demonstrative to his officers, he had congratulated Lieutenant Ratcliffe upon his good fortune in lighting on such a fine specimen of the *genus homo*, who in the nude might have posed for a statue of young Adam before the Fall. As to Billy's adieu to the ship *Rights-of-Man*, which the boarding lieutenant had indeed reported to him, but, in a deferential way, more as a good story than aught else, Captain Vere, though mistakenly understanding it as a satiric sally, had but thought so much the better of the impressed man for it; as a military sailor, admiring the spirit that could take an arbitrary enlistment so merrily and sensibly. The foretopman's conduct, too, so far as it had fallen under the captain's notice, had confirmed the first happy augury, while the new recruit's qualities as a "sailor-man" seemed to be such that he had thought of recommending him to the executive officer for promotion to a place that would more frequently bring him under his own observation, namely, the captaincy of the mizzentop, replacing there in the starboard watch a man not so young whom partly for that reason he deemed less fitted for the post. Be it parenthesized here that since the mizzentopmen have not to handle such breadths of heavy canvas as the lower sails on the mainmast and foremast, a young man if of the right stuff not only seems best adapted to duty there, but in fact is generally selected for the captaincy of that top, and the company under him are light hands and often but striplings. In sum, Captain Vere had from the beginning deemed Billy Budd to be what in the naval parlance of the time was called a "King's bargain": that is to say, for His Britannic Majesty's navy a capital investment at small outlay or none at all.

After a brief pause, during which the reminiscences above mentioned passed vividly through his mind and he weighed the import of Claggart's last suggestion conveyed in the phrase "mantrap under the daisies," and the more he weighed it the less reliance he felt in the informer's good faith, suddenly he turned upon him and in a low voice demanded: "Do you come to me, Master-at-arms, with so foggy a tale? As to Budd, cite me an act or spoken word of his confirmatory of what you in general charge against him. Stay," drawing nearer to him; "heed what you speak. Just now, and in a case like this, there is a yard-armend for the false witness."

"Ah, your honor!" sighed Claggart, mildly shaking his shapely head as in sad deprecation of such unmerited severity of tone. Then, bridling—erecting himself as in virtuous self-assertion—he circumstantially alleged certain words and acts which collectively, if credited, led to presumptions mortally inculpating Budd. And for some of these averments, he added, substantiating proof was not far.

With gray eyes impatient and distrustful essaying to fathom to the bottom Claggart's calm violet ones, Captain Vere again heard him out; then for the moment stood ruminating. The mood he evinced, Claggart—himself for the time liberated from the other's scrutiny—steadily regarded with a look difficult to render: a look curious of the operation of his tactics, a look such as might have been that of the spokesman of the envious children of Jacob deceptively imposing upon the troubled patriarch the blood-dyed coat of young Joseph.

Though something exceptional in the moral quality of Captain Vere made him, in earnest encounter with a fellow man, a veritable touchstone of that man's essential nature, yet now as to Claggart and what was really going on in him his feeling partook less of intuitional conviction than of strong suspicion clogged by strange dubieties. The perplexity he evinced proceeded less from aught touching the man informed against—as Claggart doubtless opined—than from considerations how best to act in regard to the informer. At first, indeed, he was naturally for summoning that substantiation of his allegations which Claggart said was at hand. But such a proceeding would result in the matter at once getting abroad, which in the present stage of it, he thought, might undesirably affect the ship's company. If Claggart was a false witness—that closed the affair. And therefore, before trying the accusation, he would first practically test the accuser; and he thought this could be done in a quiet, undemonstrative way.

The measure he determined upon involved a shifting of the scene, a transfer to a place less exposed to observation than the broad quarterdeck. For although the few gunroom officers there at the time had, in due observance of naval etiquette, withdrawn to leeward the moment Captain Vere had begun his promenade on the deck's weather side; and though during the colloquy with Claggart they of course ventured not to diminish the distance; and though throughout the interview Captain Vere's voice was far from high, and Claggart's silvery and low; and the wind in the cordage and the wash of the sea helped the more to put them beyond earshot; nevertheless, the interview's continuance already had attracted observation from some topmen aloft and other sailors in the waist or further forward.

Having determined upon his measures, Captain Vere forthwith took action. Abruptly turning to Claggart, he asked, "Master-at-arms, is it now Budd's watch aloft?"

"No, your honor."

Whereupon, "Mr. Wilkes!" summoning the nearest midshipman. "Tell Albert to come to me." Albert was the captain's hammock-boy, a sort of sea valet in whose discretion and fidelity his master had much confidence. The lad appeared.

"You know Budd, the foretopman?"

"I do, sir."

"Go find him. It is his watch off. Manage to tell him out of earshot that he is wanted aft. Contrive it that he speaks to nobody. Keep him in talk yourself. And not till you get well aft here, not till then let him know that the place where he is wanted is my cabin. You understand. Go.—Master-at-arms, show yourself on the decks below, and when you think it time for Albert to be coming with his man, stand by quietly to follow the sailor in."

Now when the foretopman found himself in the cabin, closeted there, as it were, with the captain and Claggart, he was surprised enough. But it was a surprise unaccompanied by apprehension or distrust. To an immature nature essentially honest and humane, forewarning intimations of subtler danger from one's kind come tardily if at all. The only thing that took shape in the young sailor's mind was this: Yes, the captain, I have always thought, looks kindly upon me. Wonder if he's going to make me his coxswain. I should like that. And may be now he is going to ask the master-at-arms about me.

"Shut the door there, sentry," said the commander; "stand without, and let nobody come in.—Now, Master-at-arms, tell this man to his face what you told of him to me," and stood prepared to scrutinize the mutually confronting visages.

With the measured step and calm collected air of an asylum physician approaching in the public hall some patient beginning to show indications of a coming paroxysm, Claggart deliberately advanced within short range of Billy and, mesmerically looking him in the eye, briefly recapitulated the accusation.

Not at first did Billy take it in. When he did, the rose-tan of his cheek looked struck as by white leprosy. He stood like one impaled and gagged. Meanwhile the accuser's eyes, removing not as yet from the blue dilated ones, underwent a phenomenal change, their wonted rich violet color blurring into a muddy purple. Those lights of human intelligence, losing human expression, were gelidly protruding like the alien eyes of certain uncatalogued creatures of the deep. The first mesmeristic glance was one of serpent fascination; the last was as the paralyzing lurch of the torpedo fish.

"Speak, man!" said Captain Vere to the transfixed one, struck by his aspect even more than by Claggart's. "Speak! Defend yourself!" Which appeal caused but a strange dumb gesturing and gurgling in Billy; amazement at such an accusation so suddenly sprung on inexperienced nonage; this, and, it may be, horror of the accuser's eyes, serving to bring out his lurking defect and in this instance for the time intensifying it into a convulsed tongue-tie; while the intent head and entire form straining forward in an agony of ineffectual eagerness to obey the injunction to speak and defend himself, gave an expression to the face like that of a condemned vestal priestess in the moment of being buried alive, and in the first struggle against suffocation.

Though at the time Captain Vere was quite ignorant of Billy's liability to vocal impediment, he now immediately divined it, since vividly Billy's aspect recalled to him that of a bright young schoolmate of his whom he had once seen struck by much the same startling impotence in the act of eagerly rising in the class to be foremost in response to a testing question put to it by the master. Going close up to the young sailor, and laying a soothing hand on his shoulder, he said, "There is no hurry, my boy. Take your time, take your time." Contrary to the effect intended, these words so fatherly in tone, doubtless touching Billy's heart to the quick, prompted yet more violent efforts at utterance—efforts soon ending for the time in confirming the paralysis, and bringing to his face an expression which was as a crucifixion to behold. The next instant, quick as the flame from a discharged cannon at night, his right arm shot out, and Claggart dropped to the deck. Whether intentionally or but owing to the young athlete's superior height, the blow had taken effect full upon the forehead, so shapely and intellectual-looking a feature in the master-at-arms; so that the body fell over lengthwise, like a heavy plank tilted from erectness. A gasp or two, and he lay motionless.

"Fated boy," breathed Captain Vere in tone so low as to be almost a whisper, "what have you done! But here, help me."

The twain raised the felled one from the loins up into a sitting position. The spare form flexibly acquiesced, but inertly. It was like handling a dead snake. They lowered it back. Regaining erectness, Captain Vere with one hand covering his face stood to all appearance as impassive as the object at his feet. Was he absorbed in taking in all the bearings of the event and what was best not only now at once to be done, but also in the sequel? Slowly he uncovered his face; and the effect was as if the moon emerging from eclipse should reappear with quite another aspect than that which had gone into hiding. The father in him, manifested towards Billy thus far in the scene, was replaced by the military disciplinarian. In his official tone he bade the foretopman retire to a stateroom aft (pointing it out), and there remain till thence summoned. This order Billy in silence mechanically obeyed. Then going to the cabin door where it opened on the quarter-deck, Captain Vere said to the sentry without, "Tell somebody to send Albert here." When the lad appeared, his master so contrived it that he should not catch sight of the prone one. "Albert," he said to him, "tell the surgeon I wish to see him. You need not come back till called."

When the surgeon entered—a self-poised character of that grave sense and experience that hardly anything could take him aback—Captain Vere advanced to meet him, thus unconsciously intercepting his view of Claggart, and, interrupting the other's wonted ceremonious salutation, said, "Nay. Tell me how it is with yonder man," directing his attention to the prostrate one.

The surgeon looked, and for all his self-command somewhat started at the abrupt revelation. On Claggart's always pallid complexion, thick black blood was now oozing from nostril and ear. To the gazer's professional eye it was unmistakably no living man that he saw.

"Is it so, then?" said Captain Vere, intently watching him. "I thought it. But verify it." Whereupon the customary tests confirmed the surgeon's first glance, who now, looking up in unfeigned concern, cast a look of intense inquisitiveness upon his superior. But Captain Vere, with one hand to his brow, was standing motionless. Suddenly, catching the surgeon's arm convulsively, he exclaimed, pointing down to the body, "It is the divine judgment on Ananias! Look!"

Disturbed by the excited manner he had never before observed in the *Bellipotent*'s captain, and as yet wholly ignorant of the affair, the prudent surgeon nevertheless held his peace, only again looking an earnest interrogatory as to what it was that had resulted in such a tragedy.

But Captain Vere was now again motionless, standing absorbed in thought. Again starting, he vehemently exclaimed, "Struck dead by an angel of God! Yet the angel must hang!"

At these passionate interjections, mere incoherences to the listener as yet unapprised of the antecedents, the surgeon was profoundly discomposed. But now, as recollecting himself, Captain Vere in less passionate tone briefly related the circumstances leading up to the event. "But come; we must dispatch," he added. "Help me to remove him" (meaning the body) "to yonder compartment," designating one opposite that where the foretopman remained immured. Anew disturbed by a request that, as implying a desire for secrecy, seemed unaccountably strange to him, there was nothing for the subordinate to do but comply.

"Go now," said Captain Vere with something of his wonted manner. "Go now. I presently shall call a drumhead court. Tell the lieutenants what has happened, and tell Mr. Mordant" (meaning the captain of marines), "and charge them to keep the matter to themselves."

Full of disquietude and misgiving, the surgeon left the cabin. Was Captain Vere suddenly affected in his mind, or was it but a transient excitement, brought about by so strange and extraordinary a tragedy? As to the drumhead court, it struck the surgeon as impolitic, if nothing more. The thing to do, he thought, was to place Billy Budd in confinement, and in a way dictated by usage, and postpone further action in so extraordinary a case to such time as they should rejoin the squadron, and then refer it to the admiral. He recalled the unwonted agitation of Captain Vere and his excited exclamations, so at variance with his normal manner. Was he unhinged?

But assuming that he is, it is not so susceptible of proof. What then can the surgeon do? No more trying situation is conceivable than that of an officer subordinate under a captain whom he suspects to be not mad, indeed, but yet not quite unaffected in his intellects. To argue his order to him would be insolence. To resist him would be mutiny.

In obedience to Captain Vere, he communicated what had happened to the lieutenants and captain of marines, saying nothing as to the captain's state. They fully shared his own surprise and concern. Like him too, they seemed to think that such a matter should be referred to the admiral.

Who in the rainbow can draw the line where the violet tint ends and the orange tint begins? Distinctly we see the difference of the colors, but where exactly does the one first blendingly enter into the other? So with sanity and insanity. In pronounced cases there is no question about them. But in some supposed cases, in various degrees supposedly less pronounced, to draw the exact line of demarcation few will undertake, though for a fee becoming considerate some professional experts will. There is nothing namable but that some men will, or undertake to, do it for pay.

Whether Captain Vere, as the surgeon professionally and privately surmised, was really the sudden victim of any degree of aberration, every one must determine for himself by such light as this narrative may afford.

That the unhappy event which has been narrated could not have happened at a worse juncture was but too true. For it was close on the heel of the suppressed insurrections, an aftertime very critical to naval authority, demanding from every English sea commander two qualities not readily interfusable—prudence and rigor. Moreover, there was something crucial in the case.

In the jugglery of circumstances preceding and attending the event on board the *Bellipotent*, and in the light of that martial code whereby it was formally to be judged, innocence and guilt personified in Claggart and Budd in effect changed places. In a legal view the apparent victim of the tragedy was he who had sought to victimize a man blameless; and the indisputable deed of the latter, navally regarded, constituted the most heinous of military crimes. Yet more. The essential right and wrong involved in the matter, the clearer that might be, so much the worse for the responsibility of a loyal sea commander, inasmuch as he was not authorized to determine the matter on that primitive basis.

Small wonder then that the *Bellipotent*'s captain, though in general a man of rapid decision, felt that circumspectness not less than promptitude was necessary. Until he could decide upon his course, and in each detail; and not only so, but until the concluding measure was upon the point of being enacted, he deemed it advisable, in view of all the circumstances, to guard as much as possible against publicity. Here he may or may not have erred. Certain it is, however, that subsequently in the confidential talk of more than one or two gun rooms and cabins he was not a little criticized by some officers, a fact imputed by his friends and vehemently by his cousin Jack Denton to professional jealousy of Starry Vere. Some imaginative ground for invidious comment there was. The maintenance of secrecy in the matter, the confining all knowledge of it for a time to the place where the homicide occurred, the quarterdeck cabin; in these particulars lurked some resemblance to the policy adopted in those tragedies of the palace which have occurred more than once in the capital founded by Peter the Barbarian.

The case indeed was such that fain would the *Bellipotent*'s captain have deferred taking any action whatever respecting it further than to keep the foretopman a close prisoner till the ship rejoined the squadron and then submitting the matter to the judgment of his admiral.

But a true military officer is in one particular like a true monk. Not with more of self-abnegation will the latter keep his vows of monastic obedience than the former his vows of allegiance to martial duty.

Feeling that unless quick action was taken on it, the deed of the foretopman, so soon as it should be known on the gun decks, would tend to awaken any slumbering embers of the Nore among the crew, a sense of the urgency of the case overruled in Captain Vere every other consideration. But though a conscientious disciplinarian, he was no lover of authority for mere authority's sake. Very far was he from embracing opportunities for monopolizing to himself the perils of moral responsibility, none at least that could properly be referred to an official superior or shared with him by his official equals or even subordinates. So thinking, he was glad it would not be at variance with usage to turn the matter over to a summary court of his own officers, reserving to himself, as the one on whom the ultimate accountability would rest, the right of maintaining a supervision of it, or formally or informally interposing at need. Accordingly a drumhead court was summarily convened, he electing the individuals composing it: the first lieutenant, the captain of marines, and the sailing master.

In associating an officer of marines with the sea lieutenant and the sailing master in a case having to do with a sailor, the commander perhaps deviated from general custom. He was prompted thereto by the circumstance that he took that soldier to be a judicious person, thoughtful, and not altogether incapable of grappling with a difficult case unprecedented in his prior experience. Yet even as to him he was not without some latent misgiving, for withal he was an extremely good-natured man, an enjoyer of his dinner, a sound sleeper, and inclined to obesity—a man who though he would always maintain his manhood in battle might not prove altogether reliable in a moral dilemma involving aught of the tragic. As to the first lieutenant and the sailing master, Captain Vere could not but be aware that though honest natures, of approved gallantry upon occasion, their intelligence was mostly confined to the matter of active seamanship and the fighting demands of their profession.

The court was held in the same cabin where the unfortunate affair had taken place. This cabin, the commander's, embraced the entire area under the poop deck. Aft, and on either side, was a small state-room, the one now temporarily a jail and the other a dead-house, and a yet smaller compartment, leaving a space between expanding forward into a goodly oblong of length coinciding with the ship's beam. A skylight of moderate dimension was overhead, and at each end of the oblong space were two sashed porthole windows easily convertible back into embrasures for short carronades.

All being quickly in readiness, Billy Budd was arraigned, Captain Vere necessarily appearing as the sole witness in the case, and as such temporarily sinking his rank, though singularly maintaining it in a matter apparently trivial, namely, that he testified from the ship's weather side, with that object having caused the court to sit on the lee side. Concisely he narrated all that had led up to the catastrophe, omitting nothing in Claggart's accusation and deposing as to the manner in which the prisoner had received it. At this testimony the three officers glanced with no little surprise at Billy Budd, the last man they would have suspected either of the mutinous design alleged by Claggart or the undeniable deed he himself had done. The first lieutenant, taking judicial primacy and turning toward the prisoner, said, "Captain Vere has spoken. Is it or is it not as Captain Vere says?"

In response came syllables not so much impeded in the utterance as might have been anticipated. They were these: "Captain Vere tells the truth. It is just as Captain Vere says, but it is not as the master-at-arms said. I have eaten the King's bread and I am true to the King."

"I believe you, my man," said the witness, his voice indicating a suppressed emotion not otherwise betrayed.

"God will bless you for that, your honor!" not without stammering said Billy, and all but broke down. But immediately he was recalled to self-control by another question, to which with the same emotional difficulty of utterance he said, "No, there was no malice between us. I never bore malice against the master-at-arms. I am sorry that he is dead. I did not mean to kill him. Could I have used my tongue I would not have struck him. But he foully lied to my face and in presence of my captain, and I had to say something, and I could only say it with a blow, God help me!"

In the impulsive aboveboard manner of the frank one the court saw confirmed all that was implied in words that just previously had perplexed them, coming as they did from the testifier to the tragedy and promptly following Billy's impassioned disclaimer of mutinous intent—Captain Vere's words, "I believe you, my man."

Next it was asked of him whether he knew of or suspected aught savoring of incipient trouble (meaning mutiny, though the explicit term was avoided) going on in any section of the ship's company.

The reply lingered. This was naturally imputed by the court to the same vocal embarrassment which had retarded or obstructed previous answers. But in main it was otherwise here, the question immediately recalling to Billy's mind the interview with the afterguardsman in the forechains. But an innate repugnance to playing a part at all approaching that of an informer against one's own shipmates—the same erring sense of uninstructed honor which had stood in the way of his reporting the matter at the time, though as a loyal man-of-war's man it was incumbent on him, and failure so to do, if charged against him and proven, would have subjected him to the heaviest of penalties; this, with the blind feeling now his that nothing really was being hatched, prevailed with him. When the answer came it was a negative.

"One question more," said the officer of marines, now first speaking and with a troubled earnestness. "You tell us that what the master-at-arms said against you was a lie. Now why should he have so lied, so maliciously lied, since you declare there was no malice between you?"

At that question, unintentionally touching on a spiritual sphere wholly obscure to Billy's thoughts, he was nonplussed, evincing a confusion indeed that some observers, such as can readily be imagined, would have construed into involuntary evidence of hidden guilt. Nevertheless, he strove some way to answer, but all at once relinquished the vain endeavor, at the same time turning an appealing glance towards Captain Vere as deeming him his best helper and friend. Captain Vere, who had been seated for a time, rose to his feet, addressing the interrogator. "The question you put to him comes naturally enough. But how can he rightly answer it?—or anybody else, unless indeed it be he who lies within there," designating the compartment where lay the corpse. "But the prone one there will not rise to our summons. In effect, though, as it seems to me, the point you make is hardly material. Quite aside from any conceivable motive actuating the master-at-arms, and irrespective of the provocation to the blow, a martial court must needs in the present case confine its attention to the blow's consequence, which consequence justly is to be deemed not otherwise than as the striker's deed."

This utterance, the full significance of which it was not at all likely that Billy took in, nevertheless caused him to turn a wistful interrogative look toward the speaker, a look in its dumb expressiveness not unlike that which a dog of generous breed might turn upon his master, seeking in his face some elucidation of a previous gesture ambiguous to the canine intelligence. Nor was the same utterance without marked effect upon the three officers, more especially the soldier. Couched in it seemed to them a meaning unanticipated, involving a prejudgment on the speaker's part. It served to augment a mental disturbance previously evident enough.

The soldier once more spoke, in a tone of suggestive dubiety addressing at once his associates and Captain Vere: "Nobody is present—none of the ship's company, I mean—who might shed lateral light, if any is to be had, upon what remains mysterious in this matter."

"That is thoughtfully put," said Captain Vere; "I see your drift. Ay, there is a mystery; but, to use a scriptural phrase, it is a 'mystery of iniquity,' a matter for psychologic theologians to discuss. But what has a military court to do with it? Not to add that for us any possible investigation of it is cut off by the lasting tongue-tie of—him—in yonder," again designating the mortuary stateroom: "The prisoner's deed—with that alone we have to do."

To this, and particularly the closing reiteration, the marine soldier, knowing not how aptly to reply, sadly abstained from saying aught. The first lieutenant, who at the outset had not unnaturally assumed primacy in the court, now overrulingly instructed by a glance from Captain Vere, a glance more effective than words, resumed that primacy. Turning to the prisoner, "Budd," he said, and scarce in equable tones, "Budd, if you have aught further to say for yourself, say it now."

Upon this the young sailor turned another quick glance toward Captain Vere; then, as taking a hint from that aspect, a hint confirming his own instinct that silence was now best, replied to the lieutenant, "I have said all, sir."

The marine—the same who had been the sentinel without the cabin door at the time that the foretopman, followed by the master-at-arms, entered it—he, standing by the sailor throughout these judicial proceedings, was now directed to take him back to the after compartment originally assigned to the prisoner and his custodian. As the twain disappeared from view, the three officers, as partially liberated from some inward constraint associated with Billy's mere presence, simultaneously stirred in their seats. They exchanged looks of troubled indecision, yet feeling that decide they must and without long delay. For Captain Vere, he for the time stood—unconsciously with his back toward them, apparently in one of his absent fits—gazing out from a sashed porthole to windward upon the monotonous blank of the twilight sea. But the court's silence continuing, broken only at moments by brief consultations, in low earnest tones, this served to arouse him and energize him. Turning, he to-and-fro paced the cabin athwart; in the returning ascent to windward climbing the slant deck in the ship's lee roll, without knowing it symbolizing thus in his action a mind resolute to surmount difficulties even if against primitive instincts strong as the wind and the sea. Presently he came to a stand before the three. After scanning their faces he stood less as mustering his thoughts for expression than as one inly deliberating how best to put them to well-meaning men not intellectually mature, men with whom it was necessary to demonstrate certain principles that were axioms to himself. Similar impatience as to talking is perhaps one reason that deters some minds from addressing any popular assemblies.

When speak he did, something, both in the substance of what he said and his manner of saying it, showed the influence of unshared studies modifying and tempering the practical training of an active career. This, along with his phraseology, now and then was suggestive of the grounds whereon rested that imputation of a certain pedantry socially alleged against him by certain naval men of wholly practical cast, captains who nevertheless would frankly concede that His Majesty's navy mustered no more efficient officer of their grade than Starry Vere.

What he said was to this effect: "Hitherto I have been but the witness, little more; and I should hardly think now to take another tone, that of your coadjutor for the time, did I not perceive in you—at the crisis too—a troubled hesitancy, proceeding, I doubt not, from the clash of military duty with moral scruple—scruple vitalized by compassion. For the compassion, how can I otherwise than share it? But, mindful of paramount obligations, I strive against scruples that may tend to enervate decision. Not, gentlemen, that I hide from myself that the case is an exceptional one. Speculatively regarded, it well might be referred to a jury of casuists. But for us here, acting not as casuists or moralists, it is a case practical, and under martial law practically to be dealt with.

"But your scruples: do they move as in a dusk? Challenge them. Make them advance and declare themselves. Come now; do they import something like this: If, mindless of palliating circumstances, we are bound to regard the death of the master-at-arms as the prisoner's deed, then does that deed constitute a capital crime whereof the penalty is a mortal one. But in natural justice is nothing but the prisoner's overt act to be considered? How can we adjudge to summary and shameful death a fellow creature innocent before God, and whom we feel to be so?—Does that state it aright? You sign sad assent. Well,

I too feel that, the full force of that. It is Nature. But do these buttons that we wear attest that our allegiance is to Nature? No, to the King. Though the ocean, which is inviolate Nature primeval, though this be the element where we move and have our being as sailors, yet as the King's officers lies our duty in a sphere correspondingly natural? So little is that true, that in receiving our commissions we in the most important regards ceased to be natural free agents. When war is declared are we the commissioned fighters previously consulted? We fight at command. If our judgments approve the war, that is but coincidence. So in other particulars. So now. For suppose condemnation to follow these present proceedings. Would it be so much we ourselves that would condemn as it would be martial law operating through us? For that law and the rigor of it, we are not responsible. Our vowed responsibility is in this: That however pitilessly that law may operate in any instances, we nevertheless adhere to it and administer it.

"But the exceptional in the matter moves the hearts within you. Even so too is mine moved. But let not warm hearts betray heads that should be cool. Ashore in a criminal case, will an upright judge allow himself off the bench to be waylaid by some tender kinswoman of the accused seeking to touch him with her tearful plea? Well, the heart here, sometimes the feminine in man, is as that piteous woman, and hard though it be, she must here be ruled out."

He paused, earnestly studying them for a moment; then resumed.

"But something in your aspect seems to urge that it is not solely the heart that moves in you, but also the conscience, the private conscience. But tell me whether or not, occupying the position we do, private conscience should not yield to that imperial one formulated in the code under which alone we officially proceed?"

Here the three men moved in their seats, less convinced than agitated by the course of an argument troubling but the more the spontaneous conflict within.

Perceiving which, the speaker paused for a moment; then abruptly changing his tone, went on.

"To steady us a bit, let us recur to the facts.—In wartime at sea a man-of-war's man strikes his superior in grade, and the blow kills. Apart from its effect the blow itself is, according to the Articles of War, a capital crime. Furthermore—"

"Ay, sir," emotionally broke in the officer of marines, "in one sense it was. But surely Budd purposed neither mutiny nor homicide."

"Surely not, my good man. And before a court less arbitrary and more merciful than a martial one, that plea would largely extenuate. At the Last Assizes it shall acquit. But how here? We proceed under the law of the Mutiny Act. In feature no child can resemble his father more than that Act resembles in spirit the thing from which it derives—War. In His Majesty's service—in this ship, indeed—there are Englishmen forced to fight for the King against their will. Against their conscience, for aught we know. Though as their fellow creatures some of us may appreciate their position, yet as navy officers what reck we of it? Still less recks the enemy. Our impressed men he would fain cut down in the same swath with our volunteers. As regards the enemy's naval conscripts, some of whom may even share our own abhorrence of the regicidal French Directory, it is the same on our side. War looks but to the frontage, the appearance. And the Mutiny Act, War's child, takes after the father. Budd's intent or non-intent is nothing to the purpose.

"But while, put to it by those anxieties in you which I cannot but respect, I only repeat myself—while thus strangely we prolong proceedings that should be summary—the enemy may be sighted and an engagement result. We must do; and one of two things must we do— condemn or let go."

"Can we not convict and yet mitigate the penalty?" asked the sailing master, here speaking, and falteringly, for the first.

"Gentlemen, were that clearly lawful for us under the circumstances, consider the consequences of such clemency. The people" (meaning the ship's company) "have native sense; most of them are familiar with our naval usage and tradition; and how would they take it? Even could you explain to them—which our official position forbids—they, long molded by arbitrary discipline, have not that kind of intelligent responsiveness that might qualify them to comprehend and discriminate. No, to the people the foretopman's deed, however it be worded in the announcement, will be plain homicide committed in a flagrant act of mutiny. What penalty for that should follow, they know. But it does not follow. *Why?* they will ruminate. You know what sailors are. Will they not revert to the recent outbreak at the Nore? Ay. They know the well-founded alarm—the panic it struck throughout England. Your clement sentence they would account pusillanimous. They would think that we flinch, that we are afraid of them—afraid of practicing a lawful rigor singularly demanded at this juncture, lest it should provoke new troubles. What shame to us such a conjecture on their part, and how deadly to discipline. You see then, whither, prompted by duty and the law, I steadfastly drive. But I beseech you, my friends, do not take me amiss. I feel as you do for this unfortunate boy. But did he know our hearts, I take him to be of that generous nature that he would feel even for us on whom in this military neces-sity so heavy a compulsion is laid."

With that, crossing the deck he resumed his place by the sashed porthole, tacitly leaving the three to come to a decision. On the cabin's opposite side the troubled court sat silent. Loyal lieges, plain and prac-tical, though at bottom they dissented from some points Captain Vere had put to them, they were without the faculty, hardly had the incli-nation, to gainsay one whom they felt to be an earnest man, one too not less their superior in mind than in naval rank. But it is not improb-able that even such of his words as were not without influence over them, less came home to them than his closing appeal to their instinct as sea officers: in the forethought he threw out as to the practical con-sequences to discipline, considering the unconfirmed tone of the fleet at the time, should a man-of-war's man's violent killing at sea of a superior in grade be allowed to pass for aught else than a capital crime demanding prompt infliction of the penalty.

Not unlikely they were brought to something more or less akin to that harassed frame of mind which in the year 1842 actuated the com-mander of the U.S. brig-of-war *Somers* to resolve, under the so-called Articles of War, Articles modeled upon the English Mutiny Act, to resolve upon the execution at sea of a midshipman and two sailors as mutineers designing the seizure of the brig. Which resolution was carried out though in a time of peace and within not many days' sail of home. An act vindicated by a naval court of inquiry subsequently convened ashore. History, and here cited without comment. True, the circumstances on board the *Somers* were different from those on board the *Bellipotent*. But the urgency felt, well-warranted or otherwise, was much the same.

Says a writer whom few know, "Forty years after a battle it is easy for a noncombatant to reason about how it ought to have been fought. It is another thing personally and under fire to have to direct the fighting while involved in the obscuring smoke of it. Much so with respect to other emergencies involving considerations both practical and moral, and when it is imperative promptly to act. The greater the fog the more it imperils the steamer, and speed is put on though at the hazard of running somebody down. Little ween the snug card players in the cabin of the responsibilities of the sleepless man on the bridge."

In brief, Billy Budd was formally convicted and sentenced to be hung at the yardarm in the early morning watch, it being now night. Otherwise, as is customary in such cases, the sentence would forthwith have been carried out. In wartime on the field or in the fleet, a mortal punishment decreed by a drumhead court—on the field sometimes decreed by but a nod from the general—follows without delay on the heel of conviction, without appeal.

It was Captain Vere himself who of his own motion communicated the finding of the court to the prisoner, for that purpose going to the compartment where he was in custody and bidding the marine there to withdraw for the time.

Beyond the communication of the sentence, what took place at this interview was never known. But in view of the character of the twain briefly closeted in that stateroom, each radically sharing in the rarer qualities of our nature—so rare indeed as to be all but incredible to average minds however much cultivated—some conjectures may be ventured.

It would have been in consonance with the spirit of Captain Vere should he on this occasion have concealed nothing from the condemned one—should he indeed have frankly disclosed to him the part he himself had played in bringing about the decision, at the same time revealing his actuating motives. On Billy's side it is not improbable that such a confession would have been received in much the same spirit that prompted it. Not without a sort of joy, indeed, he might have appreciated the brave opinion of him implied in his captain's making such a confidant of him. Nor, as to the sentence itself, could he have been insensible that it was imparted to him as to one not afraid to die. Even more may have been. Captain Vere in end may have developed the passion sometimes latent under an exterior stoical or indifferent. He was old enough to have been Billy's father. The austere devotee of military duty, letting himself melt back into what remains primeval in our formalized humanity, may in end have caught Billy to his heart, even as Abraham may have caught young Isaac on the brink of resolutely offering him up in obedience to the exacting behest. But there is no telling the sacrament, seldom if in any case revealed to the gadding world, wherever under circumstances at all akin to those here attempted to be set forth two of great Nature's nobler order embrace. There is privacy at the time, inviolable to the survivor; and holy oblivion, the sequel to each diviner magnanimity, providentially covers all at last.

The first to encounter Captain Vere in act of leaving the compartment was the senior lieutenant. The face he beheld, for the moment one expressive of the agony of the strong, was to that officer, though a man of fifty, a startling revelation. That the condemned one suffered less than he who mainly had effected the condemnation was apparently indicated by the former's exclamation in the scene soon perforce to be touched upon.

• • •

Of a series of incidents within a brief term rapidly following each other, the adequate narration may take up a term less brief, especially if explanation or comment here and there seem requisite to the better understanding of such incidents. Between the entrance into the cabin of him who never left it alive, and him who when he did leave it left it as one condemned to die; between this and the closeted interview just given, less than an hour and a half had elapsed. It was an interval long enough, however, to awaken speculations among no few of the ship's company as to what it was that could be detaining in the cabin the master-at-arms and the sailor; for a rumor that both of them had been seen to enter it and neither of them had been seen to emerge, this rumor had got abroad upon the gun decks and in the tops, the people of a great warship being in one respect like villagers, taking microscopic note of every outward movement or nonmovement going on. When therefore, in weather not at all tempestuous, all hands were called in the second dogwatch, a summons under such circumstances not usual in those hours, the crew were not wholly unprepared for some announcement extraordinary, one having connection too with the continued absence of the two men from their wonted haunts.

There was a moderate sea at the time; and the moon, newly risen and near to being at its full, silvered the white spar deck wherever not blotted by the clear-cut shadows horizontally thrown of fixtures and moving men. On either side the quarter-deck the marine guard under arms was drawn up; and Captain Vere, standing in his place surrounded by all the wardroom officers, addressed his men. In so doing, his manner showed neither more nor less than that properly pertaining to his supreme position aboard his own ship. In clear terms and concise he told them what had taken place in the cabin: that the master-at-arms was dead, that he who had killed him had been already tried by a summary court and condemned to death, and that the execution would take place in the early morning watch. The word *mutiny* was not named in what he said. He refrained too from making the occasion an opportunity for any preachment as to the maintenance of discipline, thinking perhaps that under existing circumstances in the navy the consequence of violating discipline should be made to speak for itself.

Their captain's announcement was listened to by the throng of standing sailors in a dumbness like that of a seated congregation of believers in hell listening to the clergyman's announcement of his Calvinistic text.

At the close, however, a confused murmur went up. It began to wax. All but instantly, then, at a sign, it was pierced and suppressed by shrill whistles of the boatswain and his mates. The word was given to about ship.

To be prepared for burial Claggart's body was delivered to certain petty officers of his mess. And here, not to clog the sequel with lateral matters, it may be added that at a suitable hour, the master-at-arms was committed to the sea with every funeral honor properly belonging to his naval grade.

In this proceeding as in every public one growing out of the tragedy strict adherence to usage was observed. Nor in any point could it have been at all deviated from, either with respect to Claggart or Billy Budd, without begetting undesirable speculations in the ship's company, sailors, and more particularly men-of-war's men, being of all men the greatest sticklers for usage. For similar cause, all communication between Captain Vere and the condemned one ended with the closeted interview already given, the latter being now surrendered to the ordinary routine preliminary to the end. His transfer under guard from the captain's quarters was effected without unusual precautions—at least no visible ones. If possible, not to let the men so much as surmise that their officers anticipate aught amiss from them is the tacit rule in a military ship. And the more that some sort of trouble should really be apprehended, the more do the officers keep that apprehension to themselves, though not the less unostentatious vigilance may be augmented. In the present instance, the sentry placed over the prisoner had strict orders to let no one have communication with him but the chaplain. And certain unobtrusive measures were taken absolutely to insure this point.

• • •

In a seventy-four of the old order the deck known as the upper gun deck was the one covered over by the spar deck, which last, though not without its armament, was for the most part exposed to the weather. In general it was at all hours free from hammocks; those of the crew swinging on the lower gun deck and berth deck, the latter being not only a dormitory but also the place for the stowing of the sailors' bags, and on both sides lined with the large chests or movable pantries of the many messes of the men.

On the starboard side of the *Bellipotent's* upper gun deck, behold Billy Budd under sentry lying prone in irons in one of the bays formed by the regular spacing of the guns comprising the batteries on either side. All these pieces were of the heavier caliber of that period. Mounted on lumbering wooden carriages, they were hampered with cumbersome harness of breeching and strong side-tackles for running them out. Guns and carriages, together with the long rammers and shorter linstocks lodged in loops overhead—all these, as customary, were painted black; and the heavy hempen breechings, tarred to the same tint, wore the like livery of the undertakers. In contrast with the funereal hue of these surroundings, the prone sailor's exterior apparal, white jumper and white duck trousers, each more or less soiled, dimly glimmered in the obscure light of the bay like a patch of discolored snow in early April lingering at some upland cave's black mouth. In effect he is already in his shroud, or the garments that shall serve him in lieu of one. Over him but scarce illuminating him, two battle lanterns swing from two massive beams of the deck above. Fed with the oil supplied by the war contractors (whose gains, honest or other-wise, are in every land an anticipated portion of the harvest of death), with flickering splashes of dirty yellow light they pollute the pale moonshine all but ineffectually struggling in obstructed flecks through the open ports from which the tampioned cannon protrude. Other lanterns at intervals serve but to bring out somewhat the obscurer bays which, like small confessionals or side-chapels in a cathedral, branch from the long dim-vistaed broad aisle between the two batteries of that covered tier.

Such was the deck where now lay the Handsome Sailor. Through the rose-tan of his complexion no pallor could have shown. It would have taken days of sequestration from the winds and the sun to have brought about the effacement of that. But the skeleton in the cheekbone at the point of its angle was just beginning delicately to be defined under the warm-tinted skin. In fervid hearts self-contained, some brief experiences devour our human tissue as secret fire in a ship's hold consumes cotton in the bale.

But now lying between the two guns, as nipped in the vice of fate, Billy's agony, mainly proceeding from a generous young heart's virgin experience of the diabolical incarnate and effective in some men—the tension of that agony was over now. It survived not the something healing in the closeted interview with Captain Vere. Without movement, he lay as in a trance, that adolescent expression previously noted as his taking on something akin to the look of a slumbering child in the cradle when the warm hearth-glow of the still chamber at night plays on the dimples that at whiles mysteriously form in the cheek, silently coming and going there. For now and then in the gyved one's trance a serene happy light born of some wandering reminiscence or dream would diffuse itself over his face, and then wane away only anew to return.

The chaplain, coming to see him and finding him thus, and perceiving no sign that he was conscious of his presence, attentively regarded him for a space, then slipping aside, withdrew for the time, peradventure feeling that even he, the minister of Christ though receiving his stipend from Mars, had no consolation to proffer which could result in a peace transcending that which he beheld. But in the small hours he came again. And the prisoner, now awake to his surroundings, noticed his approach, and civilly, all but cheerfully, welcomed him. But it was to little purpose that in the interview following, the good man sought to bring Billy Budd to some godly understanding that he must die, and at dawn. True, Billy himself freely referred to his death as a thing close at hand; but it was something in the way that children will refer to death in general, who yet among their other sports will play a funeral with hearse and mourners.

Not that like children Billy was incapable of conceiving what death really is. No, but he was wholly without irrational fear of it, a fear more prevalent in highly civilized communities than those so-called barbarous ones which in all respects stand nearer to unadulterate Nature. And, as elsewhere said, a barbarian Billy radically was—as much so, for all the costume, as his countrymen the British captives, living trophies, made to march in the Roman triumph of Germanicus. Quite as much so as those later barbarians, young men probably, and picked specimens among the earlier British converts to Christianity, at least nominally such, taken to Rome (as today converts from lesser isles of the sea may be taken to London), of whom the Pope of that time, admiring the strangeness of their personal beauty so unlike the Italian stamp, their clear ruddy complexion and curled flaxen locks, exclaimed, "Angles" (meaning *English*, the modern derivative), "Angles, do you call them? And is it because they look so like angels?" Had it been later in time, one would think that the Pope had in mind Fra Angelico's seraphs, some of whom, plucking apples in gardens of the Hesperides, have the faint rosebud complexion of the more beautiful English girls.

If in vain the good chaplain sought to impress the young barbarian with ideas of death akin to those conveyed in the skull, dial, and crossbones on old tombstones, equally futile to all appearance were his efforts to bring home to him the thought of salvation and a Savior. Billy listened, but less out of awe or reverence, perhaps, than from a certain natural politeness, doubtless at bottom regarding all that in much the same way that most mariners of his class take any discourse abstract or out of the common tone of the workaday world. And this sailor way of taking clerical discourse is not wholly unlike the way in which the primer of Christianity, full of transcendent miracles, was received long ago on tropic isles by any superior *savage*, so called—a

Tahitian, say, of Captain Cook's time or shortly after that time. Out of natural courtesy he received, but did not appropriate. It was like a gift placed in the palm of an outreached hand upon which the fingers do not close.

But the *Bellipotent's* chaplain was a discreet man possessing the good sense of a good heart. So he insisted not in his vocation here. At the instance of Captain Vere, a lieutenant had apprised him of pretty much everything as to Billy; and since he felt that innocence was even a better thing than religion wherewith to go to Judgment, he reluctantly withdrew; but in his emotion not without first performing an act strange enough in an Englishman, and under the circumstances yet more so in any regular priest. Stooping over, he kissed on the fair cheek his fellow man, a felon in martial law, one whom though on the confines of death he felt he could never convert to a dogma; nor for all that did he fear for his future.

Marvel not that having been made acquainted with the young sailor's essential innocence the worthy man lifted not a finger to avert the doom of such a martyr to martial discipline. So to do would not only have been as idle as invoking the desert, but would also have been an audacious transgression of the bounds of his function, one as exactly prescribed to him by military law as that of the boatswain or any other naval officer. Bluntly put, a chaplain is the minister of the Prince of Peace serving in the host of the God of War—Mars. As such, he is as incongruous as a musket would be on the altar at Christmas. Why, then, is he there? Because he indirectly subserves the purpose attested by the cannon; because too he lends the sanction of the religion of the meek to that which practically is the abrogation of everything but brute Force.

The night so luminous on the spar deck, but otherwise on the cavernous ones below, levels so like the tiered galleries in a coal mine— the luminous night passed away. But like the prophet in the chariot disappearing in heaven and dropping his mantle to Elisha, the with-drawing night transferred its pale robe to the breaking day. A meek, shy light appeared in the East, where stretched a diaphanous fleece of white furrowed vapor. That light slowly waxed. Suddenly *eight bells* was struck aft, responded to by one louder metallic stroke from forward. It was four o'clock in the morning. Instantly the silver whistles were heard summoning all hands to witness punishment. Up through the great hatchways rimmed with racks of heavy shot the watch below came pouring, overspreading with the watch already on deck the space between the mainmast and foremast including that occupied by the capacious launch and the black booms tiered on either side of it, boat and booms making a summit of observation for the powder-boys and younger tars. A different group comprising one watch of topmen leaned over the rail of that sea balcony, no small one in a seventy-four, looking down on the crowd below. Man or boy, none spake but in whisper, and few spake at all. Captain Vere—as before, the central figure among the assembled commissioned officers—stood nigh the break of the poop deck facing forward. Just below him on the quarter-deck the marines in full equipment were drawn up much as at the scene of the promulgated sentence.

At sea in the old time, the execution by halter of a military sailor was generally from the foreyard. In the present instance, for special reasons the mainyard was assigned. Under an arm of that yard the prisoner was presently brought up, the chaplain attending him. It was noted at the time, and remarked upon afterwards, that in this final scene the good man evinced little or nothing of the perfunctory. Brief speech indeed he had with the condemned one, but the genuine Gospel was less on his tongue than in his aspect and manner towards him. The final preparations personal to the latter being speedily brought to an end by two boatswain's mates, the consummation impended. Billy stood facing aft. At the penultimate moment, his words, his only ones, words wholly unobstructed in the utterance, were these: "God bless Captain Vere!" Syllables so unanticipated coming from one with the ignominious hemp about his neck—a conventional felon's benediction directed aft towards the quarters of honor; syllables too delivered in the clear melody of a singing bird on the point of launching from the twig—had a phenomenal effect, not unenhanced by the rare personal beauty of the young sailor, spiritualized now through late experiences so poignantly profound.

Without volition, as it were, as if indeed the ship's populace were but the vehicles of some vocal current electric, with one voice from slow and aloft came a resonant sympathetic echo: "God bless Captain Vere!" And yet at that instant Billy alone must have been in their hearts, even as in their eyes.

At the pronounced words and the spontaneous echo that voluminously rebounded them, Captain Vere, either through stoic self-control or a sort of momentary paralysis induced by emotional shock, stood erectly rigid as a musket in the ship-armorer's rack.

The hull, deliberately recovering from the periodic roll to leeward, was just regaining an even keel when the last signal, a preconcerted dumb one, was given. At the same moment it chanced that the vapory fleece hanging low in the East was shot through with a soft glory as of the fleece of the Lamb of God seen in mystical vision, and simultaneously therewith, watched by the wedged mass of upturned faces, Billy ascended; and, ascending, took the full rose of the dawn.

In the pinioned figure arrived at the yard-end, to the wonder of all no motion was apparent, none save that created by the slow roll of the hull in moderate weather, so majestic in a great ship ponderously cannoned.

When some days afterwards, in reference to the singularity just mentioned, the purser, a rather ruddy, rotund person more accurate as an accountant than profound as a philosopher, said at mess to the surgeon, "What testimony to the force lodged in will power," the latter, saturnine, spare, and tall, one in whom a discreet causticity went along with a manner less genial than polite, replied, "Your pardon, Mr.

Purser. In a hanging scientifically conducted—and under special orders I myself directed how Budd's was to be effected—any movement following the completed suspension and originating in the body suspended, such movement indicates mechanical spasm in the muscular system. Hence the absence of that is no more attributable to will power, as you call it, than to horsepower—begging your pardon."

"But this muscular spasm you speak of, is not that in a degree more or less invariable in these cases?"

"Assuredly so, Mr. Purser."

"How then, my good sir, do you account for its absence in this instance?"

"Mr. Purser, it is clear that your sense of the singularity in this matter equals not mine. You account for it by what you call will power—a term not yet included in the lexicon of science. For me, I do not, with my present knowledge, pretend to account for it at all. Even should we assume the hypothesis that at the first touch of the halyards the action of Budd's heart, intensified by extraordinary emotion at its climax, abruptly stopped—much like a watch when in carelessly winding it up you strain at the finish, thus snapping the chain—even under that hypothesis how account for the phenomenon that followed?"

"You admit, then, that the absence of spasmodic movement was phenomenal."

"It was phenomenal, Mr. Purser, in the sense that it was an appearance the cause of which is not immediately to be assigned."

"But tell me, my dear sir," pertinaciously continued the other, "was the man's death effected by the halter, or was it a species of euthanasia?"

"*Euthanasia*, Mr. Purser, is something like your *will power:* I doubt its authenticity as a scientific term—begging your pardon again. It is at once imaginative and metaphysical—in short, Greek—But," abruptly changing his tone, "there is a case in the sick bay that I do not care to leave to my assistants. Beg your pardon, but excuse me." And rising from the mess he formally withdrew.

• • •

The silence at the moment of execution and for a moment or two continuing thereafter, a silence but emphasized by the regular wash of the sea against the hull or the flutter of a sail caused by the helmsman's eyes being tempted astray, this emphasized silence was gradually disturbed by a sound not easily to be verbally rendered. Whoever has heard the freshet-wave of a torrent suddenly swelled by pouring showers in tropical mountains, showers not shared by the plain; whoever has heard the first muffled murmur of its sloping advance through precipitous woods may form some conception of the sound now heard. The seeming remoteness of its source was because of its murmurous indistinctness, since it came from close by, even from the men massed on the ship's open deck. Being inarticulate, it was dubious in significance further than it seemed to indicate some capricious revulsion of thought or feeling such as mobs ashore are liable to, in the present instance possibly implying a sullen revocation on the men's part of their involuntary echoing of Billy's benediction. But ere the murmur had time to wax into clamor it was met by a strategic command, the more telling that it came with abrupt unexpectedness: "Pipe down the starboard watch, Boatswain, and see that they go."

Shrill as the shriek of the sea hawk, the silver whistles of the boatswain and his mates pierced that ominous low sound, dissipating it; and yielding to the mechanism of discipline the throng was thinned by one-half. For the remainder, most of them were set to temporary employments connected with trimming the yards and so forth, business readily to be got up to serve occasion by any officer of the deck.

Now each proceeding that follows a mortal sentence pronounced at sea by a drumhead court is characterized by promptitude not perceptibly merging into hurry, though bordering that. The hammock, the one which had been Billy's bed when alive, having already been ballasted with shot and otherwise prepared to serve for his canvas coffin, the last offices of the sea undertakers, the sailmaker's mates, were now speedily completed. When everything was in readiness a second call for all hands, made necessary by the strategic movement before mentioned, was sounded, now to witness burial.

The details of this closing formality it needs not to give. But when the tilted plank let slide its freight into the sea, a second strange human murmur was heard, blended now with another inarticulate sound proceeding from certain larger seafowl who, their attention having been attracted by the peculiar commotion in the water resulting from the heavy sloped dive of the shotted hammock into the sea, flew screaming to the spot. So near the hull did they come, that the stridor or bony creak of their gaunt double-jointed pinions was audible. As the ship under light airs passed on, leaving the burial spot astern, they still kept circling it low down with the moving shadow of their outstretched wings and the croaked requiem of their cries.

Upon sailors as superstitious as those of the age preceding ours, men-of-war's men too who had just beheld the prodigy of repose in the form suspended in air, and now foundering in the deeps; to such mariners the action of the seafowl, though dictated by mere animal greed for prey, was big with no prosaic significance. An uncertain movement began among them, in which some encroachment was made. It was tolerated but for a moment. For suddenly the drum beat to quarters, which familiar sound happening at least twice every day, had upon the present occasion a signal peremptoriness in it. True martial discipline long continued superinduces in average man a sort of impulse whose operation at the official word of command much resembles in its promptitude the effect of an instinct.

The drumbeat dissolved the multitude, distributing most of them along the batteries of the two covered gun decks. There, as wonted, the guns' crews stood by their respective cannon erect and silent. In due course the first officer, sword under arm and standing in his place on the quarter-deck, formally received the successive reports of the sworded lieutenants commanding the sections of batteries below; the last of which reports being made, the summed report he delivered with the customary salute to the commander. All this occupied time, which in the present case was the object in beating to quarters at an hour prior to the customary one. That such variance from usage was authorized by an officer like Captain Vere, a martinet as some deemed him, was evidence of the necessity for unusual action implied in what he deemed to be temporarily the mood of his men. "With mankind," he would say, "forms, measured forms, are everything; and that is the import couched in the story of Orpheus with his lyre spellbinding the wild denizens of the wood." And this he once applied to the disruption of forms going on across the Channel and the consequences thereof.

At this unwonted muster at quarters, all proceeded as at the regular hour. The band on the quarter-deck played a sacred air, after which the chaplain went through the customary morning service. That done, the drum beat the retreat; and toned by music and religious rites subserving the discipline and purposes of war, the men in their wonted orderly manner dispersed to the places alloted them when not at the guns.

And now it was full day. The fleece of low-hanging vapor had vanished, licked up by the sun that late had so glorified it. And the circumambient air in the clearness of its serenity was like smooth white marble in the polished block not yet removed from the marble-dealer's yard.

The symmetry of form attainable in pure fiction cannot so readily be achieved in a narration essentially having less to do with fable than with fact. Truth uncompromisingly told will always have its ragged edges; hence the conclusion of such a narration is apt to be less finished than an architectural finial.

How it fared with the Handsome Sailor during the year of the Great Mutiny has been faithfully given. But though properly the story ends with his life, something in way of sequel will not be amiss. Three brief chapters will suffice.

In the general rechristening under the Directory of the craft originally forming the navy of the French monarchy, the *St. Louis* line-of-battle ship was named the *Athée* (the *Atheist*). Such a name, like some other substituted ones in the Revolutionary fleet, while proclaiming the infidel audacity of the ruling power, was yet, though not so intended to be, the aptest name, if one consider it, ever given to a war-ship; far more so indeed than the *Devastation*, the *Erebus* (the *Hell*), and similar names bestowed upon fighting ships.

On the return passage to the English fleet from the detached cruise during which occurred the events already recorded, the *Bellipotent* fell in with the *Athée*. An engagement ensued, during which Captain Vere, in the act of putting his ship alongside the enemy with a view of throwing his boarders across her bulwarks, was hit by a musket ball from a porthole of the enemy's main cabin. More than disabled, he dropped to the deck and was carried below to the same cockpit where some of his men already lay. The senior lieutenant took command. Under him the enemy was finally captured, and though much crip-pled was by rare good fortune successfully taken into Gibraltar, an English port not very distant from the scene of the fight. There, Cap-tain Vere with the rest of the wounded was put ashore. He lingered for some days, but the end came. Unhappily he was cut off too early for the Nile and Trafalgar. The spirit that 'spite its philosophic aus-terity may yet have indulged in the most secret of all passions, ambi-tion, never attained to the fullness of fame.

Not long before death, while lying under the influence of that magical drug which, soothing the physical frame, mysteriously oper-ates on the subtler element in man, he was heard to murmur words inexplicable to his attendant: "Billy Budd, Billy Budd." That these were not the accents of remorse would seem clear from what the attendant said to the *Bellipotent*'s senior officer of marines, who, as the most reluctant to condemn of the members of the drumhead court, too well knew, though here he kept the knowledge to himself, who Billy Budd was.

Some few weeks after the execution, among other matters under the head of "News from the Mediterranean," there appeared in a naval chronicle of the time, an authorized weekly publication, an account of the affair. It was doubtless for the most part written in good faith, though the medium, partly rumor, through which the facts must have retched the writer served to deflect and in part falsify them. The account was as follows:

"On the tenth of the last month a deplorable occurrence took place on board H.M.S. *Bellipotent.* John Claggart, the ship's master-at-arms, discovering that some sort of plot was incipient among an inferior section of the ship's company, and that the ringleader was one William Budd; he, Claggart, in the act of arraigning the man before the captain, was vindictively stabbed to the heart by the suddenly drawn sheath knife of Budd.

"The deed and the implement employed sufficiently suggest that though mustered into the service under an English name the assassin was no Englishman, but one of those aliens adopting English cognomens whom the present extraordinary necessities of the service have caused to be admitted into it in considerable numbers.

"The enormity of the crime and the extreme depravity of the criminal appear the greater in view of the character of the victim, a middle-aged man respectable and discreet, belonging to that minor official grade, the petty officers, upon whom, as none know better than the commissioned gentlemen, the efficiency of His Majesty's navy so largely depends. His function was a responsible one, at once onerous and thankless; and his fidelity in it the greater because of his strong patriotic impulse. In this instance as in so many other instances in these days, the character of this unfortunate man signally refutes, if refutation were needed, that peevish saying attributed to the late Dr. Johnson, that patriotism is the last refuge of a scoundrel.

"The criminal paid the penalty of his crime. The promptitude of the punishment has proved salutary. Nothing amiss is now apprehended aboard H.M.S. *Bellipotent.*"

The above, appearing in a publication now long ago superannuated and forgotten, is all that hitherto has stood in human record to attest what manner of men respectively were John Claggart and Billy Budd.

• • •

Everything is for a term venerated in navies. Any tangible object associated with some striking incident of the service is converted into a monument. The spar from which the foretopman was suspended was for some few years kept trace of by the bluejackets. Their knowledges followed it from ship to dockyard and again from dockyard to ship, still pursuing it even when at last reduced to a mere dockyard boom. To them a chip of it was as a piece of the Cross. Ignorant though they were of the secret facts of the tragedy, and not thinking but that the penalty was somehow unavoidably inflicted from the naval point of view, for all that, they instinctively felt that Billy was a sort of man as incapable of mutiny as of wilful murder. They recalled the fresh young image of the Handsome Sailor, that face never deformed by a sneer or subtler vile freak of the heart within. This impression of him was doubtless deepened by the fact that he was gone, and in a measure mysteriously gone. On the gun decks of the *Bellipotent* the general estimate of his nature and its unconscious simplicity eventually found rude utterance from another foretopman, one of his own watch, gifted, as some sailors are, with an artless *poetic* temperament. The tarry hand made some lines which, after circulating among the shipboard crews for a while, finally got rudely printed at Portsmouth as a ballad. The title given to it was the sailor's.

BILLY IN THE DARBIES

Good of the chaplain to enter Lone Bay
And down on his marrowbones here and pray
For the likes just o' me, Billy Budd.—But, look:
Through the port comes the moonshine astray!
It tips the guard's cutlass and silvers this nook;
But 'twill die in the dawning of Billy's last day.
A jewel-block they'll make of me tomorrow,
Pendant pearl from the yardarm-end
Like the eardrop I gave to Bristol Molly—
O, 'tis me, not the sentence they'll suspend.

Ay, ay, all is up; and I must up too,

Early in the morning, aloft from alow.

On an empty stomach now never it would do.

They'll give me a nibble—bit o' biscuit ere I go.

Sure, a messmate will reach me the last parting cup;

But, turning heads away from the hoist and the belay,

Heaven knows who will have the running of me up!

No pipe to those halyards.—But aren't it all sham?

A blur's in my eyes; it is dreaming that I am.

A hatchet to my hawser? All adrift to go?

The drum roll to grog, and Billy never know?

But Donald he has promised to stand by the plank;

So I'll shake a friendly hand ere I sink.

But—no! It is dead then I'll be, come to think.

I remember Taff the Welshman when he sank.

And his cheek it was like the budding pink.

But me they'll lash in hammock, drop me deep.

Fathoms down, fathoms down, how I'll dream fast asleep.

I feel it stealing now. Sentry, are you there?

Just ease these darbies at the wrist,

And roll me over fair!

I am sleepy, and the oozy weeds about me twist.

from All Hands Aloft!

by Lou A. Schmitt

The U.S. captured several German sailing ships during World War I and used them to transport supplies. A shortage of sailors forced the Navy to man the vessels with green cadets like Lou A. Schmitt, who in 1918 sailed aboard the square-rigger Arapahoe *on a supply run from San Francisco to the Philippines. Three weeks into the voyage, the seas began to build.*

That night the wind blew off and on and the swells built up rapidly. Several times during our watch rain came sweeping over the sea to pour down in torrential cloudbursts. The sky was inky black and at times, as the wind died away, the air felt close and muggy.

At lookout I was joined by the Finn and together we stood with our backs against the fo'c'slehead pipe rail, feet braced wide as *Arapahoe* rolled and wallowed. From overhead came the creak of rigging, the rattle of blocks and the flapping of canvas as the great masts swept the sky like pendulums of giant clocks.

Everyone seemed jumpy and nervous. It was as though we were waiting for something to happen, something frightening but which we had no power to avoid. Even the Finn was unusually quiet as we stared into the darkness and rain. Hoping to relieve the tension, I came up with a lame, "Sort of rough tonight, eh, bos'n?"

"Gon' blow hard."

"Oh, now! Wait a minute, how about that red sky this evening, don't that mean good weather?"

"Yeah, but he gon' blow lak hell firs'—typhoon, maybe."

"How can you tell when it's a typhoon?"

"Ho! Ho! Don' vorry, you gon' know all right," he answered as he felt his way to the deck.

Breakfast on Tuesday morning was calamitous on the rolling ship. From the galley came the crash of pots and pans and the curses of the cook as things slid about in confusion. Inside the fo'c'sle conditions were but little better as we lay wedged in our bunks attempting to sleep. Eventually, hot coffee was handed in, which we drank standing up with arms hooked around a stanchion. Cooking in the galley was impossible and we were lucky to have bread for the meal. On deck the starboard watch had worked since daylight snugging down the ship and making fast lines and gear. Apparently conditions had changed but little during their watch; the wind remained light with heavy squalls of rain.

The system of navigation used on *Arapahoe* was quite accurate even if a bit old-fashioned. The ship was equipped with a good chronometer and by taking morning and noon shots of the sun the Captain was able to determine fairly exact latitude and longitude.

During stormy weather with overcast skies, it became necessary to navigate by dead reckoning. This system was based on a calculation of the ship's speed and distance sailed over a certain course and from a certain fixed point. The speed and distance run were determined by an instrument known as the taffrail log. Secured to the rail at the stern of the ship, it resembled a speedometer with a dial indicating the speed and a meter showing miles traveled. Operated by a long line streaming out from the stern, one end was attached to the instrument and the other to a rotor device that caused the line to turn as it passed through the water. By keeping a careful record of the course sailed and the time we were on it, it was possible by knowing the distance run to have a pretty accurate idea of our position.

At eight bells, we came on deck to face a driving rain that made scraping or painting impossible. This was received with high glee by the cadets who figured we would be allowed to stand by in the fo'c'sle. Apparently, however, the rain presented no problem to the mate who, without doubt, had experienced like situations many times before. Soon the entire watch, except for the man at the wheel, was ordered forward to work under the fo'c'slehead.

The mate's order had aroused but slight enthusiasm, and there had been audible grumbling as we straggled forward through the downpour. Stavanger and Laurence were busily at work making a strop from a length of wire rope that had been secured from a huge roll in the 'tweendecks. Lofty and Sanbert had armed themselves with scrapers, and started "scriping and shiping" rust on the anchor windlass, making a great fuss and noise as though to impress us lowly cadets with the importance of their task.

For a moment we stood around hoping we had been forgotten when suddenly, turning to the Finn, the mate asked, "How are dese men, bos'n, are dey gud at overhauling t'ings?"

"Yes, dey're ver' gud, Sir."

"Gud. Put dem to vork overhauling de potatoes."

Before leaving San Francisco, *Arapahoe* had taken on a supply of potatoes that looked ample for a voyage around the world. In spite of the fact that they had constituted the main item of food for thirty-two men three times a day for a month, we still had a formidable amount.

Apparently, the warm sub-tropical climate or the dampness under the fo'c'slehead had agreed with the potatoes or, maybe, it was simply a desire to propagate their kind, at any rate they soon were throwing out long, green shoots.

Overhauling the potatoes consisted of removing the sprouts, cutting off any ends that had started to spoil, and picking out those that were beyond redemption. This was one job of overhauling that could be entrusted entirely to the cadets, and soon we were seated in a semicircle like old ladies at a quilting bee as we plucked at shoots, whacked off ends and threw the finished product into empty bins. For the next several weeks it was to keep us occupied when the mate could find nothing else for us to do, and I am sure that during that time I personally became acquainted with most of the ship's potatoes. Evidently the mate recognized our contribution toward working the ship and wished to record our efforts because the log for July 16th contained the following entry:

> "Scriping foreward windles and shiping rust under fore-castle head   two mend puting strops on the yard   remender overhauling the potatoes
> Course W 1/2 S lat 16°45' long 167°

According to the Finn it had been the custom on German ships to rig safety ropes from the masts out to the end of the yards in such a manner that the ropes would be at one's back. Their purpose was to prevent a fall over backward in case a hand slipped while hauling on a stubborn sail. Another precaution taken during heavy weather was safety netting; nets of wide mesh strung above the bulwarks to prevent men being washed over the side when the ship was boarded by seas. *Arapahoe* was fitted with neither of these devices, and listening to his stories of men (even whole watches) lost overboard, did nothing to decrease our nervousness.

Throughout the day it rained continually; at times the sky seemed to close in, shutting out the daylight and causing us to glance aloft. Now and then, as she rolled farther than usual, a sea would break over the side and green water rush from bulwark to bulwark before running out freeing ports in a smother of foam.

The heavy rains had furnished us an opportunity to try out our oilskins, most of which had been bought from the slop chest and were of an inferior quality. After a few hours spent lying over the yards on our stomachs, the middle of the short jackets were worn to the consistency of cheesecloth, and of about the same value in dispelling water. To make them more resistant some of the crew painted them with linseed oil, a treatment that was not permanent but effective while it lasted. Regardless of what was worn or the precautions taken, it was an impossibility to keep dry and usually by the end of the watch we were soaked.

During our afternoon watch below most of the conversation had to do with typhoons and what probably would happen if we were caught in one. Both Stavanger and the Finn claimed to have been in them, or at least on their outer edges. Both knew they went around in a circle, the wind "she blow lak hell," and came from the south. That was about the extent of their knowledge.

Pape had entered the fo'c'sle to throw off a dripping sou'wester and wiped his face with a towel. He had been aft and checked the distance of our day's run by the patent log on the taffrail. After spreading his chart on the table, he was busily engrossed pricking off our position with a pair of pointed dividers. The position of the ship was always the most interesting bit of news on *Arapahoe*, and Pape soon was surrounded by an eager group as he extended the penciled zigzag line three quarters of an inch to the west.

"Well, there you are, men," he said, snapping shut his dividers. "If we have any luck, by this time next week we may be sighting Guam."

Instantly a babble of voices broke out as questions were flung at him with regard to the extraordinary weather we were experiencing. His face became grave as he started to talk. Outside, the rain continued to come down heavily, while inside the air was hot and sticky like the interior of a Turkish bath. The fo'c'sle was hushed as he explained the phenomena of the giant waves.

"Probably," he said, they were caused by a violent storm somewhere to the south and we were catching only the swells it had kicked up. This was a welcome thought, and grasping at straws, we were all agreeing that undoubtedly this was what had occurred when his next words dashed our hopes. "Of course, that's what we'd like to think, but there's a few bad features we can't overlook. One's the time of year; late summer and fall is the typhoon season when they can happen anytime. The second is our location. This is the typhoon zone," he said, as he picked up his pencil and circled an area roughly the size of a dinner plate. Crowding closer, I noted that the circle took in the north half of the Philippines, the East China Sea, and both the Mariana and Caroline Islands. I also noted with a queasy feeling that our position only a few hundred miles east of Saipan put us well within this circle.

"Oh, well, why worry," said the easy-going Ryan, as waiting for an opportune moment between rolls he climbed onto his upper bunk, "you say it's somebody else's wind; it'll all be blown out time it gets up here."

"No, I didn't say that," answered Pape. "I said, 'probably,' it was the aftermath of a storm. What's got the Old Man worried is the glass. It's been dropping steadily for two days and still going down."

"Yeah! That damn cheap Shipping Board," began Hank, "why the hell don't we have a radio on this ship, then we'd know what's going on. Christ! Not even a storm warning. We could sink for all they give a damn! Nobody'd ever know what happened to us."

"Radio?" said Skinner with a nervous laugh. "You'd hardly expect a radio on a ship that feeds you on salt horse and tongues and sounds, and not even a place to take a bath or dry your clothes. Right now I'd settle for a can of peaches."

As a ripple of strained laughter went around the group, Pape continued in his calm voice. "I wouldn't attach too much importance to a radio if I were you. After all, what good would weather reports do? A sailing ship can't run away from a storm, we have to take it as it comes. Maybe it's better this way."

"Typhoon," a dread word filled with mysterious implications of danger, was one that many of us had never heard before shipping on *Arapahoe*. Now, as Pape went on to speak of this type of storm and its effect on a sailing ship, the full gravity of our situation slowly dawned upon us.

A typhoon, he explained, was a tropical cyclone occurring most frequently in the Indian Ocean and China Sea. A peculiar feature of these storms was the direction the wind revolved around the center, or eye, as he called it. In the Southern Hemisphere this direction was clockwise, but counter clockwise in the Northern.

The wind was said to reach terrific force as it circled around this center, often blowing from 100 to 150 miles per hour. According to Pape, the forward speed was slow and fortunately its path narrow, usually not more than ten to fifteen miles in width. This path, however, was marked by destruction of the worst kind; houses blown down, trees uprooted, and crops ruined. Originating at sea, typhoons sank small craft and damaged and destroyed shipping.

The usual method for a steamer caught in a typhoon, he said, was to head into the wind and use the power of her engines to ride out the storm. This might be easier said than done; with a ship attempting to turn in one direction and the wind pushing against her in the other, even her engines might be insufficient to bring her up into the wind and she would be caught broadside in the trough. This condition, known as broaching, was extremely dangerous, something to be avoided at all costs.

A sailing ship, with no engines, was strictly at the mercy of the elements. If caught in the fury of a typhoon, little more could be done other than heave to under bare poles and hope for the best.

A quiet and sober group watched Pape as he buttoned the strap of his sou'wester and started for the door. Turning the knob he looked back over his shoulder and said with a half grin, "Hope I haven't said anything to disturb you boys. Just remember those guys over in the trenches probably are having their troubles, too."

All during the night the wind blew fitfully from east northeast with but little change in the size of the seas. On the morning watch we again worked under the fo'c'slehead and listened to the petulant plaints of Marc and Cleo who objected to being penned up in the tiny sty. The overhauling of the potatoes was progressing slowly; with the mate aft, it came to a complete stop to be resumed briskly when he again made his appearance. With the rain we again had an ample supply of water for washing, but now there was no place to dry anything, and the dark, threatening sky made sunshine seem remote.

At eleven o'clock, Cohen came from the wheel to report that he had overheard the Captain tell the mate to be ready to take in sail. The wind was still from east northeast, and although only moderate in intensity, there was that unmistakable moan in the rigging we had learned to associate with rising weather.

As we went below at eight bells, the rain had slackened but the sky seemed darker than ever. High above, black clouds went scudding along, and spray flew over our bows as *Arapahoe* dropped into deep valleys of water. At dinner we ate as if we were starved, bracing ourselves at the swaying table to wolf down white beans and great chunks of bread. Momentarily expecting to be called out, we were strangely silent as we stood by, clinging to stanchions or holding to the edge of bunks. Now and then, as muffled shouts were heard, we would listen, each man tense and nervous.

No one was ever prepared for the chilling shout of "All hands aloft!" even though it may have been expected for hours. Suddenly it came as the door burst open to be filled by the square figure of the mate. "O.K., boys, everybody out!"

The very tone of his voice and the grimness of his face left no doubt as to the urgency of the matter, and in a minute we were rushing out on deck. Apparently, the Captain had no intention of being caught unprepared, for already the starboard watch was hauling at clew and buntlines of the fore and mizzen royals, while the halyard of the flying jib was let go allowing it to come screaming down the stay. Minutes later, Skinner, Lofty, Johnny and I were making our way aloft, pressing tightly against the fore weather shrouds as the slip rolled and pitched. It was not easy to climb to the royal yard and I experienced a few bad moments as we edged out along the footrope grasping the jackstay tightly. Up aloft we could feel the full fury of the rising wind, while about the ship the great seas surged, breaking over the deck in smothers of foaming water.

With the mizzen and foreroyals made fast, both watches were held on deck. During our watch below the wind had gradually swung around to the dangerous south and two men were at the wheel. As the afternoon waned, the word was passed that the barometer had fallen additional points and that more sail would be taken in shortly. With the wind at the new angle, *Arapahoe*'s yards were braced around sharply to starboard and we were close hauled on the port tack. The ship rode better with the wind on the quarter and despite the shift to the south, some of us tried to make ourselves believe we had seen the worst of it. There were even a few jokes bantered back and forth among the two watches gathered under the shelter of the fo'c'slehead. This feeling, however, was not shared by the A.B.s and bos'ns, especially the Finn who stared at the black sky to the south and ominously shook his bead.

That evening darkness came early, seeming to settle over the ship like a blanket as the sea took on the color of lead and an oppressive feeling filled the air. Suddenly the order came to take in the cro'jack, mizzen topgallant and the main royal. Now, we had plenty of work for all hands as these sails were clewed up to the yards. As usual, I fell heir to the royal and was soon up onto the yard, this time along with three members of the starboard watch. The wind had slowly increased in strength and the backstays were shrieking and howling as we bundled the sail up onto the yard and made it fast with the gaskets. Although the hour was early, the sky was black as we flattened against the weather rigging and, feeling cautiously for the ratlines, made our way to the deck.

The mizzen topgallant was smaller than the same sails on the fore and main and, despite the darkness and the wind slowly increasing to gale strength, we finally got it furled. During this time it had again started to rain, first in sudden squalls that, blown with the wind, felt like the sting of needles; then as the wind slacked for a moment, it changed to a torrent that fell in a solid stream of water, blinding us so that we groped about feeling uncertainly for the lines at the pinrails.

The cro'jack, a big sail, wet and heavy, was a brute to handle. As usual, the two watches divided, each watch hauling on the bunt and clewlines on their own side of the yard. Slowly, after much shouting and heaving, the big canvas was hauled up to hang flapping and beating the air. At times the ship would stagger as great seas drove into her to break over the bulwark filling the deck knee deep with water. Up on the yard we strung out on each side of the mast hanging on tight as the ship rolled in the darkness. From the port end of the yard, the bos'n was shouting something, the words blown from his lips, unintelligible to any but those beside him. In close to the mast Stavanger worked like a demon, and under his urging the center of the sail was eventually brought up and fastened with a gasket.

At first most of us standing on the footropes in the rain-swept darkness could do but little more than hang on; slowly, as our fears subsided, the training we had received came to our aid, and moving out to the weather side, we were soon hauling the heavy canvas up under our stomachs and fighting for the bottom boltrope.

Once as the ship rolled heavily to port, the yard over which I was hanging, pointed downward at a sharp angle and my feet started to slide. For an instant I thought we were capsizing and as I looked down into the dark water, I held my breath, experiencing a panic so terrifying I wanted to scream from fright. Slowly, after what seemed like ages, she started rolling back to starboard and I found myself hanging on with both hands as I slid toward the mast. Weak and shaky, I thought of the Finn's warning about falling over the side; obviously, a fall into the sea would have been a drop into eternity. With her lifeboats lashed down and covered with canvas, and the ship rushing through the black night in the mountainous seas, there could have been no possible way of effecting a rescue, even the thought of it would have been absurd.

It was nearly midnight when at last, tired, hungry and wet, we again sought shelter under the fo'c'slehead. By now it was blowing hard and the ship was laboring badly. Back in the darkness, cigarettes were lit, their ends glowing red as smokers sucked at them nervously.

At eight bells the wheel was relieved by two men from the starboard watch. In a sea such as this, the wheel was the most dangerous place on the ship. Both men were lashed to the wheelbox as a protection against the gigantic seas that came smoking up from astern. On some of the larger four-masted barks, the wheel had been placed atop a deckhouse amidships. In others, a half-circular device known as a whaleback was erected aft of the wheel. These different constructions were a protection from the great walls of green water that threatened to engulf the stern and wash the helmsman away. On *Arapahoe*, in spite of her having made numerous trips around the Horn, she had no such protection, the wheel was located on the open deck at the very end of the poop.

As the weather grew worse and the seas built up, the Captain seldom went below. Most of the time he was at the weather rail, bracing himself against the violent rolls as he watched the straining rigging. Frequently, he would look into the binnacle, staring long at the compass card as the lubber line swung wildly.

Steering in such a sea was a nightmare; it took the combined efforts of two men literally fighting the wheel to keep the big ship near her course. The freakish wind veering from southwest to south sent *Arapahoe* plunging into terrific seas. Often, great ragged combers came crashing aboard to race the length of the open deck, causing us to leap for the shrouds or hang to lifelines to keep from being bowled over by the force of the rushing water.

At four in the morning we were lit by a frightful squall, the worst we had experienced. For a time *Arapahoe* lay over with her lee rail covered as the seas lifted her to the top of great crests before dropping her into canyons of water. Quickly, the howling of the wind turned to an uproar as waves came piling over the sides and the ship lurched and reeled.

Suddenly, the dark figure of the mate appeared, bawling orders in a foghorn voice. Both the fore and main topgallants and the great mainsail were to be taken in. Following the bos'ns out onto the wildly swinging deck we found buntlines off their pins and clewlines badly tangled. To me it seemed a hopeless mess, trying to untangle lines in the dark as great walls of water came over the bulwark to rush from side to side. Often, the hatches would be covered as battering combers exploded against them to send sheets of water flying. At such times I was thankful that the hatch covers had been reinforced with planking. Nothing could have saved the ship had their coverings torn loose in that maelstrom of wind and waves.

Many times as we struggled to get the sails clewed up we were swept off our feet by the force of the water. Once, I was knocked down to go rolling over and over into the scuppers, hanging desperately to the end of a buntline as I fought to regain my footing. Sea boots and oilskins were of but little value in this kind of weather; boots filled with water were only a hindrance, while oilskins could do little more than keep out the wind.

Finally, with the topgallants clewed up we were ready to go aloft. With all hands on deck our watch would furl the fore, and the starboard the main. Climbing up the shrouds we came to the foretop; it was no time for false bravado, and I was glad to crawl through the hole in the platform instead of the dangerous route out over the futtock shrouds. As we reached the yardarm and spread out along its length we felt the force of the gale as the ship heeled over and the yard swung like a thing possessed.

The topgallant was of heavy storm canvas and felt stiff as cast iron as it defied our efforts to furl it. In the darkness we could see very little; on one side of me was a black lump of oilskins that was Sanbert, on the other, I thought I recognized Hank. Now and then I heard a hoarse shout; above everything was the roar and shriek of the wind forcing us against the yard and blowing oilskin jackets over our heads. Time seemed to stand still as we battled the thrashing sail and hung on desperately to keep from being pitched headlong into the black void below us.

Although it certainly was no time for day dreaming, I thought of the folly that had caused me to leave a comfortable home and place myself in such a situation. Surely, the life of an infantryman in the trenches could be no more hazardous or terrifying than being in this perilous spot, standing on a thin rope in the darkness high above the deck with the ship yawing drunkenly. Below there was nothing but the raging sea.

Dawn was breaking over a dismal scene as we made our way to the deck. Seas still poured over the bulwarks; from deck level they looked more gigantic and frightening than ever. Although tired and half dead from our ordeal with the topgallants, not a minute was lost by the crew, even the cabin boy and cooks were on deck to help with the mighty mainsail in response to "All Hands Aloft!"

In the fading darkness of early morning, we stared at the tremendous seas as they came roaring by the ship. More than a thousand feet in length, they were sloping on the lee side, steep-walled on the other, pushed up by the mighty force of the south wind now reaching hurricane proportions. Time and again, as huge combers crashed over the sides, it seemed *Arapahoe* would never free herself of the great weight of water. Each time she rose shuddering as green seas surged along the deck and she plunged over into the next trough—troughs so deep it seemed a two-story building might easily have been lost in their depths.

By this time most of us knew what to expect in taking in the mainsail; even so, it was a heartbreaking task, as slowly, inch by inch, the heavy, wet canvas was hoisted up to the yard. The mates stood by to slack off the sheets as we hauled at clew and buntlines, apparently unwilling to trust this important task to anyone else. In a wind such as this, it would be easy to lose control of the sail; had this occurred, it would have been blown to pieces in an instant.

Up aloft, weary and stupid from fatigue, we put in another frightful two hours before the mainsail was furled. By now it was nearly noon, and we had gone almost twenty-four hours without food or sleep. The ship was stripped down to the upper and lower topsails, the big foresail and the fore staysail. She was still overcanvased, and the word went around that the foresail and upper topsails also would have to come in.

The wind, awe inspiring, showed no indication of diminishing. Long ribbons of white streaked the tops of the swells to be blown off like smoke as we plunged into deepening valleys.

The galley was a flooded wreck and cooking was impossible, but somehow Sandy had managed to make coffee and we were allowed to go below for a much-needed break. The fo'c'sle again a shambles, had water sloshing about, its deck a jumble of broken crockery, ruined clothing and sodden books. Some of the steel lockers had broken open, spewing their contents onto the deck, adding to the mess of wreckage that washed from side to side.

Exhausted, we moved mechanically as if by instinct, dull-eyed, and with brains half functioning, rapidly reaching the stage where nothing seemed to matter. Gulping hot coffee and gnawing at sea biscuits like starving dogs, we stared at one another while some, dropping onto water-soaked bunks, immediately fell asleep. Hanging to a stanchion, I was dimly aware of a gurgling sound as water splashed around and under the bunks, and of the groan of the hull under terrific stress as the ship rolled to her extreme limits of stability.

After what seemed like only minutes, weary and half asleep, we were staggering out the lee door to be met by a wall of water. *Arap-ahoe*, running wild through seas so large they defied imagination, reeled like a drunken thing, at times heeling over so far it was impossible to keep our footing.

Eventually, as night settled down, dark and threatening, the big foresail and all three upper topsails were taken in and secured. We were now under three lower topsails and the small fore staysail; the next move could mean bare poles, a highly dangerous condition in these gigantic seas—an action to be taken only as a last resort.

Although dead tired, before either watch could go below it was necessary to bring some semblance of order out of the chaos of lines and ropes tangled and scattered about the decks. Following this, the starboard watch was dismissed but ordered to remain fully dressed and ready to turn out at a moment's notice.

With big seas breaking over the bows, the lookout's position was untenable. He was moved to the foretop and lashed to the shrouds. A man was stationed on each fo'c'sle to relay messages to and from the poop; the rest of the watch stood by, shivering under the fo'c'slehead.

By four o'clock the gale that had blown in ugly gusts throughout the night showed signs of abating, and Saturday morning, July 20th, found a faint tinge of yellow light above the eastern horizon. The seas were still mountainous, and the ship steered badly, but as the morning advanced, the sky seemed to lighten and we hoped the worst was over.

Relieved at eight bells, we were further encouraged by a breakfast of cornmeal mush, coffee, and hardtack, the first hot food we had eaten since the storm drove into us nearly two days before. Afterward, we threw ourselves onto our bunks and, as the water seeped in around the doors and splashed about in the fo'c'sle, fell into unconscious sleep.

During daylight, Saturday, we attempted to do something about the mass of tangled rigging. Although the wind had gone down somewhat, the seas were still titanic, breaking over the side to inundate the deck in an overwhelming millrace, a force that could bowl men over like tenpins.

By late afternoon it looked as though the weather might moderate still further; in the fo'c'sles blankets were wrung out, wreckage thrown over the side, and a half-hearted attempt made to bail out the water. The spirits of even the most optimistic were therefore dampened when, at the change of watch, we were suddenly ordered to take in the mizzen lower topsail.

Both watches were grumbling at this seemingly unnecessary precaution, especially those due to go below. Some of the crew coming on deck had managed to find dry clothes; their feelings were not improved when they were drenched immediately by a great wave as they leaped wildly for the life line.

The mizzen lower topsail was not one of the largest sails on *Arapahoe*, but with the ship racing ahead, straining at every shroud and backstay, taking it in was a mighty task. Our work was made extra difficult by buntlines being fouled in their blocks. On the starboard side, Brodie and Bergstrom sweated and cursed as they labored on this stubborn gear, while the rest of us, hanging on tight, braced against the gusts and waited for the lines to be freed.

With the lower topsail taken in, the mizzen was bare leaving only three sails on the entire ship, the lower topsails on the fore and main and the fore staysail on the big wire stay that ran from the foremast down to the fo'c'slehead.

Even as we reached the deck the mate was bellowing for us to get forward and take in the staysail. Waiting for a moment between rolls we rushed forward, floundering through water that surged over the deck and poured out freeing ports that banged shut as the ship rolled in the opposite direction.

Forward, the Finn let go the halyard and we hauled on the downhaul bringing the staysail down. I was thankful the jibs were in and made fast, for under the bowsprit the sea boiled upward as *Arapahoe* plunged into swells sending water cascading over the bows. We had a few bad minutes as the sheet block lashed about furiously, threatening to knock us overboard. Eventually it was secured, and throwing our weight onto the whipping canvas we furled it and made it fast.

The wind was blowing strongly as we made our way below. It had started to rain again, and although the hour was still early, the sky had assumed a strange unnatural darkness. Worn out and rapidly nearing the breaking point, the watch looked tired and drawn as we entered the dreary fo'c'sle. Overhead, with the sails off the ship, the wind blowing through the naked rigging was setting up an unearthly din. Supper that night was little more than a name. Although the galley had been flooded and cooking impossible, somewhere Sandy had discovered a few cans of corned beef; hardly enough to go around, but by filling up with hardtack and hot coffee, we were able to get by. Most of us were too nearly exhausted to be hungry, and wanted only to lie down and sleep. Even standing erect on the slanting deck had been an exertion. This, coupled with the hard work, wet, hunger and loss of sleep, was rapidly taking its toll.

Little was said as sea boots were emptied and socks wrung out. Most of us were too tired to talk, or maybe, there just was nothing to say. There was none of the banter usually flung about the fo'c'sle. Everyone was quiet, grim; even Ryan, noted for making light of the toughest situation, was silent, his eyes hollow, his face clearly showing the strain. In his cross-ship bunk, Johnny Hoculak lay quietly, his dark eyes staring straight ahead, his face looking pinched and old.

The Finn sat in the gloom of his tiny quarters, his cigarette flaring up brightly as he took enormous drags which he inhaled deeply and blew out in bluish clouds. He was a strange man from a strange land related neither to Sweden nor Norway. Finland lies between Sweden and Russia, part of it well beyond the Arctic Circle, its people of mysterious origin.

Hank, bracing himself on the edge of his bunk, suddenly shouted, his voice shrill and irritable rising above the roar of the wind and the creak and groan of the ship. "For Christ's sake, bos'n! How much longer is this going to last? Don't these damn storms ever blow over?"

"Yeah, he gon' blow over, but tonight, he gon' blow ver' bad."

"You mean to say it'll be worse tonight?"

"Shur."

"How the hell do you know?"

"I don' know how I know, but he come bad tonight. Vhy you t'ink all sail es in but lower tops'ls?"

"I don't know anything about that, but if anybody ever gets me on one of these damn windbags again—"

"Yeah, dat's O.K., but you're here now," interrupted the Finn, pointing to the deck with his forefinger. Right at that particular moment my own sentiments regarding sailing ships were most heartily in accord with Hank's.

At eight bells, wind and spray flew through the door as it opened to admit a dripping O'Connor, police on the starboard watch. After shaking each man into wakefulness, we were told that roll call at the break of the poop had been dispensed with, and that the watch would stand by under the fo'c'slehead.

It was my trick at the wheel with Stavanger, and as we stepped out the door the rain lashed at our faces with a hissing noise, while the wind whistled, roared and wailed as dark waves towered above us. For a moment we stood in the lee of the fo'c'sle, steadying ourselves against the roll and accustoming our eyes to the darkness. Grasping life lines, we edged our way aft, leaping to the mainmast fife rail to avoid seas that came sweeping the deck, and rushing to the poop companionway as the ship hesitated before heeling in the opposite direction.

As we took over the wheel from Jones and Maringo and were given the course, "West north-west," I noticed that both men were sweating freely. On the lee side from Stavanger I drew the lashing tightly around my waist and watching him closely, heaved on the spokes when needed.

Although Stavanger probably was the best helmsman on *Arapahoe*, and I made every effort to help him, steering was extremely difficult. At times she rolled almost on her beam ends before careening back in a sickening motion that kept us fighting the wheel to keep her from coming into the wind. Often waves unbelievably big and black loomed above the stern, causing me to duck and grip the spokes. Occasionally water broke over the poop to pour off the half round in rushing torrents; usually at the last moment the stern would shoot upward to hang suspended before dropping dizzily into huge troughs.

At two bells our trick was over. Two black figures, Laurence and Cohen held on to the taffrail as they moved up to us in the darkness.

Going forward I spent a dismal hour at police, crouching low behind the scuttlebutts which afforded but scant shelter. Later I relieved Skinner at lookout and, lashed to the pipe rail, peered into the murky blackness, shielding my face from the rain.

The storm was mounting in fury as I joined a shadowy group huddled under the fo'c'slehead. From aloft came an indescribable noise as the wind increased to a full gale driving *Arapahoe* before it. By midnight it was reaching its peak with the ship pitching and burying her bows in the seas. Smashed by giant waves that came crashing aboard, the lookout could no longer maintain his position and as the water surged waist deep about the deck, both watches were forced to take refuge in the fo'c'sle.

During the next several hours we hovered in a group, clinging to stanchions or braced in bunks. The ship was fighting for her life and from outside came the scream and moans of a great wind as it tore through the rigging in a bloodcurdling din. Now and then the oil lamp would flicker and smoke as seas struck the fo'c'sle with such terrific force that its steel sides would shiver and shake. We looked from one to the other in silence.

In his dark corner the Finn was talking to himself in a low tone; occasionally, a match would flare, lighting his stubbled face as he held it to a cigarette.

Of all the men crowded into the narrow space, Stavanger seemed the least perturbed. Dressed in his torn oilskins and battered sou'wester, the big overgrown fellow sat bracing himself in his lower bunk. Once, as *Arapahoe* staggered and trembled from a sea that must have engulfed the entire ship, causing water to squirt in around the doors and come trickling down from the skylight, he gave me a broad wink, rolled his eyes upward, and said with a grin:

"Yeesus Chris'! Mus' be rainin' out dere."

Stavanger was an odd character, ignorant, and frequently bragging of the most shocking acts, yet, as he talked we seemed to gain from him a sense of security and a renewed faith in our ship. Somehow, I felt less like a rat in a trap as I heard him say, "Don' vorry, she'll mek it all right. Dis is a big steel ship—she's been t'rough all dis before."

This brought a "Thank God!" from Maringo, starboard watch cadet, who, crouched in a far corner, his fingers entwined by a small silver chain, had been muttering incoherently.

"Yeah, that's fine," came the thin, rasping voice of Brodie, "while you're at it, though, you might throw in a few thanks for the Scotchmen who built her. Maybe they had something to do with it, too."

Other than this, there was but little conversation, the two watches crowding the close quarters waited quietly, the dim light of the fo'c'sle lamp shining feebly on faces deeply lined, and eyes that were tired and dull.

At last the long hours of darkness came to an end and we looked out on a world of weird half-light. Sheets of driving rain swept the ship, while overhead dark clouds raced through a sky still threatening and portentous. The seas, huge, black and formidable, seemed to be breaking in every direction, their tops blown off in spindrifts of blinding spray, to fly through the air like grey smoke.

During Sunday, the wind blew with undiminished strength, the sky had a heavy overcast, and late afternoon found dusk again settling over the ocean. At four in the afternoon we went below to eat a meager supper of boiled macaroni laced with an insipid sauce. Finished, we fell onto soggy bunks and fully clothed, dropped off into exhausted slumber.

With darkness there came a respite from the gale that had blown at near hurricane force throughout the day. Although the seas were still enormous, they were not quite so vicious as they came rolling over our weather rail to fill the waist with water.

Just before eight bells we were awakened by Bond and stumbled about the fo'c'sle, eyes swollen and brains numb from lack of sleep. Outside, the wind still howled like a banshee, the ship rolled badly, and water could be heard sloshing about the deck. Buttoning oilskins and rubbing sleep from our eyes, we made our way aft to the muster. The wheel was relieved by Sanbert and Barker, the lookout by Ryan, and I had the wretched job of police.

Later, after replacing Ryan and lashing myself to the rail, I stood staring ahead, shutting my eyes as flying spray stung my face and solid water came over the bow. Cold, wet and hungry, I was barely conscious of the dark figure that suddenly loomed beside me. It was the Finn. Crowding close he shouted above the noise of the wind.

"Hey, Louie. You hear de news?"

"News? What news?"

"De peegs!"

"Pigs? What about them?"

"Dey bof gon'—vashed over side las' night!"

"No!"

"Shur, dey gon' all right. No pork chops now."

It was true. While we sweated out the storm in the fo'c'sle, Marc and Cleo had managed to get out of their pen to fall victims of the gale. As I thought of them following old Alford about the deck begging for scraps, I realized that somehow I had never associated them with pork chops.

At ten o'clock I was relieved at lookout by Barker. Soon, I was seated at the fo'c'sle table, my head on my arms, completely oblivious to the roar of the wind and the creak and groan of the ship. The rest of the watch were gathered about me, all still in oilskins and sea boots. Some dozed as they sprawled on bunks; others sat at the table and stared into space.

Suddenly from forward came muffled shouts followed by the ringing of the bell. Instantly every man was on his feet, wide awake. The Finn, springing from his bunk, dashed out the door, bareheaded, his long hair flying in the wind as he shouted, "Qveek! Man overboard, maybe!"

Stumbling and falling in the darkness, we followed him to the fo'c'slehead to crowd around "Captain" Barker.

"What's the matter?" shouted a dozen voices.

"I saw a light over there!" he answered excitedly, pointing to the northwest.

"Over where?"

"Over there!" he repeated, continuing to point.

Every head turned in the direction indicated and stared long and hard into the darkness. By that time we were joined by both mates, while the watch below came running forward.

"Vot's de madder op haar?" shouted Mr. Knudsen.

"Oh, Barker saw a light," someone laughed.

"A light? Vare?"

"Right over there, Sir, about two points off the starboard bow."

"Are you shur? Vot did it luk lak?"

"It was a white light, Sir—burned bright for a minute and then went out."

For at least ten minutes we stood shivering, hanging onto the railing and gazing into the blackness as sheets of water came flying over the bows. Some of the watch had returned to the fo'c'sles, others were turning away with snide remarks suggesting that Barker try drinking more lime juice, or that he sleep with his hands outside the blankets, when someone shouted, "THERE IT IS, SIR!"

Turning, I saw it distinctly. Far off in the darkness, appearing no larger than the flame of a match, it burned brightly for an instant, then dimmed more and more until we found ourselves staring into empty blackness.

"What do you make of it, Sir?" someone asked.

"It's a distress signal. Bos'n, call all hands!"

In an instant *Arapahoe* became a scene of excited activity as all hands were called on deck. Suddenly from the poop a blue light illuminated the sky, outlining our rigging in a ghostly silhouette and casting an eerie glow over the water. For a full twenty seconds our answering flare burned with a luminous light, while every eye was glued to the dark in the direction we last had seen the signal.

After a long wait it came again, this time farther abeam—that same white light now appearing to be farther away, burning brightly for nearly a half minute before fading out in the distance.

Even as the signal disappeared, there came the order, "Stand by to set upper tops'ls fore and main!"

"Jesus Christ! In this wind and sea, what for?" asked someone.

"'Ve gon' udder tack purty qveek an' Ol' Man vants planty sail so her head she com' op fast," answered the Finn.

"What the hell's he going on the other tack for, bos'n?"

"Got to go udder tack or heave to. If ve don' ve go off an' leave dem."

Nearly two o'clock, after a mighty battle in the heavy wind and breaking seas we got the topsails set and were ready to go about. With additional sail *Arapahoe* went tearing through the water at an increased speed, plunging into great troughs to ship seas that came rushing down the deck to where we stood waiting at the winches.

Bringing the ship about in the darkness in high wind and heavy seas was a maneuver that called for a high degree of skill on the part of the Captain. It had to be executed with split-second timing and left no margin for error. We had tacked ship many times in fair weather, and in our training had gone through simulated drills. This was our first attempt in the teeth of a gale.

Pape, cool-headed and experienced was at the weather helm with Bond standing at the lee. Everything was in readiness and each man at his position. At a sharp command from the Captain, Pape spun the wheel to port, bringing *Arapahoe*'s head up into the wind. For a minute there was a tremendous tumult in the rigging, a whipping of canvas and banging of blocks as lee braces were cast off, and we wound furiously at winches swinging the yards around to the other tack. The topgallant and royal yards were hauled around by hand, following this, the heavy yards were trimmed by hauling at the hand braces. We were now on the starboard tack with the yards braced around against the port backstays.

Though this may seem a simple maneuver, it was actually one calling for violent physical exertion on the part of the crew and was extremely dangerous to both the men and the ship. Had she failed to come about or missed stays in the heavy gale and monstrous seas, the results could easily have been disastrous. We were unable to leave our positions at the winches, as the ship, rolling heavily, swung around into the wind and we were buffeted by great seas that came slamming over the side threatening to wash us overboard. Many times the winches were covered by foaming water, while men grimly hung on or were knocked flat, to regain their feet, sputtering, choking and cursing.

With the ship on the starboard tack, we again scanned the darkness. There was no sleep on *Arapahoe*, as every available man climbed into the lower rigging to search for the mysterious signal.

By four in the morning, although a constant watch had been kept, nothing further was seen. Sober-faced, we gathered in the fo'c'sle to discuss why there had been no further signals. The consensus was that a ship had foundered and sunk while we waited for daylight, helpless to aid them in the darkness, gigantic seas and heavy gale. Ryan, always optimistic, came up with a remark to which little heed was given when he suggested, "Maybe, they're out of matches."

The Captain, who had taken bearings on the signal, knew we were in the immediate vicinity of whatever had occurred, and wishing to remain close to the scene, ordered the ship hove to.

To stop a big square-rigger or to heave to on the ragged edge of a typhoon, required considerably more doing than reversing the engines or closing the throttle on a steamer. It was done by a complicated action known as "backing the main yards" in which the foreyards were braced in one direction and the main yards in the other. In this manner the sails on the two yards were forced to work against each other, those on the foreyards pulling ahead, while those on the main, with the wind against their front surface, pushed her back. Since the opposing forces were almost equal, the result was that the ship lay nearly broadside to the wind, wallowing in the seas, stationary except for the drift to leeward.

Additional flares were burned from off the stern during the long hours before daylight but brought no response. Silently, one after the other, men shook their heads and turned away. Apparently the mate had a similar feeling, for *Arapahoe*'s log, dated Sunday, July 21, contained only this laconic entry:

day begins with havy gale of South wind and tremendus sea running
11 kl (p.m.) sighted Distress signal on the starboard quarter
1120 called all hands and went on the other tack still seeing signals burning untill 2 kl a.m. Course W1/2S.   Wind South   Lat 17°27   Long 153°14

During the night the weather worsened, the wind blew out of the south to send waves crashing against the ship as she rolled with the mighty combers. Long before the first grey streaks of dawn we were back in the rigging and as the darkness slowly paled and turned to the gloom of a bleak Monday morning, we searched the sea with anxious eyes.

Johnny and I had established ourselves at the fore crosstree and from this high perch gazed out over the ocean. A faint haze limited visibility but now and then we would think we saw something in the distance that only turned out to be the shoulder of a ragged sea or a whitecap on the crest of a wave.

For the next two hours we searched the area while the driving wind drifted us steadily northward. Nothing was seen, not even a bit of wreckage in the boiling cauldron of water. From a position high on the mainmast, armed with a folding telescope, the mate swept the horizon long and carefully before climbing down to the deck.

It was Lofty who sighted the wreck. Clinging to the slender main topmast, and seated in a precarious position on the topgallant yard, his eagle eyes caught the movement of a dark object as it rose to the top of a swell. His hail, heard indistinctly above the roar of the wind brought the mate rushing back up the rigging. On deck we could see white faces upturned. The Captain, who stood by the starboard lifeboat with hands cupped around his mouth was shouting, but his words were snatched away by the gale.

As the mate reached the crosstree we could hear him calling up to Lofty who, extending his arm, pointed off to port. Looking in the direction he had indicated, we scanned the sea closely, at first seeing nothing but the great waste of water.

Suddenly I saw it. Far away, much farther than we had been concentrating our gaze, something that looked like tiny match sticks pointing upward. It appeared only for an instant and even as I grasped Johnny's arm it was gone,

Our attention was diverted to the deck where Brodie and the Finn were beckoning all hands down from aloft. Eight bells was striking as we hurried down to find both watches gathered at the break of the poop.

Throughout the ship excitement prevailed as the order was given to square the main yards and get the ship under way. With the main topsails filled, *Arapahoe*, close hauled, began to rush through the water, the gale heeling her over to port and mountainous seas smashing into the weather bulwark.

The mate had returned to the poop and was talking to the Captain; at times he gestured toward the south and soon the Captain climbed to the mizzen top. For some time he remained in the rigging, steadying himself against the roll as he pointed his glass southward.

Lofty had also returned to the deck and was quickly surrounded and eagerly questioned about what he had seen.

"Looked like a dismasted ship," he said in answer to our queries.

"See any signs of life?"

"Nope, too far away."

At eight-thirty the mate's shrill whistle sounded and as the morning murk gave way to the sullen light of a stormy day, we went back on the port tack. With the yards braced around hard against the starboard backstays, the port was the weather side over which green seas came pouring aboard. At the first opportunity, as the ship plunged ahead through the morning gloom, we climbed into the rigging. In a minute someone again spotted the wreck, now off our starboard bow but too far away to be seen clearly.

Bearing down rapidly, *Arapahoe* gradually closed the distance and by nine o'clock we could make out broken stumps of masts with several small dark objects in the rigging. At first what was left of the masts appeared to protrude right out of the water. As we drew closer and the wreck was lifted to the top of a swell, we saw a dark hull, which except for the stern, was flush with the sea and covered by breaking combers. Often it would drop out of sight as the hulk slid down into great valleys, each time to reappear.

When first sighted, the figures in the rigging had been nothing more than mere specks against a background of raging water. Suddenly, horrified, I realized they were men. We attempted to count them as the fury of the gale pressed us hard against the shrouds and *Arapahoe* reeled and pitched. Unable to agree on the number, some said there were four, some said six. Most of us just hung on and stared, wondering what was going to happen.

The Finn, climbing up beside me, gazed toward the tragic scene, his long hair whipping in the wind. Suddenly nudging my arm, he pointed aft. Turning, I saw the carpenter and Brodie removing the cover from the starboard lifeboat. In spite of the heavy wind and wild sea, it was evident the Captain was going to attempt a rescue.

At the mate's whistle we fell aft to assemble at the break of the poop where we stood by gravely and looked up at the Captain. For a moment he stood gazing down, his hands resting on the teak railing, before he started to speak.

"Dot wreck you see out dere vas a four-masted schooner. She's been dismasted an' is a vater logged hulk. She may break op any minute. Dere's men on her an' ve're going to tak' dem off. All right, Mr. Peterson, you hev' de vatch, pick your boat crew."

The second mate's face had a half grin as he turned to the assembled crew. "Enybody don' hev' to go if dey don' vant to. Pape—Bergstrom—Craig—" for an instant his eyes traveled over the silent group before centering on the husky figure of the carpenter. "Chips, how aboud you?" He turned to the Captain. "Boat crew's ready, Sir."

The Captain's voice was brisk and sharp as he said, "Mr. Knudsen, heave de ship to an' launch de starboard boat!"

With the main yards backed, *Arapahoe* again lay in the terrific seas, her decks awash with snarling water.

Launching a boat in the angry foam-streaked waves was an undertaking fraught with the greatest danger. There were no smiles on any faces as the grim-featured seamen, each wearing a cork-block life jacket, stood by as the boat was hoisted at the davits. Like watching a drama unfold on the screen, thrilling and unreal, these five brave men climbed into the swinging boat: first, Peterson, the second mate, middle-aged, bony and angular with high cheek bones and a bristly mustache; Pape, able-seaman, young, husky, a giant of a man; Bergstrom, also an A.B., around thirty, short, thick-set, and good-natured; Joe Craig, ordinary seaman, an ex-coast guardsman, about twenty-two, tall, slender, and of quiet demeanor; and, lastly Bauma, the ship's carpenter, a Dutchman, sturdy as an oak, a man with a cheerful disposition, a round face, and eyes that twinkled when he laughed.

The handling of lifeboats in heavy seas calls for a particular brand of seamanship but little appreciated by those who have never experienced it. Getting a boat over the side successfully and effecting a rescue, was indeed, the ultimate test in bravery and skill.

Arapahoe lay hove to, nearly broadside, rolling heavily in tremendous seas. The starboard boat was on the lee side; in order to understand the difficulties of launching, one must visualize the great seas, towering high above our decks one moment and dropping away to form deep chasms of dark, yawning water the next.

The boat was lowered from davits by tackle hooked into rings at the bow and stern. The hooks had to be released at the proper moment; failure to disengage one hook, or the slightest error in judgment could have resulted in the boat's occupants being thrown to their deaths in the sea. As the boat was lowered slowly under the direction of the mate, an attempt was made to hold it steady by lines at bow and stern. At the same time it was fended off from being smashed against our steel sides by boat hooks in the hands of Bauma and Craig.

There came a breath-taking moment as the wooden craft was raised high by a sea and, at a shout from the mate, cast off. Seconds later, with men pulling desperately on the oars, it cleared the ship and was lost to our view as a wave came aboard in a smother of flying water.

The sharp whistle of the mate again rang out as the command was given to square the yards and get the ship under way. This procedure aroused the curiosity of both watches and, as the ship gathered speed and drew away from the scene, we clustered together and discussed its meaning. By this time our boat could no longer be seen in the haze and heavy seas.

The action was made clear when the Finn was asked, "Hey, bos'n, does the Old Man know what the Christ he's doing? What's he running away for?"

"He no run avay," answered the Finn. "Our boat no can row against vind an' sea, so ve gon' tack to lee of wreck and vait for dem dere."

Any misgivings we might have had as to the Captain's running away were dispelled during the next couple of hours; during that period we worked furiously, tacking ship several times. To me it all became a blurred confusion as we cranked on winches and hauled at braces, ducking and hanging on tight as seas came roaring aboard to cover the deck and slosh around hatches in knee-deep foaming water.

Presently, as we beat up into the wind close hauled, I was called aft by the mate. As I reached the poop, Stavanger at the weather wheel with Sanbert at the lee gave me a quick wink as they battled to hold the plunging ship as close to the wind as possible.

The mate, visibly nervous, was standing at the starboard rail talking rapidly to the Captain. Turning, he ordered me to stand by atop the aft fo'c'sle to act as police and carry messages forward.

Taking my position I gazed long and carefully for some sign of our boat but could see nothing other than the heaving ocean. Remembering the mate's obvious concern, I experienced a sickening sensation as I wondered if the boat had capsized.

Suddenly I saw the wreck again off our port bow. It was still some distance away and the stubs of its masts rocked dizzily as they rose with the giant waves. Plunging her bows into the seas, *Arapahoe* was rapidly drawing nearer.

I watched the Captain as calm, cool, apparently not the slightest bit flustered, he gave his orders to the mate. Standing at the standard compass and occasionally glancing aloft, he held up his hand and, without turning his head, motioned gently to Stavanger. Something about him reminded me of a maestro standing on a podium conducting an unseen orchestra. The music was the high thin whine of the wind blowing through miles of taut rigging in counterpoint to the booming crash of seas breaking over our bows.

In another thirty minutes we had drawn abeam of the wreck on the lee side. At a command from the Captain the main yards were backed and the ship again hove to. We now lay with our port side to the weather so as to give the boat the benefit of our lee when she came alongside to be taken aboard.

The Captain's strategy was now apparent. Originally, we had hove to on the weather side of the wreck; the boat had been launched at nine o'clock, the Captain depending on the wind and seas to carry it down to the hulk. After getting the boat over the side, he had, by a master-piece of seamanship in the teeth a howling gale and gigantic seas, tacked the ship around until now, at eleven o'clock, we were hove to about two miles to the lee of the wreck, waiting for our boat to arrive.

Minutes were like hours as men peered out over the churning ocean from perches in the rigging. At first nothing could be seen but great waves, their tops blown off into flying scud, their very size beaten down and flattened by the force of the wind. Occasionally we would catch glimpses of the wreck as stumps of masts appeared momentarily before being lost in the deep troughs.

Finally there came a hail from aloft and I looked up to see an arm pointing excitedly. Soon I saw it, too; at first, far away, an object that bobbed on the crest of a huge swell and disappeared only to appear again, each time drawing closer.

Gradually the distance lessened. Often the boat would disappear for long, agonizing moments while we held our breaths in suspense. After what seemed like an eternity, it was sweeping around our stern, and I had a fleeting glimpse of a scene that was to be fixed in my memory forever. Four stalwart men, their faces pale and drawn, were straining at the oars; in the stern, one hand grasping the tiller, the other resting on the gunwale, his eyes gazing stolidly ahead, sat the second mate; near him, bareheaded, sitting erect and straight, was an old man; he had snow-white hair and a long grey beard that blew in the wind. Huddled in the bottom of the boat were several dark figures, their eyes hollow and vacant as they stared at the plunging slip.

Moments later they were off our lee with death at their elbows as the monstrous waves threatened to dash the frail craft against *Arapahoe*'s side. As the lunging boat sank far below the level of our bulwark, I hurriedly counted its occupants—fourteen in all.

To get the survivors and our crew safely aboard was a tremendous task which at first seemed almost impossible. Cargo netting and a boarding ladder were already hung over the side, while ropes were coiled down nearby and heaving lines placed in handy positions.

As the boat surged dangerously close, the second mate shouted up through cupped hands, the only word intelligible above the gale was "line." At the same time, he gestured in pantomime by holding his hands under his armpits.

Quickly a large loop was formed in a rope end and tied with a bowline knot. This was bent to a heaving line which was thrown to the boat. Minutes later, with the loop under his armpits, we were hauling a limp, palid figure aboard who babbled incoherently as he fell into the mate's powerful arms before being carried aft.

Next came the old man with the white beard who staggered as he reached the deck and was held up by two of our men. In spite of his weakened condition and being on the verge of collapse, he introduced himself to our skipper as Captain Charles Backus of the schooner *Ethel Zane*, and asked that aid be given his crew.

"Vas your men all saved?" asked our Captain.

"Yes, thank God! They were all taken off by your boat," replied the old man as, swaying unsteadily, he also was helped aft.

We worked rapidly, seriously hampered by seas that continued to come crashing aboard, threatening the lifeboat, flooding the deck, and causing the ship to roll badly. One by one, however, the dazed men were hauled aboard until all nine were accounted for. Only then did Peterson and Bauma come scrambling up the ladder, leaving Bergstrom, Craig and Pape to fend off the boat and hook on the tackle.

Bringing the lifeboat back on board was an operation equally as difficult and dangerous as launching it. It called for extreme cool headedness on the part of both the men in the boat and those on *Arapahoe's* deck. In such a sea it was essential that both falls be hooked on at precisely the right moment and the boat hauled clear of the water. After a mighty struggle with the raging seas it was back on the skids and made fast. Twelve o'clock noon, eight bells were striking as Pape, Bergstrom, and Craig crawled wearily out of the boat to be surrounded by an admiring crew. Questions were flung at them from all sides but the questioners were quickly dispersed by the mate's whistle calling the watches to square the main yards and get the ship under way.

With nine additional men on board the Captain was immediately faced with a question of quarters. Although it was some time before we learned the particulars of the wreck and rescue, we did find out that *Ethel Zane's* crew had consisted of her captain, two mates, a cook, a donkeyman, and four able-bodied seamen, all safely aboard.

The captain and two mates were to be quartered aft in the spare staterooms off the main cabin. Of these three, the second mate, who had been the first man hauled aboard, was suffering from shock and exposure and was in a critical condition. The remainder were taken to the port watch fo'c'sle where six of us gave up our bunks to these exhausted men who were in a state of semi-shock from their terrible experience with the sea. With the ship under way, the Captain lost no time in preparing quarters and providing clothing for these unfortunate seamen. They had been brought aboard with no possessions other than the water-soaked clothes they had on their backs. Soon they were fitted out with odds and ends of nondescript clothing contributed by members of the watches.

Their quarters were to be the donkey room, made over into an improvised fo'c'sle. The ship was barely back on her course when both watches were set to work under the inexhaustible Chips, bringing lumber from forward. All afternoon as the rain poured down and the wind blew in mighty gusts, we labored carrying lumber on the reeling deck, sawing and hammering in the damp, dismal donkey room until the six bunks were completed.

Far from being luxurious quarters, the room smelled of oil and rancid grease, was dark and gloomy, and with the doors closed, had little or no ventilation. The donkey engine and coal-bin took up nearly all the space leaving but scant room for the narrow bunks built along its walls. It was finished at last, fitted with extra mattresses and blankets. An oil lantern was hung from the wall, and the room was ready for its new occupants.

When first brought aboard, the shipwrecked men had been fed sandwiches and strong, hot coffee; afterward they had fallen on the bunks and were covered over with blankets. At two bells they were aroused and called to the table for a hot meal. Apparently, Sandy had outdone himself, for as the supper hour advanced, we could smell food cooking and the aroma of fresh baked rolls.

During their supper we had an opportunity to observe these six men closely for the first time. Still badly shaken and stupified with fatigue, they sat at the table and ate in silence. While they were eating, we crowded into the fo'c'sle and stood in the doors peering at them as though they were men from another world. All of us were filled with curiosity, but aware of the condition of the half-starved men, no one felt like asking questions. Once I heard one of them mutter to himself, "Damn! I never thought I'd live to eat another meal!"

Arapahoe's boat crew were also singularly quiet. Little was said by any of them; they seemed to consider it merely a part of a day's work, typical of sailing ship men, inured to danger, toil and hardship. My thoughts went back to that terrible morning when, hove to in the howling gale and crashing seas, they had, without the slightest hesitation, volunteered their services. They didn't have to go, and certainly no one would have criticized them had they refused. With nothing to gain and everything to lose, they were risking their very lives that other men might live.

I thought, too, of those heart-rending hours that seemed like a lifetime, when the tiny boat laden with its cargo of half-drowned men, fought its way foot by foot back to *Arapahoe*. Often it had disappeared in the great troughs of water while we held our breaths and wondered whether it would rise. Back on board they had quietly returned to their duties, unsung heroes who did not expect their bravery to be recorded. They were just plain men of the sea, merchant seamen manning their country's ships in time of war, undecorated, living and oftentimes dying, unnamed, unknown, and forgotten.

I recalled the grin on the face of the second mate as he said, "Eny-budy don' hev to go if dey don' vant to," and then proceeded to name his "volunteers." Knudsen, his face heavy with anxiety as he worked the ship, launched the boat in the wild seas and, somehow, got the survivors aboard with a green untried crew of boys.

Just another day in their lives, an incident of the voyage, recorded in one brief paragraph in the log:

> Monday, July 22, 1918
> 8 a.m. sighted schooner to leward, squared away getting life boat reddy to put over.
> 9 a.m. hove to 1 1/2 miles to windward of sch. put St. life boat over maned by 2nd mate Charles Peterson S.F.
> Paul Bergstrom   Joe Craig O.S.   Pape A.B.
> Bauma carpenter.   squared away droped vessel to leward of wreck name found to be *Ethel Zane* and waited for life boat. 1130 a.m. life boat along side with Capt. and 8 men during this time there was a gale blowing and a tremendious high sea running which mad rescuing of the men very hasardioues. 12' noon lifeboat on skidts lashed and vessel proceeding on her way. The posetion of the wreck Lat 17°27'   Long 152°31'
>
> HANS WILHELMSEN (master)

That was all. In his comment, "droped vessel to leward of wreck," there was little to indicate the decision he had been called upon to make, or the seamanship involved, as he skillfully maneuvered the big square-rigger into position and made the rescue possible. Neither was mention made in the log that little or no food was served in the cabin, and according to the cabin boy, the "Old Man" never removed his clothes, and his pillow was never rumpled.

from The Last Grain Race
by Eric Newby

Eric Newby (born 1919) in 1938 signed on with the Finnish crew of the four-masted merchant ship Moshulu. *The ship was bound from Ireland for Australia to pick up a load of grain. The young Newby had no nautical experience.*

On the 20th of March *Moshulu* was in a position near the Snares, a group of uninhabited islands in latitude 48° southward of New Zealand. At midnight on the 19th we had come on deck at the muster to find the ship under full sail, flying along at 13 knots with a NNW. wind, the seas boiling out from under her bows.

I had first wheel and it needed the greatest attention to keep the course. She had to be steady, so I kept my eyes and my whole attention on the card, grimly determined that if *Moshulu* was to be lost by broaching to, it wasn't going to happen while I was at the wheel.

At two bells (1 a.m.) I was relieved. Soaked through and very cold I was happily going below for a period of 'påpass' when the Mate told me to summon the watch. One by one I shook them into reluctant wakefulness whilst he roamed about impatiently on the deck above.

'Where you were all bloddy night?' he demanded when they were all finally on deck. 'Kom on. Bräck bukgårdingarna på kryss royal.'

As we stumbled aft along the slippery deck to the mizzen royal bunt-lines we cursed the Mate audibly and the Captain more secretly. By the time Yonny Valker and I had been aloft and furled the main royal, which was heavy and sodden with rain, and cleared up on deck, it was a quarter past two, and I was overdue for lookout. I need not have been anxious to reach it, for Sedelquist failed to relieve me at three and I spent an hour-and-three-quarters looking at nothing but rain.

At last the end of this interminable 'utkik' drew near. At twenty to four I saw the light lit in the starboard fo'c'sle where the 'påpass' was waking the other watch. At two minutes to I saw the dark figures con-gregating beneath the break of the midships deck for the muster. There was a short interval while the Mate counted; an interval when, finding one man short, he despatched the 'påpass' to find the missing man— in this case 'Doonkey', who had either been overlooked or was not shaken hard enough. He was greeted with jeers of disapproval when he shambled out on deck.

'Orlright,' said the Mate. 'Lösa av ror och utkik, in frivakt.' The helmsman was relieved and there was a struggle at the steel doors as the free watch went below.

'Klara lanternor,' I said to Vytautas, as he relieved me. 'It's bloody cold and you can see damn all.'

'Not so fine, yerss?' said Vytautas, who was a good deal warmer and drier than I was myself. 'She is going.'

'So am I,' I said and went off in a hurry to report 'Klara lanternor' to the officer of the watch.

Very cold and very miserable I went below resolved to do something to elevate my spirits. At 'utkik' I had decided that I would open a 5 lb. can of marmalade which had cost me 3*s* 6*d* in Port Lincoln. Now I did so and cutting myself a massive slice of bread, I spread it on thickly. The marmalade looked rather insipid but I was not prepared for it to be absolutely tasteless as well. When we had reached Port 'Veek' we found that a 5 lb. tin of jam was only 2*s* 6*d*, but I had comforted myself that the extra shilling was well spent in order to obtain a supe-rior article. I thought now of all the splendid jams I might have bought instead. Bäckmann had a big tin of peach jam, one of the most delicious things I had ever tasted. Alvar had fig, Sedelquist quince, Hermansonn loganberry—all good fully-flavoured stuff. Only I had managed, in a country with a vast growth of every kind of fruit, to pick on some with neither taste nor smell of any kind.

I soon found that nobody was very keen to offer me their jam in exchange. One day I offered my marmalade to Sedelquist. Have some jam, Sedelquist,' I said pushing my hateful marmalade towards him.

'Oh you noh,' he said, 'there's damn all oranges in your jam. It tastes of olt bolls to me.'

'Balls?'

'Yes, olt goolf bolls. You should try quince. Veree good.'

'I should like to very much—'

'It's a peety,' he went on, 'that your marmalade isn't bettair.'

Thirteen days out from Spencer's Gulf we crossed the 180th meridian and suffered two Fridays in succession. Two Fridays were not popular. Sedelquist was angry because he had been deprived of the two Sundays he had hoped for; I was depressed because it meant an extra day of 'Backstern'; only Yonny Valker, that rigid medievalist, was happy, secure in the knowledge that here was a problem nobody would have the patience to explain to him.

'Koms to blow,' said Tria to me on the afternoon of the first Friday as I came on deck to pour the washing-up water over the side.

'Good.'

'No, no. Not good. Koms to blow bad,' he replied anxiously.

I asked him how he knew.

'I don' know how I know. There's someting fonny, someting noh good in the vind.' There was nobody about on the bridge deck, so I asked him if I could look at the last entry in the logbook in the charthouse.

'Orlright,' he said reluctantly, 'Don' let Kapten see you.' The Captain did not like finding the crew in the charthouse. I looked hastily at the open book and read the noon position:

'24.3.39. Lat. 51° 4S, Long. 176° 37′ 16W. Course East. Run 282.
Barometer 4 a.m. 758 millimetres; Noon 754 millimetres. Wind WSW,
Force 4.'

I glanced at the barometer. It had been falling steadily since 4
o'clock on Wednesday morning, the 22nd. On that day, except for
some light northerly airs, we had been becalmed on a sea as grey and
unvarying as a featureless plain. The albatross had vanished. At midnight on Wednesday the wind had been a gentle breeze from the NW.
and by the afternoon of Thursday, the 23rd, *Moshulu* was logging 12
knots with WNW. wind, force 5. At 8 it had shifted to the west, the
yards were squared, the spankers and the gaff topsail were taken in and
she ran before it. The time was now 4 p.m. on the 24th, the wind
WSW. The air was full of masses of white and grey cloud moving
rapidly eastward above the ship, which was being driven and lifted forward with a slight see-saw motion on the crest of seas of immense
depth and power. These seas did not seem to be raised by wind;
instead they seemed the product of some widespread underwater con-
vulsion. All round the ship the sea was surging and hurling itself into
the air in plumes of spray, occasionally leaping over the rail by the
mizzen braces and filling the main deck with a swirl of white water.
The air was bitter; I could see Tria's breath smoking.

'It looks all right to me,' I said.

'I don' say right now,' said Tria. 'But very soon this blody ting gets so
much as she can stand. Lissun when you go aloft.'

We were joined by the Sailmaker, who stood for some time looking
up at the main royal with the wind straining in it, then over the rail at
the mounting sea. 'Going to blow,' he said.

Hilbert came racing down the deck from the 'Vaskrum' for'ard,
dressed in nothing but wooden clogs and fresh long underwear, his
teeth chattering. All he said was: 'Vind,' and vanished into the starboard fo'c'sle. The First Mate looked down at us from the midships
deck. 'Going to vind a little too mooch,' he began conversationally.

'For Christ's sake,' I said, rather too audibly.

'What the hell are you doing?' he demanded, noticing me.

'Backstern, Sir.'

'Backstern doesn't take all bloddy day. Get down in the hold with babord'svakt for knacka rost.'

I went below to where the port watch were working suspended on platforms over one of the 'tween-deck hatches. The only vacant space was next to Taanila, even more gnomelike than usual in goggles. I slipped in beside him and he turned as the platform gave a lurch. 'I tink . . .' he began. In that moment I wondered exactly what he was going to think. Was he going to think that I needed a knife inserted in some delicate part? Was he going to remind me yet again of my unfortunate nationality? Or was he going to tell me his opinion of 'knacka rost'?

'I tink it it is going to . . .'

'Don't tell me, let me guess—to vind.'

'Yo, yo. How you know?'

'Because I'm bloody clever.'

At 5 the heavy chain sheet to the fore royal parted on the port side. We just managed to get the sail in before it blew itself to pieces. The remaining royals had to come in, and the flying jib, then all hands went aloft for the main and mizzen courses. All through the night there were two helmsmen. The wind increased and the seas rose higher and began to pour into the ship again. In the watch below I lay awake listening to the clang of freeing ports along the length of the main deck as they opened to the pressure of water and closed as the ship rolled away, tipping the sea light across her so that the same process took place on the other side. With more apprehension I listened to the sound of water trickling steadily into the fo'c'sle through a cracked port above Bäckmann's bunk. This seemed to constitute a far greater threat to our comfort than the more spectacular effects outside.

At 5.30 on the morning of the second Friday, *Moshulu*, still carrying her upper topgallants, began to labour under the onslaught of the heavy seas which were flooding on to the deck like a mill race. It was quite dark as six of us clewed-up the mizzen lower topgallant, and although from where I was at the tail of the rope I could see nothing at all except the hunched shoulders of Jansson ahead of me, I could hear Tria at the head of the line exhorting us. The sail was almost up when the wind fell quite suddenly and we all knew that we were in the trough of a wave far bigger than anything we had yet experienced. It was far too dark to see it at a distance, we could only sense its coming as the ship rolled slightly to port to meet it.

'Hoold . . .' someone began to shout as the darkness became darker still and the sea came looming aver the rail. I was end man. There was just time to take a turn with the clewline round my middle and a good hold, the next moment it was on top of us. The rope was not torn from me; instead it was as though a gentle giant had smoothed his hands over my knuckles. They simply opened of their own accord and I unravelled from it like a cotton reel from the end of a thread and was swept away. As I went another body bumped me, and I received a blow in the eye from a seaboot. Then I was alone, rushing onwards and turning over and over. My head was filled with bright lights like a by-pass at night, and the air was full of the sounds of a large orchestra playing out of tune. In spite of this there was time to think and I thought: 'I'm done for.' At the same time the words of a sea poem, 'ten men hauling the lee fore brace . . . seven when she rose at last', came back to me with peculiar aptness. But only for an instant because now I was turning full somersaults, hitting myself violently again and again as I met something flat which might have been the coaming of No. 4 hatch, or the top of the charthouse, for all I knew. Then I was over it, full of water and very frightened, thinking 'Is this what it's like to drown?' No more obstructions now but still going very fast and still under water, perhaps no longer in the ship, washed overboard, alone in the Southern Ocean. Quite suddenly there was a parting of water, a terrific crash as my head hit something solid, and I felt myself aground.

Finding myself in the lee scuppers with my head forced right through a freeing port so that the last of the great sea behind me spurted about my ears, I was in a panic that a second wave might come aboard and squeeze me through it like a sausage, to finish me off.

Staggering to my feet, my oilskins ballooning with water, too stupid

from the blow on my head to be frightened, I had just enough sense
to jump for the starboard lifeline when the next wave came boiling
over the port quarter and obliterated everything from view.

Swinging above the deck on the lifeline with the sea sucking
greedily at my seaboots, I began to realize what a fortunate escape I
had had from serious injury, for the alacrity with which I had leapt
for the lifeline in spite of the great weight of sea-water inside my oilskins had convinced me that I had suffered no damage except the
bang on the head.

The sea had taken me and swept me from the pin rail of the mizzen
rigging, where I had been working, diagonally across the deck for fifty
feet past the Jarvis brace winches, on the long handles of which I could
so easily have been speared, over the fife rails of the mizzen mast, right
over the top of No. 3 hatch and into the scuppers by the main braces
outside the Captain's quarters.

'Where you bin?' demanded Tria accusingly, when I managed to
join the little knot of survivors who were forcing their way waist
deep across the deck, spluttering, cursing, and spitting sea-water as
they came.

'Paddling,' I said, relieved to find that there still six of us.

'Orlright, don' be all bloody day,' he added unsympathetically.

'Tag i gigtåget. One more now. Ooh—ah, oh, bräck dem.'

'What happened?' I asked Jansson.

'That goddam Valker let her come up too mooch,' said Jansson. 'I
bin all over the bloddy deck in that sea.'

On the second Friday *Moshulu*'s noon position was 50° 19′ S., 170°
36′ W. In 23 ½ hours she had sailed 296 miles. [*] This was the best day's
sailing with cargo she ever had with Erikson. It was only bettered by
the Germans on very few occasions. Twice in 1909 on a voyage from
Newcastle, N.S.W., to Valparaiso when loaded with nearly 5,000 tons
of coal she ran 300 miles.

[*] When running to the east in southerly latitudes a day, noon to noon, is about
23 ½ hours.

At midnight the wind was SW., force 6, and in the early hours of Saturday morning I went aloft with Hermansonn in a storm of sleet to make fast the main upper topgallant. It was now blowing a fresh gale, force 8, and the yard was swinging like a mad thing; we had a terrible time with this sail. Some of the gaskets had been caught in the buntline blocks on the yard and were immovable, others were missing. The sleet numbed our fingers until we almost cried with cold.

Below us, in the fore and mizzen rigging, eight boys were having the time of their lives furling the lower topgallants; on the mizzen two buntlines had carried away to starboard and the sail was being clewed-up to the yard with lines taken to the capstan on the main deck, where from time to time ton upon ton of white water poured over the rail, causing those heaving at the capstan bars to abandon their efforts and leap for the lifelines.

'OOH, what bloddy cold,' screamed Hermansonn. 'Ut, Kossuri, you strongbody, you rosbif, ut, ut på nock.'

As we reached the yardarm there was a great ripping sound that seemed to come from below, and we both hung dizzily over the yard to see whether the upper topsail had blown out. Then, in spite of the wind and our precarious situation, Hermansonn began to laugh. I knew then that I had suffered some dire misfortune as Hermansonn only laughed in that way when a disaster happened to someone else.

'Ho, ho!' he boomed above the gale, 'Ho, ho, focking fonny!'

'What?' I screamed in his ear. 'Tell me.'

'Your trousers, ho, ho, English, no good.'

It was true. My oilskin trousers, unable to stand the strain to which they had been subjected, had split from end to end.

This was an accident of the worst kind. To find myself half way across the Southern Ocean, in the stormiest seas in the world, with defective oilskin trousers, was calamity.

At the moment however there was no time to worry over such things. The wind was awe-inspiring. Not only was it so strong in the gusts that we could no nothing but hang on until it lessened, but it moaned in a way which I had never heard before, rising and falling like the winds heard about old houses in the wintertime. It seemed, in spite of its force, to be the last part of some even more violent disturbance that was taking place at a great distance. This then was what Tria had meant when he told me to listen when I went aloft.

But in this weather there were still worse jobs on deck where the Carpenter and two helpers were trying to caulk the closet. As the ship started to run downhill into the valley between two seas, she would bury her bows nearly to the fo'c'sle head, so that the water surged into the pipes and shot into the compartment in a solid icy column like the jet emitted by a whale, leaving them half drowned and spluttering.

At noon the wind was WSW., force 9, and there was a vicious sea running. We were carrying upper and lower topsails, the foresail, forestaysail, and jigger staysail. I spent the morning with a sail-needle, seaming up my ruined oilskins, while overhead the starboard watch struggled to reeve fresh buntlines on the mizzen lower topgallant. The outer steel doors of the fo'c'sle were fast, but not being close-fitting they let the water in. Soon there were more than six inches of water in the compartment reserved for our seaboots and oilskins, and half as much in the fo'c'sle itself. Every few minutes I had to leave my stitching and bail with a cocoa tin to prevent the fo'c'sle being flooded still more. Everyone else was asleep. As old soldiers do before an action, they were absorbing sleep greedily like medicine and lay snoring happily in the midst of tumult.

For the noise was unbelievable. In the fo'c'sle the shrieking of the wind through the shrouds and about the upper yards now bereft of sail, so awe-inspiring on the open decks, was here only a murmur subordinated to the shuddering and groaning of the hull under stress and to the sounds of water; water thundering over the ship in torrents, water sluicing out through the freeing ports, water trickling into the fo'c'sle in half-a-dozen different ways, and sloshing about the floor.

By the time I had mended the trousers, the free watch was nearly over. I was 'Backstern', and having made sure that Kroner had put on the washing-up water, I waited for a lull to dash forward to the fo'c'sle head from where I could look back along the ship.

Moshulu was running ten knots in the biggest seas I had ever seen. As I watched, the poop began to sink before my eyes and the horizon astern was blotted out by a high polished wall, solid and impenetrable like marble. The poop went on dropping until the whole ship seemed to be toppling backwards into the deep moat below the wall of water that loomed over her, down and down to the bottom of the sea itself. At the moment when it seemed that this impregnable mass must engulf us, a rift appeared in its face and it collapsed, burrowing beneath the ship, bearing her up so that what a moment before seemed a sluggish, solid hulk destined for the sea bed was now like a bird skimming the water, supported by the wind high above the valley.

This was noon.

In the first part of the afternoon the barometer was low, 742 millimetres. At one moment *Moshulu* would be riding the crests in brilliant sunshine, the next swooping down a great incline of water peppered by rain and hailstones, yawing a little from her course and beginning to roll, taking sea as high as her charthouse. Everyone was soaking wet and none of us had any more dry clothes. Everything in the Vuitton was wet as well. All through the afternoon we were kept busy making new wire buntlines, cold work with no movement in it, but by coffee-time one of my shirts had dried over the galley fire and I put it on rejoicing. But not for long.

As soon as I came out on deck I heard a voice calling me. It was the Captain, in leather coat and tweed cap, like a huge backwoods peer I had seen in a *Tatler* that the Sailmaker had somehow saved from destruction.

'Here you,' he said. 'Take up some slack on the crojack sheet.'

I plunged down on to the maindeck, where I was immediately knocked flat by a sea coming inboard. After this initial soaking, I no longer cared whether I was wet or not, only leaping for the lifelines when big dangerous seas came aboard.

At six there was a slight easing in the wind. I happened to be coming from the wheel, when once more the Captain had something in mind for me.

'We'll see what she can stand,' he said, looking aloft in a speculative way like a gambler about to stake a large sum on an uncertainty.

'Aloft and break out the main lower topgallant. Lively now.' As I went I heard Sedelquist, who had been at the wheel with me, say: 'Crazy focker.' Privately agreeing with him, I swung myself on to the pin rail and into the main rigging. Aloft the wind seemed as strong as ever, and I looked down to a deck as narrow as a ruler on which the tiny figures of the watch were clustered, waiting to perform the ticklish job of sheeting home the sail which I was about to loose from its gaskets.

A distant cry borne on the wind told me that they were ready.

I cast off the gaskets on the weather side, hauled up a good slack on the buntlines, and, scuttling into the rigging, clung to the shrouds for my life. The yard began to plunge and whip, the bunt-lines plucked at the blocks seized to the shrouds, making the rat-lines tremble underfoot.

'She'll never stand it,' was the general verdict when I regained the deck.

With the sail sheeted home there was too much strain on the entire sail structure and at eight o'clock the upper topsail sheet carried away and the sail had to be taken in, together with the lower topgallant we had recently set.

Thus reduced, we drove on in the darkness with both topsails set on the fore and mizzen, the main lower topsail, the foresail and one fore-and-aft sail—the jigger staysail.

This was the night of the second Friday, March 24th. We were wet and fed up and though we cursed *Moshulu* and the Captain too, we were pleased with him for pushing her to the limit.

'This Kapten is proper strongbody for vind,' said Sandell after an issue of rum and a good dinner of Lobscouse—a sustaining hash made from pounded hard bisuit, potato, and 'Buffelo'.

'—the Kapten,' replied Sedelquist who was absolutely cynical about all men. 'Vonts to get his name in the papers, I shouldn't vonder.'

'We'll be in it too, if he does,' I said.

'Yes, in the bloddy paper but on the front with beeg black lines all round "missing". That's what we'll be.'

It was too cold to argue. I slipped into my bunk dressed in my soaking long underwear with two pullovers on top. On my head was a very hairy balaclava helmet, so that I looked like the subject of some hitherto unpublished photograph of a military man in the lines about Sebastopol.

The fo'c'sle no longer seemed a human habitation. There were several inches of water on the floor, and trousers, seaboots, and oilskins that had slipped from their hooks were moving gently backwards and forwards the whole length of it with a sucking sound. Wedging myself as firmly as I could in a steady position, I tried to read the *Times* leader on the dismissal of Dr. Schacht, but the subject seemed so remote and unimportant and the light was so bad that when Alvar said 'Light ut' I extinguished it without argument.

Just before midnight the voice of the 'påpass' woke me. My long underwear was steaming like a kettle. Outside it was fearfully cold. Because it was my 'utkik' I put on as many layers as I could: a wet hairy shirt and trousers that I had bought in the East India Dock Road, two more pullovers in addition to the two I was sleeping in, and my heavy pilot coat. Everything was dripping with water.

'Remember *Admiral Karpfanger* [*]—keep good 'utkik', plenty ice around here, maybe,' screamed Tria cheerfully in my ear, and left me.

At the lookout I peered ahead of the ship and could see nothing. The air was full of spray which rose like mist about the ship. The wind was strong enough to lean on. High above in the darkness the rest of the watch was bending afresh chain-sheet for the main upper topsail.

With the new sheet bent we started to wind the yard into position. The gearing on the winch was very low and it was a slow job to raise it. By three in the morning it was in position and we had set the sail, together with the main lower topgallant which the Captain was determined she should carry.

But it was no use. The barometer continued to fall, and at five the

[*] German schoolship ex *L'Avenir* lost with all hands in the Southern Ocean, February 1938.

starboard watch bad to furl it again. This was on the morning of March 25th.

'Going to blow, I tink,' said Tria.

'What do you think it's doing now?' I asked him.

'Notting.'

'Golly.'

After breakfast I was at 'Backstern', extremely bad-tempered because I had been washed away when crossing the foredeck to the starboard fo'c'sle and had lost all the hot water.

Suddenly Taanila appeared. 'Kom,' he said.

'Why? I'm "Backstern".'

'Styrman, he say "BRÄCK GÅRDINGARNA PÅ STOR ÖVRE MÄRS".'

'This is it,' said Kroner as I went aft. 'Upper topsails. It's going to be really big.'

'It's the blasted "Backstern" that worries me. There's no water.'

'I'll put some on for you,' he answered. 'It'll be there when you come back.'

'Maybe I shan't,' I said, nearer the mark than usual.

When we were all assembled the Mate slacked away the handbrake of the upper topsail halliard winch and set it spinning. The eighty-foot yard began to descend in its greased track on the fore part of the mizzen mast, and as the weather sheet was progressively eased we clewed-up to windward and manned the buntlines. With the weather clew up, the lee side was easier and the sail was furled without incident.

The fore upper topsail was the most difficult. All the buntlines jammed and more than half the robands securing the topsail to the jackstay had gone. The outer buntline block had broken loose and was flailing in the air, so that when we reached the lowered yard eighty feet above the sea, we hesitated a moment before the 'Horry ops' of the Mates behind us drove us out on to the footropes, hesitated because the bunt of the sail was beating back over the yard. The wind was immense. It no longer blew in the accepted sense of the word at all; instead it seemed to be tearing apart the very substance of the atmosphere. Nor was the sound of it any longer definable in ordinary terms.

It no longer roared, screamed, sobbed, or sang according to the various levels on which it was encountered. The power and noise of this wind was now more vast and all-comprehending, in its way as big as the sky, bigger than the sea itself, making something that the mind balked at, so that it took refuge in blankness.

It was in this negative state of mind that could accept anything without qualm, even the possibility of death, that I fell off the yard backwards. I was the last man out on the weather side and was engaged in casting loose a gasket before we started to work on the sail, when without warning it flicked up, half the foot of a topsail, 40 feet of canvas as hard as corrugated iron, and knocked me clean off the footrope.

There was no interval for reflection, no sudden upsurge of remorse for past sins, nor did my life pass in rapid review before my eyes. Instead there was a delightful jerk and I found myself entangled in the weather rigging some five feet below the yard, and as soon as I could I climbed back to the yard and carried on with my job. I felt no fear at all until much later on.

It needed three-quarters of an hour to make fast the weather side. Time and time again we nearly had the sail to the yard when the wind tore it from our fingers.

My companion aloft was Alvar.

'What happened?' he said when we reached the deck.

'I fell.'

'I din' see,' he said in a disappointed way. 'I don' believe.'

'I'm damned if I'm going to do it again just because you didn't see it.'

'I don' believe.'

'Orlright,' I said. 'The next time I'll tell you when I'm going to fall off.'

'Dot's bettair,' said Alvar.

At noon on Saturday, the 25th, our position was 50° 7' S., 164° 21' W. In the 23 ½ hours from noon on the 24th *Moshulu* had sailed 241 miles and made 228 between observed positions. Her previous day's runs were 296 and 282, but the violence of the sea and the necessary reduction in canvas were slowing her increasingly.

The barometer fell and fell, 746, 742, 737 millimetres. The sun went down astern, shedding a pale watery yellow light on the undersides of the deep black clouds hurrying above the ship. It was extremely cold, colder than it had ever been, blowing a strong gale, force 9. Big seas were coming aboard. I felt very lonely. The ship that had seemed huge and powerful was nothing now, a speck in the Great Southern Ocean, two thousand miles eastwards of New Zealand, three thousand from the coast of South America, separated to the North from the nearest inhabited land, the Cook Islands and Tahiti, by two thousand miles of open sea; to the South there was nothing but the Antarctic ice and darkness. She was running before seas that were being generated in the greatest expanse of open ocean, of a power and size unparalleled because there was no impediment to them as they drove eastwards round the world. She was made pigmy too by the wind, the wind that was already indescribable, that Tria said had only now begun to blow.

At this moment, for the first time I felt certain of the existence of an infinitely powerful and at the same time merciful God. Nearly everyone in the ship felt something of this, no one spoke of it. We were all of us awed by what we saw and heard beyond the common experience of men.

I had second wheel in the watch till midnight with Jansson to help me. We relieved Yonny Valker and Bäckmann.

'Törn om,' I said, mounting the platform next to Yonny and feeling with my foot for the brake pedal.

'Törn om,' repeated Yonny, showing me that he was ready to be relieved.

'Othhnordotht,' he lisped, giving me the course (we were running before the storm ENE.), and then added as he relinquished the wheel: 'No more babords.'

It seemed reasonable. The ship was pointing ENE½E., but with the rolling it was difficult to keep her right on course and I supposed that he had already given her as much port helm as she needed.

I was soon disillusioned. Yonny had left me with the wheel hard to starboard and she continued to run off in that direction.

Before Tria awoke to what was happening *Moshulu* was pointing south east. Unfortunately he lost his head; shrieking wildly he began to turn the binnacle hood towards Jansson so that he could see the card, but only turned the hood sufficiently for the card to be invisible to both of us. At this moment the First Mate arrived and, thinking Jansson was at fault, began to give him hell. Not even the fact that I was standing on the weather side convinced him that I was helmsman.

It needed the four of us to return the ship to her course, and she took some terrific seas aboard. Afterwards the Mate laid into Jansson until the latter's nose began to glow red.

'It was my fault,' I shouted, trying to make my voice heard above the wind.

'Shot op, shot op!' bellowed the Mate with such violence that I dared not say another word. 'Shot op, or by *helvete* be jus' too bloddy bad.'

I shut up.

'I'm sorry,' I said to Jansson afterwards.

'Orlright,' he said, 'not dead, but nearly. We'll make some cocoa in the "Doonkey Hus".'

As the barometer went on falling, the wind rose. At 4 a.m. it fell to 733 metres and the wind blew force 10, Beaufort notation, a whole gale of wind. The starboard watch took in the main upper topsail at three o'clock and the ship ran before the storm under lower topsails and the foresail; the whole of the after deck was inundated.

'A liddle more,' said Sandell, 'she'll take a liddle more than this.'

Day broke at last, slowly because clouds, black as night, pressed upon the ship. Hail, driving rain, and flurries of snow fell. At five the watch was called. We knew the reason before the Mate gave the order.

'Undra märs skot,' said Sedelquist. 'Got to slack those lower topsail sheets before it's too late.'

The main deck was like a reef with occasionally the tops of the winches and the hatches breaking the surface, and it seemed strange to me that a week ago, when we had been securing the hatch covers with heavy timbers, the precautions had seemed superfluous, almost too adequate, and yet now I found myself wondering what would happen if one of those awful cliff-like seas caught up with the ship and pooped her.

On the deck we were caught in a roaring flood and jumped for the lifelines, hanging on minutes at a time, but with her topsails eased she ran better and there was less danger of the sail blowing out.

At six o'clock, cold yet exultant, we went below for coffee.

'She's a real ship,' said Sandell. 'I've never seen a ship like this. Blows like strongbody. Mos' ships you'd have the foresail off her and heave-to. Lovs vind, lovs it. But my God if ve have to take the foresail, be someting.'

The clouds cleared and a whole gale of wind blew out of a clear blue sky. At eight the wind reached its greatest velocity, force 11 on the Beaufort scale, a wind in which a wooden ship might well have foundered, and a lesser than *Moshulu* would have hove to, drifting to leeward, lying on the wind under a storm trysail.

All through the storm the pigs had been setting up despairing cries, as well they might, cooped in their narrow steel coffins. At six o'clock we cleaned out their sties, a difficult job in a ship running before a great gale. It took three of us to do it.

'For Chrissake don' let them go,' grunted Tria, as we levered the iron troughs through the door of the sty with crowbars.

He had no sooner said this than Auguste and Filimon, believing that the ship was about to founder, charged the barricade of hatch covers with which we had fenced them in, intent on finding a place in the boats. The barricade collapsed and Filimon, who was leading, shot between Tria's legs, upsetting him in the nasty mess we were shovelling up. Auguste followed him closely, and they both went glissading away on their behinds into the lee scuppers, from which we had difficulty in rescuing them.

'Better eat them before they go overside,' I said as we struggled with Auguste, who was threshing about under water.

'I don' care how soon we eat that Filimon,' Tria said.

Moshulu continued to carry her sail and the storm entered its last and most impressive phase. We were cold and wet and yet too excited to sleep. Some stood on the fo'c'sle head but only for a short time as the force of the wind made it difficult to remain on two feet. Others stood beneath it and gazed out along the ship, watching the seas rearing up astern as high as a three-storeyed house. It was not only their height that was impressive but their length. Between the greatest of them there was a distance that could only be estimated in relation to the ship, as much as four times her entire length, or nearly a quarter of a mile. The seas approached very deliberately, black and shiny as jet, with smoking white crests gleaming in the sunshine, hissing as they came, hurling a fine spume into the air as high as the main yard.

I went aloft in the fore rigging, out of the comparative shelter of the foresail, into the top, and higher again to the cross-trees, where I braced myself to the backstays. At this height, 130 feet up, in a wind blowing 70 miles an hour, the noise was an unearthly scream. Above me was the naked topgallant yard and above that again the royal to which I presently climbed. I was now used to heights but the bare yard, gleaming yellow in the sunshine, was groaning and creaking on its tracks. The high whistle of the wind through the halliards sheaf, and above all the pale blue illimitable sky, cold and serene, made me deeply afraid and conscious of my insignificance.

Far below, the ship was an impressive sight. For a time the whole of the after deck would disappear, hatches, winches, everything, as the solid water hit it, and then, like an animal pulled down by hounds, she would rise and shake them from her, would come lifting out of the sea with her freeing ports spouting.

Opening my camera, I attached the lens hood, but the wind blew it into the sea. The mist of spray rising all about the ship made it almost impossible to see anything through the viewfinder. There was no need for the range-finder. I simply set the scale to infinity and pressed the button, and even that was difficult enough.

Later, I was standing on deck just aft of the charthouse when a monster wave reared over the main rail and exploded on the house itself. As it came I shut the camera but was too late to shut the case.

In an agony of mind I went down to the fo'c'sle. The camera was very wet. The film was undamaged. I up-ended it and a thin trickle of water ran out of the Compur shutter. The rest of the watch were observing me with interest.

'I'll have to take it to pieces or it'll rust up,' I explained.

'Good,' said everybody. 'Now.'

'No, when the storm finishes. The thing's full of springs.'

'Put it in the offen,' said Sedelquist. 'I should ask the "Kock". Dry heem out.'

By noon *Moshulu* had again run 228 miles. Since the storm began we had crossed 18 degrees of longitude. Now the barometer rose steadily. The starboard watch reset the fore and main upper topsails and all through the afternoon we were resetting sail. Big seas were still coming aboard and we frequently deserted the halliard winches for the lifelines. Sent aloft to overhaul the buntlines, I returned in a filthy temper because I had dropped my knife overboard.

By 9 p.m. the gale had passed, the wind had fallen, but there was still a tremendous sea running. The weather was clear and cold with overhead a thin crescent moon. At two in the morning of Monday, the 27th, we reset the main royal and in an hour or two more we were in full sail again.

acknowledgments

Many people made this anthology.

At Thunder's Mouth Press and Avalon Publishing Group:
Thanks to Ghadah Alrawi, Will Balliett, Sue Canavan, Maria Fernandez, Linda Kosarin, Dan O'Connor, Neil Ortenberg, Paul Paddock, Susan Reich, Simon Sullivan, David Riedy, and Mike Walters for their support and hard work.

At The Writing Company:
Nate Hardcastle and March Truedsson did most of the research. Shawneric Hachey oversaw rights research and negotiations. Thanks also to Kate Fletcher, Mark Klimek, Nat May and Taylor Smith.

At the Portland Public Library in Portland, Maine:
Thanks to the librarians for their assistance in finding and borrowing books and other publications from around the country.

Finally, I am grateful to the writers whose work appears in this book.

p e r m i s s i o n s

b i b l i o g r a p h y

The selections used in this anthology were taken from the editions and publications listed below. In some cases, other editions may be easier to find. Hard-to-find or out-of-print titles often are available through inter-library loan services or through Internet booksellers.

Conrad, Joseph. *Great Short Works of Joseph Conrad.* New York: Harper and Row, 1967. (For "Youth".)

Dana, Jr., Richard Henry. *Two Years Before the Mast: A Personal Narrative.* New York: The Modern Library, 2001.

Forester, C.S. *Lieutenant Hornblower.* New York: Pinnacle Books, 1976.

Hall, James Norman. *Doctor Dogbody's Leg.* New York: Henry Holt & Company, 1998.

Harvey, Robert. *Cochrane: The Life and Exploits of a Fighting Captain.* New York: Carroll & Graf, 2000.

Lewis, Jon E. (editor). *The Mammoth Book of Life Before the Mast: An Anthology of Eyewitness Accounts from the Age of Fighting Sail.* New York: Carroll & Graf, 2001. (For "Frigate Engagement: HMS Macedonian v. USS United States" by Samuel Leech and "A Pressed Man" by Robert Hay.)

Marryat, Frederick. *Mr. Midshipman Easy.* Ithaca, New York: McBooks Press, 1998.

Melville, Herman. *Billy Budd.* New York: Washington Square Press, 1999.

Newby, Eric. *The Last Grain Race.* New York: Granada Publishing, 1981.

Nordhoff, Charles, and James Norman Hall. *Mutiny on the Bounty.* New York: Little, Brown & Company, 1960.

O'Brian, Patrick. *The Ionian Mission.* New York: William Collins, 1981.

Schmitt, Lou A. *All Hands Aloft.* New York: Howell-North Books, 1956.

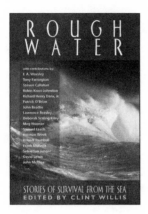
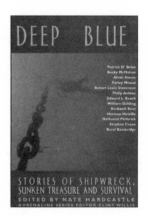

Exciting titles from Adrenaline Books

EXPLORE: Stories of Survival from Off the Map

Edited by Jennifer Schwamm Willis
Series Editor, Clint Willis
Adventurers endure storms, starvation, predators and disease for the thrill of discovery in 19 gripping stories. Selections from writers such as Edward Marriott, Tim Cahill, Andrea Barrett, Redmond O'Hanlon and Harold Brodkey bring readers to places where genuine discovery is still possible.
$16.95 ($27.95 Canada); 384 pages

WILD: Stories of Survival from the World's Most Dangerous Places

Edited by Clint Willis
The wilderness—forest, desert, glacier, jungle—has inspired some of the past century's best writers, from Edward Abbey and Jack London to Norman Maclean and Barry Lopez. *Wild* contains 13 selections for people who love the wilderness and readers who love great writing.
$17.95 ($29.95 Canada), 336 pages

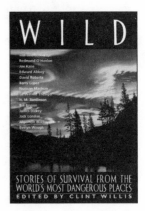

RESCUE: Stories of Survival from Land and Sea

Edited by Dorcas S. Miller; Series Editor, Clint Willis
Some of the world's best adventure writing tells stories of people in trouble and the people who come to their aid. *Rescue* gathers those stories from mountain ledges, sea-going vessels, desert wastes, ice flows and the real Wild West. It includes work by some of the world's best writers, from Antoine de St. Exupéry to Spike Walker and Pete Sinclair.
$16.95 ($27.95 Canada), 384 pages

Exciting titles from Adrenaline Books

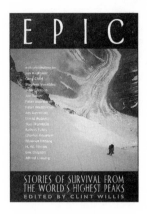

EPIC: Stories of Survival from the World's Highest Peaks

Edited by Clint Willis
A collection of 15 gripping accounts of legend-making expeditions to the world's most challenging mountains, including selections by Greg Child, David Roberts and Maurice Herzog.
$16.95 ($27.95 Canada), 352 pages

HIGH: Stories of Survival from Everest and K2

Edited by Clint Willis
The first anthology ever to focus exclusively on the two highest, most formidable mountains in the world. Includes accounts by Chris Bonington, Robert Bates, Charles Houston and Matt Dickinson.
$16.95 ($27.95 Canada), 336 pages

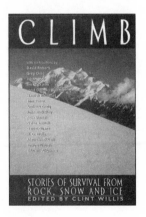

CLIMB: Stories of Survival from Rock, Snow and Ice

Edited by Clint Willis
This collection focuses on the most exciting descriptions of the hardest climbing in the world. From the cliffs of Yosemite to the windswept towers of Patagonia to the high peaks of Alaska and the Himalaya, *Climb* offers more than a dozen classic accounts.
$16.95 ($27.95 Canada), 272 pages

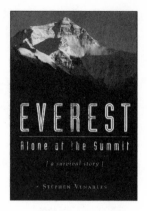
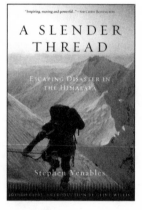

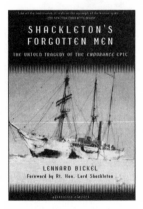

Exciting titles from Adrenaline Books

WILD BLUE: Stories of Survival from Air and Space

Edited by David Fisher and William Garvey
Series Editor, Clint Willis

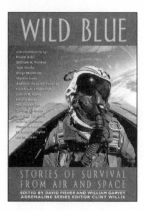

Wild Blue collects the most gripping accounts of what may be the greatest achievement of the century: manned flight. From flying a Piper Cub over the Rockies at the age of 16 to a nigh-time carrier approach, *Wild Blue* puts you right in the cockpit.
$17.95 ($29.95 Canada), 352 pages

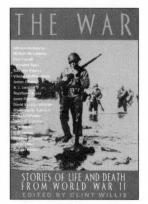

THE WAR: Stories of Life and Death from World War II

Edited by Clint Willis

The greatest writing about the War, from Okinawa to Normandy. This entry in the Adrenaline Books series is about courage, conscience, and loss. It features work by Stephen E. Ambrose, A. J. Liebling, William Manchester, Paul Fussell, and 13 others. $16.95 ($27.95 Canada), 384 pages

BLOOD: Stories of Life and Death from the Civil War

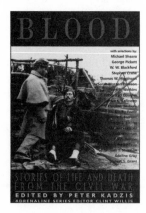

Edited by Peter Kadzis; Series Editor, Clint Willis
The most dramatic moment in this nation's history, also produced some of our greatest literature. From tragic charges to prison escapes to the desolation wrought on those who stayed behind, *Blood* is composed mainly of the vivid stories of those who were there. Includes accounts by General George Pickett, Walt Whitman, Ulysses S. Grant, Michael Shaara and Shelby Foote among others. $16.95 ($27.95 Canada); 320 pages